DOMESTIC VIOLENCE AND INTERNATIONAL LAW

Domestic Violence and International Law argues that certain forms of domestic violence are a violation of international human rights law. The argument is based on the international law principle that, where a state fails to protect a vulnerable group of people from harm, whether perpetrated by the state or private actors, it has breached its obligations to protect against human rights violations.

This book provides a comprehensive legal analysis of why a state should be accountable in international law for allowing women to suffer extreme forms of domestic violence. The state's breach of its responsibility is in its failure to act effectively in domestic violence cases; and in its silent endorsement of the violence, it becomes complicit.

The book seeks to reformulate academic and political debate on domestic violence and the responsibility of states under international law. It is based on empirical data combined with an honest assessment of whether or not domestic violence is recognised by the international community as a human rights violation.

Domestic Violence and International Law

Bonita Meyersfeld

·HART·
PUBLISHING

OXFORD AND PORTLAND, OREGON
2012

Published in the United Kingdom by Hart Publishing Ltd
16C Worcester Place, Oxford, OX1 2JW
Telephone: +44 (0)1865 517530
Fax: +44 (0)1865 510710
E-mail: mail@hartpub.co.uk
Website: http://www.hartpub.co.uk

Published in North America (US and Canada) by
Hart Publishing
c/o International Specialized Book Services
920 NE 58th Avenue, Suite 300
Portland, OR 97213-3786
USA
Tel: +1 503 287 3093 or toll-free: (1) 800 944 6190
Fax: +1 503 280 8832
E-mail: orders@isbs.com
Website: http://www.isbs.com

British Library Cataloguing in Publication Data
Data Available

ISBN: 978-1-84113-991-1 (Hardback)
978-1-84946-357-7 (Paperback)

Typeset by Hope Services, Abingdon
Printed and bound in Great Britain by
CPI Antony Rowe Ltd, Chippenham, Wiltshire

To Sandra and Charles
With Love

Foreword

Harold Hongju Koh*

Until recently, the juxtaposition of domestic violence and international law would have seemed an oxymoron. For by its nature, violence that is 'domestic' would seem, by definition, to stand outside the scrutiny of 'international law'. For generations, domestic violence has lived beyond the shadows not just of international law, but of all law. Banished from international law's gaze, and too often treated as an immutable face of particular cultures, domestic violence has too often been typecast as a 'soft' social issue that must take a back seat to other, 'more pressing' economic and political issues.

Today, this is finally changing. Increasingly, governments, courts and policy-makers are recognising systemic forms of domestic violence as an important international problem. Not only does domestic violence shatter lives and homes, it carries with it tangible and damaging economic and communal consequences. Over the last decade, various parts of the United Nations, including the Office of the Secretary-General, the Special Rapporteur on torture and the Special Rapporteur on violence against women, have turned their attention to systemic forms of domestic violence, finally recognising it for what it is: one of the most pervasive and pressing human rights concerns faced by the international community. Following the call of non-governmental organisations and community representatives, the world is finally taking note that just because some violence begins at home, that does not mean that it lacks global consequences.

Until now, no single volume has captured the arguments that view systemic domestic violence through an international law lens. There are no existing studies arguing for the internationalisation of extreme and systemic forms of domestic violence in a way that so comprehensively addresses both academic and practical needs. *Domestic Violence and International Law* fills that gap, by providing an original, provocative and much needed legal framework for the coherent development of a norm prohibiting systemic forms of domestic violence in international human rights law.

I have known the author, Dr Bonita Meyersfeld, for many years as a talented human rights lawyer, dedicated academic, and shrewd political policy adviser. Whilst gaining human rights expertise in many fields, Dr Meyersfeld has developed a thoroughgoing analysis that asks and addresses the most difficult questions often neglected by academics, lawyers and activists who dismiss the

* The Legal Adviser, United States Department of State (2009–); US Assistant Secretary of State for Democracy, Human Rights & Labor 1998–2001; Martin R Flug '55 Professor of International Law (on leave) and Dean, Yale Law School, 2004–09.

possibility that systemic forms of violence against women might violate international law.

This book advances the frontiers of academic and political thought on this important intellectual debate. It analyses the current position and history of international law regarding the practice of systemic forms of domestic violence, investigates what an emerging norm against that practice might look like, explores how meaningful reform could be achieved, and explains why the problem of domestic violence would benefit from articulation of clearer rules of international law.

Domestic Violence and International Law breaks new ground and will surely provide a valuable resource for lawyers, judges and policymakers for many years to come. Dr Meyersfeld creatively reformulates academic and political debate on domestic violence to focus upon the responsibility of states under international law to protect citizens from certain extreme forms of what she dubs 'systemic intimate violence'. Dr Meyersfeld focuses her attention in this book on violence perpetrated by men against women. But her analysis transcends this focus, and offers a useful and important blueprint for possible development of international law principles applicable to state responsibility for all forms of systemic intimate violence committed by private persons.

This book offers lawyers the legal arguments necessary to galvanise change, whether in international, regional or national courts. Judges can find in these pages balanced guidance on the jurisprudence in the field and considerations to guide their decisions. And policymakers at the national, regional and international levels will find tools and standards necessary to enhance protections for victims and survivors of domestic violence.

Most fundamentally, this book is memorable for the hope and optimism it expresses about the transformative possibilities of international law. Without compromising such intensely human values as privacy, autonomy and cultural identity, Dr Meyersfeld moves her reader with an abiding conviction: that international law, buoyed by the power of transnational actors, can propel public actors to protect abused and vulnerable people in their most private worlds.

Acknowledgement

This book has its source in the pain and fear of countless people who have endured the terrible shock of violence. It also has its source in the intellectual, ideological and emotional fortitude of many people, for whose encouragement and love, I thank you.

My deepest gratitude to Professor Harold Hongju Koh of Yale Law School, whose commitment to the vulnerable and whose consistent intellectual acumen have been driving forces behind this book. Thank you to Professors Michael Reisman, Judith Resnik and Jim Silk for your guidance and dedication to the completion of this project, and to the librarians at Yale Law School, who sourced a great deal of the material on which I have relied. Thank you too to Irum Khan-Lodhi for her selfless and excellent research assistance.

I am indebted to the reviewers and the staff at Hart Publishing, who contributed to the creation of this book. In particular, Ruth Massey has refined and edited this book with patience, skill and unfaltering attention to detail.

To my family who are my friends and my friends who are my family—and my parents (natural, in-laws and adopted)—thank you for your endless support.

There are two people who have been at the heart of this book and to whom this book is dedicated. To my mother Sandra Du Trevou, you are my hero and inspiration in all I do. Thank you. To my husband Charles Young, thank you for reading, re-reading, questioning, editing and dissecting this book. Thank you for enduring this process and making me as happy as you do.

Contents

Table of Cases

Table of International and Regional Instruments

Table of National Legislation

Introduction

Many claim that domestic violence is a human rights violation. I, along with others who have studied and practised in the field of domestic violence, who have seen its fundamental inhumanity, agree. The substance and nature of domestic violence can be so severe that it is a clear and unquestionable violation of the basic rights of the victim. But can we claim that there is an international legal principle, an international *law*, prohibiting domestic violence?

Identifying a legal principle in international law is not simple. There are many sources of law and several theories about these sources. In this book I analyse international instruments and state practice to determine whether we can say that there is an international law that requires states to respond in a particular manner to domestic violence. While there is a clear legal norm prohibiting *discrimination* against women, the honest conclusion is that there may not be a similarly authoritative principle regarding domestic violence. But things are changing. International bodies and the states they represent tend to agree that domestic violence requires a response that is global and effective.

The analysis in chapter one demonstrates that there is a developing norm in international law prohibiting domestic violence as a human rights violation. This norm is in the process of maturing into a universally binding principle of customary international law. While more needs to be done to crystallise this norm (a matter I address in chapter two), international lawyers ought to be aware of this developing jurisprudence.

In chapter two I distil the constitutive elements that make extreme, severe and systemic forms of domestic violence against women an international human rights violation. Not all forms of domestic violence are appropriate for regulation by international law. While it is uncomfortable to distinguish between degrees of violence, it would be wrong to hold a state liable for all acts of domestic violence that are neither extreme nor systemic. There are forms of domestic violence which, on the one hand, are egregious and systemic and receive no state response. On the other hand, there is abuse that is intermittent and involves only minor and/or one-off incidents. This book examines states' duty to react to the former only, that is, extreme and systemic forms of physical, and non-physical, cumulative violence. I refer to this type of violence as 'systemic intimate violence'.

If systemic intimate violence is a violation of an international human right, the state must have a corresponding duty to protect that right. The content of this duty must be precise and easily ascertainable. The corresponding duty is that states take reasonable steps and implement basic measures that fit within the peculiar context of systemic intimate violence. While such guiding principles are important, it is also necessary to give states far more detailed guidance as to how properly to respond to the nuanced and strange form of harm that is systemic intimate violence.

I discuss the theoretical application of the principles of state responsibility in international law in chapter three. If the substance of systemic intimate violence is such that the harm factually falls within international human rights law, a government's failure to assist abused women ought to fall within the rules of state responsibility. This means that if states fail to protect women from systemic intimate violence, technically they are in breach of international law and the principles of state responsibility apply.

The final question of international law's usefulness for victims and survivors of domestic violence is addressed in chapter four. Why is it at all useful to formulate a theory of domestic violence in international law? I turn to international law as an institution designed to induce states to remedy the deficiencies within their own individual domestic legal systems. The enunciation of a norm in international law acts as a guide to be used by national governments, state institutions, non-governmental organisations and individuals to improve legislation and policies in respect of systemic intimate violence. I do not maintain that international law has the same force as a state's domestic laws. Nor do I propose that international human rights law is an additional body of law with which states must comply. Rather, I turn to international law as a standard-setting spectrum, an enunciation of norms to which states can aspire and on which individuals can rely in holding their governments to account.

Based on the theory of non-coercive state compliance, I argue that there are two ways in which international law may serve to improve states' response to domestic violence. First, international law has an expressive value: it stipulates norms, which define the content of rights and concomitant state obligations. This expressive function facilitates the creation of new norms and laws to address harm for which no regulation exists. The second function of international law is its implementing capability. This process of international law compels states to modify their laws in accordance with international standards, thereby implementing better legal and statutory practices.

A common question is whether the term 'victim' or 'survivor' should be used when referring to a woman who suffers abuse. The concern is that the word 'victim' connotes weakness and vulnerability. But 'survivor' is problematic in its implied commentary on those women who either kill or are killed as a result of the abuse. Using this term risks implying that women who do not escape their abuse are failures, are weak, or in some way consented to the abuse. In reality a woman who does not flee and 'survive' is no weaker than the one who does. Therefore, while neither term is ideal, I choose to refer to women in domestic violence situations as victims and to the process of harm as victimisation. In no way is the term 'victim' used to suggest inferiority or weakness. Where necessary, I refer to 'survivors' of domestic violence to denote that the cycle of violence is over. Furthermore, because this book analyses the intersection between violence and gender, I refer to the victim as female and the perpetrator as male. I do this because it is this particular subset of violence which I have cho-sen to examine and certainly not because all forms of intimate violence are per-petrated by men against women. This analysis may well be used as a template for investigating state responsibility for harm committed in private in general. Women are not the only victims of domestic violence and men are not the only perpetrators. Children, the elderly, the disabled, men and non-human animals all endure such harm.

But the gendered analysis is necessary because domestic violence against women is particularly prolific due to historic gender-based differentiation and discrimination. This type of violence is the most serious cause of women's ill-health worldwide, including death and disability among women aged 15 to 44; more so than cancer, malaria, traffic accidents and war. It is the coalescence of violence and discrimination against women specifically that occupies this book, and that I believe requires further analysis from the point of view of inter-national law.

This book is not an attempt to change human nature. I do not maintain that amending laws, policies or government will change the fact of domestic vio-lence. Rather, it is an attempt to change the way our communities and states respond to the predicament in which so many women find themselves. State institutions cannot stay the blow of a violent fist. However, once charged with the knowledge of such violence, they can provide an effective response, a haven for recuperation, facilities for rehabilitation, and an expression of remorse and condemnation of such violence. Such measures would radically change the experience of the victim, limiting her pain to the period of the violence and not a moment beyond. To that end, this book attempts to lay the foundations by which international law can, and should, be used to place greater pressure on states to combat systemic intimate violence.

Postscript to the Paperback Edition, March 2012

Since the publication of this book, there have been important developments in international law regarding the prohibition on violence against women and, specifically, domestic violence. In 2011, the Inter-American Commission on Human Rights (the Commission) held that the United States had violated its international and regional obligations to protect individuals from domestic vio-lence. In 2011, in the case of *Jessica Lenahan (Gonzales) et al v United States*,[1] the Commission found that the United States had systemically failed to meet its due diligence obligations to protect women and children from domestic vio-lence. The Commission further confirmed that domestic violence is a serious

---

[1] *Jessica Lenahan (Gonzales) et al v United States*, Report No. 80/11 Case 12.626, July 21, 2011.

human rights violation and an extreme form of discrimination, for which states must be held accountable.

The same year saw the emergence of the Council of Europe Convention on Preventing and Combating Violence against Women and Domestic Violence ("Convention").[2] This Convention joins a small number of treaties imposing specific obligations on member states to prevent and address violence against women. The Convention is notable both for its encapsulation of best practices in combating violence against women and for its confirmation that all forms of violence against women, including domestic violence, are human rights violations for which states are responsible.

These developments confirm the principle that domestic violence is indeed a human rights violation for which states have responsibility.

---

[2] Council of Europe Convention on Preventing and Combating Violence against Women and Domestic Violence, May 12, 2011 [hereinafter Convention].

1

Domestic Violence as a Violation of International Human Rights Law

The twentieth century will be remembered as a century marked by violence. It burdens us with its legacy of mass destruction, of violence inflicted on a scale never seen and never possible before in human history . . .

Less visible, but even more widespread, is the legacy of day-to-day, individual suffering. It is the pain of children who are abused by people who should protect them, women injured or humiliated by violent partners . . . This suffering . . . is a legacy that reproduces itself, as new generations learn from the violence of generations past, as victims learn from victimizers, and as the social conditions that nurture violence are allowed to continue. No country, no city, no community is immune.

But neither are we powerless against it.

Nelson Mandela[1]

INTRODUCTION

DOMESTIC VIOLENCE IS one of the most serious causes of illness, poverty, homelessness and disability in women around the world. Women as a group are affected by this form of violence more than any other group and, in every country in the world, when women ask their courts, police and prosecutors for help, repeatedly their requests are ignored. Clearly domestic violence violates a person's human rights; but can we claim that there is an international legal principle, an international *law*, prohibiting domestic violence?

If one considers the plethora of international instruments and statements that deal with violence against women, it seems clear that international bodies and the states they represent have identified domestic violence as a global human rights concern. If, however, one takes a traditional approach to the creation of international law, and what constitutes international law, it is less clear whether there is a binding international rule regarding domestic violence.

---

[1] Nelson Mandela, 'Foreword' in Etienne G Krug, *World Report on Violence and Health* (World Health Organization, 2002) ix.

Why is this? Currently there is a binding principle of international law that *discrimination* against women is prohibited. The prohibition on discrimination against women forms part of the right to equality in several international covenants, and is the focus of the Convention on the Elimination of All Forms of Discrimination against Women (CEDAW),[2] an international treaty signed by a large majority of members of the United Nations (UN). This treaty, however, contains no reference to violence against women in general or to domestic violence specifically. As I discuss in detail below, there is a *regional* treaty prohibiting violence against women in the Inter-American system, and a plethora of UN and treaty body interpretations of CEDAW prohibit violence against women as a form of discrimination. But there is no *international* treaty provision that prohibits domestic violence per se.

Treaties are of course not the only source of international law. A staggering number of declarations and statements have been made by the UN Secretary-General, General Assembly, treaty bodies and Special Rapporteurs regarding violence against women in general, many of which include domestic violence within their scope. There is very clear jurisprudence from regional courts and treaty-monitoring bodies that domestic violence is a human rights violation and there is a wealth of reputable and respected writing on domestic violence as a human rights violation from academics and experts in the field of international law.

The question, then, is whether the resolutions, declarations and statements of the UN Secretary-General, General Assembly and treaty bodies, and the jurisprudence of regional courts (all of which I discuss in detail below) collectively can be said to create a principle of international law that prohibits domestic violence. We could also phrase the question slightly differently: do these resolutions, declarations, statements, regional treaty, judgments and academic literature constitute *evidence* of international law? The answer is—it depends.

If one takes a strictly traditional view of the creation and development of international law, it is unlikely that these instruments constitute international law. If, however, one takes a new approach to the sources and evidence of international law, it is possible either that the international instruments themselves constitute international law or that they may be *evidence* of customary international law.

This chapter examines all the international instruments, jurisprudence and academic literature that relate to domestic violence. I undertake this analysis in order to clarify precisely where we are in international law, whether there is currently a legal rule prohibiting domestic violence, and, if there is, what it entails.

---

[2] Convention on the Elimination of All Forms of Discrimination against Women (CEDAW) (adopted 18 December 1979, entered into force 3 September 1981) 1249 UNTS 13, UN Doc A/RES/34/830, (1980) 19 ILM 33. CEDAW established the CEDAW Committee 'For the purpose of considering the progress made in the implementation of the present Convention'. For a list of states that have signed and ratified CEDAW see www.un.org/womenwatch/daw/cedaw/states.htm. See also a list of parties that have entered reservations to CEDAW at www.un.org/womenwatch/daw/cedaw/reservations-country.htm.

I conclude that there is evidence in international law of a *developing* norm that domestic violence against women is a human rights violation and that this norm is in the process of maturing into a universally binding principle of international law.[3] In the last decade international bodies and state representatives have developed the principle of state responsibility for domestic violence to the point where we can say, *at least*, that there is an *emerging* principle of international human rights law that prohibits domestic violence. On the basis that the norm is growing, I explore the question of what steps are necessary to mature this norm into a universally binding and authoritative rule of law.

Many query whether domestic violence is sufficiently egregious to constitute an international human rights violation. This is addressed in chapter two. Others may wonder how international law could be beneficial to domestic violence victims, and I address this in chapter four. This chapter focuses solely on the status of violence against women, and domestic violence specifically, in international law.

SOURCES OF INTERNATIONAL LAW

In light of the fact that the world community has no parliament or legislature, how do we identify which norms are binding rules of international law? And specifically, how do we determine whether a rule prohibiting domestic violence exists in international law? UN bodies have developed over time to act as legislative entities by facilitating inter-state treaties and adopting declarations, but it is not always clear which instruments have the power of law.[4]

There are four generally accepted sources of international law, being, in descending order of authority: treaties; customary international law; the general principles of law as recognised by civilised nations; and legal jurisprudence, which includes judgments of international tribunals, jurisprudence of nations, and the teachings of respected academics.[5] These are not the only sources of international law.[6] Increasingly, resolutions and declarations made by UN

---

[3] See Amnesty International, *Men's Violence against Women in Intimate Relationships: An Account of the Situation in Sweden* (19 April 2004), www2.amnesty.se/svaw.nsf/mvaw/$File/mvaw.pdf, indicating (at 4) that violence in intimate relationships is a human rights violation.

[4] See generally, O Schachter, 'United Nations Law' (1994) 88 *American Journal of International Law* 1.

[5] Statute of the International Court of Justice (ICJ Statute), Art 38. See also the description of criminal law to be applied by the International Criminal Court in terms of Art 21(1) of the Rome Statute, which includes first the Rome Statute itself, second, where applicable, 'treaties and the principles and rules of international law, including the established principles of the international law of armed conflict and third, as a last resort, general principles of law derived from national legal systems'. United Nations Diplomatic Conference of Plenipotentiaries on the Establishment of an International Criminal Court, Rome Statute of the International Criminal Court (1998) UN Doc A/CONF.183/9, Art 7 (hereinafter Rome Statute).

[6] Alan Boyle and Christine Chinkin, *The Making of International Law* (Oxford, Oxford University Press, 2007).

bodies and officials are recognised as evidence of international law or interpretations of principles of international law.[7] Certain resolutions of the General Assembly, the Human Rights Council and treaty bodies are binding on Member States of the UN, while others are recommendatory, with varying degrees of majority support. Resolutions and declarations may be evidence of custom or usage and, in the case of human rights law, they are a barometer of developments in this area of international law.[8] It is also important to note the contribution of the International Law Commission (ILC), which is empowered by the General Assembly to promote the progressive development of international law and its codification; many international conventions and treaties are drawn from the work of the ILC.[9]

I now turn to examine these sources of law to determine whether domestic violence is a human rights violation for the purposes of international law.

The first and most authoritative source of international law comprises conventions and treaties. For the purposes of implementing and enforcing international law in national courts, treaty law is the most authoritative.[10] International conventions and treaties are the culmination of an agreement between two or more nations.[11] States expressly accede to the principles contained in a treaty, thereby making a commitment to fulfil specific legal obligations. Treaties are not automatically binding on states that have not signed them unless the provisions of the treaty are, or become, rules of customary international law or a *jus cogens* principle, that is, a principle so foundational that one cannot refuse to be bound thereby, such as the prohibition of genocide.[12] In 1969, the International Court of Justice (ICJ) in the *North Sea Continental Shelf* case held that treaty provisions could apply to non-signatories if the provisions qualify as customary inter-

[7]   ibid, 108–09.

[8]   ibid, 226–29.

[9]   Statute of the International Law Commission (1947), adopted by UNGA Res 174 (II) (21 November 1947), as amended by UNGA Res 485 (V) (12 December 1950), 984 (X) (3 December 1955), 985 (X) (3 December 1955) and 36/39 (18 November 1981).

[10]   See eg *Secretary of State for the Home Department v K (FC) and Fornah (FC) v Secretary of State for the Home Department* [2006] UKHL 46, para 10, per Lord Bingham (noting that the interpretation of international obligations must begin with the text of the Refugee Convention itself, 'because it expresses what the parties to it have agreed'). See also *Januzi v Secretary of State for the Home Department* [2006] UKHL 5, [2006] 2 WLR 397, para 4. Unincorporated human rights treaties may also bind states if their principles have developed into customary international law. See *European Roma Rights Centre v Immigration Officer at Prague Airport and the Secretary of State for the Home Department* [2004] UKHL 55, [2005] 2 AC 1, paras 98–101, per Baroness Hale. For a discussion of the incorporation of international law in the UK, see A Lester and B Meyersfeld, 'International Human Rights Codes and UK Law' in A Lester, D Pannick and J Herberg (eds), *Human Rights Law and Practice*, 3rd edn (London, LexisNexis, 2009) 823.

[11]   Schachter (n 4) 2 (describing the origins and development of 'norm-creating' treaties in the UN system).

[12]   Some maintain that rules of customary international law can emerge by virtue of the treaty negotiation process, even before the treaty is signed. See H Charlesworth, 'The Unbearable Lightness of Customary International Law' (1998) 92 *American Society of International Law Proceedings* 44 and 46, citing Louis Sohn, '"Generally Accepted" International Rules' (1986) 61 *Washington Law Review* 1073, 1074.

national law.[13] This will happen if a provision is of a 'fundamentally norm-creating character such as could be regarded as forming the basis of a general rule of law'.[14] In order to determine whether the provision in question (regarding equidistance) was fundamental, the ICJ considered: (1) the fact that the treaty provision was secondary to the 'primary obligation to effect delimitation by agreement'; (2) the fact that the equidistance principle was subject to a 'special circumstances' exception, which raised 'further doubts as to the potentially norm-creating character of the rule'; and (3) the fact that the treaty in question permitted reservations, which eroded the fundamental nature of the equidistance principle.[15] Slama extracts three factors from this case which can be used to determine whether a particular principle is of a 'fundamentally norm-creating character' necessary to constitute a binding obligation: '(1) Whether the principle involved imposes a primary obligation; (2) Whether the principle is subject to any exceptions; or (3) Whether a State may exclude itself from the obligation of the principle by an expression of its intent not to be bound by such.'[16]

The most obvious starting point in a discussion of treaties and violence against women is CEDAW, which is often referred to as the Bill of Rights for women. It was adopted unanimously by the UN General Assembly in 1979 and envisions the eradication of discrimination against women. CEDAW was followed by a range of global and regional declarations, recommendations and comments addressing various rights of women, resulting in a body of international law that deals exclusively with the needs and well-being of women.[17]

---

[13] *Federal Republic of Germany v Denmark; Federal Republic of Germany v Netherlands* (*North Sea Continental Shelf* case) [1969] ICJ Rep 3, paras 70–71.

[14] ibid, paras 41–42, determining whether the equidistant principle might be said to be a rule of customary international law.

[15] ibid, paras 42–43.

[16] JL Slama, 'Opinio Juris in Customary International Law' (1990) 15 *Oklahoma City University Law Review* 603, 651.

[17] These instruments include: Convention on the Nationality of Women (OAS Treaty Series No 4, 38, entered into force 29 August 1934); Convention on the Political Rights of Women (193 UNTS 135, entered into force 7 July 1954); CEDAW; Optional Protocol to the Convention on the Elimination of All Forms of Discrimination against Women (CEDAW Optional Protocol), UNGA Res 54/4, Annex (22 December 2000) UN Doc A/Res/54/4; Declaration on the Protection of Women and Children in Emergency and Armed Conflict, UNGA Res 3318 (XXIX) (14 December 1974) UN Doc A/9631; Declaration on the Elimination of Violence against Women (DEVAW), UNGA Res 48/104 (20 December 1993) UN Doc A/RES/48/104; *Report of the Fourth World Conference on Women* (Beijing, 4–15 September 1995) (hereinafter Beijing Conference) and Beijing Declaration and Platform for Action (15 September 1995) UN Doc A/CONF.177/20/Rev.1 (1995) and A/Conf.177/20/Add.1 (1995) (hereinafter Beijing Declaration); Protocol to Prevent, Suppress and Punish Trafficking in Persons, especially Women and Children, Supplementing the United Nations Convention against Transnational Organized Crime, UNGA Res, Annex II 55/25 (15 November 2000) UN Doc A/RES/55/25 (hereinafter UN Convention against Transnational Organized Crime); United Nations High Commissioner for Human Rights, *Principles and Guidelines on Human Rights and Trafficking* (2002) UN Doc E/2002/68/Add.1; Office of United Nations High Commissioner for Refugees, *Guidelines on International Protection: Gender-Related Persecution within the Context of Art 1a(2) of the 1951 Convention and its 1967 Protocol Relating to the Status of Refugees* (2002) UN Doc HCR/GIP/02/01; UN Commission on Human Rights Res 45 (4 March 1994) UN Doc E/CN.4/RES/1994/45 on the question of integrating the rights of women into the human rights mechanisms of the United Nations and the elimination of violence against women (hereinafter

CEDAW itself, however, does not contain a provision dealing with violence against women specifically. While there are non-treaty instruments that address this subject, the text of CEDAW itself does not. It also has one of the highest rates of reservations against its key provisions.

In addition to CEDAW, there is a regional treaty on violence against women. The Inter-American Convention on the Prevention, Punishment and Eradication of Violence against Women, known as the Convention of Belem Do Para, binds signatories of the Inter-American system and demonstrates a regional commitment to the eradication of violence, as well as discrimination, against women.[18] However, this is only a regional instrument and is not directly binding on all nation states.

The omission in CEDAW has been remedied to some extent by the General Assembly's 1993 Declaration on the Elimination of Violence against Women (DEVAW)[19] and CEDAW's General Recommendation 19 (discussed below), but this does not change the fact that the text of CEDAW omits entirely any specific reference to preventing violence against women.[20] Therefore, on a strict interpretation of international law, there is currently no prohibition of violence against women or, specifically, domestic violence in any international treaty. The question, then, is whether the range of international instruments that followed CEDAW and the Inter-American system's regional treaty, collectively constitute a binding obligation such that one can conclude that there is a principle of international law prohibiting domestic violence.

Customary international law constitutes the second broad category of international law, and is the process by which certain norms become international law by virtue of states customarily and intentionally acting in accordance with those norms. Because there is no global treaty prohibiting violence against women, customary international law is potentially the most authoritative

UNCHR Resolution 1994/45). UNCHR Resolution 1994/45 (which was adopted at the Fifty-sixth meeting of the UNHCR) established the mandate of the Special Rapporteur on violence against women, its causes and consequences; Inter-American Convention on the Granting of Civil Rights to Women (signed at the Ninth International Conference of American States, 30 March–2 May 1948, entered into force 17 March 1949) OAS Treaty Series No 23 (1948); Inter-American Convention on the Granting of Political Rights to Women (signed at the Ninth International Conference of American States, 30 March–2 May 1948, entered into force 29 December 1954) OAS Treaty Series No 3 (1948); Inter-American Convention on the Prevention, Punishment and Eradication of Violence against Women (Convention of Belem Do Para) (adopted 9 June 1994, entered into force 5 March 1995) (1994) 33 ILM 1534; Protocol to the African Charter on Human and Peoples' Rights on the Rights of Women in Africa, adopted by the 2nd Ordinary Session of the Assembly of the Union, Maputo, CAB/LEG/66.6 (13 September 2000), reprinted in 1 *African Human Rights Law Journal* 40, entered into force 25 November 2005 (hereinafter Protocol to the African Charter on the Rights of Women in Africa); UNSC Res 1325 on women, peace and security (31 October 2000) UN Doc S/RES/1325; and UNSC Res 1820 on sexual violence in conflict (19 June 2008) UN doc S/RES/1820.

[18]   Convention of Belem Do Para, ibid.

[19]   DEVAW (n 17).

[20]   UN Committee for the Elimination of All Forms of Discrimination against Women, 'General Recommendation 19: Violence against Women' (1992) UN Doc A/47/38. See also Sally Engle Merry, *Human Rights and Gender Violence: Translating International Law into Local Justice* (Chicago, University of Chicago Press, 2005) 65.

source of an established legal norm prohibiting such violence. I therefore discuss this source in detail throughout this chapter.

The third source of international law comprises the general principles of law recognised by so-called 'civilised' nations. Apart from the unhappy connotations of the term 'civilised nations', this source of law is generally not contentious. Essentially, it is a reference to the collection of norms that underpin many legal systems. Finally, the judgments of international tribunals, scholarly works and the jurisprudence of other nations have also been used as interpretive or guiding sources of international law, and these too are discussed below.

COMPLEXITIES OF CUSTOMARY INTERNATIONAL LAW

In light of the fact that there is no global treaty governing domestic violence per se, it is necessary to consider other sources of international law to determine its status. For this reason it is necessary to engage the complexities of customary international law to assess whether or not there is a norm in international law that prohibits domestic violence.

The Elements of Customary International Law

Customary international law is an international custom which evidences a general practice accepted by states as law.[21] It is said to consist of two elements: (1) the conduct element, which is the consistent practice of states; and (2) the mental element, known as *opinio juris*, which is the state's belief that what it is doing is obligatory or right or that it is acting in accordance with a principle of law.[22] The test for determining whether a state acted through a sense of obligation is a subjective one.[23] In order for domestic violence to be prohibited in

---

[21] ICJ Statute (n 5), Art 38(b). For a discussion of the incorporation of principles of customary international law into the UK (specifically in respect of refugee law) see *European Roma Rights Centre v Immigration Officer at Prague Airport* (n 10) paras 22–24. See also *Paquete Habana; The Lola*, 175 US 677 (1900) 20 S Ct 290; 44 L Ed 320, holding that the conclusion of treaties and the adoption of certain practices by states are evidence of the existence of customary international law.

[22] *Opinio juris* stands for *opinio juris sive necessitates*, the belief that something is obligatory or right. See Sohn (n 12) 1073: 'It is universally agreed that "usages generally accepted as expressing principles of law" constitute one of the main sources of international law . . . Ordinarily, a rule is considered generally accepted when it is supported by constant practice of states acting on the conviction that the practice is obligatory.' See also American Law Institute, Restatement of the Foreign Relations Law of the United States (Third) vol 1, 1986, para 102(2), (3) and commentary (hereinafter American Law Institute, Restatement): 'c. Opinio juris. For a practice of states to become a rule of customary international law it must appear that the states follow the practice from a sense of legal obligation (opinio juris sive necessitatis).'

[23] See Hurst Hannum, 'The Status of the Universal Declaration of Human Rights in National and International Law' (1995/1996) 25 *Georgia Journal of International and Comparative Law* 287, 319. See also W Michael Reisman, 'Jonathan I Charney: An Appreciation' (2003) 36 *Vanderbilt Journal of Transnational Law* 23.

customary international law there must be uniform and constant use of such practice, and states practising that custom must also recognise that they are acting in accordance with a rule of international law.[24]

The elements of customary international law raise a number of questions: how many states must practise a rule in order for it to become law? Inversely, how many dissenting states are required to show that there is *not* a principle of customary international law? How does one determine the presence or absence of *opinio juris*? What if states agree that a rule is law but fail to comply with its requirements? Is there a difference between what states say and what they do as far as evidencing customary international law, and which is weightier, custom or *opinio juris*? Is it appropriate to use customary international law to determine human rights law, especially given the circularity of the elements of customary international law when determining whether new law has been created? And, how in fact do we recognise these two elements of customary international law?

For the most part, customary international law is ambiguous since it lacks the clarity and express consensus of binding treaties and relies instead on 'widespread state practice and *opinio juris*—a sense of legal obligation'.[25] It is not necessary that the consent to the rule be express.[26] At the same time, however, states are endowed with the ability to dissent from a rule of customary international law. This 'persistent objector' principle provides that if a state has objected persistently to a custom, that state is not bound by the rule. The dissent does not negate the legality of the rule vis-a-vis other states. It simply does not bind the objecting state. And yet it is the very fact of uniformity of practice that is required for a custom to become a principle of international law. This has been described as 'a delicate, indeed precarious, equilibrium between opposite concerns: on the one hand, to permit customary rules to emerge without demanding the individual consent of every state; on the other hand, to permit individual states to escape being bound by any rule they do not recognize as such'.[27]

How many states, therefore, are needed to raise a collective norm, such as the prohibition on domestic violence, to the level of a principle of customary international law? Is it enough that a reasonable number of states practise this rule,

---

[24] American Law Institute, Restatement (n 22). The ICJ Statute provides that the court shall use 'international custom, as evidence of a general practice accepted as law'. This was confirmed by the American Law Institute, Restatement at para 102(2) and (3): '(2) Customary international law results from a general and consistent practice of states followed by them from a sense of legal obligation. (3) International agreements create law for the states parties thereto and may lead to the creation of customary international law when such agreements are intended for adherence by states generally and are in fact widely accepted.'

[25] Andrew Guzman, 'A Compliance Based Theory of International Law' in Oona A Hathaway and Harold Hongju Koh (eds), *Foundations of International Law and Politics* (New York, Foundation Press, 2005) 58, 70.

[26] Slama (n 16), citing TL Stein, 'The Approach of the Different Drummer: The Principle of the Persistent Objector in International Law' (1985) 26 *Harvard International Law Journal* 469.

[27] Prosper Weil, 'Towards Relative Normativity in International Law?' (1981) 77 *American Journal of International Law* 413, 433–34.

or must different regional groups and different political, economic and ideological approaches be represented in order for the rule to be universal?[28] This is important with regard to domestic violence, which is often not criminalised or prohibited by states in certain regions. A sensible response is that there must be a modicum of generality about the norm evidenced by a reasonable number of states from a variety of regions. Complete universality, however, is not required and the fact that a few states object to the establishment of a new rule or to a revision of an old one does not prevent the birth of the rule.[29]

According to some academics, there is much evidence of deviations from purported customary international law norms, and very little 'general and consistent state practice'.[30] If this is the case, at what point do the deviations become the norm, requiring a change in the content of the law? For example, if all states practise racism, believing that it is not internationally prohibited, will racism become a principle of customary international law? This is an obvious nonsense and is addressed by the notion that there are certain practices that are right (ie lawful) and others that are wrong (ie unlawful). However, while it is clear that the consistent practice of racism (or corruption or torture) does not make racism lawful, can we say the same about domestic violence? At the level of international law this is, at best, unclear.

This complexity is compounded by the fact that states must behave consistently, *with the understanding* that they are under a legal obligation to act in that way. This begs the question, 'How can custom create law if its psychological component requires action in conscious accordance with law pre-existing the action?'[31] Some commentators argue that, for new law to be created, it is not necessary to believe that one is complying with a *legal* norm; rather, states must simply perform in a particular manner because they regard their conduct to be 'obligatory' or 'right'.[32] Nonetheless, the circularity involved renders this examination, at best, vague.

The natural question, then, is, how does one know whether a practice is sufficiently uniform that a principle of customary international law exists? Given the high degree of violence against women condoned by states, and the persistent reluctance of states to intervene to mitigate such violence, it is difficult to

[28] Sohn (n 12) maintains that 'One of the major elements determining the obligatory character of a particular rule of customary international law is its generality . . . [W]hat is sought . . . is a general recognition among states of a certain practice as obligatory' (p 1074). He proposes that two main factors have to be taken into account: 'first, express acceptance of the rule by a reasonable number of states belonging to various regional groups and representing different political, economic and ideological approaches; second, acquiescence by other states.' See also Andrew T Guzman, *How International Law Works: A Rational Choice Theory* (Oxford, Oxford University Press, 2008) 189–90.

[29] Sohn (n 12) 1074.

[30] Jack L Goldsmith and Eric A Posner, 'Further Thoughts on Customary International Law' (2001) 23 *Michigan Journal of International Law* 191, 191–92.

[31] Anthony A D'amato, *The Concept of Custom in International Law* (Ithaca, Cornell University Press 1971) 73. See also Charlesworth (n 12) 44.

[32] Hans Kelsen, *Principles of International Law* (Clark, Law Book Exchange, 2003) 307.

assert either that states act consistently to prevent domestic violence, or that they believe they have a legal obligation to do so.[33]

There is no one accepted process of unravelling these questions, but there are two broad approaches to customary international law that can be taken, namely, traditional theories and contemporary principles of customary international law.[34] An examination of each in respect of domestic violence is informative.

Traditional Theories of Customary International Law

Traditional theories examine the balance between custom and *opinio juris*. There are three dominant views on this issue. The first view is that *opinio juris* is the primary or only relevant element and that custom can exist by virtue of the psychological element alone.[35] In 1965, Bin Cheng argued that if *opinio juris* can be established conclusively, there is no need for 'usage at all in the sense of repeated practice'.[36] This became known as 'instant custom', a term which contradicts the intuitive temporal component of customary international law and the sense that it develops over a long period of time. The second view articulates the opposite, prioritising custom over *opinio juris*. Proponents of this view argue that usage is the most important, or indeed the *only*, element in the formation of custom and that the belief that a custom is legal in nature is not necessary.[37]

The third and most widely accepted view is a combination of the two. It is attributed to Gény's theory that *opinio juris*, the psychological element, is necessary to determine whether usage is motivated by an intention to comply with a legal requirement.[38] This approach, combining the two elements, was evident in an investigation undertaken by the International Law Commission (ILC), which confirmed that there are five strands to customary international law:

---

[33] Patrick Kelly, 'The Twilight of Customary International Law' (2000) 40 *Virginia Journal of International Law* 452.

[34] See: D'amato (n 31) 74–87; Arthur A Weisburd, 'Customary International Law: The Problem of Treaties' (1988) 21 *Vanderbijlt Journal of Transnational Law* 1, 10; Chen's theory of 'instant custom', Lung-Chu Chen, 'United Nations Resolutions on Outer Space: "Instant" International Customary Law?' (1965) 5 *Indian Journal of International Law* 23, 46–47 (arguing that a rule of customary international law may be developed instantly by the articulation of the belief that a particular norm constitutes customary international law); Goldsmith and Posner's positive theoretical account of customary international law, Jack L Goldsmith and Eric A Posner, 'A Theory of Customary International Law' (1999) 66 *University of Chicago Law Review* 1113; and Goldsmith and Posner (n 30) 191. This is countered by the traditionalist defence of Detlev F Vagts, 'International Relations Looks at Customary International Law: A Traditionalist's Defence' (2004) 15 *European Journal of International Law* 1031. See also Sohn (n 12) 1073 (noting that 'the methods of developing new rules of customary international law have greatly changed since the Second World War').

[35] Slama (n 16) 613 (citing Puchta and Savigny in describing the historical evolution of the principle of *opinio juris* in customary international law); see also D'amato (n 31).

[36] Slama (n 16) 615.

[37] Kelsen (n 32) 450–51. See also Slama (n 16) 614–16.

[38] Slama (n 16) 614 (describing the development of *opinio juris* in customary international law).

(a) concordant practice by a number of states with reference to a type of situation falling within the domain of international relations; (b) continuation or repetition of the practice over a considerable period of time; (c) a conception that the practice is required by, or consistent with, prevailing international law; (d) general acquiescence in the practice by other States; . . . [and the establishment of] the presence of each of these elements . . . by a competent international authority.[39]

Another version, based on the International Court of Justice's interpretation of customary international law and proposed by certain academics, involves a four-part test:

(1) state practice—the 'quantitative' element; (2) *opinio juris*—the 'psychological' element; (3) the norm must be adhered to by a majority of 'specially affected' states—the 'qualitative' element; and (4) the practice must be continued over some period of time—the 'temporal' element.[40]

Notwithstanding the various formulations, it is possible to conclude that the two components of customary international law—the mental component and the practice of a custom—are inextricably linked.

Contemporary Theories of Customary International Law

Recently, new theories regarding the determinative elements of customary international law have developed. These so-called 'new' or 'contemporary' theories of customary international law recognise rules 'from rights and principles proclaimed in international human rights instruments that have their basis in the Charter of the UN and other treaties of a universal character'.[41] The rules may be evident from diplomatic correspondence, policy statements delivered by states, press releases, the opinions of official legal advisers, official manuals on legal questions, executive decisions and practices, comments made by governments on drafts produced by the ILC on various legal subjects, state legislation, international and national judicial decisions, recitals in treaties and other international instruments, a pattern of treaties in the same form, the practice of international organs, and resolutions relating to legal questions in the UN General Assembly.[42]

Members of the UN have indicated that UN declarations may by custom become recognised as laying down rules binding upon states. UN resolutions

[39] Slama (n 16) 616 (citing Manley O Hudson, 'Article 24 of the Statute of the International Law Commission' (1950) 2 *Yearbook of the International Law Commission* 24, 26).
[40] Slama (n 16) 617–18 (citing the formula for custom creation summarised by Professor Dennis Arrow and based on the jurisprudence of the ICJ and prevailing international law scholars).
[41] Thomas Buergenthal, Dinah Shelton and David Stewart, *International Human Rights in a Nutshell* (St Paul, West, 2002) 395. See also Schachter (n 4) 3 (noting that 'some treaties such as codification conventions express preexisting customary law').
[42] Ian Brownlie, *Principles of Public International Law*, 7th edn (Oxford, Oxford University Press, 2008) 3. See also Sohn (n 12) 1074.

and decisions are part of the official records of the UN and 'constitute formal expressions of the opinion or will of UN bodies'.[43] However, the components of custom and *opinio juris* are still required to endorse the declaration, either at the time of its creation or later.[44]

Professor Schachter notes that 'a large area of international regulation has been developed by the specialized [UN] agencies'.[45] Schachter's theory of the creation of authoritative international obligations, based in part on the New Haven School, is summarised by Professor Koh as:

> (1) the designation of a behavioral requirement; (2) the indication that persons with competence and authority have made the designation; (3) an indication of the capacity and willingness of those concerned to make the designated requirement effective; (4) transmittal of the requirement to the target audience; and, (5) creation in the target audience of psychological and operational responses that indicate that the designated requirement is regarded as authoritative and hence, as likely to be complied with in the future.[46]

Some have proposed that the activities of non-governmental organisations (NGOs) should be regarded as contributing to the expansion of customary international law.[47] Others maintain that UN declarations are not customary international law but comprise 'a new body of international law, "declarative" international law', which are rules that, lacking either one of the two elements of customary international law (either practice or *opinio juris*), are 'declared as law by a majority of States but not actually enforced by them, or rules that are both practiced and accepted as law, but only by a minority of States'.[48]

In general, contemporary principles of customary international law potentially emerge from the UN system and its interaction with the international community. This is actually quite sensible, considering that the UN and its treaty bodies are roughly 60 years old and customary international law developed long before the existence of these international bodies. Globalisation and information technology have also drawn back the veil concealing government activity and we know that the needs and values of individuals within a state are not always represented by their governments. In fact, it may not be appropriate to determine principles of human rights law by looking at what a state's government does or

---

[43] For details of the purpose and make-up of UN documents see United Nations Official Records and Resolutions at www.lib.msu.edu/foxre/unres.html. See also www.lib.msu.edu/foxre/unres.html for details of the status in international law of the various UN bodies and their subsidiary organs.

[44] Sohn (n 12) 1079 (citing a Memorandum of the Office of Legal Affairs of the Secretariat, UN Doc E/CN.4/L.610, para 4, quoted in 34 UN ESCOR Supp (No 8) at 15, UN Doc E/3614/Rev 1 (1962)).

[45] Schachter (n 4) 5.

[46] Oscar Schachter, 'Towards a Theory of International Obligation' (1968) 8 *Virginia Journal of International Law* 300, 307. See also Harold Hongju Koh, 'Why do Nations Obey International Law?' (1997) 106 *Yale Law Journal* 2599, 2603 fn 113.

[47] Charlesworth (n 12) 44 (citing Isabelle Gunning, 'Modernizing Customary International Law: The Challenge of Human Rights' (1991) 31 *Virginia Journal of International Law* 211).

[48] See Hiram E Chodesh, 'Neither Treaty Nor Custom: The Emergence of Declarative International Law' (1991) 26 *Texas International Law Journal* 87, 89 (arguing that 'declarative law is not accepted as law by a generality of states').

says; rather, it would be preferable to look at what the citizens of that state demand or need. A somewhat nuanced approach to customary international law, especially in the context of human rights, is quite practical.

What is the outcome if we apply these theories to domestic violence?

APPLYING CUSTOMARY INTERNATIONAL LAW TO DOMESTIC VIOLENCE

Traditional Theories of Customary International Law

If one takes the view that customary international law exists and is evidenced only by consistent usage and the concomitant belief that such usage is required by law, how does one know which states at what time complied with which principle? Various mechanisms could provide an answer; for example, we could look at the laws, customs and behaviour of every state within a delineated time frame and draw conclusions as to the customary nature of the practice. If we adopt this modus operandi to determine whether domestic violence is a violation of customary international law, the answer is likely to be—it depends. Traditionally, very few states created law around domestic violence. Increasingly, though (and only recently), more and more states are adopting legislation prohibiting domestic violence and acknowledging that they have a responsibility to respond to the needs of domestic violence victims and survivors. If one focuses on the latter development, then one might conclude that states in fact are consistently acting against domestic violence, although this still leaves open the question of critical mass and how many states must enact domestic violence legislation in order for this to be a global law.

One would then have to ask whether these states are addressing domestic violence with the belief that they are required to do so by law. Once again it is possible to argue both ways. Many states that adopt domestic violence legislation actually incorporate a reference to CEDAW, DEVAW or other international instruments in their legislation. This certainly links the conduct of the state to an international law imperative and evinces some mental belief that enacting such legislation is at least conduct in compliance with international law, although the absence of an express reference to international law in national legislation does not necessarily mean that the state does not deem itself bound by a principle of international law. Add to this broil the fact that, even where states have enacted domestic violence legislation, the violence continues. If a state allows high levels of domestic violence to continue, irrespective of the existence of anti-violence legislation, is this evidence of a persistent objector? Does it mean that there really is no custom against domestic violence? Or does it simply mean that the legislation is not effective?

Finally, to whom do we look to represent the mind of the state? Do we look to the motivation of the government and, if so, which administration? If the government is not democratically elected or if it is not representative of women, do we accept its actions as custom even though it may be acting without the endorsement of some or all of its citizens?[49] This is an important question as regards countries that practise overt gender discrimination. Do women endorse these governments and, if not, is that relevant to the formulation of a customary international law on domestic violence?

While it is largely accepted that, based on the prohibition of discrimination against women in CEDAW, there is an international rule prohibiting sex discrimination, the obligation this imposes on states in respect of domestic violence is less clear. Not all states would agree that they have an international obligation to protect women from domestic violence:[50] some may present economic justifications for their failure to prevent disproportionate levels of violence against women; others acquiesce to violence against women based on the politicisation of religious beliefs or cultural practices.[51]

This raises an important policy question. Can we really look for human rights norms using traditional methods of customary international law? If customary international law depends on the practice and *opinio juris* of states, and states are run by governments which may (and often do) act at odds with the human rights or needs of their citizens, can we really determine the rules of customary international law with reference to state behaviour? Such an approach is arguably inappropriate, particularly in the context of violence against women. For example, in 1998 the CEDAW Committee noted that despite the efforts of many countries, 'overall global discrimination is worsening'.[52] On a strict interpretation of customary international law, there is little evidence of state practice to support the claim that domestic violence is factually prohibited.

Contemporary Theories of Customary International Law

The quandary is mitigated slightly if one accepts that customary international law may be evidenced by UN resolutions, declarations and treaty provisions in respect of non-signatories.[53] In general, these documents give us an objective benchmark and provide probative evidence of the mental element of states. UN resolutions and declarations may well evidence the existence of a customary

---

[49]   See Boyle and Chinkin (n 6) 37.

[50]   See *Town of Castle Rock v Gonzales* 125 S Ct 2796 (2005). See also Joel Richard Paul, 'Cultural Resistance to Global Governance' (2000) 22 *Michigan Journal of International Law* 9.

[51]   See Jimmy Carter, 'The Words of God do Not Justify Cruelty to Women' *The Observer* (London, 12 July 2009), www.guardian.co.uk/commentisfree/2009/jul/12/jimmy-carter-womens-rights-equality. For a detailed discussion of the ways in which religious extremism target women in countries such as Afghanistan and Pakistan, see Jan Goodwin, *The Price of Honor: Muslim Women Lift the Veil of Silence on the Islamic World*, rev edn (New York, Plume Printing, 2003).

[52]   Valerie A Dormady, 'Status of the Convention on the Elimination of All Forms of Discrimination against Women (CEDAW) in 1998' (1999) 33 *International Law* 637, 642.

[53]   See Kelly (n 33) 454–55. See also Koh (n 46) 2603 fn 113.

international law norm prohibiting domestic violence. In fact, this is where we find the bulk of 'authority' for most of the international law dealing with violence against women. This view of customary international law is particularly compelling where resolutions or declarations are made unanimously by the relevant UN body. However, it has been cautioned that even 'a UN declaration adopted unanimously will have diminished authority as law if it is not observed by states particularly affected'.[54]

It is also possible that what we may perceive as non-endorsement of a norm is in fact non-compliance with a norm due to a failure to 'operationalise' it.[55] Therefore, the degree to which states *do not* protect women against domestic violence is not necessarily a sign that an international law principle prohibiting such violence does not exist; rather it suggests that the law is poorly implemented.

The views of contemporary customary international law proponents are well supported but they remain contentious. While contemporary or 'new' customary international law has found support in recent decisions of the ICJ, it is criticised for evidencing neither custom nor *opinio juris*.[56] Whether or not this is accepted as a source of international law remains a matter for debate.

IS THERE AN EMERGING NORM PROHIBITING DOMESTIC VIOLENCE?

For the reasons discussed above, if one adopts the traditional approach to customary international law, looking both to the conduct of states and to the psychological motivation behind that conduct, it is not clear that there is an authoritative norm prohibiting domestic violence. This is because most states fail to prioritise and combat domestic violence, making it difficult to substantiate a claim that there is consistent and universal state practice with respect to mitigating domestic violence. In respect of domestic violence, there is no obvious 'concordant practice by a number of states with reference to a type of situation falling within the domain of international relations',[57] although many states are taking domestic violence and violence against women increasingly seriously. While there has been an increase in domestic violence legislation in many states, this has not necessarily happened over 'a considerable period of time'.[58] On the other hand, it is possible to argue that the increased attention paid by such states to issues of domestic violence is based on a conception that the practice is required by, or consistent with, prevailing international law, or at least 'the right thing to do'.[59] The jury, so to speak, is still out.

---

[54] Schachter (n 4) 3.
[55] Allen Buchanan, *Justice, Legitimacy, and Self-Determination* (Oxford, Oxford University Press, 2006) 75.
[56] Kelly (n 33) 484–85.
[57] ibid, 616 (citing Hudson).
[58] ibid. See also Slama (n 16) 613, 617–18.
[59] Kelly (n 33) 616 (citing Hudson).

The contemporary approach to customary international law may give us a different answer, however. International bodies of varying degrees of authoritative status have produced a multitude of resolutions, declarations, studies, statements and reports on the subject of domestic violence and violence against women. Potentially, a degree of international consensus can be found in this wide range of literature, evincing a move towards the recognition of a right to be free from domestic violence with a conjoint obligation on the state to do all it can to protect against and prevent this violence. Whether the norm is articulated by states' governments, NGOs or international representatives and entities, the fact is that states and international organisations around the world are turning their attention to the economic cost, social disruption and personal violation caused by domestic violence. This at least indicates a degree of international consensus that the problem is pervasive and global.

Therefore, within the strict framework of international law, it is unclear how one would categorise the various international and regional instruments prohibiting domestic violence. Perhaps they are evidence of the two elements of customary international law, namely, consistent state practice and/or *opinio juris*. Or perhaps they are evidence of norms which are developing into law notwithstanding the contrary behaviour of certain states. It is precisely this quandary that demands a thorough analysis of domestic violence in international law, which I now turn to do.

WOMEN'S RIGHTS IN INTERNATIONAL LAW— HISTORICAL OVERVIEW

International human rights law prohibits the violation of certain rights. A list of inviolable rights appeared in 1948, in the UN's Universal Declaration of Human Rights (UDHR).[60] The UDHR, a declaration and not a treaty, became a reflection of customary international law, encompassing a list of mandatory norms that apply to all nations. The UDHR was followed by the two rights covenants, namely the International Covenant on Civil and Political Rights (ICCPR) and the International Covenant on Economic, Social and Cultural Rights (ICESCR).[61] Based largely on the events of World War Two and the Holocaust, the rights articulated in these instruments reflect 'the inherent dignity and the equal and inalienable rights' of all people.[62]

[60] Universal Declaration of Human Rights (UDHR) (adopted 10 December 1948) UNGA Res 217 A(III).

[61] International Covenant on Civil and Political Rights (ICCPR) (adopted 16 December 1966, entered into force 23 March 1976) 999 UNTS 171; International Covenant on Economic, Social and Cultural Rights (ICESCR) (adopted 16 December 1966, entered into force 3 January 1976) 993 UNTS 3.

[62] UDHR, preamble. For a brief discussion of the development of human rights in international law see Myres S McDougal, Harold D Lasswell and Lung-chu Chen, *Human Rights and the World Public Order: The Basic Policies of an International Law of Human Dignity* (New Haven, Yale University Press, 1980) 4–5.

Over the course of the last 30 years, however, women and women's groups have identified various ways in which the needs and rights of women are not addressed by these instruments. Theorists have argued that women are abused as a group, and endure a particular form of harm relating to their gender which intersects with their ethnicity, race or religion. While the provisions of the UDHR arguably could be extrapolated to apply to gender-based violence and discrimination, some maintain that this is insufficient and does not 'provide the type of special protection women need by virtue of the different nature of their body and reproductive functions'.[63] This call for precise and express rights for women[64] has resulted in the development of international instruments, bodies and organisations that specifically address the rights of women in international law.[65]

From an institutional point of view, the demarcation of women's rights began as early as 1946, when the UN established the Commission on the Status of Women (CSW).[66] The CSW is a division of the UN Economic and Social Council, the entity responsible for the implementation of the provisions of the ICESCR. The administrative division of the CSW, the Division for the Advancement of Women, is responsible for some of the major developments in women's rights in international law and exists today as an effective, albeit under-used, body.[67] As mentioned above, the most important development for women in international law was the adoption of CEDAW and the creation of the CEDAW Committee to oversee its enforcement.[68]

---

[63] See Surya P Subedi, 'Protection of Women against Domestic Violence: The Response of International Law' (1997) 6 *European Human Rights Law Review* 587, 592–93. See also Dorothy Q Thomas and Michele E Beasley, Esq, 'Domestic Violence as a Human Rights Issue' (1993) 15 *Human Rights Quarterly* 36, 39 (describing the inadequacy of international law to prevent violence against women).

[64] For a comprehensive discussion of the history of women's rights in international law, see Arvonne S Fraser, *Becoming Human: The Origins and Development of Women's Human Rights* (Maryland, Johns Hopkins University Press, 1999) (originally published in (1999) 21 *Human Rights Quarterly* 853).

[65] See McDougal et al (n 62) 612–52.

[66] For a discussion of the history of this organisation see Peace Women (Women's International League for Peace and Freedom), UN Commission on the Status of Women, www.peacewomen.org/un/ecosoc/CSW/CSWindex.html. See also Division for the Advancement of Women, Commission on the Status of Women: Overview, www.un.org/womenwatch/daw/csw (hereinafter CSW Overview).

[67] See CSW Overview, ibid. The Division for the Advancement of Women acted as the substantive secretariat for the Beijing Conference (n 17) in 1995, the largest conference in the history of the UN, and was responsible for the preparations for the three previous World Conferences on Women (Mexico 1975, Copenhagen 1980, Nairobi 1985). See 'Division for the Advancement of Women: Brief History', www.un.org/womenwatch/daw/daw.

[68] This was not the first treaty to address one specific right or group of people: the same had been done in the prohibition of racial discrimination and would continue in respect of refugees, torture survivors, children's rights and the rights of indigenous and tribal peoples. See eg International Convention on the Elimination of All Forms of Racial Discrimination (adopted 21 December 1965, entered into force 4 January 1969) 660 UNTS 195; Convention relating to the Status of Refugees (adopted 28 July 1951, entered into force on 22 April 1954) 189 UNTS 150; Convention against Torture and Other Cruel, Inhuman or Degrading Treatment or Punishment (adopted 10 December 1984, entered into force 26 July 1987) 1465 UNTS 85, (1984) 23 ILM 1027 (hereinafter Torture Convention); Convention on the Rights of the Child (adopted 20 November 1989, entered into force 2 September 1990) 1577 UNTS 3, (1989) 28 ILM 1456 (hereinafter Children's Convention).

These instruments and bodies developed several major themes concerning women's rights, including health, reproductive and family rights, political and legal representation, economic and employment equality, the eradication of prostitution and cultural stereotypes, education, and safety. These themes have been addressed by international laws and institutions with varying degrees of success. One such theme is the right to be safe from violence.

VIOLENCE AGAINST WOMEN IN INTERNATIONAL LAW— HISTORICAL OVERVIEW

In the early 1970s, the UN General Assembly proclaimed 1975 International Women's Year, which was expanded to the UN Decade for Women from 1975 to 1985.[69] During this period, three World Conferences on Women took place, in Mexico, Copenhagen and Nairobi (the fourth and most recent conference was held in Beijing in 1995).[70]

The first World Conference on Women was held in Mexico in 1975. The World Plan of Action adopted at this conference did not expressly refer to violence against women, but 'drew attention to the need for the family to ensure dignity, equality and security of each of its members'.[71] It is clear that violence against women was not on the radar of international law at this stage and, when CEDAW was adopted four years later in 1979, violence against women was not incorporated into the original text.

At the second World Conference on Women in Copenhagen in 1980, reference was made to family violence, and the conference participants adopted a resolution on 'battered women and violence in the family'.[72] At the third World Conference, which took place in Nairobi in 1985, violence against women was a far more prominent theme, emerging as 'a serious international concern'.[73] The Forward-Looking Strategies adopted by the conference linked peace and equality to the eradication of violence against women in both the public and private spheres.[74]

Meanwhile, one year prior to Nairobi, in 1984, the UN Economic and Social Council passed Resolution 1984/14 on violence in the family.[75] Based on this

---

[69] UN Division for the Advancement of Women, 'Information Note, United Nations Work on Violence against Women', www.un.org/womenwatch/daw/news/unwvaw.html hereinafter Information Note.

[70] See UN Division for the Advancement of Women, *Report of the World Conference to Review and Appraise the Achievements of the United Nations Decade for Women: Equality, Development and Peace* (Nairobi, 15–26 July 1985) UN Doc A/CONF.116/28/Rev.1, www.un.org/womenwatch/daw/beijing/otherconferences/Nairobi/Nairobi%20Full%20Optimized.pdf, para 2 (hereinafter Nairobi Principles). See in general www.un.org/womenwatch/daw/beijing/nairobi.html.

[71] Information Note (n 69).

[72] ibid.

[73] ibid. See also the Nairobi Principles (n 70).

[74] Information Note (n 69) ('The conference included violence as a major obstacle to the achievement of development, equality and peace, the three objectives of the Decade'). See also the Nairobi Principles (n 70).

[75] UNESC Res 14 (24 May 1984) UN Doc ESC Res 1984/14, on Violence in the family.

Resolution, a year later the UN General Assembly passed Resolution 40/36 on domestic violence, which invited states to 'take specific action urgently in order to prevent domestic violence and to render the appropriate assistance to the victims thereof'[76] and called for UN research on domestic violence 'from a criminological perspective to formulate distinct action-oriented strategies'.[77] The Resolution laid the foundation for compelling legislative reform, but it was weak in its language: it 'invites' Member States, inter alia, to enact and implement criminal and civil legislation, to provide temporary shelter relief for victims, to curb domestic violence through a process of education and research, and to improve the accessibility of social, legal and health services.[78] The Resolution was not authoritative or mandatory, using instead the language of invitation and suggestion; however, it did lead to an Expert Group Meeting on Violence in the Family in 1986, which focused on the manner in which women are affected by domestic violence.[79]

In 1989 the UN released a report on Violence against Women in the Family, which was one of the significant marks of change in the international legal landscape.[80] The report established four important factors. First, it described domestic violence as a problem in almost every country, giving it an international profile.[81] Second, domestic violence was cited as one of the more serious causes of ill-health amongst women, thereby linking it to the existing international right to health. Third, the report established that domestic violence is not random but is 'associated with inequality between women and men, and strategies to perpetuate or entrench that inequality'.[82] Finally, the report initiated a change in the emphasis in international law from protection of the family to protection of individuals *within* the family.

This last factor is important because many human rights instruments promote the protection of the family unit as the 'natural and fundamental group

---

[76] UNGA Res 40/36 (29 November 1985) UN Doc A/RES/40/36, Art 2 (hereinafter 1985 UN Resolution).

[77] ibid, Art 3. Art 5 also calls for inter-agency support for domestic violence within the UN.

[78] ibid, Art 7(a).

[79] See Information Note (n 69).

[80] UN Centre for Social Development and Humanitarian Affairs, 'Violence against Women in the Family' (1989) UN Doc ST/CSDHA/2, 14. It was also at this time that the CEDAW Committee recommended that states include a discussion of violence against women in their reports to the CEDAW Committee. See General Recommendation 19 (n 20) Art 2.

[81] 'Violence against Women in the Family', ibid.

[82] ibid. See also Helen O'Connell, *Equality Postponed: Gender, Rights and Development* (Oxford, World View, 1996) 11.

[83] UDHR, Art 16(3). See also Art 18(1) of the African Charter on Human and Peoples' Rights (adopted 27 June 1981, entered into force 21 October 1986) (1982) 21 ILM 58 (hereinafter African Charter or Banjul Charter), describing the family as 'the natural unit and basis of society'. Art 29(1) states that the 'individual shall also have the duty . . . to preserve the harmonious development of the family and to work for the cohesion and respect of the family'. Art 17(1) of the ICCPR provides that 'No one shall be subjected to arbitrary or unlawful interference with his privacy, family, home or correspondence, nor to unlawful attacks on his honour and reputation'. Art 23(1) of the ICCPR echoes the UDHR, stating that the 'family is the natural and fundamental group unit of society and is entitled to protection by society and the State'.

unit of society' which is 'entitled to protection by society and the state'.[83] But as far as domestic violence is concerned, the family is the locus of the harm. The emphasis on the protection and sanctity of the family unit in basic international human rights instruments sheds some light on the tendency of so many people to see all family activity, including intimate violence, as a private issue, falling outside the purview of the law. Therefore, the report, by acknowledging that domestic violence is both a manifestation of discrimination against women and a perpetuating force of gender inequality, helped to mitigate some of this exaggerated respect for the family unit.[84]

In 1990, the UN General Assembly adopted General Resolution 45/114 on domestic violence, which noted the serious lack of information and research on domestic violence globally and the need 'for exchange of information on ways of dealing with this problem'.[85] This Resolution was nuanced, identifying the need for 'common policies' and 'specialised approaches'; the particular needs of women, children and the elderly; the diverse approaches of different cultures to domestic violence; and the impact of domestic violence on 'attitudes and behaviour, such as increased tolerance to violence in society as a whole'.[86] Once again, using suggestive language, the Resolution 'urged' states to adopt and implement multidisciplinary policies to prevent domestic violence, protect its victims and provide appropriate treatment for offenders.[87]

Possibly the most important aspect of the 1990 Resolution was its globalising effect. By urging Member States to 'exchange information, experience and research findings', the Resolution shifted domestic violence into the mainstream realm of international justice and public affairs and acknowledged the global pervasiveness of this problem.[88] Domestic violence was now a recognised pandemic.

In 1992 the CEDAW Committee incorporated violence against women into its jurisprudence with the adoption of General Recommendation 19, which confirmed expressly that domestic violence impedes gender equality and that the 'full implementation of the Convention require[s] states to take positive measures to eliminate all forms of violence against women'. General Recommendation 19 laid down a framework, the value of which cannot be discounted. It broadened the definition of violence against women to include physical, sexual and psychological harm, including 'threats of such acts, coercion or arbitrary deprivation of liberty, whether occurring in public or private life'.[89] It demonstrated that violence between intimates affects women disproportionately, demarcating women as a group in need of proactive state protection. It recommended that states take

---

[84] For a discussion of this see Hilary Charlesworth, Christine Chinkin and Shelley Wright, 'Feminist Approaches to International Law' (1991) 85 *American Journal of International Law* 613, 636.

[85] Preamble to UNGA Res 45/114 (14 December 1990) UN Doc A/RES/45/114 (hereinafter 1990 UN Resolution).

[86] ibid. However, Art 2 emphasises criminal sanctions for domestic violence, which, as discussed in ch 2, is not necessarily the ideal approach.

[87] ibid, Art 1(a)–(d).

[88] ibid, Arts 3, 4.

[89] General Recommendation 19 (n 20) para 6.

specific steps to reduce domestic violence by improving women's legal protection, through legislative amendments and gender-sensitive training for the judiciary;[90] gathering statistics in order to identify the nature and extent of the problem;[91] and creating complaint mechanisms and places of refuge for women escaping violent circumstances.[92] Finally, it incorporated reference to the so-called 'due diligence' standard to determine what diligent states should do to fulfil the objectives contained in General Recommendation 19.[93]

Then, in 1993, the World Conference on Human Rights in Vienna witnessed one of the strongest global calls yet for the recognition of violence against women as an international human rights violation.[94] The incorporation of the human rights of women in the Vienna Declaration and Programme of Action led, inter alia, to the appointment of the Special Rapporteur on violence against women, its causes and consequences, and the confirmation of female genital cutting (FGC) as an international human rights violation.[95]

The internationalisation of measures preventing violence against women gained significant momentum in 1994 with the adoption of the General Assembly's Declaration on the Elimination of Violence against Women. DEVAW defined violence against women as 'any act of gender-based violence that results in, or is likely to result in, physical, sexual or psychological harm or suffering to women, including threats of such acts, coercion or arbitrary deprivation of liberty, whether occurring in public or private life'.[96] DEVAW adopted the same principles as the CEDAW Committee's General Recommendation 19, identifying the need for

> a clear and comprehensive definition of violence against women, a clear statement of the rights to be applied to ensure the elimination of violence against women in all its forms, a commitment by States in respect of their responsibilities, and a commitment by the international community at large to the elimination of violence against women.[97]

---

[90] ibid, para 24(b).

[91] ibid, para 24(c).

[92] ibid, paras 24(i), (k), (r).

[93] ibid, para 9 ('States may also be responsible for private acts if they fail to act with due diligence to prevent violations of rights or to investigate and punish acts of violence, and for providing compensation').

[94] See 'Vienna Declaration and Programme of Action', World Conference on Human Rights (Vienna, 14–25 June 1993) UN Doc A/CONF.157/24 (12 July 1993) 20 (hereinafter Vienna Declaration).

[95] See UNCHR Resolution 1994/45 (n 17) and the establishment of the mandate of the Special Rapporteur on violence against women (n 17).

[96] DEVAW (n 17), Art 1. Art 4(c) requires states to 'Exercise due diligence to prevent, investigate and, in accordance with national legislation, punish acts of violence against women, whether those acts are perpetrated by the State or by private persons'. See also *Report of the Fiftieth Session of the Committee on the Elimination of Discrimination against Women* (31 May 1995) UN Doc A/50/38 (31 May 1995) (hereinafter CEDAW Fiftieth Session). Art 5 of DEVAW enjoins UN bodies and other international organisations to include the protection of women from violence in their respective fields of competence.

[97] DEVAW (n 17) preamble.

In the same year, the General Assembly of the Organization of American States (OAS) adopted the Inter-American Convention on the Prevention, Punishment and Eradication of Violence against Women, which became known as the Convention of Belem Do Para.

In 1995, at the fourth World Conference of Women in Beijing, violence against women was identified as one of the 12 areas of women's lives requiring urgent action.[98] The consequent Beijing Declaration and Platform for Action adopted the definition of violence against women in DEVAW and expanded it to include violence perpetrated against women in war.[99]

At this point, the focus on violence against women shifted from non-state violence to crimes of conflict and the development of the norm prohibiting mass rape as a weapon of war, which characterised the genocides in Rwanda and the Former Yugoslavia during the 1990s.[100] The jurisprudence of women's international rights was further augmented by the decisions of the International Criminal Tribunals for the Former Yugoslavia and Rwanda, which established the precedent and legal rationale that led to the criminalisation of mass rape as a weapon of war, a crime against humanity and an instrument of genocide under the Rome Statute in 1998.[101]

In 2000, the UN General Assembly adopted the Optional Protocol to the Convention on the Elimination of All Forms of Discrimination against Women. This enabled the CEDAW Committee to receive communications by, or on behalf of, individuals who have grievances falling within the scope of CEDAW.[102] It also gave the CEDAW Committee investigative powers, significantly augmenting the

---

[98]   See Chapter Three of the Beijing Declaration (n 17).

[99]   ibid, paras 101, 110(d).

[100]   See Anika Rahman and Nahid Tubia, *Female Genital Mutilation: A Guide to Laws & Policies Worldwide* (London, Zed Books, 2000). See also generally Kelly D Askin, 'Prosecuting Wartime Rape and Other Gender-Related Crimes under International Law: Extraordinary Advances, Enduring Obstacles' (2003) 21 *Berkeley Journal of International Law* 288, 347 (discussing the jurisprudence of rape as a weapon of war/genocide or as a crime against humanity). The culmination of these developments was thoroughly addressed by Elizabeth Schneider in her examination of the law regarding battered women from a feminist perspective, Elizabeth M Schneider, *Battered Women & Feminist Lawmaking* (New Haven, Yale University Press, 2002) 95. FGC was prohibited specifically in DEVAW (n 17), Art 2(a), which includes female genital cutting in the definition of violence against women.

[101]   The International Criminal Tribunal for Rwanda (ICTR) was established by UNSC Res 955 (8 November 1994) UN Doc S/RES/955. See also its Statute, www.ictr.org/ENGLISH/basicdocs/statute/2007.pdf (hereinafter ICTR Statute). The International Criminal Tribunal for the Former Yugoslavia (ICTY) was established by UNSC Res 808 (22 February 1993) UN Doc S/RES/808. See also its Statute, www.icty.org/sid/135 (hereinafter ICTY Statute). See also *Prosecutor v Furundzija* (Judgment) (1999) ICTY-95-17/1-T, (1999) 38 ILM 317, 353 (indicating that although 'No international human rights instrument specifically prohibits rape . . . In certain circumstances . . . rape can amount to torture'); *Prosecutor v Rutaganda* (Judgment) (1999) ICTR-96-3-T, (1999) 39 ILM 557, 570 (identifying, inter alia, rape and torture as crimes against humanity). Art 7 § 1(k) of the Rome Statute (n 5) defines crimes against humanity as conduct that is 'widespread, systematic and focused on a segment of a population, including, rape, sexual slavery, enforced prostitution, forced pregnancy, enforced sterilisation, or any other form of sexual violence of comparable gravity'.

[102]   CEDAW Optional Protocol (n 17) Art 2.

status of CEDAW. That same year, in March, the UN Human Rights Committee (which is the UN committee responsible for implementation of the ICCPR) adopted General Comment No 28, entrenching equality of rights between men and women.[103] This was an important moment in women's rights jurisprudence. The UN Human Rights Committee authorised the interpretation of Article 3 of the ICCPR, which enjoins states to ensure the equal right of men and women to enjoy all civil and political rights, as requiring proactive conduct by states to 'ensure to men and women equally the enjoyment of all rights provided for in the Covenant'.[104] General Comment No 28 acknowledged what feminists had claimed for over three decades—that the harm and inequality that are unique to women had not been addressed by mainstream international law and that positive action was necessary to offset the negative effects of the historic legacy of gender differentiation and discrimination.[105]

On 8 September 2000, 189 nations adopted the Millennium Declaration, which established the eight Millennium Development Goals (MDGs).[106] The third MDG aims to promote gender equality and empower women through equal education, literacy, waged employment and parliamentary representation.[107] However, no mention is made of violence against women specifically.

On 9 October 2006, the office of former Secretary-General Kofi Annan issued a report classifying violence against women—whether in the home or elsewhere—as a human rights violation. The report confirmed that states are obliged by international human rights standards to hold perpetrators to account.[108] The report is a breakthrough, confirming that (1) violence against women is not inevitable; (2) violence against women continues because of discrimination against women; and (3) the continued prevalence of violence against women indicates that 'States have yet to tackle it with the necessary political commitment, visibility and resources'.[109]

Today, almost every UN body has a policy on violence against women, including 'a resource manual on strategies for confronting domestic violence' prepared under the supervision of the UN Centre for Crime Prevention and Criminal Justice.[110] In addition, the UN Children Fund has produced a report

---

[103] Human Rights Committee, 'General Comment No 28: Equality of Rights between Men and Women (article 3)' (29 March 2000) UN Doc CCPR/C/21/Rev.1/Add.10. See also Carin Benninger-Budel, *Violence Against Women: 10 Reports/Year 2000 for the Protection and Promotion of the Human Rights of Women* (Geneva, World Organization against Torture, 2000) 10.

[104] General Comment No 28, ibid, para 3.

[105] ibid.

[106] United Nations Millennium Declaration, UNGA Res 55/2 (18 September 2000) UN Doc A/Res/55/2.

[107] See www.unmillenniumproject.org/goals/index.htm.

[108] UN Secretary-General, 'In-depth Study on All Forms of Violence against Women' (2006) UN Doc A/61/122/Add.1 (hereinafter Study of the Secretary-General).

[109] ibid, i.

[110] See Information Note (n 69) ('Other parts of the United Nations system and its related entities, such as the International Labour Organization and the World Health Organization, addressed specific forms of violence against women within their specific mandates').

on *Domestic Violence against Women and Girls*, describing the types, causes and consequences of domestic violence.[111]

Where does that leave us as far as international law is concerned? A detailed analysis of relevant international and regional treaties, instruments, statements and jurisprudence shows that, although not in treaty, most international bodies and many states identify domestic violence as a responsibility of states and as a human rights violation. What is less clear and requires more work is precisely what states should be doing to prevent domestic violence and at what stage states can be said to be responsible for domestic violence. The developments I discuss below, many of which match the indicia identified by Koh, Schachter and others, have helped to clarify the muddy waters of a prohibition in customary international law; but a distilled, authoritative and applicable principle of international law prohibiting domestic violence is still being developed.

DOMESTIC VIOLENCE IN INTERNATIONAL LAW—HISTORICAL OVERVIEW AND STATUS QUO: 1946–2000

Domestic violence was one of the earliest forms of gender-based violence to generate international action.[112] This was followed by a long history of international institutions and instruments which together comprise weighty evidence that domestic violence is a breach of states' international human rights obligations.

The following analysis examines the international instruments and institutions that address domestic violence in one form or another. I divide the analysis into two periods: 1946–2000 and 2000–09. The development of domestic violence as a subject in international law from 1946 to 2000 is stilted and haphazard. From 2000, however, the lens of international law begins to focus on domestic violence as a specific manifestation of violence against women. It is precisely this specification by general treaty-monitoring bodies and UN institutions (and not only the gender-specific bodies) that evidences the growing universal acknowledgement of domestic violence as a human rights violation.

1946: Commission on the Status of Women

The CSW was the first international body to deal with women's rights. As a functional commission of the Economic and Social Council of the UN, it is a political body made up of 45 members (who are representatives of Member States) elected

---

[111] United Nations Children's Fund (UNICEF), *Domestic Violence against Women and Girls* (Italy, Innocenti Research Centre, 2000), www.unicef-icdc.org/publications/pdf/digest6e.pdf. UNIFEM also administers the Trust Fund in Support of Action to Eliminate Violence against Women, which provides financial support for projects to eradicate gender-based violence, as well as mounting innovative regional and international advocacy campaigns involving grassroots activists.

[112] See Information Note (n 69) ('Initially the development of policy within the United Nations with regard to violence against women was concentrated on violence against women in the family').

by the Economic and Social Council.[113] The object of the CSW is 'to promote implementation of the principle that men and women shall have equal rights'.[114] Originally, the CSW's mandate was to prepare recommendations and reports for the Economic and Social Council on promoting women's rights in political, economic, social and educational fields.[115] Later, this was expanded to include the promotion of equality, development and peace. The CSW was required to monitor the implementation of measures for the advancement of women and the progress thereof at sub-regional, regional and international levels.[116]

The work of the CSW is closely linked with the four World Conferences on Women's Rights discussed above. The CSW helped to organise these conferences and is responsible specifically for the implementation of the Beijing Platform for Action. It is also responsible for mainstreaming a gender perspective in UN activities.[117]

The CSW has an impressive legacy but it has not been used to its full potential. As the initial UN body responsible for developing women's rights, the CSW was established as part of the Economic and Social Council (the UN organ responsible for the coordination of economic, social and related work of the other UN specialised agencies), which falls under the purview of the ICESCR. The ICESCR has been the weaker of the two rights covenants due to a fear of judicial intervention in the policies of the executive branch of government and the fact that it requires state resources and governments to fulfil their socio-economic obligations only to the extent that they have the resources to do so. As a result, many governments fail to comply with the covenant, citing a lack of resources and priorities as justification.

The CSW has a communications mechanism which allows it to hear communications that reveal 'a consistent pattern of reliably attested injustice and discriminatory practices against women'.[118] However, the CSW does not make decisions on such communications but rather takes into account forms of violence against women in developing its policy work.[119] It has also been suggested that 'it is less powerful and effective than other UN commissions'.[120] In general,

---

[113] CSW Overview (n 66).

[114] ibid.

[115] ibid. For a discussion of the CSW see Merry (n 20) 65.

[116] Merry (n 20) 66.

[117] CSW Overview (n 66) . See also Merry (n 20) 65–68.

[118] Information on the communications mechanism is available at www.un.org/womenwatch/daw/csw/communications_procedure.html. See Buergenthal et al (n 41) 106 (noting that the CSW 'used these communications principally as a source of information for its studies rather than as an instrument designed to prod governments to address the specific complaints'). See also Jessica Neuwirth, 'Inequality before the Law: Holding States Accountable for Sex Discriminatory Laws under the Convention on the Elimination of All Forms of Discrimination against Women and through the Beijing Platform for Action' (2005) 18 *Harvard Human Rights Journal* 19, 49 (discussing 'a little known and hardly used communications procedure for consideration of communications').

[119] See CSW, 'Commission on Status of Women Considers Secretary-General's Report on Reforming Human Rights Communications Procedures' WOM/1275 (UN online press release, 9 March 2001), www.un.org/News/Press/docs/2001/wom1275.doc.htm.

[120] Merry (n 20) 66.

the CSW has been more effective at promoting women's rights than at engaging and remedying specific violations of women's rights.[121]

1979: CEDAW

CEDAW is a binding treaty in international law.[122] As of May 2009, 186 countries—over 90 per cent of the UN's members—are party to CEDAW.[123] The content of CEDAW can be broken down into three parts: (1) substantive provisions; (2) recommendations to states; and (3) provisions relating to the CEDAW Committee.

Article 2 is the central provision that places an international obligation on states to end discrimination against women in all its forms. It requires states to pursue 'by all appropriate means and without delay a policy of eliminating discrimination against women'.[124] This includes amending national constitutions and legislation to 'embody the principle of equality of men and women'.[125] States are also required to prohibit by law discrimination against women and to impose sanctions where this prohibition is breached.[126] Apart from legislative reforms, states are required to amend civil, political, social, educational and cultural institutions to implement all the provisions of CEDAW.[127]

CEDAW calls on states to change the way public and private entities and individuals treat women. This is important in relation to domestic violence because it brings the state into the private realm. It compels the state to equalise private relationships (ie the way individuals treat women and not only the way the state treats women) and to intervene when discrimination marks both public and private affairs.[128]

---

[121] See Buergenthal et al (n 41) 105–06 (describing the limited powers of the CSW).

[122] The operation of treaties is governed by the Vienna Convention on the Law of Treaties (adopted 23 May 1969, entered into force 27 January 1980), 1155 UNTS 331, (1969) 8 ILM 679 (hereinafter Vienna Convention). This is founded, in part, on the notion of *pacta sunt servanda*, ie that 'Every treaty in force is binding upon the parties to it and must be performed by them in good faith' (Art 26). See Buergenthal et al (n 41) 82. See also Rebecca J Cook, 'Reservations to the Convention on the Elimination of All Forms of Discrimination against Women' (1990) 30 *Virginia Journal of International Law* 634, 663.

[123] See www2.ohchr.org/english/law/cedaw.htm. There are 98 signatories and there have been 182 ratifications, accessions and successions.

[124] CEDAW, Art 2.

[125] ibid, Art 2(a).

[126] ibid, Art 2(b).

[127] ibid, Arts 3, 4, 5. Reforms include: judicial reform to ensure equality before the law, especially as regards marriage (Arts 15 and 16); education reform (Art 10); labour reform (Arts 11 and 6, which prohibits the exploitation of women by trafficking or prostitution); the meaningful political enfranchisement of women (Arts 7, 8 and 9; Art 15 requires equality before the law and focuses on equality within the state); improved healthcare for women (Art 12); economic reform (Arts 13 and 14); and the adoption of 'all necessary measures at the national level aimed at achieving the full realization of the rights' (Art 24).

[128] ibid, Art 5(a) (describing the obligation to modify the social and cultural patterns of conduct of men and women to eliminate prejudice). See Cook (n 122) 649–50.

However, the only provisions in CEDAW that relate to violence against women are those prohibiting trafficking and prostitution.[129] Aside from these provisions, which deal with non-family forms of violence, there is no broad prohibition on violence against women.[130] While the omission of any reference to violence in the text of CEDAW has been remedied to some extent by DEVAW and General Recommendation 19, the original text of CEDAW remains an unrefined tool that by itself does not address the extent and severity of domestic violence against women.[131]

It is certainly possible to extrapolate a prohibition on violence from the other provisions of CEDAW. For example, its definition of discrimination against women refers to 'any distinction, exclusion or restriction made on the basis of sex which has the effect or purpose of impairing or nullifying the recognition, enjoyment or exercise by women . . . of human rights and fundamental freedoms in the political, economic, social, cultural, civil or any other field'.[132] A state's failure to protect women from violence constitutes a restriction made on the basis of sex, which has the effect of impairing or nullifying women's enjoyment or exercise of their human rights. The principles relating to violence against women are now part of the jurisprudence of CEDAW, as discussed below, but it is a profound omission that the goal of eradication of violence against women is not expressly stipulated in the treaty itself.

Another key deficiency of CEDAW is the number of reservations that have been entered in relation to its seminal provisions. A reservation is a unilateral statement made by a state whereby it excludes or modifies the legal effect of certain provisions of the treaty.[133] Most reservations are lawful unless they are specifically prohibited by the treaty in question or if the reservation is incompatible with the object and purpose of the treaty. A reservation modifies the treaty as between the reserving state and the other signatories but generally does not modify the treaty as between the other non-reserving signatories inter se. Under certain circumstances, parties to the treaty may object to reservations entered by other state parties, although this does not change the nature of the reservation.[134] The reservations entered against CEDAW have limited the extent to which a norm of international law can be said to have developed from this treaty to become applicable to non-signatories.[135] After all, the interpretation of a treaty

[129] CEDAW, Art 6.

[130] See Sally Engle Merry, 'Constructing a Global Law—Violence against Women and the Human Rights System' (2003) 28 *Law and Social Inquiry* 941, 952 (confirming that violence against women was not included in the original CEDAW text but that it has been developed with the denunciation of violence against women in DEVAW).

[131] See ibid.

[132] CEDAW, Art 1.

[133] Vienna Convention (n 122), Art 2. The international law of treaties provides that, when signing a treaty, a state may enter a so-called reservation to such treaty. See Vienna Convention, Art 19(c).

[134] ibid, Art 20.

[135] *North Sea Continental Shelf* case (n 13) 42–43. See Cook (n 122) 651 fn 35 (discussing the value of multi-party treaties as expanding customary international law and citing the *Barcelona Traction* case) and 649–50 (describing the advantages and disadvantages of allowing reservations in international human rights law).

and the existence of its provisions in customary international law vis-a-vis non-signatory states are determined with reference to the text of the treaty and the language of the reservations thereto.[136]

Human rights treaties are outliers, different from all other treaties in international law because they operate for the benefit of the individual, often against the interests of the state.[137] Allowing the state to enter reservations to its own obligations can, and does, impede the extent to which the treaty benefits the individuals in question.[138] CEDAW is an example of this. Whilst it boasts one of the highest numbers of Member States to have signed and ratified the treaty, most state signatories have entered significant reservations to some of its seminal provisions.[139] The injunction in the Vienna Convention on the Law of Treaties that reservations may not be 'incompatible with the object and purpose'[140] of a treaty has not stopped some states from entering reservations against CEDAW's core provisions, such as Article 2, with the result that many state parties have explicitly discriminatory laws on their books and in practice.[141]

The result is a treaty which on its face prohibits the discrimination of women but whose Member States actively and openly discriminate against their female citizens.[142] For example, whilst certain individual states within Nigeria have passed domestic violence legislation, Amnesty International reports that a bill addressing domestic violence and implementing CEDAW failed to be enacted in the National Assembly 22 years after Nigeria had ratified the Convention.[143] Algeria, Yemen and Mali are other examples of states where broad reservations to rights that would have required a change in domestic law have effectively meant that 'No real international rights or obligations have thus been accepted'.[144]

---

[136] See Cook (n 122) 653 (citing the IAC death penalty case).

[137] See ibid, 645–46.

[138] Art 28(1) of CEDAW allows signatory states to enter reservations upon ratification or accession. See William A Schabas, 'Reservations to the Convention on the Elimination of All Forms of Discrimination against Women and the Convention on the Rights of the Child' (1997) 3 *William and Mary Journal of Women and the Law* 79, 82, 84–86 (describing the nature of reservations entered against CEDAW). See also Dormady (n 52) 637 (describing the problematic nature of reservations to CEDAW because 'ratification of the treaty had not translated into compliance through legislative and policy changes by many state parties').

[139] See Jo Lynn Southard, 'Protection of Women's Human Rights Under the Convention on the Elimination of All Forms of Discrimination against Women' (1996) 8 *Pace International Law Review* 1, 20–21 (describing the number of states and the nature of the reservations they have entered against seminal provisions of CEDAW).

[140] Vienna Convention (n 122), Art 28(2).

[141] See Neuwirth (n 118) 19–20 (describing the sex discriminatory laws in several countries which have ratified CEDAW. See also Merry (n 130) 953 (discussing the problem of reservations to CEDAW); Cook (n 122) 687 (describing the reservation by Bangladesh with regard to Art 2 of CEDAW on the basis that it conflicts with Shari'a law).

[142] See Neuwirth (n 118) 23–25 (describing the extent of sex discriminatory laws in countries such as Yemen, Sudan, Algeria, Mali and Nigeria).

[143] Amnesty International, *The State of the World's Human Rights: Universal Declaration on Human Rights: 60 Years On* (27 May 2008), thereport.amnesty.org.

[144] This concern was raised by the Human Rights Committee in its general comment on reservations. See Neuwirth (n 118) 30.

This is not to say that reservations have rendered CEDAW nugatory, but it does call into question the extent to which the protection of women against violence—which does not form part of CEDAW's text—is a principle of customary international law. This is particularly true if one adopts a traditional approach to determining customary international law, which requires, inter alia, concordant practice over time by a majority of 'specially affected' states.

1979: CEDAW Committee

The CEDAW Committee is one of six UN treaty bodies responsible for implementing its constituting treaty.[145] It was established to monitor the implementation of CEDAW by Member States,[146] which are required to submit regular reports to the CEDAW Committee on the 'legislative, judicial, administrative or other measures' adopted to give effect to the provisions of CEDAW.[147] The majority of the CEDAW Committee's work involves examining these reports, interviewing state representatives, and proposing ways in which states can enhance gender equality.[148]

The CEDAW Committee is historically one of the least empowered UN bodies, having been established with fewer resources, less financial support and less power than other treaty bodies.[149] Its original remit was to meet for no more than two weeks annually, during which time it was to review all country reports, hold dialogues with states, prepare comments and recommendations on state reports and provide feedback to the Secretary-General. Remuneration is minimal,[150] and the time limitation as originally envisaged did not exist in respect of any other treaty body.[151] Although its resources and meeting capacity have since

---

[145] The treaty bodies are: the Human Rights Committee established in terms of Art 28 of the ICCPR; the Committee against Torture, established in terms of Art 17 of the Torture Convention; the Committee on the Elimination of Discrimination against Women, created in terms of Art 17 of CEDAW; and the Committee on the Rights of the Child, established in terms of Art 43 of the Children's Convention (n 68).

[146] CEDAW, Art 17. The CEDAW Committee is responsible for monitoring 'the progress made in the implementation' of CEDAW, which it does predominantly by receiving state reports on the status of women and holding dialogues with state representatives on the content of such reports, in terms of Art 17(1) read together with Art 18 of CEDAW.

[147] A Member State is required to submit a report within one year after entry into force of CEDAW for the state concerned, and thereafter, at least every four years or whenever the CEDAW Committee requests (CEDAW, Art 18).

[148] Submissions are made to the Secretary-General of the UN, for consideration by the CEDAW Committee (CEDAW, Art 17).

[149] For a discussion of the difficulties faced by the CEDAW Committee see Margareth Etienne, 'Addressing Gender-Based Violence in an International Context' (1995) 18 *Harvard Women's Law Journal* 139.

[150] It has been reported that CEDAW Committee members are paid $3,000 a year for their work. This includes eight weeks of meeting time and considerable preparation between meetings (Merry (n 20) 238 fn 6).

[151] Southard (n 139) 23 (describing the limitations of the CEDAW Committee due to weak UN support).

improved, it continues to share the same deficiency as most human rights bodies, namely, a lack of enforcement power.[152]

While CEDAW has deficiencies in its content and enforcement capabilities, the treaty is not a sinking ship. As anthropologist Sally Engle Merry states, 'CEDAW is law without sanctions. But a close examination of the way in which the CEDAW process operates suggests that although it does not have the power to punish, it does important cultural work'.[153] I would go further and argue that it does important policy work, leading to political and legal reform. First, it sets a precedent for the development of women's rights law in international law. Secondly, one of CEDAW's more effective tools lies in the reporting procedures whereby states are required to report on the status of women's rights in their country. This has the surprising effect of naming and shaming, a process which should not be undervalued if one views international human rights as a 'cultural system whose coin is admission into the international community of human-rights-compliant States'.[154] The process of norm acculturation, that principles of international law infiltrate state practice, is discussed in chapter four below. Legal and practical changes actually do take place, with varying degrees of success, in countries which have varying records of human rights compliance. The CEDAW Committee forms an important part of this process.

1985: UN Resolution

UN resolutions are passed by the General Assembly of the UN. According to traditional views of customary international law, they are not binding on states, although there are arguments within the school of contemporary customary international law that they constitute customary international law and, therefore, are binding and authoritative.[155] Because the members of the UN vote on them in the General Assembly, it is arguable that resolutions constitute proof of customary international law, articulating the *opinio juris* of nation states. Within the context of customary international law, therefore, a UN resolution may be evidence of the existence of an international norm, especially in an area in which several such resolutions have been voted for by overwhelming majorities.[156] At the very least, resolutions set a standard, albeit an advisory one, recommending how states ought to behave.

[152] See Andrea Vesa, 'International and Regional Standards for Protecting Victims of Domestic Violence' (2004) 12 *American University Journal of Gender, Social Policy and the Law* 309, 312 (arguing that the major deficiency in international law generally—and in respect of domestic violence specifically—is the lack of enforcement mechanisms.). See also Merry (n 130) 942 (identifying the lack of enforcement mechanisms as CEDAW's main weakness).

[153] Merry (n 20) 72.

[154] Merry (n 130) 942–43.

[155] See Slama (n 16) 647.

[156] ibid (describing the opinions of the ICJ in the *Western Sahara* and *Nicaragua* cases, which 'make clear that *opinio juris* may be manifested in the Resolutions of the United Nations . . . the cumulative impact of many resolutions when similar in content voted for by overwhelming majorities and

In 1985 the UN General Assembly passed Resolution 40/36 on domestic violence, inviting states to 'take specific action urgently in order to prevent domestic violence and to render the appropriate assistance to the victims thereof'.[157] The 1985 Resolution was one of the first to refer to the public effects of domestic violence.[158] It focuses, inter alia, on the negative impact of domestic violence on children, the family and the victim[159] and invites governments to make broad changes to their justice systems to deal with the punishment of abusers and the protection of victims.[160] The Resolution suggests that states are responsible for preventing domestic violence and assisting victims. However, this suggestion is directed only at the 'Member States concerned', not at 'all' Member States. This is a linguistic nuance but it does contribute to a generally permissive impression that the Resolution is advisory and tentative, rather than authoritative and binding.

The 1985 Resolution does not claim to be anything more than a point of departure from which the international law of domestic violence should be developed by international organisations and by states.[161] It 'invites' Member States to adopt certain measures, with a view to 'making the criminal and civil justice system more sensitive in its response to domestic violence'.[162] Once again, the language is permissive and not mandatory, in keeping with the legal nature of the Resolution. However, notwithstanding that the Resolution merely invites states to amend their legal systems, it does constitute an expression of the way the law ought to be, thereby creating a standard of state behaviour as regards domestic violence. As an initial statement on the matter, the 1985 Resolution is an important expression of minimal government action. It is also quite nuanced and includes approaches other than purely criminal justice provisions. The Resolution invites states to introduce civil and criminal legislation addressing domestic violence, enforce such legislation, protect battered family members and punish the offenders.[163]

As early as 1985 the UN recognised the necessity of finding 'alternative ways of treatment for offenders, according to the type of violence'.[164] The Resolution identifies the 'special and sometimes delicate position of the victim' and compels

---

frequently repeated over a period of time may give rise to a general *opinio juris* and thus constitute a norm of customary international law'). See also Brownlie (n 42) 3 (describing resolutions of the General Assembly as evidence of customary international law).

[157] 1985 UN Resolution (n 76) Art 2.

[158] Art 3 of the 1985 UN Resolution (n 76), for example, requests 'the Secretary General to intensify research on domestic violence from a criminological perspective'.

[159] See ibid, paras 4–8 and 10 of the preamble. Specifically, the 1985 UN Resolution notes the 'situation of women as victims of crime' (Art 1) and invites 'Member States concerned to take specific action urgently in order to prevent domestic violence and to render the appropriate assistance to the victims thereof' (Art 2).

[160] ibid, Art 7.

[161] ibid, Art 3 and Arts 4–6 (inviting other bodies within the UN to address domestic violence as a component of their mandates).

[162] ibid, Art 7.

[163] ibid, Art 7(a).

[164] ibid.

states to be respectful of victims 'in particular in the manner in which the victim is treated'.[165] The delicacy of the victim's position includes the recognition that urgent and temporary solutions are required, such as 'shelters and other facilities and services for the safety of victims'.[166]

The Resolution identifies the preventative steps that states should take. They should provide support and counselling to families 'in order to improve their ability to create a non-violent environment, emphasizing principles of education, equality of rights and equality of responsibilities between men and women, their partnership and the peaceful resolution of conflicts'.[167] States should oppose the normalisation of domestic violence through social endorsement; recognise the connection between inequality, ignorance and gender-based harm; and address each link in the chain of violence.[168]

The Resolution raises the tension between intervention on the one hand and the protection of privacy on the other.[169] Any intervention by state authorities to protect victims of domestic violence must be balanced against the right to privacy. Laws prohibiting domestic violence may be robust and effective without giving the state exaggerated powers or limiting the protection of the parties' privacy. This is an important theme, and one I address in detail in chapter two below.

The implementation of the 1985 Resolution included the 1986 Expert Group Meeting on Violence in the Family, with special emphasis on the effects of this form of violence on women. This Meeting adopted specific recommendations regarding legal reform, training of the police, prosecutorial and health sectors, and the provision of social and resource support for victims. Significantly, it clarified that domestic violence is an underreported, global phenomenon.[170]

1990: UN Resolution

The preamble to the 1990 UN Resolution introduces the concern of Member States that 'domestic violence [is] an urgent problem deserving focused attention and concerted action'.[171] Domestic violence is now an international concern and

[165] ibid, Art 7(b). In addition, Art 7(e) calls on states to provide 'specialized assistance to victims of domestic violence'.

[166] ibid, Art 7(f). Art 7(g) refers to 'specialized training and units for those who deal in some capacity with victims of domestic violence'.

[167] ibid, Art 7(c).

[168] This is confirmed in the 1985 UN Resolution (n 76) in Art 7(d) (calling on states to create public awareness of the problem of domestic violence, specifically as regards 'serious acts of violence perpetrated against children'). Art 7(h) also requires states to 'research and collect data on the background, extent and types of domestic violence'.

[169] ibid, Art 7(i) (inviting states to make 'legal remedies to domestic violence more accessible and, in view of the criminogenic effects of the phenomenon, in particular on young victims, to give due consideration to the interests of society by maintaining a balance between intervention and the protection of privacy').

[170] Information Note (n 69).

[171] 1990 UN Resolution (n 85) preamble (making several references to the family and to the destructive force of domestic violence in the family unit).

Resolution 1990 records a type of international consensus against domestic violence that was absent in the 1985 Resolution.

The 1990 Resolution takes a tentative step in the direction of recognising domestic violence as having an impact not only on the immediate lives of the victims but also on broader society.[172] This public component is reflected in the Resolution's proposal that domestic violence be combated through 'multidisciplinary policies, measures and strategies, within and outside of the criminal justice system'.[173] The detail of these steps is left to be determined by states themselves, as is the formulation of the approach to be taken in their criminal justice systems.[174] States are urged to cooperate with each other and with NGOs, but as regards research findings, there is no stipulation as to what states should do with such information.[175]

The 1985 and 1990 Resolutions are progressive for that period, but there are shortcomings in their substance and in their authoritative status.[176] The Resolutions did what was necessary at the time—they called on states to include domestic violence in their criminal justice systems and to work domestic violence into their social policies. Understandably, the injunctions are vague and non-specific. It is left to the proper autonomy of each state to decide how it will implement the Resolutions. The 1990 Resolution marks remarkable progress in terms of understanding the psychological components of domestic violence, the negative impact it has on other family members and the fact that the intimate nature of the violence should not preclude a public and, if necessary, criminal response.[177] However, neither Resolution addresses the *nature* of the right to be free from domestic violence, the enforceability of the concomitant international obligation and the relevance internationally of domestic violence as a human rights violation. The Resolutions fall short of constituting a statement on domestic violence as a violation of women's human rights. This was to come later.

Ultimately, despite the Resolutions lacking any authoritative status under a traditional approach to customary international law, they contribute to the body of evidence that proves that domestic violence is an international concern, requiring attention at an international level, and that the activities of private individuals in the context of domestic violence are in fact the responsibility of states.

---

[172] ibid, paras 10, 14, 15, and 17 of the preamble.

[173] ibid, Art 1. The Resolution also makes reference to 'legal, law enforcement, judicial, societal, educational, psychological, economic, health-related and correctional aspects'.

[174] ibid, Art 2, although it should be noted that the Resolution requests the Secretary-General 'to convene a working group of experts, within existing or with extrabudgetary resources, to formulate guidelines or a manual for practitioners concerning the problem of domestic violence for consideration at the Ninth United Nations Congress on the Prevention of Crime and the Treatment of Offenders and its regional preparatory meetings, taking into account the conclusions of the report of the Secretary-General on domestic violence' (Art 5).

[175] ibid, Art 3.

[176] Both the 1985 and 1990 Resolutions were adopted 'without vote'. See www.un.org/Depts/dhl/res/resa40.htm and www.un.org/Depts/dhl/res/resa45.htm.

[177] 1990 UN Resolution (n 85) Art 4.

1992: CEDAW Committee General Recommendation 19

Violence against women became increasingly important in CEDAW Committee meetings around the time of General Recommendation 19.[178] General Recommendations 12 and 19, passed in 1989 and 1994 respectively, were official statements of the CEDAW Committee, incorporating violence against women, including domestic violence, into the treaty's framework.[179]

The CEDAW Committee has the power to 'make suggestions and general recommendations based on the examination of reports and information received from the State Parties'.[180] General Recommendations 12 and 19 are examples of this power. Recommendation 12 urges states to consider the seriousness of violence against women and requires that statistics on gender-based violence be gathered.[181] General Recommendation 19 is more comprehensive. It amends the textual gap in CEDAW and states expressly that the definition of discrimination includes gender-based violence, which 'may breach specific provisions of the Convention, regardless of whether those provisions expressly mention violence'.[182] Gender-based violence is defined as 'violence that is directed against a woman because she is a woman or that affects women disproportionately'.[183] General Recommendation 19 recognises so-called violence in the family as

> one of the most insidious forms of violence against women. It is prevalent in all societies. Within family relationships women of all ages are subjected to violence of all kinds, including battering, rape, other forms of sexual assault, mental and other forms of violence, which are perpetuated by traditional attitudes. Lack of economic independence forces many women to stay in violent relationships. The abrogation of their family responsibilities by men can be a form of violence, and coercion. These forms of violence put women's health at risk and impair their ability to participate in family life and public life on a basis of equality.[184]

General Recommendation 19 creates an express link between discrimination and violence. It confirms that sex inequality and 'Traditional attitudes by which women are regarded as subordinate to men' leads to a tolerance of violence against women.[185] It also shows how violence against women as a group inhibits that group's ability to enjoy rights and freedoms.[186] This is a logical extrapolation

---

[178]   This is analysed in ch 4 below.

[179]   UN Committee for the Elimination of All Forms of Discrimination against Women, 'General Recommendation 12: Violence against Women' (1990) UN Doc A/44/38 (hereinafter General Recommendation 12) (establishing that violence against women was prohibited by CEDAW). This was confirmed in General Recommendation 19 (n 20) 5.

[180]   CEDAW, Art 21(1).

[181]   General Recommendation 12 (n 179).

[182]   General Recommendation 19 (n 20) Art 6.

[183]   ibid, Art 6.

[184]   ibid, para 23.

[185]   ibid, Art 11.

[186]   ibid, Art 7(b) (citing violence as 'a form of discrimination that seriously inhibits womens' [*sic*] ability to enjoy rights and freedoms on a basis of equality with men').

of CEDAW to violence against women: the obligation to end discrimination against women must include the prevention of violence against women if violence against women is a manifestation of, and exacerbates, discrimination.[187] This is the first important element of General Recommendation 19.

The Recommendation also makes a bold statement about cultural autonomy. It rejects traditional 'prejudices and practices [which] may justify gender-based violence as a form of protection or control of women'[188] where the effect of such practices is continued discrimination and low levels of political participation, education, skills and work opportunities.[189] It furthermore prohibits a wide range of violence. In general, violence against women is said to include 'acts that inflict physical, mental or sexual harm or suffering, threats of such acts, coercion and other deprivations of liberty'[190] which deprive women of their equal enjoyment, exercise and knowledge of human rights and fundamental freedoms.[191] The following forms of violence against women are listed specifically: family violence and abuse; forced marriage; dowry deaths; acid attacks; female circumcision;[192] prostitution;[193] trafficking;[194] rape in general;[195] sexual assault in armed conflict;[196] sexual harassment;[197] dietary restrictions for pregnant women;[198] sexual exploitation of rural women;[199] and compulsory sterilisation and abortion.[200]

'Family violence' forms a separate heading within General Recommendation 19. It is described as one of the most insidious forms of violence against women, which affects women of all ages.[201] The Recommendation explains that family violence is universal and prevalent in all societies.[202] It sets out the variety of types of harm, such as 'battering, rape, other forms of sexual assault, mental and other forms of violence . . .', and describes men's 'abrogation of their family responsibilities' as a form of violence and coercion.[203] It reveals that many women are unable to leave abusive situations because a 'Lack of economic independence forces [them] to stay in violent relationships'.[204] It concludes by

---

[187] ibid, para 4 (noting that the 'full implementation of the Convention required States to take positive measures to eliminate all forms of violence against women').

[188] ibid, Art 11.

[189] ibid.

[190] ibid, Art 1.

[191] ibid, Art 11.

[192] ibid.

[193] ibid, Arts 13, 15.

[194] ibid, Arts 14, 16.

[195] ibid, Art 15.

[196] ibid, Art 16.

[197] ibid, Art 17.

[198] ibid, Arts 19, 20.

[199] ibid, Art 21.

[200] ibid, Art 22.

[201] ibid, Art 23.

[202] ibid.

[203] ibid.

[204] ibid.

stating that 'These forms of violence put women's health at risk and impair their ability to participate in family life and public life on a basis of equality'.[205]

General Recommendation 19 covers violence 'perpetrated by public authorities'[206] but it is not 'restricted to action by or on behalf of Governments'.[207] States are also required to protect women from violence 'by any person, organisation or enterprise', including private persons.[208] States may be responsible for private acts if they fail to act with due diligence to prevent violations of rights or to investigate and punish acts of violence.[209] If they fail in that obligation they may be obliged to provide compensation.[210]

General Recommendation 19 makes several recommendations to state parties.[211] In respect of domestic violence, states are required to 'take appropriate and effective measures to overcome all forms of gender-based violence, *whether by public or private act*' (emphasis added).[212] These measures include criminal penalties and civil remedies;[213] removing by legislation the defence of honour for crimes of assault against or murder of female family members;[214] ensuring victims' immediate safety by supplying refuges, counselling and rehabilitation programmes[215] (including rehabilitation programmes for the perpetrators of domestic violence[216]); and providing support services to families in cases of incest or sexual abuse.[217] State parties are encouraged to comment on the implementation of these steps in their reports to the CEDAW Committee.[218]

To some extent, General Recommendation 19 closes the textual gap in the original CEDAW text and makes it clear that the obligation to end discrimination against women includes the duty to prevent violence against women. It also formed the basis for DEVAW, and can therefore be seen as one of a series of triggers which, so to speak, brought violence against women into the mainframe of international law.[219] But does this take us closer to asserting that domestic violence is a violation of international law?

General recommendations made by UN treaty bodies are not automatically binding on states, not even to the states party to the treaty in question. They are used to explain or interpret provisions within the governing treaty.[220] Of course

---

[205] ibid.
[206] ibid, Art 8 ('Such acts of violence may breach that State's obligations under general international human rights law and under other conventions, in addition to breaching this Convention').
[207] ibid, Art 9.
[208] ibid.
[209] ibid.
[210] ibid.
[211] ibid, Art 24.
[212] ibid, Art 24(a).
[213] ibid, Art 24(r)(i).
[214] ibid, Art 24(r)(ii).
[215] ibid, Art 24(r)(iii).
[216] ibid, Art 24(r)(iv).
[217] ibid, Art 24(r)(v).
[218] ibid, Art 24(v).
[219] See Merry (n 20) 76.
[220] ibid, 75.

they may evidence a rule of customary international law and, cumulatively with other instruments and declarations, General Recommendation 19 is an important instrument in relation to domestic violence. However, it is not an amendment to CEDAW and, again, depending on whether one adopts a 'traditional' or 'new' approach to customary international law, it is not clear whether it is binding on Member States.[221] After all, this is not a resolution or declaration of the community of states represented in the General Assembly. It is an interpretation made by the committee endowed with the power to administer the treaty, and the extent to which this could be viewed as binding customary international law is contentious.

Even though there is sufficient content in General Recommendation 19 to argue that states are obliged to investigate, prosecute and punish domestic violence, *and* pay compensation if they fail to do so (the obligation in respect of other human rights violations), there is no express statement to this effect.

The theory underlying General Recommendation 19 is that 'improving women's status with relation to men will reduce their vulnerability to violence'.[222] In other words, the Recommendation links violence against women to discrimination. This is correct: violence against women is a direct consequence of discrimination; but, practically and politically, linking violence against women to gender discrimination may not be the most efficacious approach in international law. Many states actively practise gender discrimination or gender *differentiation* but nonetheless strive to eradicate violence against women.

By linking violence to discrimination in such absolute terms, it becomes difficult for states that practise gender stratification to ally themselves with these principles. For example, Palestinian women have argued for a reinterpretation of Islam that would grant them greater safety without requiring the equivalent treatment of men and women, which would contradict the tenets of Islam.[223] This is a difficult line to walk. It is counter-intuitive to discuss the reduction of violence against women without a commitment to gender equality. While it is far from ideal, it should still be possible to lobby in certain states for the safety of women, albeit at the most basic level, within the confines of gender stratification. I emphasise, though, that this is not the ideal.

1994: DEVAW

The Declaration on the Elimination of Violence against Women is the most explicit international instrument relating to domestic violence. DEVAW, based largely on the provisions of General Recommendation 19, states that three forms of violence may constitute violations of women's human rights, namely, violence in the family, public violence, and violence that is condoned by the

---

[221] Kelly (n 33) (rejecting customary international law as a source of international law).
[222] Merry (n 20) 77.
[223] ibid.

state, irrespective of where it occurs.[224] DEVAW requires states to make the justice system accessible to injured women[225] and stipulates that states should exercise 'due diligence to prevent, investigate and, in accordance with national legislation, punish acts of violence against women, whether those acts are perpetrated by the State or by private persons'.[226]

It has been argued that DEVAW is evidence or a manifestation of customary international law.[227] The 'contemporary' theory of customary international law would recognise DEVAW as evidence of a norm prohibiting violence against women that is binding on states. According to this thinking, 'declaratory resolutions . . . if accepted by an overwhelming majority of the General Assembly, usually by consensus or by an almost unanimous vote, can also constitute "generally accepted" principles of international law'.[228] DEVAW effectively does what women had been demanding for decades: it requires the state to get involved.

As a statement of an authoritative institution it sets an international precedent that violence against women is objectionable. As a declaration, however, its authority is limited. Whether or not it can be demarcated as a principle of international law remains the subject of much debate.[229] The least contentious position is that it is a guide to how states ought ideally to prevent and address violence against women. It is possible to conclude that DEVAW 'was never intended to be the end of this process, but rather a first solid foundation on the basis of which States were supposed to take actions at all levels designed to eliminate violence against women'.[230]

But the issue remains as to whether DEVAW is of sufficient status that it constitutes a universally binding norm in customary international law with regard to violence against women.

---

[224] Art 2 of DEVAW refers to private, communal and state perpetrated violence, including: 'Physical, sexual and psychological violence occurring in the family, including battering, sexual abuse of female children in the household, dowry-related violence, marital rape, female genital mutilation and other traditional practices harmful to women, non-spousal violence and violence related to exploitation.'

[225] ibid, Art 4(d).

[226] ibid, Art 4(c).

[227] Subedi (n 63) 598–99 (arguing that if declarations and resolutions are coupled with state practice and *opinio juris*, this may give rise 'to the emergence of new rules of customary international law'). See also Kelly (n 33) 484–85 (describing the so-called new or contemporary principles of customary international law which maintain that 'unanimous and near-unanimous resolutions and declarations of the UN General Assembly and other international fora constitute a consensus in legal norms providing clear evidence of the *opinio juris* of nations'); Sohn (n 12) 1074–77 (maintaining that, based on statements made by the ICJ, 'once a principle is generally accepted at an international conference, usually through consensus, a rule of customary international law can emerge without having to wait for the signature of the convention'). Others view this as 'declarative' law, which is distinct from customary international law. For a discussion of this view, see Chodesh (n 48) 87.

[228] Sohn (n 12) 1078.

[229] See ibid. See also Michael Reisman, 'The Cult of Custom in the Late 20th Century' (1987) 17 *California Western International Law Journal* 133; Chodesh (n 48); Kelly (n 33).

[230] Subedi (n 63) 602.

1995: Beijing Platform for Action

The Beijing Platform for Action was a turning point in international women's rights law. The fourth World Conference on Women was held in Beijing in 1995. The conference reviewed and assessed the implementation of the Nairobi Forward-Looking Strategies for the Advancement of Women and drafted and passed the Beijing Declaration and the Platform for Action for speeding up the implementation of the Nairobi Strategies.

The Declaration called on states and the international community to provide sufficient resources at both the national and international levels to implement the Platform for Action. The Platform for Action detailed major problems facing women in various countries and laid out strategies and measures to resolve these problems. It focused on poverty, education and health care and affirmed and called for the elimination of all forms of discrimination and violence against women so as to ensure women's equal participation in economic and social development.

Thanks to an admirable strength of will and organisation, women's rights groups succeeded in changing the general view that violence against women is private and intermittent. They demonstrated its global pervasiveness and highlighted its public nature, thereby ending the demarcation of violence against women as a private and quasi-legal phenomenon. Beijing had a positive effect on the adoption and implementation of, and compliance with, CEDAW, leading to increased national reform by state parties.[231] States entered objections to reservations made by other states and the reserving states began to rescind their original reservations.[232]

One reason for the success of Beijing was its pure size. The extent of the conference and its global and eclectic list of attendees made it one of the more visible UN-hosted international events.[233] However, it has been criticised for its lack of enforcement mechanisms and for the fact that its follow-up procedure does not allow for state-specific assessment.[234]

Undoubtedly Beijing's key strength is its representative value. The conference saw the 'oppressed' group talking out about the needs of its members and it presented a consensus amongst millions of women that violence in their homes was a violation that needed to be addressed on an international level. The Beijing Declaration, which was drafted by the governments in attendance at Beijing, stated that those governments 'are determined to . . . prevent and eliminate all

---

[231] Neuwirth (n 118) 46.

[232] ibid, 43 (describing the impact of the Beijing Conference on the reservations made to key CEDAW provisions).

[233] ibid, 47.

[234] ibid, 51. See also Charlesworth (n 12) 46 (arguing that the Vienna Conference on Human Rights and the Beijing Declaration 'contain relatively modest initiatives to improve the situation of women and reinforce a stereotype of women as wives and mothers. In any event, the compliance requirements in the official documents are very weak').

forms of violence against women and girls'.[235] It identified increased domestic violence as one of the 'health issues of growing concern to women'[236] but it also brought domestic violence within the rubric of human rights violations:

> Violence against women both violates and impairs or nullifies the enjoyment by women of human rights and fundamental freedoms . . . [G]ender-based violence, such as battering and other domestic violence, sexual abuse, sexual slavery and exploitation, and international trafficking in women and children, forced prostitution and sexual harassment, as well as violence against women, resulting from cultural prejudice, racism and racial discrimination, xenophobia, pornography, ethnic cleansing, armed conflict, foreign occupation, religious and anti-religious extremism and terrorism are incompatible with the dignity and the worth of the human person and must be combated and eliminated. Any harmful aspect of certain traditional, customary or modern practices that violates the rights of women should be prohibited and eliminated. Governments should take urgent action to combat and eliminate all forms of violence against women in private and public life, whether perpetrated or tolerated by the State or private persons.[237]

Does the reference to domestic violence in the Beijing Declaration make domestic violence an international legal issue? By 1995 it constituted a strong statement on domestic violence, but is it evidence that domestic violence is a violation of international human rights law? The language of Beijing states that domestic violence 'impairs or nullifies the enjoyment by women of human rights and fundamental freedoms' but it does not state that domestic violence itself is a human rights violation. Perhaps this would be unnecessarily pedantic, but what one can conclude without contention is that the governments at Beijing committed themselves to an obligation to prevent domestic violence, both because of its consequences for women's health and because it impedes women's enjoyment and fulfilment of their rights and freedoms.

The issue remains, however, as to whether one can say that this constitutes international consensus that there is an obligation on states to prevent and protect women as a group from domestic violence. There were 17,000 representatives from 189 countries at Beijing, the largest UN conference to have taken place at that time, but very few Heads of State were in attendance (although several First Ladies were there).[238] Undoubtedly Beijing proved that there is an

---

[235] Beijing Declaration (n 17) para 29.
[236] ibid, para 100. Para 106(q) refers to the training of primary healthcare workers to recognise and address domestic violence.
[237] ibid, para 224.
[238] See Ministry of Foreign Affairs of the People's Republic of China, 'The Fourth World Conference on Women met in Beijing in September, 1995' (17 November 2000), www.fmprc.gov.cn/ eng/ziliao/3602/3604/t18026.htm. Statements of senior government officials included the Prime Minister of the People's Republic of Bangladesh, Begum khaleda zia, www.un.org/esa/gopher-data/ conf/fwcw/conf/gov/950904215436.txt; President of Iceland, Madam Vigdis Finnbogadottir, www.un.org/esa/gopher-data/conf/fwcw/conf/gov/950904203248.txt; Prime Minister of the Islamic Republic of Pakistan, Mohtarma Benazir Bhutto, www.un.org/esa/gopher-data/conf/fwcw/conf/ gov/950904202603.txt; Queen Fabiola of Belgium, www.un.org/esa/gopher-data/conf/fwcw/conf/ gov/950905205005.txt; and His Excellency Jiang Zemin, President of the People's Republic of China, www.un.org/esa/gopher-data/conf/fwcw/conf/gov/950905171157.txt.

international movement regarding violence against women. While UN conferences and associated declarations are not traditional sources of international law,
the Beijing Declaration and its conclusions are generally used as the point of departure in almost all international instruments regarding violence against women.[239]

DOMESTIC VIOLENCE IN INTERNATIONAL LAW— HISTORICAL OVERVIEW AND STATUS QUO: 2000–09

2000: The CEDAW Optional Protocol

The Optional Protocol is an addendum to CEDAW and requires signature and
ratification like any other treaty.[240] It was adopted by the General Assembly on
6 October 1999 and entered into force on 22 December 2000.[241] As of 8 March
2009, 79 states had ratified the Optional Protocol.[242] Reservations are not
permitted.[243]

The Optional Protocol enables the CEDAW Committee to receive communications by or on behalf of individuals who have grievances falling within the
scope of CEDAW.[244] It also gives the CEDAW Committee investigative powers,
significantly augmenting the status of CEDAW. Only countries that have ratified
the Protocol are subject to the CEDAW Committee's jurisdiction.[245] There are
substantive and procedural requirements that must be satified in order for a communication to be admissible, including the exhaustion of local remedies.[246] If a
communication is manifestly ill-founded or not sufficiently substantiated, it will
be inadmissible.[247] Provision is made for interim urgent relief to avoid irrepara-
ble damage to the victim.[248] States have six months in which to respond to an
allegation.[249] Once the CEDAW Committee has evaluated the communication

---

[239] See eg UNSC Resolution 1325 (n 17), 'Recalling also the commitments of the Beijing
Declaration and Platform for Action (A/52/231) . . .'; UNSC Resolution 1820 (n 17), 'Recalling the
commitments of the Beijing Declaration and Platform for Action (A/52/231) as well as those contained in the outcome document of the twenty-third Special Session of the United Nations General
Assembly entitled "Women 2000: Gender Equality, Development and Peace for the Twenty-first
Century" (A/S–23/10/Rev.1), in particular those concerning sexual violence and women in situations
of armed conflict'.

[240] See CSW Overview (n 66).

[241] ibid. The Optional Protocol was open for signature on 10 December 1999, Human Rights
Day. On 22 December 2000, following receipt of the 10th instrument of ratification, the Optional
Protocol entered into force.

[242] See treaties.un.org/Pages/ViewDetails.aspx?src=TREATY&id=128&chapter=4&lang=en#top.

[243] CEDAW Optional Protocol (n 17) Art 17.

[244] ibid, Arts 1 and 2. Such individuals must be citizens of a state party in order to be able to claim
to be victims of a violation of a right protected by CEDAW.

[245] The CEDAW Committee can only entertain communications concerning a state which is a
party of both CEDAW and the Optional Protocol (CEDAW Optional Protocol, Art 3).

[246] ibid, Art 4, 4(1).

[247] ibid, Art 4(2)(c).

[248] ibid, Art 5.

[249] ibid, Art 6.

and made its recommendations available to the state and the parties in question, the state party is required to consider the recommendations and respond in writing within six months.[250] The CEDAW Committee may initiate investigations *meru moto*[251] and, if warranted, visit the territory of the state in question, with the state's consent.[252] Most inquiries are conducted confidentially.[253] Thereafter, the procedure mirrors the communications process: the CEDAW Committee examines the findings of the inquiry, submits its findings to the state party, and the state party has six months to respond.[254] While reservations to the Optional Protocol are not permitted, a state party is entitled to declare that it does not recognise this particular competence of the Committee.[255]

Case Law

The decisions of the CEDAW Committee under the Optional Protocol constitute some of the strongest evidence of customary international law as its decisions are binding on 79 signatories, 69 of which have ratified the Protocol. As one of the categories of sources of international law identified in the ICJ Statute, the decisions of international and national judicial bodies and tribunals are an important source to consider in determining whether domestic violence is a violation of international human rights law.[256] It is useful to analyse some of the cases that have been considered by the CEDAW Committee.[257]

Ms B-J v Germany

The first application, *Ms B-J v Germany*, involved a divorced woman who had been unable to secure a final maintenance hearing in Germany and was living in a state of dire financial uncertainty.[258] The CEDAW Committee declared the application inadmissible on the basis that the applicant had not exhausted local remedies and that the CEDAW Committee was precluded *ratione temporis* from considering certain aspects of the complaint.[259] In a separate opinion, two CEDAW Committee members dissented from the majority opinion, maintaining that the domestic proceedings regarding the allocation of maintenance were

---

[250] ibid, Art 7(4).

[251] The CEDAW Committee may initiate investigations if it receives 'reliable information indicating grave or systematic violations by a State Party of rights set forth in the Convention'. Under such circumstances, the state party is invited 'to cooperate in the examination of the information' and to submit observations (ibid, Art 8(1)).

[252] ibid, Art 8(2).

[253] ibid, Arts 6(1), 8(5).

[254] ibid, Art 8(3)–(4).

[255] ibid, Art 10(1).

[256] ICJ Statute (n 5) Art 38.

[257] The CEDAW Committee has considered 10 cases as at the date of writing.

[258] *Ms B-J v Germany* (Decision of inadmissibility) CEDAW Committee (views adopted 14 July 2004) Communication No 1/2003 UN Doc CEDAW/A/59/38, paras 8.4, 8.5, 8.8(a).

[259] ibid.

unreasonably prolonged.[260] The majority applied a narrow, black letter analysis to the facts, which demonstrates a legally sound approach to decision-making. This is important for the integrity of the CEDAW Committee. The minority's view is also important. It focused on the complainant's enduring status quo, which breaches both the letter and the spirit of CEDAW. At the very least, the complaint against Germany proves that the mechanism is functional and respectable.

Ms AT v Hungary

The next communication made to the CEDAW Committee under the Optional Protocol dealt directly with domestic violence.[261] In *Ms AT v Hungary*, a Hungarian citizen claimed, inter alia, that Hungary had failed to protect her from extreme and repetitive forms of domestic violence, thereby violating its obligations under CEDAW.[262] While criminal proceedings had been initiated against the abuser, LF, they were lengthy and provided no immediate protection to the victim. At the time (2003), Hungary had no system of protection orders or restraining orders, with the result that there were no state institutions or laws that prevented the abuse from continuing.

Hungary did not dispute the allegations and indicated that it would take steps to improve its laws and policy regarding domestic violence.[263] It referred to the fact that domestic violence is a problem in Hungary and that its laws must be adjusted to address this.[264] Importantly, Hungary made specific reference to standards of protection that are 'internationally expected',[265] and as a result of its interaction with the CEDAW Committee Hungary has made meaningful amendments to its domestic violence laws, most notably to incorporate protection orders, which, prior to the submission of the communication, did not exist.[266]

---

[260] See Individual opinion of Committee members Krisztina Morvai and Meriem Belmihoub-Zerdani (dissenting) (since the complainant was an older woman who had dedicated three decades of her life to supporting her family and husband, the lack of certainty of her financial income five years after the divorce was 'rightly considered to be unacceptable and a serious violation of her human rights in and of itself' (p 13)).

[261] *Ms AT v Hungary* (Decision) CEDAW Committee (views adopted 26 January 2005) Communication No 2/2003 UN Doc CEDAW/C/32/D/2/2003.

[262] The communication maintains that 'the irrationally lengthy criminal procedures against LF [the abuser], the lack of protection orders or restraining orders under current Hungarian law, and the fact that LF has not spent any time in custody, constitute violations of her [the petitioner's] rights under the Convention as well as violations of General Recommendation 19 of the Committee. She maintains that these criminal procedures can hardly be considered effective and/or immediate protection' (ibid, para 3.2). See also paras 9.3 and 9.4 for the CEDAW Committee's acceptance of the role of the state in allowing the violence to be prolonged.

[263] ibid, para 5.6.

[264] ibid, para 5.7. Hungary refers to the CEDAW Committee's instructions regarding domestic violence in response to Hungary's combined fourth and fifth periodic report in 2002.

[265] ibid, para 7.4.

[266] ibid, paras 2.1, 3.2, 5.7, 9.3, 9.4.

The CEDAW Committee concluded its opinion with recommendations that Hungary 'take immediate and effective measures to guarantee the physical and mental integrity' of the claimant and her family, and to ensure that the claimant 'is given a safe home in which to live with her children, receives appropriate child support and legal assistance and that she receives reparation proportionate to the physical and mental harm undergone and to the gravity of violations of her rights'.[267] The CEDAW Committee confirmed that a state can be held responsible for the conduct of non-state actors and imposed liability on Hungary for the following:

> For four years and continuing to the present day, the author has felt threatened by her former common law husband—the father of her two children. The author has been battered by the same man, i.e. her former common law husband. She has been unsuccessful, either through civil or criminal proceedings, to temporarily or permanently bar L.F. from the apartment where she and her children have continued to reside. The author could not have asked for a restraining or protection order since neither option currently exists in the State Party. She has been unable to flee to a shelter because none are equipped to take her in together with her children, one of whom is fully disabled. None of these facts have been disputed by the State Party and, considered together, they indicate that the rights of the author under articles 5 (a) and 16 of the Convention have been violated.[268]

The case posits domestic violence as a serious consideration for the CEDAW Committee, which recognised the systemic nature of the violence and the social and legal reluctance to intervene in this form of gender-specific and intimate violence. Both the CEDAW Committee and Hungary acknowledged that the state's failure to assist the claimant constituted a violation of human rights. When Hungary conceded that its legal and institutional system was not yet ready 'to ensure the internationally expected, coordinated, comprehensive and effective protection and support for the victims of domestic violence',[269] it accepted that such a standard exists and that it is bound to comply with it. This is indisputably a strong and authoritative indication of a state recognising a principle of international law, and may constitute evidence of customary international law. Under the traditional treatise of customary international law, the state obviously lacked the conduct element (it failed to protect its citizens from domestic violence), but it clearly demonstrates the belief, the *opinio juris*, that there is a standard in international law with which it ought to have complied. It is also a policy statement by a Member State which, according to the academic literature, may be evidence of customary international law according to contemporary principles.[270]

---

[267] ibid, para 9.6. The CEDAW Committee also makes several general recommendations regarding domestic violence and women in Hungary.
[268] ibid, para 9.4.
[269] ibid, para 7.4.
[270] Koh (n 46) 2603 fn 113.

The decision is authority for the fact that (1) extreme and systemic forms of domestic violence are violations of the victim's human rights; (2) as such, the state has an obligation to protect individuals from this violation; and (3) where it fails to do so, it is in breach of international law.

Goekce (deceased) v Austria

In this case the Vienna Intervention Centre against Domestic Violence and the Association for Women's Access to Justice submitted a complaint on behalf of Goecke, who had been killed by her husband.[271] The deceased's first report of violence on 2 December 1999 indicated that her husband had attempted to strangle her, and a form of temporary (10 day) protection order was granted. The law in Austria required authorisation from the spouse (or a direct descendant living in the same household as the accused) to prosecute the offender for making a 'criminal dangerous threat'[272] but the deceased did not give authorisation and reportedly refused to testify against her husband. The state brought charges against the husband for the offence of causing bodily harm but he was acquitted because her injuries were too minor.

Less than a year later, a further interim protection order was granted but the prosecutor's request that the husband be detained was denied (according to the state this was because the deceased had failed to give evidence against her husband).[273] Over the course of the following two years (2000–02) the police were called to the deceased's home five times in relation to violent incidents. During this period the relevant welfare authorities in Austria began looking into the well-being of the minor children. The deceased and her husband tried to give the impression that the home was stable in order to ensure that their children were not taken away.[274]

In 2002 a further temporary (10 day) protection order was granted for acts of violence, including attempted strangulation, blows to the face and a death threat. The deceased pressed charges against her husband for bodily harm and for 'making a criminal dangerous threat' but the request was denied,[275] apparently in part because the deceased indicated that she wished to remain with her husband.[276] The state reported that the deceased repeatedly tried to play down the incidents to avoid her husband being prosecuted.[277] Less than two weeks later a protection order of three months' duration was issued against the

---

[271] *The Vienna Intervention Centre against Domestic Violence and the Association for Women's Access to Justice on behalf of Hakan Goekce, Handan Goekce, and Guelue Goekce (descendants of the deceased) v Austria* (Decision) CEDAW Committee (views adopted 6 August 2007) Communication No 5/2005 UN Doc CEDAW/C/39/D/5/2005.

[272] ibid, para 2.3.

[273] ibid, para 2.4.

[274] ibid, paras 4.4, 5.5.

[275] ibid, para 2.6.

[276] ibid, para 4.7.

[277] ibid, para 4.8.

husband, which he reportedly violated. Both the deceased's father and brother had given statements to the police regarding the danger posed to the deceased, which the police did not record. Neither did the police pursue an allegation that the husband had a gun in contravention of the weapons prohibition that was in force against him.[278]

A month later the public prosecutor stopped the prosecution of the husband for causing bodily harm and making a criminal dangerous threat on the grounds that there was insufficient evidence to prosecute him.[279] Two days later the husband shot and killed the deceased in their apartment, in front of their two daughters.[280] The night before the deceased had called the police, asking for protection.[281]

The state argued that the fact that the deceased had decided not to leave her husband and her ambivalence towards his incarceration and prosecution made it difficult for the police to protect her.[282] One can imagine the frustration of the authorities who were required continuously to intervene in the deceased's case, but their response may have been different if they had had the necessary knowledge of the nature and nuances of domestic violence.

There may be many reasons for ambivalence on the part of the victim, which is not unique to this deceased. As opposed to stranger violence, victims of domestic violence must engage with the authorities about a person with whom they have created a life and with whom they may have had children. The option of believing in the abusive partner's rehabilitation may be more compelling than the option of engaging with the criminal justice system. This may be compounded by the abuser's threats to harm the victim or her relatives (in this case the deceased's husband had threatened to harm her relatives), economic dependence on the abuser or, more poignantly, by his promises of reform.

The case of Goekce reveals how delicate the balance is between providing protection to domestic violence victims while also respecting the choices and autonomy of the victim and her family.[283]

The Committee reviewed the question of whether state parties can be held accountable for the conduct of non-state actors, stating that 'discrimination under the Convention is not restricted to action by or on behalf of Governments' and that 'under general international law and specific human rights covenants, states may also be responsible for private acts if they fail to act with due diligence to prevent violations of rights or to investigate and punish acts of violence, and for providing compensation'.[284] It noted that although Austria had a comprehensive policy addressing domestic violence, including civil and criminal

---

[278] ibid, para 2.9.
[279] ibid, para 2.10.
[280] ibid, para 2.11.
[281] ibid, para 5.5.
[282] ibid, paras 4.13–4.14.
[283] ibid, para 4.16.
[284] ibid, para 12.1.1.

remedies, awareness raising, education and training, shelters and counselling, the system was not supported by the state's agents.[285] This was evidenced by the fact that the husband had a gun in violation of a weapons prohibition issued against him (which was known to the police) and that, notwithstanding the three years of violence recorded between the deceased and her husband, the police had not responded to the deceased's emergency call several hours before she was killed.[286] The Committee found that 'in light of the long record of earlier disturbances and battering, by not responding to the call immediately, the police are accountable for failing to exercise due diligence to protect Şahide Goekce'.[287]

As regards the need to balance the rights of the accused abuser against the rights of the deceased, the Committee expressed the view that the perpetrator's rights cannot supersede 'women's human rights to life and to physical and mental integrity'.[288] Given the continued occurrence of extreme and dangerous violence, the Committee found that the prosecutor should not have denied the request to detain the perpetrator. As such, the state had violated its obligations under CEDAW read in conjunction with Recommendation 19, namely, to embody the principle of equality of men and women in legislation and to ensure the practical realisation of this principle, especially as regards the commission of acts of violence against women. The state had violated the rights of the deceased.[289] This conclusion confirms that domestic violence may constitute a violation of a woman's right to equality and that the state's duty to prevent this form of violence against women forms part of its general non-discrimination obligations under CEDAW.

The Committee noted the sophistication of the state's domestic violence laws and focused its recommendations on implementation. It recommended that the state: (1) strengthen its domestic violence laws by providing sanctions against the police for the failure to prevent and respond to violence against women;[290] (2) speedily prosecute perpetrators of domestic violence to convey the social condemnation of domestic violence;[291] (3) improve coordination among law enforcement and judicial officers and ensure that those involved in the criminal justice system cooperate with NGOs;[292] and (4) strengthen the training of judges, lawyers and law enforcement officials in domestic violence.[293]

---

[285] ibid, para 12.1.2.
[286] ibid, para 12.1.3.
[287] ibid, para 12.1.4.
[288] ibid, para 12.1.5.
[289] ibid, para 12.1.6–12.1.7.
[290] ibid, para 12.3(a).
[291] ibid, para 12.3(b).
[292] ibid, para 12.3(c).
[293] ibid, para 12.3(d).

Ms NSF v The United Kingdom

The claimant in this case was a Pakistani woman who was contesting her deportation from the UK back to Pakistan, where she claimed that her life was at risk from her former husband and that the Pakistani Government was unable to protect her.[294] The case was not admissible on the basis that the claimant had not exhausted her domestic remedies (she had not sought judicial review to fight her deportation and she had not yet raised the issue of discrimination based on sex at the national level).

The decision shows the seriousness with which the Committee takes its role in the hierarchy of decision-making bodies. It will not intervene in a national adjudicative process unless all remedies have been pursued. This type of judicial constraint is important. It demonstrates the Committee's commitment to process and the rules according to which it operates. The Committee was not mute regarding substance. It also noted 'the situation in which women who have fled their country because of fear of domestic violence often find themselves'[295] and intimated that the Home Office, when considering the claim for asylum, should consider the impact of sex discrimination on the claimant's need to remain in the UK.[296]

Ms Zhen Zhen Zheng v The Netherlands

In this case, the petitioner was born in China and was allegedly trafficked into the Netherlands, where, having escaped, she applied for permanent residence.[297] Her application failed. The petitioner claimed that the state party had failed to fulfil its obligations under Article 6 of CEDAW, which requires states to 'take all appropriate measures, including legislation, to suppress all forms of traffic in women and exploitation of prostitution of women'.

According to the petitioner, the state had failed to inform her of her rights under Dutch law, namely that victims of trafficking could obtain a residence permit under certain circumstances; that the state should have realised during the various immigration proceedings that she had been a victim of trafficking; that trafficked women who report the perpetration of this crime are vulnerable to acts of retaliation by the perpetrators; that the state had not been sensitive to the fact that she was an uneducated, illiterate, orphaned minor when she was trafficked and therefore could not be expected to remember the details of her experience (such as the names of people with whom she had travelled and how she had arrived in the Netherlands); and that the state's immigration policy placed the burden of blame on the victim if she could not give this information.[298]

---

[294] *Ms NSF v The United Kingdom* (Decision) CEDAW Committee (views adopted 12 June 2007) Communication No 10/2005 UN Doc CEDAW/C/38/D/10/2005.

[295] ibid, para 7.3.

[296] ibid.

[297] *Ms Zhen Zhen Zheng v The Netherlands* (Decision) CEDAW Committee (views adopted 17 February 2009) Communication No 15/2007 UN Doc CEDAW/C/42/D/15/2007.

[298] ibid, paras 3.1–3.7.

The CEDAW Committee held that the claim was inadmissible because the petitioner had a review application pending and because she had not raised the state's obligations under CEDAW during the asylum proceedings. The decision is of course not ideal for the petitioner, but it has a positive side-effect in that it demonstrates the Committee's commitment to the principle that all domestic remedies must have been pursued before it will intervene.

In a dissenting opinion, the decision gives us an insight into the substantive elements of the state's obligations vis-a-vis trafficking, which are similar to the obligations that states ought to meet in respect of domestic violence.[299] The dissenting opinion notes that, in light of the vulnerability of victims of trafficking, the state has an obligation 'to protect victims of an international crime such as trafficking' and 'to have law enforcement officials adequately trained so as to identify victims of such crimes and to inform them of the avenues under which they can seek protection'.[300]

The dissenting Committee members identified the need for a more nuanced response to the elements of trafficking and the fact that trafficked persons are often uneducated, illiterate and orphaned. These characteristics enable traffickers to abduct individuals from their community with very little disruption. This opinion explains these nuances, how the law should be designed to identify these characteristics, and how officials should be trained to respond accordingly.[301]

Fatma Yildirim (deceased) v Austria

In the second domestic violence case against Austria, the petitioner, again representing the deceased and her family, claimed that the deceased was a victim of the state's violation of its obligations under CEDAW.[302] As opposed to the *Goekce* case, the deceased was consistent in her reports to the police and her requests that her husband be detained. He had been physically and psychologically violent and on several occasions had threatened to kill the deceased both in her home and, after she had moved out of the family home, at her place of work. On two occasions the deceased asked that her husband be detained. She had instituted divorce proceedings against him and several expulsion and 'prohibition to return' orders had been granted against her husband.

The details of the case reveal the deficiencies in the implementation of legislation, which otherwise was progressive and robust. When the deceased's husband became violent she told him that she wanted a divorce, but he threatened to kill her and her children if she divorced him. Following several death

---

[299] See Individual opinion of Committee members Mary Shanthi Dairiam, Violeta Neubauer and Silvia Pimental (dissenting), ibid, paras 8.1–9.2.

[300] ibid, para 8.1.

[301] ibid, para 9.1.

[302] *The Vienna Intervention Centre against Domestic Violence and the Association for Women's Access to Justice on behalf of Banu Akbak, Gülen Khan, and Melissa Özdemir (descendants of the deceased), alleged victim: Fatma Yildirim (deceased) v Austria* (Decision) CEDAW Committee (views adopted 1 October 2007) Communication No 6/2005 UN Doc CEDAW/C/39/D/6/2005.

threats and violent episodes the deceased moved out of the joint home and, after further violence against her, she reported her husband to the police.

Over a period of three months, the deceased took the following actions: she reported her husband to the police for assault and making a criminal dangerous threat, which resulted in an expulsion and prohibition order, which was reported to the relevant city department on domestic violence and to the public prosecutor; the deceased twice requested that her husband be detained and twice this was refused; the deceased applied on her own behalf and on behalf of her minor daughter for an interim injunction against her husband and the court alerted the police to this application; when the deceased was harassed by her husband at work she called the police but they did not report the incident to the public prosecutor; on the same day the husband threatened the deceased's adult son, who reported the incident to the police; the deceased reported further incidents of abuse and death threats at her workplace and the police responded by speaking to him in person and on his mobile phone; the husband again visited the deceased's workplace and made a further threat to kill her, which again was reported to the police and the complaint was passed to a special division within the police department; the deceased engaged the help of an NGO (the author of the complaint) which informed the police of the death threats; the deceased again gave the police information about her husband's threats and again asked that he be detained and again this was refused; the deceased then filed a petition for divorce and a further interim injunction was ordered against the husband. Ten days later the deceased was murdered by her husband.[303]

The petitioner alleged that the state was responsible for the following systemic failures: that the criminal justice system predominantly and disproportionately negatively affects women and that women are more affected than men by the practice of not appropriately prosecuting and punishing offenders in domestic violence cases; that women are disproportionately affected by the lack of coordination between law enforcement and judicial personnel; that these distinctions resulted in inequality in practice and the denial of the deceased's human rights; that Austria's criminal justice personnel failed to act with due diligence to investigate and prosecute acts of violence; that there was a prevailing lack of seriousness with which violence against women is viewed by the authorities; that prosecutors and judges specifically consider domestic violence to be a social or domestic problem, a minor or petty offence that happens in certain social classes (in this case the deceased was an Austrian national of Turkish origin); that the police ought to have taken the threats seriously, especially in light of the fact that the husband was dependent on the deceased for his right to remain in Austria;[304] and that the legal system was deficient because the deceased could not appeal the decision of the public prosecutor not to detain her husband.[305]

---

[303] ibid, paras 2.1–2.13.
[304] ibid, paras 3.3–3.7.
[305] ibid, para 7.4.

The state had taken the view that it was correct not to detain the deceased's husband because:

> the imposition of detention constitutes massive interference with a person's funda-
> mental freedoms . . . The proportionality assessment is a forward-looking evaluation
> of how dangerous the person concerned is and whether that person will commit an
> offence that must be weighed against a suspect's fundamental freedoms and rights
> . . . [The husband] had no criminal record, did not use a weapon and appeared quiet
> and cooperative to the police officers who intervened . . . [The deceased] had no appar-
> ent injuries.[306]

Therefore, the police decided not to arrest the husband because from an '*ex ante* point of view—this would not have been proportionate'.[307]

The test employed by the state would be appropriate in some incidents of criminal conduct but not in respect of domestic violence. Why is this? Domestic violence cases are typified by an escalation of violence and the behaviour of the abuser towards the abused is rarely visible in public. The abuser's cooperation with officials is typical behaviour, which forms part of the abusive process and sets a precedent for the victim that the abuser has a relationship with law enforcement officials which protects him from legal sanction. In this case, the message was correct. Notwithstanding the myriad complaints and protection orders, the only action taken by the police was to talk to the husband.

Balancing the rights of an accused abuser and those of the abused is a difficult challenge. The state is correct in its assessment that detention should be a last resort. If, however, officials understood the fluid, repetitive and escalating vio-lence that characterises domestic violence they would be better equipped to judge whether detention is in fact necessary. This can be achieved only if there is auto-matic communication between various state institutions (usually between the police and public prosecutors but also between health authorities, housing authorities and child welfare authorities), which collectively could identify the cumulative nature of the violence. I discuss this aspect of domestic violence more fully in chapter two.

The inherent nature of domestic violence, in other words, requires a carefully tailored set of criteria to determine the extent of danger. Possession of weapons and previous convictions are not necessarily appropriate indicia. This is because perpetrators of domestic violence are not necessarily social deviants or crimi-nally-minded. There may very well be no other aspect of the abuser's personal-ity or actions that reveal his potential for violence. And the reason for this is that, as experts have claimed for decades, violence against women occurs in large part because there is no real social disapprobation. The *Yildrim* matter is a case in point. Apart from the expulsion order and the interaction between the police and the husband, which proved blatantly ineffective, there was no state response, no

---

[306] ibid, para 4.3.
[307] ibid.

matter how many times the deceased complained and notwithstanding the fact that the threats took place in public, at her place of work, and in violation of court orders against him.

The Committee's response is illuminating. It took the view that the failure to detain the husband was a breach of the state's due diligence obligation to protect the deceased.[308] In the case of domestic violence, 'the perpetrator's rights cannot supersede women's human rights to life and physical and mental integrity'.[309] The Committee also made various recommendations to the state: to strengthen the implementation and monitoring of its domestic violence legislation and to provide sanctions against state authorities that fail to implement it; to prosecute perpetrators of domestic violence, not only to bring them to justice but also to send a signal to the public that society condemns domestic violence; that due consideration is given to the balance of the perpetrator's rights and those of the abused; to improve coordination between law enforcement and judicial officers; and to improve training of law enforcement officials.[310]

The Committee's opinion gives the state (and other CEDAW signatories) guidance as to how to fulfil its obligations in respect of domestic violence. It also shows quite systematically the ways in which a legal framework can break down and fail to protect victims of domestic violence.

Investigation of Ciudad Juárez, Mexico

The first and, as at the date of writing, only investigation launched by the CEDAW Committee under the Optional Protocol relates to violence against women in Mexico. Towards the end of 2002, the CEDAW Committee received information about the murder, rape and disappearance of hundreds of women in the Mexican city of Ciudad Juárez, in the State of Chihuahua.[311] The CEDAW Committee launched an investigation into the situation under the terms of Article 8 of the Optional Protocol.[312]

It found that over a decade approximately 400 to 600 disappearances and murders of women and girls, usually between the ages of 15 and 25, had been reported in Ciudad Juárez.[313] A substantial number of the killings were linked

[308] ibid, para 12.1.5.
[309] ibid.
[310] ibid, para 12.3.
[311] See CEDAW Committee, *Report on Mexico* (27 January 2005) UN Doc CEDAW/C/2005/OP.8/MEXICO (hereinafter CEDAW Committee Ciudad Juárez Report), para 3.
[312] ibid, 1.
[313] See Center for Reproductive Rights (CRR) (formerly Center for Reproductive Law and Policy), 'Letter to the Committee on the Elimination of Discrimination against Women (CEDAW) entitled, Supplementary Information on Mexico Scheduled for Review by CEDAW in August, 2002' (19 June 2002), www.crlp.org/pdf/sl_mexico_eng_2002.pdf. See also Inter-American Commission on Human Rights, Organization of American States, *The Situation of the Rights of Women in Ciudad Juárez, Mexico: The Right to be Free from Violence and Discrimination* (7 March 2003) EA/Ser.L/V/II.117 Doc 44 (hereinafter OAS Report).

to domestic and intra-familial violence.[314] For the most part, the police and judiciary remained inert.[315]

There are a number of factors which make the violence against women in Ciudad Juárez remarkable. I discuss these in some detail since the substantive nature of the crimes, many of which are described as domestic violence, and the structural and systemic nature of the state's response, demonstrate the advances made in international law as regards domestic violence. The first aspect relates to the increasing number of women who have disappeared over the last decade. Due to inconsistencies between the various reports it is impossible to determine the exact number of missing women, with estimates raging from 350 to a few thousand.[316] It is not only the high number of disappearances that is shocking but also the consistent manner in which the disappearances took place and the fact that the violence has persisted and escalated for over a decade. The second relevant factor is the evidence of rape and torture committed on the bodies that have been found.[317] Not only is the violence particularly cruel, the murders are preceded by periods of captivity and mutilated corpses are 'then abandoned on waste ground and eventually discovered by passers-by, not by the police'.[318] Thirdly, the victims apparently fit a profile. They are usually young, attractive women, who are very poor, working in the *maquiladoras* (export processing plant industry) or studying.[319] In general the victims are vulnerable and, due to their poverty, they and their families receive very little respect from the community and the authorities. The fourth factor is the pattern by which the victims were abducted and murdered. At first, the victims would disappear while on their way to or from their homes (they had to cross deserted, unlit areas at night or in the early morning).[320] Increasingly, however, the disappearances occurred in broad daylight, in the city centre.[321]

The fifth relevant aspect of the crimes in Ciudad Juárez is the reaction of state officials. The objectivity of the state authorities has been called into question and there is evidence that individual members of the police have participated in the disappearance and murder of victims.[322] Police officials have refused to investigate disappearances when they are reported and have abandoned cases

---

[314] See OAS Report, ibid, para 57 ('The killing of women in Ciudad Juárez is strongly linked to and influenced by the prevalence of domestic and intrafamilial violence').

[315] ibid, para 11. Many citizens of Ciudad Juárez complained about the 'insufficient response of the police and judiciary to these killings' (para 69).

[316] ibid, para 36, p 11; para 73, p 16; para 135, p 24.

[317] ibid, para 61, p 15 (indicating that one third of the murdered women had been 'brutally raped').

[318] ibid, para 37, p 11.

[319] ibid, para 63, p 15.

[320] ibid.

[321] ibid, para 65, p 15. According to the CEDAW Committee, 'the method of these sexual crimes begins with the victims' abduction through deception or by force. They are held captive and subjected to sexual abuse, including rape and, in some cases, torture until they are murdered; their bodies are then abandoned in some deserted spot.'

[322] ibid, para 87, p 17.

which are 'too old'; families are instructed by the police to look for disappeared women themselves and are denied access to court files. Evidence is removed from court files, destroyed or marred, and there is evidence that internal organs of corpses are missing. Families are told to identify bodies as their relatives when the remains of the bodies look nothing like their relatives; officials present skeletons which have been picked clean; officials cover certain parts of the bodies and refuse to reveal them to families. Outspoken families and members of society are intimidated, threatened and followed; complaints made against police officials are lost or delayed. In general, cases are delayed indefinitely with no information regarding their progress. The hostile behaviour of state officials towards victims' families, together with almost complete impunity, has exacerbated the intensity of the crimes and accelerated their occurrence.[323]

The sixth factor is the general status of women within the local community, combined with the extreme poverty that exists in Ciudad Juárez. It is reported that violence committed against women is 'marked by hatred and misogyny'.[324] A rigid framework of classism and sexism supports a certain inertia towards the violence, leading to the CEDAW Committee's conclusion that 'the root causes of gender violence in its structural dimension and in all its forms—whether domestic and intra-family violence or sexual violence and abuse, murders, kidnappings, and disappearances must be combated'.[325]

Due to the peculiarly rapid growth of Ciudad Juárez and the employment of women rather than men in the *maquilas*, the 'traditional dynamic of relations between the sexes, which was characterized by gender inequality', has worsened.[326] The increasing employability of women set against traditional patriarchal attitudes creates a tension which has perpetuated and exacerbated 'the stereotyped view of men's and women's social roles'.[327] An entire community cannot be labelled as woman-hating, but there appears to be a great number of individuals in Ciudad Juárez who are hostile towards women, and it seems that such hostility is not challenged by the authorities.

Many of the crimes are committed within the context of personal or intimate relationships. According to the Mexican government, the State of Chihuahua acknowledges that 334 women were murdered between 1993 and May 2004. Of those, '66 per cent were the result of intra-family, domestic or ordinary violence involving husbands, boyfriends or other close family members'.[328]

The final relevant factor is the role of international actors. The CEDAW Committee describes the role of NGOs as follows:

---

[323] ibid ('Thus far in the cases involving sex crimes, the murderers have acted with full impunity').

[324] ibid, paras 23 and 26, p 9 (describing how violence against women is regarded as 'a "normal" phenomenon within the context of systematic and generalized gender-based discrimination').

[325] ibid, para 34, p 10.

[326] ibid, para 25, p 9.

[327] ibid.

[328] ibid, para 3.1, p 55. See also ibid, para 245, p 39 (describing high rates of incest and violence against women in the family).

The NGOs which have provided information to the Committee are the forces which, for the longest time and with the greatest persistence, have taken the lead in reporting this clear violation of human rights and demanding justice. They are also a source of truthful, heartrending testimony, criteria and evidence which are essential to the effort to shed light on many of the circumstances under which the crimes have taken place.[329]

Several NGOs and international organisations have visited the area and raised public awareness of the problem.[330] Various international officials have visited Ciudad Juárez, including the Special Rapporteur on women's rights of the Inter-American Commission on Human Rights; the Special Rapporteur of the Commission on Human Rights on extrajudicial, summary or arbitrary executions; the UN Special Rapporteur on violence against women; and, in 2001, the UN Special Rapporteur on the independence of judges and lawyers.[331] There are over 300 civil society organisations publicising and campaigning against denials of justice in Ciudad Juárez and, as a result of national and international pressure, the city has been the subject of public and political concern.[332]

When the brutality of, and fear associated with, the so-called 'serial' killings attracted public attention, the inaction of the Chihuahua authorities triggered international concern.[333] A decade after the killings commenced, investigations began in earnest.

Initially, the Mexican government's response to international pressure was that the victims were immoral women who lived double lives and were responsible for their own victimisation.[334] This approach fuelled the discussion of impunity, revealing disquieting details about Chihuahua's failure to protect women from public and domestic violence.[335] The authorities who were responsible for investigating the crimes and prosecuting the perpetrators were reportedly negligent, for example by causing delays in the initiation of investigations into reports of disappearances; using minimal effort in the initial investigation; failing to collect or record evidence; losing evidence; mistreating the family of

---

[329] ibid, para 255, p 40.
[330] The recommendation that the CEDAW Committee launch an investigation into the disappearances in Ciudad Juárez came from local and international NGOs. See ibid, para 3, p 4.
[331] ibid, paras 30–31, p 10.
[332] ibid, para 244, p 39. See eg US Congress, Concurrent Resolution (3 May 2006) (109th Congress 2 session) H Con Res 90, condemning the violence against women in Ciudad Juárez, thomas.loc.gov/cgi-bin/query/z?c109:H.CON.RES.90.RDS. See also 'US Lawmakers Urge Calderón to Fight Violence Against Women', Washington Office on Latin America (WOLA Newsroom) (Washington, 9 August 2007), www.wola.org/index.php?option=com_content&task=viewp&id=544&Itemid=8; www.wola.org/media/Violence%20Against%20Women/solis%20letter%20english.pdf (referring to a letter from the US House of Representatives to Mexican President Felipe Calderón to intensify the probes into the killings of women in Ciudad Juárez).
[333] OAS Report (n 313) para 244, p 39 (noting that many of the killings were 'manifestations of violence based on gender').
[334] CRR (n 313) 5.
[335] OAS Report (n 313) paras 34, 54, 70.

the victim; and failing to provide information as to the status of the investigation or the workings of the legal process.[336]

It became increasingly evident that there were no support services for the families of those who had been killed and there was a dearth of convictions or prosecutions of perpetrators.[337] In this way, the overall administration of justice was ineffective and political will to improve the status quo was seemingly absent.[338] The impunity not only sanctioned past offences, but also led to a rise in criminal conduct.[339]

In 1998, in response to international pressure, the officials of Chihuahua created a Special Prosecutor's Office to address the matter of the killings.[340] However, the practice of denigrating the victims and holding them responsible for their own victimisation continued. The officials reportedly blamed the victims for their disappearance, referring in a derogatory manner to their way of dressing or lifestyles, revealing a lack of understanding regarding the exigency of economic conditions for many women, and betraying a sexist view regarding the choices women make and the extent to which they may or may not conform to the traditional roles expected of them. One of the problems highlighted by the OAS Report is the fact that the increase in the number of jobs for women was a departure from accepted cultural patterns, which led to further tensions 'in a society marked by historical inequalities between men and women and few resources to assist in changing those attitudes'.[341]

Prejudice against the victims remained, with the official view being that 'violence against women—most illustratively domestic violence—is not a serious crime'.[342]

The vulnerability of women as a group is stark. The story of Ciudad Juárez is not an isolated peculiarity but a theme that is common in more countries than should be acceptable.

How does this concentration of violence against women help in the evaluation of CEDAW?[343] The CEDAW Committee's efficacy lies in its most uncertain power, that of publication and publicity. The media attention generated by the

---

[336] ibid, para 48 ('Because of the lack of basic information, family members . . . have expressed a profound lack of confidence in the willingness or the ability of the authorities to clarify what happened or pursue accountability').

[337] ibid, para 70.

[338] ibid, para 34. Many families had requested DNA tests to determine and/or confirm the identity of a deceased and either waited without response or their requests were denied immediately ('even with a missing person's report, the response was neither rapid nor comprehensive'). It should be noted, however, that the Chihuahua officials have taken steps to improve the facilities and capabilities of the Unit for Attention to Victims of the Special Prosecutor's Office (para 55).

[339] ibid, para 34.

[340] ibid, para 33.

[341] ibid, para 40.

[342] ibid, para 36.

[343] CEDAW Committee Ciudad Juárez Report (n 311) para 256, p 40 (describing the opinion of NGOs that the intervention of the Committee compelled the Mexican authorities to recognise the problem).

controversy outlined above has brought the world to Ciudad Juárez and Ciudad Juárez to the world. One element of the Committee's objectives is to provide states with the opportunity 'to assess the weakness in the procedures, the legal and administrative institutions and implementation processes of the legal system that do not allow women to obtain the benefit of the law as intended and to take remedial action'.[344]

As a result of the CEDAW Committee's investigation and the publicity surrounding the events in Ciudad Juárez over the last decade, Mexico is implementing practical and policy changes, albeit slowly. In November 2009, the Inter-American Court of Human Rights held that Mexico had violated basic human rights by failing to investigate the disappearance and murders of several women over a 15 year period.[345]

Appraisal of the Optional Protocol

While the Optional Protocol does call on states to take all appropriate steps to ensure that individuals under their jurisdiction are not subjected to ill-treatment or intimidation as a consequence of communicating with the Committee, it is possible that fear of state recrimination may dissuade individuals from communicating with the CEDAW Committee.[346]

When a communication is brought to the attention of the state party concerned, the Optional Protocol provides for a confidential process. The same is true of Article 8 inquiries, in terms of which the CEDAW Committee may investigate allegations of grave or systemic violations by a state party of Convention rights. This process is also confidential. Confidentiality is important and enables a diplomatic approach to be taken to a given situation, which, on occasion, may yield beneficial results. On the other hand, without the interface of the media and the element of publicity in these processes, the intimidation of individuals who have communicated with the CEDAW Committee may go undetected. It also decreases the efficacy of one of the main methods of enforcing international human rights law: the naming and shaming process is absent in the case of confidential hearings.[347]

---

[344] *Ms Zhen Zheng v The Netherlands* (n 297). See particularly the Individual opinion of Committee members Mary Shanthi Dairiam, Violeta Neubauer and Silvia Pimental (dissenting), at para 9.2.

[345] Inter-American Court of Human Rights, *González et al ('Cotton Field') v Mexico*. Preliminary Objection, Merits, Reparations and Costs, judgment of 16 November 2009, Series C No 205, www.corteidh.or.cr/docs/casos/articulos/seriec_205_esp1.pdf (in Spanish) (hereinafter *Cotton Field* case).

[346] CEDAW Optional Protocol (n 17), Art 11.

[347] This is not the case with all Optional Protocol proceedings. See CEDAW Optional Protocol (n 17) Art 13 (calling on state parties to facilitate access to information about the views and recommendations of CEDAW).

The Optional Protocol has led to greater UN support for the CEDAW Committee.[348] However, while it expands CEDAW's powers of investigation, it does not expand its powers of enforcement.[349] Its inability to compel state conduct, coupled with the confidentiality requirements and the ability of state parties to reject the competence of the CEDAW Committee under certain circumstances, means that the Optional Protocol actually imports limited power.

It does, however, bring the CEDAW Committee and the local individual into contact. Where communications and recommendations are made public, a powerful tool develops. It is in global announcements that we see the efficacy of international human rights bodies and organisations. It is through universal condemnation and public damnation that change potentially takes root. For whatever reason, the state officials who were inert in the face of the victims' families may now be alert in the face of the camera. If cameras were to be placed in police stations, jails and police vehicles, the freedom with which officials could pursue their own agenda would decrease. The watchdog of the world—the fallibility of the human ego and its need to be seen in the best possible light—gives the Optional Protocol and the CEDAW Committee a modicum of enforcement capability.

2000: UN General Comment No 28

General Comment No 28 was adopted by the UN's Human Rights Committee, which is the committee responsible for the implementation of the ICCPR. It revises the Human Rights Committee's comment on Article 3 of the ICCPR, which requires state parties 'to ensure the equal rights of men and women to the enjoyment of all civil and political rights set forth in the present Covenant'.[350] As described above, whether or not General Comment No 28 constitutes customary international law depends on the method used to determine the rules of customary international law.

According to Article 3 of the Comment, states are required to ensure that the rights of women and men are equally protected.[351] Having identified this obligation, it goes on to describe the steps that states must take to fulfil this obligation.[352]

The Human Rights Committee confirmed that the fulfilment of civil and political rights requires both negative measures (ie abstention from harmful state conduct) and positive measures (ie the creation of facilities to implement

---

[348] This is evidenced by the General Assembly's request that the Secretary-General of the UN 'provide the staff and facilities necessary for the effective performance of the functions of the Committee under the Protocol' (CEDAW Optional Protocol (n 17) para 6).

[349] See Neuwirth (n 118) 49 (criticising the lack of enforcement mechanisms in the Optional Protocol).

[350] ICCPR (n 61), Art 3.

[351] General Comment No 28 (n 103) para 2.

[352] ibid, para 3 (describing the steps, which include 'the removal of obstacles to the equal enjoyment of such rights, the education of the population and of State officials in human rights, and the adjustment of domestic legislation so as to give effect to the undertakings set forth in the Covenant').

civil and political rights).[353] State parties, therefore, are required to end discrimination on the ground of sex specifically and 'to put an end to discriminatory actions, both in the public and the private sector'.[354] It is important to note
that this posits sex discrimination *in the private sector* as a civil and political
issue.

In keeping with the approach of General Recommendation 19 and DEVAW,
General Comment No 28 raises the thorny issue of culture.[355] It requires state
parties to ensure that 'traditional, historical, religious or cultural attitudes are
not used to justify violations of women's rights to equality before the law and to
equal enjoyment of all Covenant rights'.[356] However, it provides no information or guidelines as to how states should achieve this. This issue is particularly
important since many governments rely on the support of such traditional or
cultural communities in order to stay in power. International instruments
should include helpful and reasonable guidance as to how to implement international standards in a variety of contexts which are structured according to
gendered hierarchies.

There is an overall obligation on states to provide information regarding the
'actual role' of women in society.[357] States are required to take account of the
factors that impede the equal enjoyment by women of the rights contained in
the ICCPR. General Comment No 28 spells out the type of information that
states should record.[358] Specifically, they must provide information on legal
measures to protect women with regard to domestic violence, rape, safe termination of pregnancies occurring as a result of rape, forced abortion/sterilisation
and FGC,[359] and analyse laws that confine women to the home.[360]

This is an example of the integration of domestic violence into the work of
the other UN committees. It helps to demonstrate that the confinement of
domestic violence victims to their homes (either through physical force, coercion or threats, economic need or as a result of depression) is of the same ilk as
state detention. This form of detention, though it is not perpetrated by the state
authorities, now falls within the scope of the ICCPR's arrest and detention provisions. The connection made between formal arrest and the isolation engen-
dered by domestic violence is a major step forward in recognising the fact that
intimate violence is no less cruel than violence committed by state authorities.

---

[353] ibid ('The State Party must not only adopt measures of protection, but also positive measures
in all areas so as to achieve the effective and equal empowerment of women').
[354] ibid, para 4.
[355] ibid, para 5.
[356] ibid.
[357] ibid, para 3.
[358] ibid, para 6.
[359] ibid, para 11.
[360] ibid, para 14. This request is made in the context of Art 9 of the ICCPR (n 61), which prohibits
arbitrary arrest and detention, usually associated with state incarceration. The comment refers to
'any laws or practices which may deprive women of their liberty on an arbitrary or unequal basis,
such as by confinement within the house'.

In referring to access to justice, the Comment insists that women should be able to 'give evidence as witnesses on the same terms as men'.[361] This affects the so-called cautionary rule of evidence in terms of which women's testimony is traditionally viewed with caution, as is a child's, due to their 'tendency' to provide unreliable information. This is particularly important in cases of rape and domestic violence where, with only two witnesses, the woman's testimony is usually pitted against that of the man. General Comment No 28 requires women to have direct and autonomous access to the courts, which includes equal access to legal aid. It emphasises the importance of this in 'family matters', thereby acknowledging that this is the realm in which women need particular legal assistance.

General Comment No 28 is a departure from some of the ambiguous and non-committal language of other relevant international instruments. Its recommendations are accompanied by examples or explanations of why certain positive steps need to be taken to ensure that women are able to enjoy the rights contained in the ICCPR. It also makes an authoritative statement about the long debate regarding positive and negative rights, namely that proactive steps are necessary to entrench civil and political rights. It represents a significant step in the direction of mainstreaming gender discrimination issues and taking women's specific circumstances into account in all rights and not only those which are gender-specific. It is one of the many factors that reflect the emergence of a concrete, definitive and authoritative norm in international law prohibiting domestic violence.

2004: General Assembly Resolution on the Elimination of Domestic Violence against Women

A landmark in international law, General Assembly Resolution 58/147 invokes the connection between domestic violence and discrimination against women.[362] It recognises that domestic violence is a societal problem and a 'manifestation of unequal power relations between women and men', which it reinforces with reference to the need for equal pay for equal work, increased job opportunities, credit and saving schemes, and property and inheritance rights, all of which may mitigate to women's increased vulnerability to domestic violence.[363] The preamble also states clearly that 'domestic violence against women and girls is a human rights issue'.

The Resolution's description of domestic violence is progressive and reflects the nuances that comprise this type of violence. It approaches domestic violence as violence that occurs in the private sphere between 'individuals who are related through blood or intimacy'.[364] This widens the scope of the Resolution

---

[361] ibid, para 18.
[362] UNGA Res 58/147 (19 February 2004) UN Doc A/RES/58/147, on the elimination of domestic violence against women (hereinafter Res 58/147).
[363] ibid, para 7(m).
[364] ibid, para 1(a).

(and states' obligations in respect of domestic violence) to embrace violence that occurs in all manner of intimate contexts, not only marital relationships. The Resolution responds to the decades of insistence that domestic violence may be 'private' but is one of the 'most common and least visible forms of violence against women and its consequences affect many areas of the lives of victims'.[365] Within the concept of domestic violence, the Resolution includes physical, psychological, sexual and economic harm and, importantly, reference is also made to the isolation of the victim, all of which 'cause imminent harm to the safety, health or well-being of women'.[366]

The reference to 'imminent' harm is extremely useful in helping us to understand the immediacy of domestic violence, especially where abused women kill their abusers. In such cases it is common that the abused woman will not kill in direct response to the violence she experiences; normally she will wait until the abuser is incapacitated, asleep or vulnerable. This type of conduct lacks the immediacy required for traditional defences such as self-defence (discussed further in chapter two). The notion of battered woman syndrome has helped to explain that the planning involved in this type of murder forms part of a continuum of self-defence; that while it seems that the there is no threat of real and imminent harm (as required for self-defence), in the abused's mind the threat of harm is both real and imminent. We also now understand that the threat of harm is *not* only in the mind of the abused but, because she often is unable to escape the abuse, is *in fact* real and imminent. Legal systems have for the most part been unable to grasp that the context of violence, while appearing to lack immediacy of harm, is constant and 'imminent' and that the murder by an abused of her abuser may in fact be an act of self-defence. It is not clear whether this was the reason why the word 'imminent' was used in the Resolution, but it certainly helps to move the discussion of domestic violence in a more reasoned and realistic direction.

One of the most important components of the Resolution is its recognition that domestic violence is a 'public concern [which] requires States to take serious action to protect victims and prevent domestic violence',[367] especially where gender-based violence in the family is 'condoned by the State'.[368] The Resolution engages the Special Rapporteur's emphasis on due diligence to prevent, investigate and punish the perpetrators of domestic violence and that a failure to do so 'violates and impairs or nullifies the enjoyment of their human rights and fundamental freedoms'.[369]

The Resolution makes recommendations regarding legislative steps (to strengthen legislation or enact legislation), spanning criminal and civil measures, such as social assistance, restraining orders[370] and the establishment of 'one-stop

---

[365] ibid, para 1(b).
[366] ibid, para 1(c) and (e).
[367] ibid, para 1(d).
[368] ibid, para 3.
[369] ibid, para 5.
[370] ibid, para 7(a)–(e).

centres' and safe havens for domestic violence victims.[371] This recommendation is extremely important due to its pragmatic nature, confirming that all levels of state may have a role to play in addressing one incident of domestic violence while also dismantling the systemic obstacles that too often prevent domestic violence victims from obtaining public assistance, such as re-victimisation and gender-insensitive laws and practices.[372] The Resolution also confirms that states may not invoke custom, tradition or religion to avoid their obligations to protect women from domestic violence.[373]

One of the most interesting elements of the Resolution is its confirmation that domestic violence is global and that in every country it has implications for the advancement of women and the broader social and economic development of the state in question. Obviously this requires funds, and the Resolution emphasises 'the need for technical and financial assistance to developing countries'.[374]

Does this Resolution confirm that domestic violence is a human rights violation for which states are responsible? It would be difficult to argue that it does not, especially if one adopts the contemporary approach to customary international law, namely that it is created by the declarations and instruments of international human rights bodies, especially the General Assembly. On a more traditional understanding of customary international law, however, the answer is not so clear.

1994–2009: Reports of the Special Rapporteur on violence against women, its causes and consequences

In March 1994, the UN Commission on Human Rights (the predecessor of the UN Human Rights Council) appointed a Special Rapporteur on violence against women, its causes and consequences.[375] The mandate of the Special Rapporteur, set out in Resolution 1994/45 and adopted on 4 March 1994, is to obtain information on violence against women and to recommend measures to eliminate this violence. The Special Rapporteur's reports have covered military sexual slavery in wartime, rape in the community, trafficking and forced prostitution of women, female genital cutting, cultural autonomy and violence against women, women's reproductive rights, migrant rights, honour killings and domestic violence. The Special Rapporteur has also undertaken country-specific missions and proposed strategies to address gender-based violence against women.[376]

The Special Rapporteur's work on domestic violence has profoundly changed the international order's understanding of and demands vis-a-vis domestic

---

[371] ibid, para 7(f)–(g).
[372] ibid, para 7(h)–(l).
[373] ibid, para 7(n).
[374] ibid, para 8.
[375] UNCHR Resolution 1994/45 (n 17).
[376] See Information Note (n 69).

violence.[377] The Special Rapporteur has confirmed that domestic violence is not 'a mere domestic criminal justice concern'[378] and that it has a global nature, occurring in both developed and developing countries.[379] The first Special Rapporteur, Radhika Coomaraswamy, took the firm position that domestic violence is a violation of international human rights law, although it is not clear whether the source of this is customary international law or whether it is evidenced by the plethora of UN instruments on violence against women, notwithstanding the absence of a treaty or convention on domestic violence. The second Special Rapporteur, Yakin Ertürk, has taken the view that on the basis of practice and *opinio juris*, it can be concluded that there is a rule of customary international law that obliges states to prevent and respond to acts of violence against women with due diligence.[380]

Role of the State and Due Diligence Standard

The work of the Special Rapporteur has resulted in a detailed understanding of the state's role in respect of domestic violence,[381] and has confirmed that the 'greatest cause of violence against women is government inaction'.[382]

In her preliminary report in 1994, the first Special Rapporteur evoked the precedent that the state is responsible for violations of women's human rights by private actors where it fails to exercise due diligence to control private individuals.[383]

---

[377] See UN Special Rapporteur on violence against women, '15 Years of the United Nations Special Rapporteur on violence against women, its causes and consequences 1994–2009—A Critical Review' (25 November 2008), www2.ohchr.org/english/issues/women/rapporteur/docs/15YearReviewofVAWMandate.pdf (hereinafter Special Rapporteur 15 Year Review).

[378] UNCHR, *Report of the Special Rapporteur on violence against women, its causes and consequences: Further Promotion and Encouragement of Human Rights and Fundamental Freedoms, Including the Question of the Programme and Methods of Work of the Commission Alternative Approaches and Ways and Means within the United Nations System for Improving the Effective Enjoyment of Human Rights and Fundamental Freedoms* (6 February 1996) UN Doc E/CN.4/1996/53, para 29 (hereinafter Special Rapporteur 1996 Report) (highlighting the incongruous elements of intimacy and aggression that comprise domestic violence, its gendered nature and the universality of state-tolerated violence).

[379] UNCHR, *Preliminary Report submitted by the Special Rapporteur on violence against women, its causes and consequences, Ms Radhika Coomaraswamy, in accordance with Commission on Human Rights Resolution 1994/45: Further Promotion and Encouragement of Human Rights and Fundamental Freedoms, Including the Question of the Programme and Methods of Work of the Commission: Alternative Approaches and Ways and Means within the United Nations System for Improving the Effective Enjoyment of Human Rights and Fundamental Freedoms* (22 November 1994) UN Doc E/CN.4/1995/42 (hereinafter Special Rapporteur 1994 Report).

[380] UNCHR, *The Due Diligence Standard as a Tool for the Elimination of Violence against Women—Report of the Special Rapporteur on violence against women, its causes and consequences, Yakin Ertürk* (30 January 2006) UN Doc E/CN.4/2006/61, para 29 (hereinafter Special Rapporteur 2006 Report).

[381] Special Rapporteur 1994 Report (n 379) para 48.

[382] ibid, para 72.

[383] ibid, paras 72, 102–03 (citing Cook (n 122) and Thomas and Beasley (n 63) 36–62. See also Kenneth Roth, 'Domestic Violence as an International Human Rights Issue' in Rebecca Cook (ed), *Human Rights of Women: National and International Perspectives* (Philadelphia, University of Pennsylvania Press, 1994) 72.

By 1996 it was accepted by the Special Rapporteur that the principles of state responsibility impose on states a duty to protect women from this form of violence.[384] The Special Rapporteur focused on the state obligation to exercise due diligence;[385] the obligation to provide equal protection of the law;[386] the obligation to prevent torture, cruel, inhuman and degrading treatment;[387] and the norm prohibiting discrimination.[388] In 1998, based on a detailed analysis of domestic violence standards, statistics, laws and progress in several countries, the Special Rapporteur concluded that states were failing in their international obligations to prevent, investigate and prosecute violence against women in the family.[389] She also importantly pointed out the pressure that is placed on the NGO sector to fill the governance gap.[390]

The Special Rapporteur's report of 2006 focused on the due diligence standard as a tool in eliminating violence against women.[391] The report noted that states' application of the due diligence standard tended to concentrate on legislative reform. Relatively little work had been done on the general obligation of prevention.[392] This report called on states to focus on transforming the societal values and institutions that sustain gender inequality.[393]

Definition of Family

In 1999, the Special Rapporteur expanded the state's obligation to protect women in diverse family forms.[394] The definition of 'family' for the purposes of domestic violence grew to encompass intimate-partner and interpersonal relationships, including non-cohabiting partners, previous partners and domestic workers. This has meant that 'wives, live-in partners, former wives or partners, girl-friends (including girl-friends not living in the same house), female relatives (including but not restricted to sisters, daughters, mothers) and female household workers'[395] may be recipients of state protection.

[384] Special Rapporteur 1996 Report (n 378) paras 29–31.
[385] ibid, paras 32–39.
[386] ibid, paras 40–41.
[387] ibid, paras 42–50.
[388] ibid, paras 51–53.
[389] UNCHR, *Violence against Women in the Family—Report of the Special Rapporteur on violence against women, its causes and consequences, Ms Radhika Coomaraswamy* (10 March 1999) UN Doc E/CN.4/1999/68, para 242 (hereinafter Special Rapporteur 1999 Report).
[390] ibid, para 243.
[391] Special Rapporteur 2006 Report (n 380).
[392] ibid, para 15.
[393] ibid, para 17.
[394] In 1999 Coomaraswamy returned to the theme of violence against women in the family, focusing on states' compliance 'with their international obligations with respect to violence against women in the family'. Special Rapporteur 1999 Report (n 389) paras 16, 18. See also Special Rapporteur 15 Year Review (n 377) pp 10–11.
[395] Special Rapporteur 15 Year Review (n 377) pp 10–11.

Cultural Relativism

The Special Rapporteur has also taken on the argument of cultural relativism and consistently and definitively rejected cultural autonomy as a justification or explanation for violence against women, including domestic violence. In 1999 Coomaraswamy confirmed that in all communities the root causes of domestic violence are similar, even when the justifications for such violence or the forms of such violence vary.[396] This captured the universality of the right to be free from domestic violence (and other forms of violence against women).

In 2002 the Special Rapporteur considered cultural practices in the family that are violent towards women.[397] This naturally engaged the issue of cultural relativism and again the Special Rapporteur confirmed the link between the prevalence of domestic violence and the stereotyped roles of men and women, and the denial of equality and dignity in 'all cultures'[398] that perpetuates cultural practices that are violent towards women.[399]

In 2007 the Special Rapporteur again confirmed that no custom, tradition or religious consideration can be invoked to justify violence against women.[400] The report identifies the myths surrounding cultural discourses and outlines general guidelines for an effective strategy to counter and transform culture-based discourses which constitute one of the major obstacles to the implementation of women's rights.[401]

Draft Model Legislation

The addendum to the Special Rapporteur's report on violence in the family sets out a framework for model legislation on domestic violence to assist states in meeting their obligations to protect women in the private sphere.[402] The proposed model law (discussed in further detail in chapter two) includes civil and criminal remedies, in addition to mandating coordinated emergency and non-emergency support services, and training of police, counsellors and the judiciary to ensure effective implementation of the law.[403] The focus on the legislative

---

[396] Special Rapporteur 1999 Report (n 389) para 32.

[397] UNCHR, *Cultural Practices in the Family that are Violent towards Women—Report of the Special Rapporteur on violence against women, its causes and consequences, Ms Radhika Coomaraswamy* (31 January 2002) UN Doc E/CN.4/2002/83.

[398] ibid, p 3.

[399] Such as FGC, honour killings, the pledging of girls for economic and cultural appeasement, witch hunting, caste, marriage, discriminatory laws, son preference, restrictive practices, practices that violate women's reproductive rights, beauty, and incest. It also identified female sexuality and masculinity and violence as ideologies that perpetuate violence against women.

[400] UN Human Rights Council, *Intersections between Culture and Violence against Women—Report of the Special Rapporteur on violence against women, its causes and consequences, Yakin Ertürk* (17 January 2007) UN Doc A/HRC/4/34 (hereinafter Special Rapporteur 2007 Report).

[401] ibid, p 3.

[402] Special Rapporteur 1999 Report (n 389).

[403] Special Rapporteur 15 Year Review (n 377) pp 10–11.

responsibility of states regarding domestic violence gave impetus to legislative advocacy and led to the enactment of specific domestic violence legislation in various countries.[404]

The Special Rapporteur's examination considered violence against women at the individual level;[405] the creation of a 'cultural negotiation' at the communal level;[406] the unequivocal opposition to violence against women at the state level, in all branches of governance;[407] and, importantly, imposing the due diligence standard at the transnational level.[408] She detailed the broader obligations of the state towards violence prevention through public policies and public education. This includes legal support and health, safety and shelter requirements for domestic violence survivors.[409] The Special Rapporteur also identified the responsibility of states that has arisen out of transnational trends, such as migrant activity[410] and the vast number of women who provide low-wage and flexible labour to the globalised labour markets through immigration and off-shore production.[411]

Domestic Violence Intersecting with Torture, Health, Equality and Other International Human Rights Principles

The Special Rapporteur has confirmed that domestic violence is a form of torture. This is one of the most important developments in the internationalisation of domestic violence. Coomaraswamy authoritatively extracted the elements of domestic violence that equate to torture, namely severe physical and/or mental pain which is intentionally inflicted for the purpose of intimidation and control and with some form of state involvement, which in the case of domestic violence is the state's failure to protect and punish.[412] She used this characterisation of domestic violence to call on treaty bodies to investigate domestic violence within their mandates (as discussed below).

The Special Rapporteur has applied international standards of equality and non-discrimination in the context of marriage and the family, upholding the right to privacy, sexual health (including sexual orientation) and reproductive rights within the context of family.[413] In 2003, the second Special Rapporteur, Yakin Ertürk, submitted her first report on developing guidelines for the practical implementation of international law relating to the universal human rights

---

[404] ibid. By 2006, 89 states were reported to have legislation addressing domestic violence; of these, 60 states had specific domestic violence laws, seven had violence laws, and about 20 had draft legislation on domestic violence in various stages of development. ibid.

[405] Special Rapporteur 2006 Report (n 380) paras 78–81.

[406] ibid, paras 85–88.

[407] ibid, paras 89–93.

[408] ibid, paras 94–99.

[409] Special Rapporteur 1994 Report (n 379) p 10.

[410] ibid, paras 69–70.

[411] Special Rapporteur 2006 Report (n 380) para 70.

[412] Special Rapporteur 1996 Report (n 378) para 43.

[413] Special Rapporteur 15 Year Review (n 377) pp 10–11.

of women.[414] The report emphasised the universality of violence against women, the multiplicity of its forms and the intersectionality of diverse kinds of discrimination against women and its linkage to a system of domination that is based on subordination and inequality (and the impact of HIV on violence).[415] In her treatment of domestic violence, Ertürk further dissipated the public/private dichotomy, especially in the context of discriminatory HIV/AIDS policies, occupation, racism, socio-economic marginalisation and restrictive immigration policies, which exacerbate domestic violence.[416]

2005–06: Resolutions and Action by the Office of the High Commissioner for Human Rights

In 2005 the Office of the High Commissioner for Human Rights (the UN body mandated to promote human rights around the world) passed Resolution 2005/41, focusing on violence against women and the recommendations of the Special Rapporteur. The Resolution stresses the 'affirmative duty' of states to protect women from violence and exercise due diligence to prevent, investigate and punish violence against women, including domestic violence.[417]

This was followed by the establishment of the Women's Human Rights and Gender Unit in 2006 in the Office of the High Commissioner for Human Rights.[418] This unit is responsible for legal standard setting with respect to inequalities involved in accessing justice. At the date of writing, the focus of the Office has been on the prosecution of sexual violence in the context of conflict and the concomitant impact on women's social and economic rights. There is every hope that this unit may pursue the delineation of a precise and authoritative duty on states to prevent domestic violence.

2001–08: Resolutions of the Commission on Human Rights and the Human Rights Council

The Commission on Human Rights, which was later replaced by the Human Rights Council, paid increasingly nuanced and detailed attention to the inter-

---

[414] UNHCR, *Towards an Effective Implementation of International Norms to End Violence against Women—Report of the Special Rapporteur on violence against women, its causes and consequences, Yakin Ertürk* (26 December 2003) UN Doc E/CN.4/2004/66.

[415] ibid, p 2.

[416] Special Rapporteur 15 Year Review (n 377) pp 10–11.

[417] UNCHR Res 2002/50 (23 April 2002) UN Doc E/CN.4/RES/2002/50, Integrating the Human Rights of Women throughout the United Nations System, para 17 (hereinafter UNCHR Res 2002/50).

[418] For information relating to the unit and its research papers, see 'The OHCHR Women's Human Rights and Gender Unit (WRGU)—Conceptual Framework and Main Priorities', www2.ohchr.org/english/issues/women.

national law relating to private violence against women. The 2001 Commission on Human Rights Resolution calls specifically for the elimination of all forms of gender-based violence in the family.[419] It affirms that the definition of violence against women includes domestic violence[420] and that the obligations of states under CEDAW include the obligation to prevent and punish violence against women.[421] The Resolution innovatively covers: the importance of sex-disaggregated data on the causes and effects of violence against women;[422] the role of men and reforming abusive behaviour;[423] and the reform of immigration and asylum policies to recognise gender-related persecution as a ground for asylum.[424] It also encourages other human rights bodies, specialised agencies and intergovernmental organisations to consider violence against women, including domestic violence, in their work.[425]

In 2002 the Commission on Human Rights passed Resolution 2002/50 on the integration of women's human rights throughout the UN system.[426] The Resolution documents the inclusion of gender in the Economic and Social Council and comments specifically on the incorporation of gender in the activities of the other UN bodies.

The importance of these Resolutions, coming from a mainstream (and not gender-specific) UN body, is self-evident. In addition to their progressive and considered substance, the Resolutions implement recommendations of the CEDAW Committee and the Special Rapporteur to integrate gender into the work of other human rights UN bodies.

The newly formed UN Human Rights Council (which replaced the Commission on Human Rights) has addressed violence against women in several resolutions.[427] In December 2007 it undertook to integrate the human rights of women throughout the UN system.[428] This includes the integration of gender both into the structure of the UN system and its staff and into the substantive work of the UN and its Member States. This was reaffirmed the next year in Resolution 7/24, which extended the mandate of the Special Rapporteur on violence against women, its causes and consequences.[429]

---

[419] UNHCR Res 2001/49 (24 April 2001) UN Doc E/CN.4/2001/49, Elimination of violence against women, para 2 (hereinafter Res 2001/49).
[420] ibid.
[421] ibid, para 6.
[422] ibid, para 10(f).
[423] ibid, para 10(g).
[424] ibid, para 19.
[425] ibid, paras 22–26.
[426] UNCHR Res 2002/50 (n 417).
[427] UNGA Res 60/251 (3 April 2006) UN Doc A/RES/60/251, Human Rights Council (establishing the Human Rights Council) (hereinafter Res 60/251).
[428] UN Human Rights Council (UNHRC) Res 6/30 (14 December 2007) UN Doc A/HRC/6/30, on integrating the human rights of women throughout the United Nations system (hereinafter UNHRC Res 6/30).
[429] UNHRC Res 7/24 (28 March 2008) UN Doc A/HRC/6/30, on the elimination of violence against women (hereinafter UNHRC Res 7/24).

In both Resolutions, the Human Rights Council emphasises the connection between discrimination against women, the vulnerability of disadvantaged and marginalised women and the degree of violence committed against women.[430] The earlier Resolution takes up the call that other human rights bodies and treaty bodies should look at how women are affected (through analysis and the collection of sex-disaggregated data) within their specific areas of specialisation (such as torture and discrimination).[431] It refers to UN General Assembly Resolution 61/143 of 19 December 2006 (discussed below) regarding the prioritising of violence against women in the Human Rights Council's work. It also 'encourages' Member States to include gender in their budgetary and institutional measures.[432] The later Resolution emphasises the connection between discrimination, vulnerability and violence against women. It specifically includes the 'elimination of all forms of gender-based violence *in the family*' (emphasis added).

On one level this continued 'confirmation', 'affirmation' and encouragement is frustratingly repetitive. Women in (and of course outside of) the UN system have been making these statements for decades. On the other hand, the Resolutions of the Human Rights Council specifically are profoundly important developments in creating a norm prohibiting domestic violence in international law. The Human Rights Council is an inter-governmental body within the UN and its main mandate is to address and make recommendations to end human rights violations. It does this through the mechanism of Universal Periodic Review, which, for the purposes of international lawmaking, is a particularly important institution because it is state-driven. More than other UN bodies, the Human Rights Council could be said to represent the consensus of the states involved in this system of, to a certain extent, peer review. So it is arguable that the robust adoption of women's rights, with particular emphasis on violence against women, is 'proof' that Member States believe that they are bound by a legal duty to protect women from violence—and this includes violence within the family.

2004–09: Further General Assembly Resolutions

Since 2004, the General Assembly has adopted several resolutions pertaining to violence against women, some of which make specific and authoritative reference to domestic violence.

In February 2005 the General Assembly passed a resolution on the elimination of all forms of violence against women which urges states to protect women from violence occurring in public and private life.[433] Later that same year,

---

[430] UNHRC Res 6/30 (n 428) para 1 and UNHRC Res 7/24 (n 429) preamble and paras 1–2.

[431] UNHRC Res 6/30 (n 428) paras 5, 7, 9.

[432] ibid, para 2.

[433] UNGA Res 59/167 (22 February 2005) UN Doc A/RES/59/167, para 8, on the elimination of all forms of violence against women, including crimes identified in the outcome document of the twenty-third special session of the General Assembly, entitled 'Women 2000: gender equality, development and peace for the twenty-first century'.

in October 2005, the General Assembly passed Resolution 60/1 on the outcome of the 2005 World Summit.[434] The summit affirmed the Millennium Development Goals and the UN's commitment to development. The Resolution includes reference to the elimination of violence against women in situations of conflict.[435] The only reference to domestic violence, however, is in connection with children's rights.[436] No reference is made to the right of women to safety in the private realm in the context of the Millennium Development Goals.

On 30 January 2007, the General Assembly passed Resolution 61/143 on the intensification of efforts to eliminate all forms of violence against women.[437] The Resolution is more nuanced and precise than preceding general statements on violence against women; for example, it explores the link between poverty, lack of empowerment and marginalisation and violence.[438] It also recognises the three levels at which violence must be addressed (as devised by the Special Rapporteur on violence against women), which are namely the state level, the level of the community and the level of the family. Confirming that violence against women is global and persists in every country in the world, the Resolution 'stresses' that the definition of 'violence against women' includes violence occurring in public or private life.[439] It specifically calls on states to eliminate and criminalise 'all forms of gender-based violence in the family'.[440]

One of the more important steps taken in this Resolution is the authoritative position adopted by the General Assembly that custom, tradition and religion are not justifications for violence against women.[441] It also recognises that there are obstacles to the implementation of international standards.[442] It accepts the due diligence standard and the fact that states have a responsibility under international law to protect women from violence, which, as per the definition adopted by the Resolution, includes domestic violence.

The Resolution is more specific in its recommendations, evoking the need for multiple sectors to be involved in targeting gender-based violence.[443] Some of the more nuanced proposals include: a reduction in homelessness or poor housing that increase women's vulnerability to violence;[444] the effect of macroeconomic policies and the role of the Bretton Woods institutions in reducing

---

[434] UNGA Res 60/1 (24 October 2005) UN Doc A/RES/60/1 (hereinafter Res 60/1).
[435] ibid, paras 58(f) and 116.
[436] ibid para 141.
[437] UNGA Res 61/143 (30 January 2007) UN Doc A/RES/61/143, Intensification of efforts to eliminate all forms of violence against women (hereinafter Res 61/143).
[438] ibid, preamble.
[439] ibid.
[440] ibid, para 4.
[441] ibid, para 5.
[442] ibid, para 6.
[443] ibid, para 8.
[444] ibid, para 8(e).

gender-based violence;[445] and the need to improve resources for the UN bodies that specialise in women's rights.[446]

This was followed in 2007 by General Assembly Resolution 61/145 regarding the implementation of the Beijing Declaration and Platform for Action and the outcome of the 23rd special session of the General Assembly.[447] The Resolution 'reaffirms' states' obligation to exercise due diligence to prevent violence against women, protect victims and prosecute perpetrators, but makes no reference to family violence.[448] Although the Resolution emphasises gender mainstreaming (both nationally and in the UN system), it is not a meaningful statement vis-a-vis domestic violence.

Less than two weeks later, the General Assembly submitted a report to the Human Rights Council on the activities of the human rights treaty bodies regarding gender equality and women's rights.[449] This is a profound development in the integration of violence against women into the work of the treaty monitoring bodies. Apart from the factual information it presents, the report demonstrates a shift in the importance placed on mainstreaming gender in the UN's work. It also confirms the concept that domestic violence is a human rights violation that falls within the rubric of multiple forms of human rights violations. So, for example, the report notes that the Human Rights Committee[450] had included one or more recommendations regarding women's rights in almost all of its concluding observations, many of which focused on domestic violence.[451] These recommendations are made under the framework of the ICCPR, importing domestic violence into that rubric of international law.[452] The Human Rights Committee also made some sensible recommendations regarding crisis-centre hotlines and victim support centres equipped with medical, psychological and legal facilities and shelters that accommodate women with their children; reducing economic dependence on abusive partners that prevent women from reporting the violence; and increasing sentencing for 'honour killings'.[453] The Committee on the Elimination of Racial Discrimination had

---

[445] ibid, paras 10 and 13.

[446] ibid, para 16.

[447] UNGA Res 61/145 (7 February 2007) UN Doc A/RES/61/145, Follow-up to the Fourth World Conference on Women and full implementation of the Beijing Declaration and Platform for Action and the outcome of the twenty-third special session of the General Assembly.

[448] ibid, para 8.

[449] UNGA, *Report of the Secretary-General on the Implementation of Resolution 2005/42, Integrating the Human Rights of Women throughout the United Nations System* (15 February 2007) UN Doc A/HRC/4/104 (hereinafter UNGA Report).

[450] Not to be confused with the Human Rights Council; the Human Rights Committee is responsible for the implementation of the ICCPR.

[451] UNGA Report (n 449) paras 2, 4.

[452] ibid, para 4. The recommendations include the adoption and implementation of laws and policies to prevent and combat domestic violence, end marital rape and grant assistance to victims of such violence.

[453] ibid, para 4.

also addressed the particular vulnerability of foreign and indigenous women to domestic violence and the lack of appropriate strategies to deal with this.[454]

Possibly the most important developments were brought about by the Committee against Torture. This committee made profound statements not only about the nature of violence against women but also regarding *all* states' responsibility to treat violence against women as a human rights violation. In 2006 the Torture Committee found that rape constituted torture and that the deportation of rape victims back to their country of origin where they had been raped by state agents would be a violation of Article 3 of the Convention against Torture.[455] The Committee also reported widespread prevalence of domestic violence and, as with the Human Rights Committee, brought domestic violence specifically into the realm of the *jus cogens* norm prohibiting torture.[456] While theorists have for years compared domestic violence to torture, the inclusion of domestic violence in the Torture Committee's analysis brings it squarely within the substance of this severe human rights violation.

The General Assembly's report also commented on the seriousness of domestic violence for indigenous peoples. This had been raised by the Special Rapporteur, who reported that almost half the women using Women Refugee Services in New Zealand are Maori and that of major concern was the unacceptably high level of domestic violence against San and Khoe women in South Africa.[457] The violence reportedly includes murder and assault with weapons and often is associated with alcohol abuse and structural side-effects experienced by marginalised communities.[458]

In 2008, the General Assembly adopted the second of three resolutions on the intensification of efforts to eliminate all forms of violence against women.[459] The Resolution refers to sustainable development[460] and the role of Bretton Woods institutions in the elimination of violence against women.[461] It also calls on the Secretary-General to intensify his efforts in developing indicators regarding violence against women and to report to specific UN bodies (including the CSW and General Assembly) on institutional developments within the UN to eradicate violence against women.[462] The next day (31 January 2008) the

[454] ibid, para 13.

[455] ibid, para 14.

[456] ibid, para 17.

[457] ibid, para 36.

[458] The Special Rapporteur on the independence of judges and lawyers focused on the representation of women in the profession and the ability of the legal profession to investigate and prosecute violence against women, including specifically domestic violence (ibid, para 40).

[459] UNGA Res 62/133 (7 February 2008) UN Doc A/RES/62/133, Intensification of efforts to eliminate all forms of violence against women (hereinafter Res 62/133). The first resolution on this topic in 2007 is UNGA Res 61/143 (n 437). The third resolution is UNGA Res 63/55 (30 January 2009) UN Doc A/RES/63/155, Intensification of efforts to eliminate all forms of violence against women (hereinafter UNGA Res 63/155).

[460] UNGA Res 62/133, ibid, preamble.

[461] ibid, para 4.

[462] ibid, paras 7, 8.

General Assembly published Resolution 62/132 on Violence against Women Migrant Workers.[463] The Resolution acknowledges the 'feminisation of migration' and mentions the impact of 'domestic and family violence' in its preamble.

Several days later, on 12 February 2008, the General Assembly called for significant improvements in the resources of the CEDAW Committee in Resolution 62/218.[464] This included authorisation to increase the number and duration of sessions[465] and a request to the Secretary-General to increase the CEDAW Committee's resources and funding.[466] The CEDAW Committee had been calling for an improvement in its resources for decades. The General Assembly's Resolution reflects a turning point in terms of the seriousness with which the UN is now taking violence against women. On the same date, in Resolution 62/136 on the improvement of the situation of women in rural areas, the General Assembly called on states to include domestic violence in their national policies regarding rural women.[467]

On 30 January 2009 the General Assembly passed its third Resolution on the intensification of efforts to eliminate all forms of violence against women, Resolution 63/155.[468] There is a marked development in the nuance, specificity and understanding of states' obligations in respect of domestic violence. The Resolution recognises the 'important role of the family in preventing and combating violence against women and girls and the need to support its capacity to prevent and combat violence against women'.[469] It condemns all forms of violence against women, whether perpetrated by private persons or non-state actors, and calls specifically for the elimination of gender-based violence in the family and violence which is condoned by the state.[470] It once again confirms that custom, tradition and religion may not be invoked as reasons not to comply with this obligation.[471] The Resolution includes reference to the role of men and boys in eliminating violence against women and again calls for a multi-sectoral approach to violence.[472]

In addition to commenting on education,[473] financial support[474] and reforming policies to meet the needs of women who have been subjected to violence,[475] the Resolution makes useful and practical recommendations regarding

[463] UNGA Res 62/132 (31 January 2008) UN Doc A/RES/62/132, Violence against women migrant workers.
[464] UNGA Res 62/218 (12 February 2008) UN Doc A/RES/62/218.
[465] ibid, paras 14, 15.
[466] ibid, para 21.
[467] UNGA Res 62/136 (12 February 2008) UN Doc A/RES/62/136, Improvement of the situation of women in rural areas, para 2(h).
[468] UNGA Res 63/155 (n 459).
[469] ibid, para 6.
[470] ibid, para 8.
[471] ibid, para 9.
[472] ibid, paras 15–16.
[473] ibid, para 16(i).
[474] ibid, para 16(g).
[475] ibid, para 14.

homelessness and inadequate housing;[476] measures to prevent the victim's consent from becoming an impediment to bringing perpetrators of violence to justice (while ensuring that appropriate safeguards to protect the victim are in place); ensuring that women have legal assistance and effective remedies for the harm suffered;[477] establishing and supporting integrated centres which provide shelter, legal, health, counselling and other services to victims of violence;[478] the rehabilitation of offenders;[479] and the invocation of the role of Bretton Woods institutions to assist in implementing the Resolution's recommendations.[480]

Resolution 63/152 of 11 February 2009 on the implementation of the outcome of the World Summit for Social Development and of the 24th special session of the General Assembly refers specifically to domestic violence as part of a growing threat to security.[481]

2006–08: Work of the Secretary-General

In 2006 the Secretary-General produced the groundbreaking *In-Depth Study on all Forms of Violence against Women*.[482] The report is an authoritative, detailed and specific statement regarding violence against women and domestic violence in particular.

The report makes three important contributions to the concretisation of a norm prohibiting domestic violence in international law. First, it confirms that domestic violence is specifically included in states' obligation to end violence against women and, as such, domestic violence is brought squarely into the realm of international human rights law.[483] Secondly, it is very clear about the steps that states should take to comply with their international obligation. Finally, the Secretary-General's authority means that domestic violence now has the 'stamp of approval' of one of the most important figures in international law.

In addition to the nuanced and detailed understanding of domestic violence,[484] the report authoritatively and clearly brings domestic violence within the realm of the principles of state responsibility.[485] It confirms that state inaction leaves in place discriminatory laws and policies that undermine women's

---

[476] ibid, para 16(f).
[477] ibid, paras 16(l)–(m).
[478] ibid, para 16(q).
[479] ibid, para 16(s).
[480] ibid, para 21.
[481] UNGA Res 63/152 (11 February 2009) UN Doc A/RES/63/152, Implementation of the outcome of the World Summit for Social Development and of the twenty-fourth special session of the General Assembly, para 18.
[482] Study of the Secretary-General (n 108).
[483] ibid, paras 28–37.
[484] ibid, paras 111, 113, 108, table 2.
[485] ibid, paras 39, 242.

human rights, including the right to be free from domestic violence.[486] The report recognises that this tends to shift responsibility for preventive and remedial measures to NGOs and other groups in civil society. Importantly, the report recognises that this inertia is

> acquiescence in the violence itself. State inaction with regard to the proper functioning of the criminal justice system has particularly corrosive effects as impunity for acts of violence against women encourages further violence and reinforces women's subordination. Such inaction by the State to address the causes of violence against women constitutes lack of compliance with human rights obligations.[487]

The report confirms that intimate partner violence is the most common form of violence experienced by women globally.[488] It emphasises the pervasiveness of such violence and confirms that it is a public concern.[489] It provides a practical breakdown of the challenges and obstacles that prevent the implementation of international standards of safety for women around the world.[490] These include a lack of political will; structural imbalances of power that prevent substantive equality; discriminatory socio-cultural attitudes and economic inequalities that reinforce subordination of women; backlash against advances in the status of women, including cultural or religious 'fundamentalism' that puts pressure on governments to reverse advances in women's rights; controversies over strategies and approaches; inadequate and uneven data, which impede informed analysis and policymaking; a continued dire lack of funding for the UN Trust Fund to End Violence against Women (which had received less than $2million per year during the decade following its creation); and the failure to implement or mainstream gender across sectors.

The report also includes a vital discussion of the economic consequences of violence against women and domestic violence, confirming that the costs 'go beyond lowered economic production and reduced human capital formation but also include the costs associated with political and social instability through intergenerational transmission of violence, as well as the funds required for programmes for victims/survivors of violence'.[491] The costs of domestic violence involve the loss of the individual's contribution to society; the drain on the resources of social services, the justice system, healthcare agencies and employers; and the impact on businesses, the state, community groups and individuals.[492] These are useful considerations for governments when deciding on budget allocations. They serve to demonstrate that it makes good financial sense to

---

[486] ibid, para 96.
[487] ibid.
[488] ibid, para 112. The report notes that the UN bodies working in the area of domestic violence have demonstrated that domestic violence is a significantly underreported global phenomenon that is committed in different contexts (para 28).
[489] ibid, para 172.
[490] ibid, paras 55–64.
[491] ibid, para 107.
[492] ibid, para 171.

allocate funds to prevent domestic violence.[493] In other words, this is one area in which spending money will save money. The report identifies three categories of costs: the direct cost of services in relation to violence against women; the indirect cost of lost employment and productivity; and the value placed on human pain and suffering.[494]

Does this report create or confirm the existence of a legal principle that domestic violence is a violation of international human rights law? Once again the answer depends on the position one adopts regarding the creation of international law. But even if one takes a traditional approach to customary international law, it is increasingly difficult to claim that there is *no* domestic violence norm or that states have no sense of legal duty to take steps to protect women from domestic violence.

In December 2006, the Secretary-General established a coordinated database on the extent, nature and consequences of all forms of violence against women, and on the impact and effectiveness of policies and programmes and best practices in combating such violence.[495] The database also provides information on promising developments and best practices, including, in relation to law, the provision of services and preventative measures.[496]

Following the General Assembly's Resolutions on the intensification of efforts to eliminate violence against women, the Secretary-General published two reports, one in 2007 and the other in 2008.[497] The reports sets out the improvements that states have made in terms of their national policies on domestic violence following the internationalisation of this issue. For the purposes of assessing the status of domestic violence in international law, it is important that almost every paragraph of these reports addresses domestic violence specifically.

In February 2008 the new UN Secretary-General Ban Ki-moon launched a campaign entitled 'UNite to End Violence against Women', a multi-year effort aimed at preventing and eliminating violence against women globally. The campaign situates violence against women in the context of the Millennium Development Goals and calls on civil society, women's organisations, young people, the private sector, the media and the entire UN system to address the global pandemic of violence against women and girls. It 'builds on existing Women and Men United to End Violence against Women and Girls international legal and policy frameworks and harnesses the strong momentum

---

[493] ibid, para 172.

[494] ibid, para 173.

[495] See UN Secretary-General's Database on Violence against Women, webapps01.un.org/vawdatabase/home.action?request_locale=en.

[496] See UN Secretary-General's Database on Violence against Women: Good Practices, webapps01.un.org/vawdatabase/goodpractices.action.

[497] UNGA, *Report of the Secretary-General: Advancement of Women, Intensification of Efforts to Eliminate All Forms of Violence against Women* (3 August 2007) UN Doc A/62/201 (hereinafter Secretary-General 2007 Report); UNGA, *Report of the Secretary-General: Advancement of Women, Intensification of Efforts to Eliminate All Forms of Violence against Women* (4 August 2008) UN Doc A/63/214.

around the issue, reflected in a growing number of initiatives by UN system partners, Governments and NGOs'.[498]

In December 2008 the UN Development Fund for Women submitted a report to the Human Rights Council and the CSW on the activities of the Fund in eliminating violence against women, which addresses some of the detail that is needed to begin the process of ending violence against women.[499]

2000–09: Work of the Treaty Monitoring Bodies

As described above, in 2000, the Human Rights Committee indicated that domestic violence may constitute a violation of the right not to be subjected to torture or ill-treatment under Article 7 of the ICCPR.[500] The Committee required states to provide information on national laws and practice with regard to domestic and other types of violence against women, including rape.[501]

Eight years later, on 15 January 2008, the Special Rapporteur on torture, Manfred Nowak, submitted his second thematic report to the Human Rights Council.[502] The report dealt exclusively with the protection of women from torture. The report is one of the most important developments in terms of establishing an international norm prohibiting domestic violence. It authoritatively categorises domestic violence as a component of torture. Further, in response to the Special Rapporteur on violence against women, the report reviews the working principles of the international law of torture to ensure that the state's obligation to prevent and protect against torture includes torturous conduct in private, committed by non-state actors.

The aim of making the torture framework gender-inclusive is twofold. It provides an extensive framework of obligations and, as the report confirms, classifying an act as 'torture' carries considerable additional weight in terms of its status as a human rights violation.[503] The categorisation also helps to shake off the stigma of shame that is often associated with gender-specific harm such as rape and domestic violence. Survivors of rape and domestic violence describe an element of shame and self-blame. While these emotions may at times apply to survivors of state-approved torture, there is a difference in the way society perceives the survivors of these two forms of harm. Political prisoners are often

---

[498] See 'UN Secretary-General's Campaign to End Violence against Women', www.un.org/women/endviolence.

[499] UNGA, *Note by the Secretary-General transmitting the Report of the Development Fund for Women on the Elimination of Violence against Women (E/CN.6/2008/9)* (18 December 2008) UN doc A/HRC/10/43–E/CN.6/2009/10.

[500] General Comment No 28 (n 103) para 11.

[501] ibid.

[502] UNHRC, *Report of the Special Rapporteur on torture and other cruel, inhuman or degrading treatment or punishment, Manfred Nowak: Promotion and Protection of All Human Rights, Civil, Political, Economic, Social and Cultural Rights, Including the Right to Development* (15 January 2008) UN Doc A/HRC/7/3 (hereinafter Special Rapporteur on torture 2008 Report).

[503] ibid, para 26.

perceived as heroes pursuing a political or ideological objective, whereas domestic violence survivors are not. Therefore, bringing private violence within the definition of torture changes the public perception both of the seriousness of the violence and of the status of its survivors.

The report also proposes changes to the definition of torture. The traditional definition of torture contains four elements: severe pain and suffering, whether mental or physical; intent; purpose; and state involvement. The Special Rapporteur suggests adding to these elements the criterion of powerlessness:

> A situation of powerlessness arises when one person exercises total power over another, classically in detention situations, where the detainee cannot escape or defend him/herself. However, it can also arise during demonstrations, when a person is not able to resist the use of force any more, e.g. handcuffed, in a police van etc. Rape is an extreme expression of this power relation, of one person treating another person as merely an object. Applied to situations of 'private violence', this means that the degree of powerlessness of the victim in a given situation must be tested. If it is found that a victim is unable to flee or otherwise coerced into staying by certain circumstances, the powerlessness criterion can be considered fulfilled.[504]

The report confirms that a society's indifference to, or even support for, the subordinate status of women, together with the existence of discriminatory laws and a pattern of state failure to punish perpetrators and protect victims, creates the conditions under which women may be subjected to systematic physical and mental suffering, despite their apparent freedom to resist.[505] The importance of this statement in international law is profound.

The second important commentary in the report relates to the part of the definition of torture that requires the act of harm to be for some 'purpose'. With regard to violence against women, according to the report, the purpose element is always fulfilled if the acts can be shown to be gender-specific. This is because discrimination is one of the elements mentioned in the definition of torture in the Convention against Torture.[506] If it can be shown that an act had a specific purpose, the intent can be implied.[507]

The third change is more a confirmation regarding the role of the state in the torture definition. The definition of torture is restricted to acts 'inflicted by or at the instigation of or with the consent or acquiescence of a public official or other person acting in an official capacity'.[508] The Special Rapporteur notes that this had frequently been used to exclude violence against women outside direct state control from the scope of protection of the Convention against Torture.[509] The report confirms that the language concerning consent and acquiescence by a public official 'clearly extends state obligations into the private sphere and

---

[504] ibid, para 28.
[505] ibid, para 29.
[506] ibid, para 30.
[507] ibid.
[508] ibid, para 31.
[509] ibid.

should be interpreted to include state failure to protect persons within its jurisdiction from torture and ill-treatment committed by private individuals'.[510]

The Special Rapporteur makes specific reference in this regard to the due diligence standard. The failure of a state to exercise due diligence to prevent harm and provide remedies to victims of torture facilitates and enables non-state actors to commit acts impermissible under the Torture Convention with impunity. The state's indifference or inaction provides a form of encouragement and/or de facto permission.[511]

Part of the report is dedicated to torture and ill-treatment in the private sphere and specifically domestic violence.[512] The report cites the World Health Organization, confirming that 'the most current form of violence against women around the world is that perpetrated by husbands or other intimate partners'.[513] It describes in detail the physical and psychological elements of domestic violence that constitute torture, referring again to the powerlessness element.[514] It also addresses the various forms of state acquiescence to domestic violence, including discriminatory laws that may trap women in abusive circumstances.[515]

State responsibility may also be engaged if domestic laws fail to provide adequate protection against any form of torture and ill-treatment in the home (including the criminalisation of marital rape)[516] and if law enforcement agencies and prosecution services fail to respond to domestic violence cases.[517] The Committee against Torture has also stressed the need to take action in cases where a woman is reportedly being confined against her will by members of her family and the importance of ensuring that fair standards of proof are required.[518]

The long-term and increasingly specific approbation of domestic violence in international law evidences the growth of a principle of international law that domestic violence is a violation of women's human rights. The growth of this norm is accelerated and concretised if one considers the impact of regional law regarding domestic violence.

THE APPROACH OF REGIONAL HUMAN RIGHTS LAW AND BODIES TO DOMESTIC VIOLENCE

Inter-American System

In 1994, the General Assembly of the Organization of American States (OAS) adopted the Inter-American Convention on the Prevention, Punishment and

[510] ibid.
[511] ibid, para 32.
[512] ibid, paras 44–49. The report also deals with FGC and trafficking.
[513] ibid, para 44 fn 40.
[514] ibid, para 45 fn 40.
[515] ibid, para 46 fn 40.
[516] ibid.
[517] ibid, para 47 fn 40.
[518] ibid, para 48 fn 40.

Eradication of Violence against Women, which became known as the Convention of Belem Do Para.[519] An even more expansive definition of violence against women was incorporated into this regional instrument.[520] The Convention identified violence as one of the historic impediments to sex equality and women's right to dignity.[521]

In many respects, the Convention of Belem Do Para is a stronger and more authoritative legal instrument than DEVAW (CEDAW is equivalent in terms of discrimination but, as discussed above, its text omits violence). The Convention of Belem Do Para is a binding treaty, whereas DEVAW is a declaration, constituting an interpretation of a treaty (CEDAW) and, at best, reflecting an emerging principle of customary international law. While both the Convention of Belem Do Para and DEVAW prohibit public and private violence that is condoned or administered by the state, the regional instrument contains a more express and detailed prohibition of domestic violence per se.[522] It refers to physical, sexual and psychological violence that 'occurs within the family or domestic unit or within any other interpersonal relationship, whether or not the perpetrator shares or has shared the same residence with the woman, including, among others, rape, battery and sexual abuse'.[523]

The Convention of Belem Do Para importantly establishes a specific right 'to be free from violence in both the public and private spheres'[524] and places responsibility on state parties to fulfil that right, an express obligation that DEVAW does not emulate.[525] Finally, the Convention of Belem Do Para allows individuals to lodge petitions with the Inter-American Commission on Human Rights. By contrast, only recently have individual petitions been catered for in the Optional Protocol to CEDAW.

In 1998 the first case raising the issue of domestic violence as a violation of human rights was brought before an international tribunal, the Inter-American Commission on Human Rights.[526] In the case against *Trinidad and Tobago re Indravani Pamela Ramjattan*, Ms Ramjattan was convicted of murdering her common law husband and sentenced to death. The courts refused to take into account evidence of the years of abuse and violence she had suffered—including beatings, death threats and rape. They also failed to take into account the fact that she had tried to escape the deceased several times and each time he would find her, beat her and, on the final such occasion before he died, ask each of her

[519] Convention of Belem Do Para (n 17). For a discussion of the development of a norm against sex discrimination in the Inter-American system, see McDougal et al (n 62) 644–45.

[520] See Convention of Belem Do Para (n 17).

[521] ibid, preamble.

[522] ibid, Arts 1, 2.

[523] ibid, Art 2(a).

[524] ibid, Art 3.

[525] The nature of this responsibility is described in Chapter III of the Convention. See ibid, Arts 7, 8.

[526] Inter-American Commission on Human Rights, *Trinidad and Tobago, Indravani Pamela Ramjattan* (3 November 1998) Report No 92/98, Case 11.837, www.cidh.oas.org/annualrep/98eng/Admissibility/T&T%2011837.htm.

six children whether or not he should kill their mother. Despite this evidence she was convicted of murder, which carries a mandatory death sentence. Following a major campaign, in 1999 an appeal court reduced her murder conviction to manslaughter and sentenced her to a total of 13 years' imprisonment, based on psychiatric evidence which showed that at the time of the murder she was suffering from 'battered woman syndrome'.

The case is a clear example of the interlacing of international pressure and international law improving the situation of individuals. It is also interesting to note that at the time of the conviction there were only six shelters in the entire country—each having room for six to eight people for a maximum stay of four months.[527]

In 2001 the Inter-American Commission on Human Rights concluded that Brazil had failed to exercise due diligence to prevent and respond to a domestic violence case despite the clear evidence against the abuser and the seriousness of the charges. The Commission found that the case could be viewed as 'part of a general pattern of negligence and lack of effective action by the state in prosecuting and convicting aggressors' and that it involved 'not only failure to fulfil the obligation with respect to prosecute and convict, but also the obligation to prevent these degrading practices'.[528]

In November 2009, the Inter-American Court of Human Rights applied both the Convention of Belem Do Para and the American Convention on Human Rights,[529] holding that Mexico was in breach of these instruments by failing to investigate the disappearance and murders of several women over a 15 year period.[530]

As a regional (rather than international) instrument, the Convention of Belem Do Para is limited evidence of an international principle regarding domestic violence. Undoubtedly, though, at the very least it demonstrates the growth of a norm prohibiting domestic violence in international law. The fact that domestic violence is extremely common in many of the states that have signed this Convention does not negate its importance in advancing a norm in international human rights law. This is a treaty which expressly binds state parties and their non-compliance may reflect on the efficacy or otherwise of international law, but it does not dilute the principle prohibiting domestic violence established by the Convention.

---

[527] Amnesty International, *Broken Bodies, Shattered Minds: Torture and Ill-treatment of Women* (6 March 2001) AI-Index ACT 40/001/2001, 20, web.amnesty.org/library/Index/engact400012001.

[528] Inter-American Commission on Human Rights, *Maria da Penha Maia Fernandes (Brazil)* (16 April 2001) Report No 54/01, Case 12.051, para 56.

[529] American Convention on Human Rights (adopted at the Inter-American Specialized Conference on Human Rights, 22 November 1969, entered into force 18 July 1978) OAS Treaty Series No 36, 1144 UNTS 123.

[530] *Cotton Field* case (n 345).

European System

Council of Europe

The Convention for the Protection of Human Rights and Fundamental Freedoms (the European Convention) prohibits sex discrimination as an impermissible basis for differentiation.[531] It also requires states to respect the individual's 'private and family life, his home and his correspondence'.[532] This right may be limited, inter alia, when it is in accordance with the law and is necessary for the protection of the rights and freedoms of others.[533] Protocol 7 to the European Convention protects the equality of rights and responsibilities of spouses both between themselves and in their relations with their children.[534]

The Parliamentary Assembly of the Council of Europe also recognises domestic violence as the major cause of death and disability of women between the ages of 16 and 44.[535] In Recommendation 1582, the Parliamentary Assembly proposed various steps that Member States ought to take to prevent domestic violence and punish its perpetrators. It did not comment on the status of domestic violence as a human rights violation but noted that acts of domestic violence are criminal acts.[536]

While the right to privacy and family life is entrenched, it is not absolute and there is room for state intervention in the family affairs of individuals. This caveat is crucial as it is within the family context that the most extreme and common form of violence against women occurs.

In 1985, the Committee of Ministers of the Council of Europe passed Recommendation No R(85)4 on violence in the family.[537] This was followed in 1990 by Recommendation No R(90)2 on social measures concerning violence in the family.[538] In 1998, the Steering Committee for equality between women and men of the Council of Europe organised a forum on domestic violence in Europe. The report confirmed that it is internationally accepted that the use of violence against women is a violation of basic human rights and that, increasingly, violence in the private sphere was becoming the subject of attention in the global context.

---

[531] Convention for the Protection of Human Rights and Fundamental Freedoms (European Convention on Human Rights, as amended) (ECHR) (adopted 4 November 1950, entered into force 3 September 1953) 213 UNTS 222, Art 14.

[532] ibid, Art 8.

[533] ibid.

[534] ibid.

[535] Parliamentary Assembly of the Council of Europe, 'Recommendation 1582 (2002) Domestic violence against women' (27 September 2002) § 2.

[536] ibid, § 4.

[537] Parliamentary Assembly of the Council of Europe, 'Recommendation No R (85) 4 of the Committee of Ministers to Member States on Violence in the Family' (26 March 1985).

[538] Parliamentary Assembly of the Council of Europe, 'Recommendation No R (90) 2 of the Committee of Ministers to Member States on Social Measures Concerning Violence within the Family' (15 January 1990).

In 2002, the Committee of Ministers of the Council of Europe produced a recommendation on the protection of women against violence.[539] The report is a strong and detailed document, which sets out innovative and precise recommendations in respect of domestic violence. The recommendation acknowledges the structural nature of violence against women and, in line with the developments at the UN, calls on states to ensure a multi-sectoral, coordinated approach to violence against women.[540]

The recommendation contains excellent and detailed proposals, particularly with regard to domestic violence. They cover: the collation of data disaggregated by gender, including the social and economic costs of violence against women;[541] the training of police, judicial and medical personnel to deal with domestic violence and manage crisis situations;[542] and the particular difficulties faced by immigrant women who experience domestic violence and the independent right of such women to residence in order to enable them to leave their violent husbands without having to leave the host country.[543]

The report makes an interesting recommendation that victims of violence should be compensated for the harm endured and that a system be established which will compensate victims and, if necessary, pursue the perpetrators of violence for reimbursement.[544] This is a notable departure from the situation in the USA, where, two years prior to the Council of Europe recommendation, the Supreme Court struck down the Violence against Women Act which enabled victims of violence to pursue civil claims against their perpetrators.

In 2004, in recommendation 1681, the Parliamentary Assembly initiated the pan-European campaign to combat domestic violence against women in Europe.[545] The recommendation confirmed that

> member states have an obligation under international law to act with due diligence to take effective steps to end violence against women, including domestic violence, and to protect its victims/survivors. If they do not themselves want to be held responsible, states must take effective measures to prevent and punish such acts by individuals and to protect the victims/survivors.[546]

In 2005 the Council of Europe Task Force to Combat Violence against Women, including Domestic Violence (EG-TFV) was set up following a decision taken at the Third Summit of Heads of State and Government of the Council of Europe

---

[539] Council of Europe, 'The Protection of Women against Violence, Recommendation Rec (2002) 5 of the Committee of Ministers to Member States on the Protection of Women against Violence Adopted on 30 April 2002 and Explanatory Memorandum' (30 April 2002) (hereinafter CoE Rec (2002) 5).

[540] ibid, para 4.

[541] ibid, para 5.

[542] ibid, paras 8–10.

[543] ibid, paras 24, 59.

[544] ibid, paras 36–37.

[545] Council of Europe, 'Recommendation 1681 (2004) Campaign to Combat Domestic Violence against Women in Europe' (8 October 2004).

[546] ibid, para 2.

held in Warsaw on 16 and 17 May 2005.[547] The Action Plan adopted at the Summit defines future action by the Council of Europe and envisages activities to combat violence against women, including domestic violence. This includes the creation of a pan-European campaign to combat domestic violence.[548]

It is interesting to note the name given to the Task Force. Domestic violence is included in the title as a specific manifestation of violence against women. This shows the Council of Europe's commitment to combating domestic violence. It also implies that domestic violence is not always automatically included in the discussion of violence against women in international law, hence the need for specification in the Task Force's title.

In 2006, under Resolution 1512, European parliaments united in combating domestic violence against women through various forms of collaborative action, including legislative and budgetary measures.[549] The Resolution authoritatively confirms that domestic violence against women results in 'serious violations of human rights'[550] and is 'one of the most widespread violations of human rights and must be combated in all Council of Europe member states'.[551] The Assembly rejected all arguments based on cultural or religious relativism as a justification for avoiding this obligation. This was followed in the same year by Recommendation 1759,[552] which, inter alia, called on the Committee of Ministers to make the fight against domestic violence a priority activity in 2006–08.[553]

In 2008 the EG-TFV issued its final activity report.[554] The report describes the shift in international law from protecting individuals against the state to the state's role in protecting individuals from harm by non-state actors.[555] The report echoes the multi-sectoral and coordinated approach proposed by the Council of Europe's 2002 recommendation.[556] The message of the campaign regarding domestic violence specifically was that joint, coordinated action is necessary; domestic violence is a human rights violation, and it damages the whole of society and not only the individuals subject to the abuse.[557]

---

[547] Council of Europe Task Force to Combat Violence against Women, including Domestic Violence (EG-TFV), *Final Activity Report* (Council of Europe, Strasbourg, September 2008), www.coe.int/t/dg2/equality/domesticviolencecampaign/Source/Final_Activity_Report.pdf   (hereinafter   CoE Domestic Violence Final Activity Report).

[548] ibid.

[549] Council of Europe, 'Resolution 1512 (2006), Parliaments United in Combating Domestic Violence against Women' (28 June 2006) para 5, assembly.coe.int/Main.asp?link=/Documents/AdoptedText/ta06/Eres1512.htm.

[550] ibid, para 1.

[551] ibid, para 2.

[552] Council of Europe, 'Recommendation 1759 (2006), Parliaments United in Combating Domestic Violence against Women' (28 June 2006), assembly.coe.int/Main.asp?link=/Documents/AdoptedText/ta06/Erec1759.htm.

[553] ibid, para 4.

[554] CoE Domestic Violence Final Activity Report (n 547).

[555] ibid, p 6, para 1.2.

[556] ibid, pp 7–8.

[557] ibid, p 11.

The Task Force, which calls for a legally binding convention on state responsibility aimed at protecting women from domestic violence, undertakes the difficult project of identifying minimum standards and principles in the provision of services which governments should provide and respect in order to meet their international obligation to exercise due diligence in preventing, investigating and punishing acts of domestic violence and providing protection to victims.[558] The Task Force adopted seven key indicators: any and every act of violence against women is to be considered a criminal offence; violence perpetrated by a partner or former partner is to be punished more severely than violence among strangers; victims should be able to seek justice in a humane manner (eg through specialised courts dealing with domestic violence, specialised units within the police, the public prosecutor's office or the judiciary); there ought to be a national emergency helpline available round the clock, free of charge, for victims of domestic violence; sufficient numbers of safe shelters for victims of domestic violence must be established; administrative data on victims of domestic violence to be collected; and recognition that domestic violence is not a private matter but a human rights violation to be addressed by all state organs and every individual.[559]

In 2009, the Secretary-General of the Council of Europe announced the preparation of a Europe-wide convention on action against violence against women.[560] The development is late in comparison with its equivalent in the Inter-American system, but it recognises the need to create a specific and regional, legally binding framework for national legislation and policies to protect, prevent and prosecute violence against women.

European Union

The European Union has not yet issued a legally binding instrument on the protection of women against gender-based violence, although the European Parliament and Council have established the 'Daphne III programme'.[561] This programme aims to prevent and combat all forms of violence, especially violence of a physical, sexual or psychological nature, against children, young people and women. It is designed to cover the period 2007–13 and supplements

---

[558] ibid, p 14. See also Liz Kelly and Lorna Dubois, *Combating Violence against Women: Minimum Standards for Support Services* (Council of Europe, Strasbourg, 2008) EG-VAW-CONF(2007) Study rev, www.coe.int/t/e/human_rights/equality/05._violence_against_women/075_EG-VAW_CONF_2007_Study_rev.asp.

[559] CoE Domestic Violence Final Activity Report (n 547) p 17.

[560] See Terry Davis, Secretary-General of the Council of Europe, 'Violence against Women: The Council of Europe takes its Campaign to a New Level' (6 April 2009) Council of Europe Press, wcd.coe.int/ViewDoc.jsp?id=1428509&Site=DC&BackColorInternet=F5CA75&BackColorIntranet=F5CA75&BackColorLogged=A9BACE.

[561] Decisions adopted Jointly by the European Parliament and the Council, Decision No 779/2007/EC (20 June 2007), establishing for the period 2007–13 a specific programme to prevent and combat violence against children, young people and women and to protect victims and groups at risk (Daphne III programme) as part of the General Programme 'Fundamental Rights and Justice'.

existing anti-violence programmes in Member States.[562] The programme targets families, teachers, social workers, police, border guards, local, national and military authorities, medical and paramedical staff, judicial staff, NGOs, trade unions and religious communities.[563] For the rest, measures to prevent and combat violence against women remain within the regulatory powers of each Member State.[564]

In 2004 the European Parliament adopted a Resolution on the current situation in combating violence against women and any future action, calling on Member States and the European Commission to consider violence against women as a human rights violation and to adopt appropriate legal and policy measures to improve the protection of women against all forms of violence.[565]

In 2007 the European Council issued a recommendation on the prevention of injury and the promotion of safety, calling on Member States to take measures to prevent injuries, including those caused by intentional violence, particularly domestic violence against women and children.[566]

The European Court of Human Rights (ECtHR) has made some of the more progressive decisions vis-a-vis state responsibility for harm committed by private actors. It is informative to explore three cases in detail.

A v The United Kingdom

In this case the ECtHR considered whether caning a child constituted torture or inhuman or degrading treatment, as prohibited by Article 3 of the European Convention.[567] The ECtHR concluded that Article 3, read together with Article 1, places an obligation on state parties to take measures to ensure that their citizens are not subjected to torture or inhuman or degrading treatment or punishment, 'including such ill-treatment administered by private individuals'.[568] The Court emphasised the state's responsibility to protect children and 'other vulnerable individuals . . . against such serious breaches of personal integrity'.[569] This laid the foundation for the state duty to protect vulnerable groups from violence perpetrated by non-state actors, which is discussed in chapter three below.

---

[562] ibid, Art 1.

[563] ibid, Art 6.

[564] ibid, Art 16. See also CoE Domestic Violence Final Activity Report (n 547) p 26.

[565] European Parliament, 'Resolution on the Current Situation in Combating Violence against Women and any Future Action' (2004/2220(INI)).

[566] Council Recommendation of 31 May 2007 on the prevention of injury and the promotion of safety (2007/C 164/01).

[567] *A v The United Kingdom* (App No 25599/94) (1999) 27 EHRR 611.

[568] ibid, para 22.

[569] ibid.

Kontrová v Slovakia

This was a landmark decision in the protection of women from violence.[570] The applicant had been beaten and subjected to psychological and physical violence by her husband. Despite reports being made to the police, they failed to bring criminal charges or investigate the complaints. Eventually, the applicant's husband shot their two children and then himself. The ECtHR held that the state had a positive obligation to take preventive operational measures to protect the applicant's children from severe beatings and psychological abuse in the applicant's family, which was known to the local police department; the police had an array of specific obligations with which they had failed to comply;[571] and the direct consequences of these failures was the death of the applicant's children.

This failure constituted a violation of Article 2 (the right to life). In the view of the Court, the police's obligation in light of a serious threat in a situation of domestic violence included

> duly registering the applicant's criminal complaint, launching a criminal investigation and commencing criminal proceedings against the applicant's husband immediately, keeping a proper record of the emergency calls and advising the next shift of the situation [as well as] taking action in respect of the allegation that the applicant's husband had a shotgun and had made violent threats with it.[572]

Opuz v Turkey

In October 2008, the ECtHR heard arguments in the case of *Opuz v Turkey*, in which the applicant claimed a violation of the Convention on the basis of Turkey's failure to take action against the applicant's husband, who had repeatedly subjected her and her mother to domestic violence and eventually killed her mother.

The case was an opportunity for regional recognition that states have enforceable and justiciable positive obligations to take reasonable steps to protect individuals from domestic violence. In a groundbreaking decision, the ECtHR held that there had been a violation of the right to life (Article 2), the right to be free from torture, inhuman and degrading treatment or punishment (Article 3) and the right to equal protection and enjoyment of the rights in question (Article 14).[573]

Over a period of 12 years the applicant's husband, HO, repeatedly threatened to kill the applicant and her mother (and on occasion the applicant's children) and committed acts of physical violence against the applicant and her mother,

---

[570] *Kontrová v Slovakia* (App No 7510/04) ECtHR (31 May 2007), concerning the failure of the police to act on threats made by the applicant's husband to kill the applicant and their common children. As a result, he shot himself and their children on 31 December 2002.

[571] ibid, paras 52–54.

[572] ibid, para 53.

[573] *Opuz v Turkey* (App No 33401/02) ECtHR (9 June 2009).

including beatings sufficient to endanger life. Eventually HO shot and killed the applicant's mother.[574] The abuse against the applicant continued even when the case came before the ECtHR. On at least five occasions the applicant and/or her mother had sought the protection of the state. The details of the violence, the nature of the state's response and the Court's findings under Articles 2, 3 and 14 of the Convention are discussed in detail in chapters two and three respectively.[575]

The Court's decision that the state had violated Article 3 in the context of domestic violence is unprecedented and addresses three important legal concepts regarding domestic violence in international law. First, the Court held that the violence suffered by the applicant, in the form of physical injuries and psychological pressure, were sufficiently serious to amount to ill-treatment within the meaning of Article 3 of the Convention.[576] This confirms that domestic violence can be so extreme that it meets the standard of harm required to trigger international law. Secondly, the Court examined and relied upon international law developments in relation to domestic violence to confirm that the local authorities had not done enough to protect the applicant from this form of ill-treatment, nor had they met their obligation to protect the applicant's mother's right to life.[577] According to the Court, the authorities should have done more than merely impose a small fine on HO, which was payable in instalments, as punishment for stabbing the applicant seven times.[578] Further, the authorities should not have relied on the applicant for a specific request to implement the law, especially taking into account the overall amount of violence perpetrated by HO against the applicant and her mother.[579] This reveals the nuanced and serious nature of the violence and that it operates on a continuum and cannot be judged on a case-by-case basis. Finally, the Court held that the state had not only failed in the specific instance of protecting the applicant, it should have pursued the protection of the applicant and her mother in the public interest, and the public interest in the safety of women outweighed HO's right to privacy within the family.[580]

The Court's decision is a profound development in the jurisprudence of international law, violence against women and state responsibility. The ECtHR, although a regional body, is a source of international law. As a judicial body, its jurisprudence both informs and reflects the development of international law and this decision concretises the principle that domestic violence may be a violation of the Convention and all Member States are bound to ensure that they exercise due diligence in protecting and preventing this form of harm.

---

[574] ibid, para 54.
[575] See ch 2, pp 135–142 and ch 3, pp 220–224.
[576] *Opuz v Turkey* (n 573) para 161.
[577] ibid, paras 162–65.
[578] ibid, para 169.
[579] ibid, para 171.
[580] ibid, paras 168–69.

African System

In contrast to the European system, Africa has experienced little of the successful application and enforcement of human rights. The original African Charter on Human and Peoples' Rights took positive strides in imposing on Member States the obligation of actively ensuring that women enjoy a safe home environment.[581] However, both the formulation of the right (coupled with the rights of the child) and the implementation of the right are deficient. The right is a sub-right, forming part of the larger right to have a family unit based on 'traditional values recognized by the community'.[582] The practical outcome of this right does not afford women any real benefit or elevation in status, especially where such 'traditional values' have placed women and children under the authority of the male household member, whose control and authority is rarely subject to restraint or intervention.[583] Various initiatives have been introduced to address this situation, including the special addendum on the eradication of all forms of violence against women and children (1998) to the 1997 Southern African Development Community's Declaration on Gender and Development[584]

The new African Union, established on 9 July 2002, seeks, inter alia, 'to build a partnership between governments and all segments of civil society, in particular women, youth and the private sector, in order to strengthen solidarity and cohesion among our peoples'.[585] While the founding document of the African Union (AU), the Constitutive Act (which incorporates and augments the Banjul Charter), undertakes to promote gender equality, the document itself is wanting in respect of defining, defending and promoting women's rights.[586] The Constitutive Act is also potentially disappointing for human rights lobbyists in its continued commitment to sovereign immunity and its dedication to 'non-interference by any Member State in the internal affairs of another'.[587] However, it should be borne in mind that the nature of the instrument is to detail the objectives of the new AU, which include unifying the various African nations and not necessarily pursuing a new human rights regime.

---

[581] Banjul Charter (n 83) (requiring states to 'ensure the elimination of every discrimination against women and also censure the protection of the rights of the woman and the child').

[582] ibid, Art 61.

[583] See Jennifer Nedelsky, 'Violence against Women: Challenges to the Liberal State and Relational Feminism' in Ian Shapiro and Russell Hardin (eds), *Political Order* (New York, NYU Press, 1996) 454, 457–58, 472–73, 479–80. In writing about the patriarchal structure of a liberal state, Nedelsky raises the question of how fundamental change can be effected within a system, the foundation of which is based on tradition which is at odds with basic egalitarian values (484–85). A statement made at the Beijing Conference (n 17) recognises that the empowerment of women may well conflict with 'regional particularities' and cultural norms but insists that these norms must be disregarded if they resist promotion and protection of fundamental rights and freedoms. Beijing Declaration (n 17) 11. See also O'Connell (n 82) 9.

[584] Secretary-General 2007 Report (n 497) para 50.

[585] Constitutive Act of the African Union (adopted 11 July 2000, entered into force 26 May 2001) (2000), preamble, www.africa-union.org/root/au/index/index.htm.

[586] ibid, Art 4(l).

[587] ibid, Art 4(g).

In July 2003 the AU adopted the Protocol on the Rights of Women in Africa as a supplement to the Banjul Charter, which came into force in 2005.[588] Of the 53 Member States of the AU, 45 have signed the Protocol.[589] This is a powerful statement in international law regarding the right of women to be free from domestic violence and a corresponding obligation on states to protect that right. Although the Protocol does not refer to domestic violence as such, Article 4 establishes that every woman has a right to life, integrity and security of the person and that all forms of exploitation, cruel, inhuman or degrading punishment and treatment are prohibited. It is the responsibility of the state to protect this right. This obligation includes the enactment and enforcement of laws 'to prohibit all forms of violence against women including unwanted or forced sex whether the violence takes place in private or public'.[590]

The Protocol recognises that there is a right to be safe from violence in private and a corresponding obligation on the state to protect that right through legislative, administrative and other social and economic measures, the allocation of sufficient monetary and other resources, and equal access to justice.[591] This targets many of the state institutions which historically have not assisted victims of domestic violence and, through this omission, have exacerbated the violence. This is actually an interesting characteristic of the Protocol as a whole. It expressly articulates the rights of women to established, mainstream human rights, such as equal protection before the law,[592] the right to education,[593] the right to participation in the political process[594] and the right to health.[595] It may be said that women technically have these rights under the African Charter, but a specific pronouncement was necessary to clarify both the existence of women's rights in countries where uncertainty exists *as well as* the detailed evocation of the corresponding duties on states, under international law, to protect those rights.

The Protocol is an important source of international law and provides evidence of the existence of a right and a corresponding state duty to protect women from domestic violence in international human rights law. The Protocol is a treaty, signed by a significant number of state parties all consenting to this obligation. As at the date of writing (January 2010), 45 of 53 countries had signed the Protocol and 26 countries had ratified it. Its enforcement and efficacy are a different matter, but for the purposes of identifying a right in international law to be free from domestic violence, the Protocol is a strong sign of a binding principle in international law.

[588] Protocol to the African Charter on the Rights of Women in Africa (n 17).

[589] See List of countries which have signed or ratified/acceded to the Protocol to the African Charter on Human and Peoples' Rights on the Rights of Women in Africa, www.africa-union. org/root/au/Documents/Treaties/List/Protocol%20on%20the%20Rights%20of%20Women.pdf.

[590] Protocol to the African Charter on the Rights of Women in Africa (n 17) Art 4(2)(a).

[591] ibid, Arts 4 (right to life, integrity and security of the person), 5 (elimination of harmful practices) and 8 (access to justice and equal protection before the law).

[592] ibid, Art 8.

[593] ibid, Art 12.

[594] ibid, Art 9.

[595] ibid, Art 14.

An unprecedented public commitment to women's rights occurred in July 2004, when Heads of State adopted the Solemn Declaration on Gender Equality at the AU Summit meeting.[596] This undertaking calls for the implementation of gender-specific economic, social and legal measures and the protection of women against violence and discrimination.[597] As regards violence against women, the state parties agree to

> Initiate, launch and engage within two years sustained public campaigns against gender based violence as well as the problem of trafficking in women and girls; Reinforce legal mechanisms that will protect women at the national level and end impunity of crimes committed against women in a manner that will change and positively alter the attitude and behaviour of the African society.[598]

In October 2005 the First African Union Conference of Ministers Responsible for Women and Gender was held in Dakar, Senegal, hosted by the AU's Women, Gender and Development Directorate. In that same month the Union adopted the Implementation Framework of the Solemn Declaration on Gender Equality in Africa.[599] The Framework seeks to eliminate gender-based violence by 2015.

The commitment of AU state parties to ending violence against women is evident, but its mode of implementation is uncertain. There is little doubt, however, that in Africa women have a defined, specific and recognised legal right to be free from domestic violence.

Regional bodies are actively pursuing an agenda prohibiting domestic violence and delineating the precise obligations on states to protect women from such violence. States are part of this process and, while a strict, traditional approach to customary international law may require more evidence of state practice and/or *opinio juris*, this bulk of precise, detailed and ever-growing regional law regarding domestic violence as an international human rights violation for which states are responsible cannot be ignored.

SPECIFICATION OF CERTAIN FORMS OF VIOLENCE AGAINST WOMEN IN INTERNATIONAL LAW

Alongside the international and regional instruments dealing with violence against women there are now also international instruments that address

---

[596] Heads of State and Government of Member States of the African Union, 'Solemn Declaration on Gender Equality in Africa' (Addis Ababa, Ethiopia, July 2004) Assembly/AU/Decl. 12 (111) Rev 1 (hereinafter Solemn Declaration on Gender Equality in Africa).

[597] For a discussion of this meeting see AU Directorate of Women, Gender and Development, '5th Consultative Meeting on Gender Mainstreaming in the African Union Aide-Memoire' (Abuja, Nigeria, 25–26 January 2005), www.africa-union.org/summit/jan2005/Gender/Aide%20memoire.doc.

[598] Solemn Declaration on Gender Equality in Africa (n 596) Art 4.

[599] First African Union Conference of Ministers Responsible for Women and Gender, 'Implementation Framework of the Solemn Declaration on Gender Equality in Africa' (Dakar, Senegal, October 2005) AU/MIN/CONF/WG/3 (I), www.africa-union.org/root/AU/Conferences/Past/2006/October/WG/English-IMPLEMENTATION_FRAMEWORK.doc.

specific forms of violence against women, namely, mass rape as a weapon of war, FGC, and trafficking of women and girls. I discuss in this section the legal recognition of these specific manifestations of violence against women in order to demonstrate the analogous process of internationalisation that is underway with respect to domestic violence.

While there are clear differences between mass rape, FGC, trafficking and domestic violence generally, I discuss these specific instances of violence against women in order to demonstrate a trend in international law towards the articulation of various specific forms of violence against women. Broad principles in international law have been used to identify specific laws and rules with a view to better protecting women against the harm in question. I do not suggest that the nature and severity of, and the harm resulting from, domestic violence generally is the same as that of mass rape, FGC and trafficking. Rather, I discuss these other forms of violence only to establish precedent for the specification in international law of certain forms of gender-based violence.

Mass Rape

Prior to 1994, rape in a conflict was not prosecuted as a breach of humanitarian law or the laws of war.[600] In an effort to address mass rape within the laws of war, jurists extrapolated established international legal principles and applied them to this particular form of sexual violence.[601] And so in 1998, in the case of *Prosecutor v Akayesu*, the International Criminal Tribunal for Rwanda (ICTR), for the first time in legal history, tried and convicted an individual for genocide and crimes against humanity for his role in orchestrating and encouraging the mass rape of women.[602]

The Tribunal also refined the legal definition of mass rape to include command responsibility and incitement to mass rape. Akayesu was found guilty of mass rape, not because he had committed an act of rape himself but on the basis of command responsibility by virtue of the fact that he had endorsed the mass rape of Tutsi women with supportive and encouraging statements. In this case, the ICTR recognised rape as a form of torture, holding that:

> Like torture, rape is used for such purposes as intimidation, degradation, humiliation, discrimination, punishment, control or destruction of a person. Like torture, rape is a violation of personal dignity, and rape in fact constitutes torture when it is inflicted by

---

[600] See Jennifer Green, Rhonda Copelon, Patrick Cotter and Beth Stephens, 'Affecting the Rules for the Prosecution of Rape and Other Gender-Based Violence before the International Criminal Tribunal for the Former Yugoslavia: A Feminist Proposal and Critique' (1994) 5 *Hastings Women's Law Journal* 171, 176.

[601] ibid, 183–84.

[602] See also James R Mchenry III, 'The Prosecution of Rape under International Law: Justice that is Long Overdue' (2002) 35 *Vanderbilt Journal of Transnational Law* 1269, 1272; Sherrie L Russell-Brown, 'Rape as an Act of Genocide' (2003) 21 *Berkeley Journal of International Law* 350.

or at the instigation of or with the consent or acquiescence of a public official or other person acting in an official capacity.[603]

It was necessary for the Tribunal to go into the detail of the definition of sexual violence to demonstrate that it was not just an unhappy side-effect of war, an indulgence of the needs of soldiers separated from their spouses, but an act of war designed to bring harm to a group as a whole through the violation of women's bodies.

The ICTR redefined the crime of rape as an act of aggression and not an act of sexual desire, recognising that 'rape is a form of aggression and that the central elements of the crime of rape cannot be captured in a mechanical description of objects and body parts'.[604] According to the Tribunal, sexual violence is not limited 'to physical invasion of the human body and may include acts which do not involve penetration or even physical contact'.[605] It also recognised the nuances of mass rape, namely that coercion need not manifest itself in physical force but includes threats, intimidation, extortion and 'other forms of duress which prey on fear or desperation'.[606]

This decision was followed by the judgment of the International Criminal Tribunal for the Former Yugoslavia (ICTY) in the case of *Prosecutor v Kunarac*, which cemented the *Akayesu* precedent, confirming widespread rape as a war crime and a crime against humanity.[607] In the infamous case of *Prosecutor v Delalic et al*, otherwise known as the *Celebici* case, the Trial Chamber held that the rape of any person is a despicable act which strikes at the very core of human dignity and physical integrity and that the condemnation and punishment of rape becomes all the more urgent where it is committed by, or at the instigation of, a public official, or with the consent or acquiescence of such an official.[608] The Tribunal, in keeping with *Akayesu*, employed the language of torture in describing the severe pain and suffering, both physical and psychological, caused by rape. It also acknowledged that psychological suffering may be exacerbated by social and cultural conditions and can be particularly acute and long lasting.[609]

The Tribunals also revisited the element of 'lack of consent' in proving the crime of rape. The requirement of proving that the victim did not consent deterred women from participating in the Yugoslav and Rwandan Tribunals. The ICTY held that free will and consent must be assessed in the context of the surrounding circumstances. In *Prosecutor v Furundzija*, the trial chamber held that 'any form of captivity vitiates consent'.[610] This was reproduced in the rules

---

[603] *Prosecutor v Akayesu* (Judgment) ICTR-96-4-T, T Ch I (2 September 1998) para 597.
[604] ibid, para 687.
[605] ibid, para 688.
[606] ibid.
[607] *Prosecutor v Kunarac* (Judgment) ICTY-96-23-T (22 February 2001) para 437. For a comparison of the *Akayesu* and *Kunarac* judgments, see Mchenry (n 602) 1284.
[608] *Prosecutor v Delalic and Others* (Judgment) ICTY-96-21-T (16 November 1998) para 543.
[609] ibid.
[610] *Prosecutor v Furundzija* (Judgment) (1999) ICTY-95-17/1-T, (1999) 38 ILM 317, para 271.

of procedure and evidence of the International Criminal Court, which state that consent cannot be inferred from the words or the acts of the victim when there is an oppressive or coercive context, or where the person is incapable of giving genuine consent, or by reason of the silence or lack of resistance on the part of the victim.[611] The rules of all these institutions prohibit the submission of evidence regarding the prior sexual conduct of the victim.

Systematic and widespread rape was brought within the definitions of ethnic cleansing and genocide—recognised war crimes—creating an understanding of how the violent rape of women facilitates the destruction of a people.[612] By identifying its constitutive elements, the ICTY and ICTR had the legal tool to hold officials responsible for their failure to protect individuals from mass rape, even if the accused himself or herself had not committed the act.[613] Today, the express norm prohibiting mass rape can lead to criminal responsibility if a commander knowingly allows the mass rape of hundreds of women.[614]

In 2000, the jurisprudence of the ad hoc tribunals was codified in the Rome Statute of the International Criminal Court, which prohibits various forms of sexual or reproductive violence against women in a variety of contexts. For example, the crime of genocide includes the imposition of measures intended to prevent births within a group (Article 6(d)); crimes against humanity include rape, sexual slavery, enforced prostitution, forced pregnancy, enforced sterilisation, or any other form of sexual violence of comparable gravity (Article 7(1)(g)); and war crimes include rape, sexual slavery, enforced prostitution, forced pregnancy, enforced sterilisation or any other form of sexual violence constituting a grave breach of the Geneva Conventions (Article 8(2)(b)).

On 31 October 2000, UN Security Council Resolution 1325 on Women, Peace and Security was passed unanimously. This was the first resolution ever passed by the Security Council that specifically addresses the impact of war on women, and women's contribution to conflict resolution and sustainable peace.[615]

Eight years later, on 19 June 2008, the UN Security Council voted unanimously to classify rape as a tactic of war and a threat to international security. This became UN Security Council Resolution 1820, which demands the immediate and complete cessation by all parties to armed conflict of all acts of sexual violence

[611] ICC Rules of Procedure and Evidence adopted by the Assembly of State Parties, Rule 70 (2002) UN Doc ICC-ASP/1/3.
[612] See Mchenry (n 602) 1271–72. See also Askin (n 100) 355.
[613] See Mchenry (n 602) 1272. Carrie Sperling, 'Mother of Atrocities: Pauline Nyiramasuhuko's Role in the Rwandan Genocide' (2005–06) 33 *Fordham Urban Law Journal* 637.
[614] See Mchenry (n 602) and Sperling (n 613).
[615] UNSC Resolution 1325 (n 17) (recognising the urgent need to mainstream a gender perspective into peacekeeping operations and post-conflict reconstruction). The potential of this is uncertain. Its recognition of women as 'agents for social change' was muted, particularly in its language, which advocates the participation of women 'where possible'. See Centre for Criminal Justice and Human Rights, Blog (2 July 2008) (referring to Madeleine Reese, Head of Women's Rights and Gender Unit, Office of the UN High Commissioner for Human Rights), www.ucc.ie/law/blogs/ccjhr/2008/07/panel-2-security-council-resolution.html.

against civilians.[616] It is authority that rape and other forms of sexual violence can constitute war crimes, crimes against humanity or a constitutive act with respect to genocide. The Resolution confirms that women and girls are particularly targeted by the use of sexual violence, including in some cases as a tactic of war to humiliate, dominate, instil fear in, disperse and/or forcibly relocate civilian members of a community or ethnic group.

The decisions of the ICTY and ICTR, the provisions of the Rome Statute and Resolutions 1325 and 1820 collectively prohibit rape and sexual violence as a crime against humanity, a grave breach of the customs and laws of war and a form of torture. These are now clear principles of international law, placing specific obligations on states, UN bodies and non-state actors.

Domestic violence is set on a similar developmental course. As with mass rape before the *Akayesu* decision, the generic prohibitions under current international law of discrimination against women are inadequate to target the specific state role in the perpetuation and prevention of domestic violence. Although international law has developed a great deal of jurisprudence on domestic violence, it has not yet attained the precision or authority that marks mass rape in international law, but it is certainly on the same trajectory.

Female Genital Cutting

The practice of FGC triggered discord between adherents of cultural autonomy and proponents of universal human rights. There are those who argue that it is the cultural right of societies that practise this procedure to do so and 'western' intervention is an improper incursion into the cultural autonomy of such groups. Human rights activists, on the other hand, argue that physical integrity and the right not to be cut is a universal right that trumps cultural justifications of the practice.

This tension impeded the application of international human rights law in countries where FGC is practised.[617] For example, international activists initially argued that FGC is a form of child abuse and violates the Children's Convention. Parents of circumcised children were outraged at the allegation that they abused their children and refused to end this long-standing traditional practice. The designation of FGC as a form of child abuse reinforced the gap between local communities' perceptions of cutting as a form of purification and initiation and the internationalist interpretation of cutting as a human rights violation.[618] Real change only began when international bodies identified the

[616] UNSC Resolution 1820 (n 17).

[617] See John Tochukwu Okwubanego, 'Female Circumcision and the Girl Child in Africa and the Middle East: The Eyes of the World are Blind to the Conquered' (1999) 33 *International Law* 159, 174.

[618] Kirsten Bowman, 'Bridging the Gap in the Hopes of Ending Female Genital Cutting' (2005) 3 *Santa Clara Journal of International Law* 132.

context of the practice and sought to understand its causes, rationales and sustaining elements and to propose alternative practices to achieve the same cultural objectives.[619]

This debate caused some uncertainty as to whether or not FGC is a violation of international human rights law.[620] Initially, the international position regarding FGC was based on established norms contained in the UDHR, the Convention on the Rights of the Child,[621] CEDAW,[622] and the Convention against Torture.[623] However, these general tenets of established international law did not provide a satisfactorily clear and precise prohibition of FGC. The international community recognised that a deficiency remained since 'international law failed to provide a strong, feasible solution for the eradication of the practice'.[624] A clearer, more authoritative standard was necessary. And so the specification of this particular form of violence against women developed so as to identify a clear legal principle in international law and a corresponding obligation on states to assist its victims.

This specification process is most evident in refugee law. In the case of *In Re Kasinga*, the US immigration authorities accepted the practice of FGC as a possible basis for asylum due to the consequences of permanent disfigurement and the 'risk of serious, potentially life-threatening complications'.[625] In the UK, the Law Lords considered whether fear of FGC constituted a ground for asylum under the Refugee Convention in the case of *Secretary of State for the Home Department v K (FC) and Fornah (FC) v Secretary of State for the Home Department*.[626] The Law Lords unanimously held that the appellant, a woman from Sierra Leone, had a well-founded fear of persecution (which would take the form of FGC) by reason of her membership of a particular social group, as required by Article 1A(2) of the Refugee Convention. The Law Lords differed as to the demarcation of the social group (whether it applied to all women or only women who might be subject to FGC), but all agreed that the threat of FGC constituted a ground for protection under the Refugee Convention.[627]

---

[619]   ibid.

[620]   See Rahman and Tubia (n 100). See in general Bowman (n 618).

[621]   Children's Convention (n 68).

[622]   See Bowman (n 618) 7 (indicating the deficiencies of CEDAW in that countries would enter reservations against the treaty, having been 'offended by the notion that their customs and traditions are seemingly disposable').

[623]   Since the mid-1980s, the UN has made several attempts to mitigate the harm of FGC, predominantly through education and awareness raising (ibid, 6–7).

[624]   ibid, 6. Of course, it is unclear that the internationalisation of FGC has achieved such opposition, but this will be discussed in the context of the benefit of international law in ch 4 below.

[625]   See *In Re Kasinga*, Interim Dec 3278, 1996 WL 379826 (BIA, 13 June 1996). The basis of the Board of Immigration's decision was that the claimant could not escape the FGC procedure and could not expect assistance from her government. See Megan Annitto, 'Asylum for Victims of Domestic Violence: Is Protection Possible after In Re R-A-?' (2000) 49 *Catholic University Law Review* 785, 795.

[626]   *Secretary of State for the Home Department v K (FC) and Fornah (FC) v Secretary of State for the Home Department* [2006] UKHL 46.

[627]   Lord Bingham found that the 'social group' was all women in Sierra Leone because 'it is clear that women in Sierra Leone are a group of persons sharing a common characteristic which, without a fundamental change in social mores is unchangeable, namely a position of social inferiority as

A common element in these approaches to FGC is the absence of protection by the state. The role of the state as endorsing and, thereby, entrenching this form of violence against women became the focus in international law. In the same way, the ferocity of domestic violence between intimates takes place not in a vacuum but rather within a context of social, cultural and behavioural rules, which, as with FGC, leave women without protection from the state. As international law develops to take these externalities into account, regulation of the harm improves. A similar shift is underway in the development of international law on domestic violence.

Trafficking

On 15 November 2000, the General Assembly adopted the UN Convention against Transnational Organized Crime and two optional protocols on trafficking in persons and smuggling of migrants.[628] Born out of the international prohibition of slavery,[629] the conceptualisation of this form of violence against women was moulded by the 'principle that trafficking in women is sex discrimination and a violation of human rights'.[630] While both genders may be victims of trafficking, the fact remains that 'the large majority of people trafficked throughout the world are women and girl children'.[631]

Originally the generic prohibitions on slavery and sex discrimination in international law were inadequate to address the specific problem of trafficking. The problem was reformulated as having a 'particular genesis in gender oppression'

compared with men . . . it is a characteristic which would exist even if FGM were not practised, although FGM is an extreme and very cruel expression of male dominance' (ibid, para 31). Baroness Hale defined the social group as Sierra Leonean women belonging to those ethnic groups where FGM is practised (para 114). Both Baroness Hale and Lord Bingham included in the group women who had been subject to FGC and those who had not yet been subjected to the procedure. The remaining Law Lords (Lords Hope, Rodger and Brown) took the view that 'the particular social group is composed of uninitiated indigenous females in Sierra Leone', excluding those who have already been initiated because they could not be said still to be at risk (para 56 per Lord Hope; Lords Rodger and Brown expressed similar views at paras 72–80 and para 119 respectively).

[628] UN Convention against Transnational Organized Crime (n 17). For a brief discussion of this instrument see Sean D Murphy, 'International Trafficking in Persons, Especially Women and Children' (2001) 95 *American Journal of International Law* 407.

[629] See Susan Feanne Toepfer and Bryan Stuart Wells, 'The Worldwide Market for Sex: A Review of International and Regional Legal Prohibitions Regarding Trafficking in Women' (1994) 2 *Michigan Journal of Gender and Law* 83, 94–104 (describing the early history of the international law of trafficking in women, including the Convention for the Suppression of Traffic in Persons and of the Exploitation of the Prostitution of Others in 1949, CEDAW in 1979, and the Convention against Sexual exploitation). Fitzpatrick dates this back as early as 1904. See Joan Fitzpatrick, 'Trafficking as a Human Rights Violation: The Complex Intersection of Legal Frameworks for Conceptualizing and Combating Trafficking' (2003) 24 *Michigan Journal of International Law* 1143, 1144, 1157–58. See also Murphy (n 628) and Shelley Case Inglis, 'Expanding International and National Protections against Trafficking for Forced Labor Using a Human Rights Framework' (2001) 7 *Buffalo Human Rights Law Review* 55.

[630] Toepfer and Wells (n 629) 84.

[631] Inglis (n 629) 61.

and highlighted the need to formulate laws accordingly and specifically to meet the nuances of this crime, such as the creation in the USA of a non-immigrant 'T' visa for aliens who are victims of severe forms of trafficking.[632] By recasting the violence in the light of the reality of the coercion, financial exigency and extreme nature of the enslavement, lawyers were able to fashion specific and more appropriate legislation to address female trafficking, at both the national and international levels.[633] Europe too has recognised the need to take specific steps to deal with this harm. The Council of Europe's Convention on Action against Trafficking in Human Beings identifies the responsibility of states in respect of this crime that encompasses slavery, violence against women and organised crime.[634]

The specification of trafficking as a particular form of violence against women and the identification of the precise role of the state has led many governments to adopt trafficking policies in their criminal justice and immigration systems. It is precisely this type of specific legislative and policy approach that is developing in respect of domestic violence.

THE WRITINGS OF RESPECTED AUTHORS AND SCHOLARS

So far I have considered treaties, UN instruments, regional instruments, and UN and regional jurisprudence to determine whether there is a norm in international law prohibiting domestic violence. In this section I discuss the final source of international law, being the academic writings of respected authors and scholars.

Since the beginning of the 1990s, the international community has begun to listen to the call of theorists to 'recharacterize internationally protected human rights to accommodate women's experience of injustice'.[635] In 1991, Hilary Charlesworth, Christine Chinkin and Shelly Wright observed that 'International law is a thoroughly gendered system'.[636] This was a bold statement in a time marked by 'the immunity of international law to feminist analysis',[637] and with it came a range of feminist commentary on the substance, procedures and politics of international law and women.

---

[632] Murphy (n 628) 410 (citing the Trafficking Victims Protection Act of 2000 § 107(e)).

[633] For example, the elements of coercion, deception and abuse of power in relationships between the perpetrator and the captive led to the realisation that if the victim ultimately consents to the exploitation, such consent shall be irrelevant. See Fitzpatrick (n 629) 1149–50. See also Home Office and Scottish Executive, 'UK Action Plan on Tackling Human Trafficking' (March 2007), www.homeoffice.gov.uk/documents/human-traffick-action-plan?view=Binary.

[634] Council of Europe Convention on Action against Trafficking In Human Beings (adopted 16 March 2005, entered into force 1 February 2008) CETS No 197.

[635] Rebecca J Cook, 'Women's International Human Rights Law: The Way Forward' (1993) 15 *Human Rights Quarterly* 230, 231. See in general Thomas and Beasley (n 63) 52 (describing how states universally fail to protect women from domestic violence). See also Subedi (n 63) (describing the universal nature of domestic violence and maintaining that it affects women predominantly).

[636] Charlesworth et al (n 84) 614.

[637] ibid.

In the early 1990s, scholars increasingly analysed the reasons for the marginalisation of violence against women in international law.[638] Authors such as Celina Romany identified the negative effect on women resulting from the distinction drawn at international law between public and private conduct, with the former being addressed by the law and the latter being left largely unregulated.[639] The battered women's movement highlighted the severity of domestic violence, revealing it as a serious legal issue.[640]

More than a decade ago, activists in the field began to draw on an analogy to torture to describe the experience of domestic violence victims.[641] In 1994, Rhonda Copelon framed the comparison between intimate violence and torture as defined by the Convention against Torture.[642] Other authors have engaged torture terminology in their discussion of violence against women, comparing battery to physical torture and prison life.[643] The culmination of these developments was thoroughly addressed by Elizabeth Schneider in her examination of the law regarding battered women from a feminist perspective, where the various motivations for, and implications of, domestic violence as an international human rights violation are garnered.[644]

The parallel between domestic violence and state-approved torture was part of the initiation of the discussion that violence at home could be as egregious as violence in public.[645] Amnesty International, a leading authority on torture in international law, applied the language and lore of the Torture Convention to sexual violence and other types of intimate harm, confirming the view that violence against women may constitute torture for which the state is accountable when it is of a nature and severity envisaged by the concept of torture in international standards and where the state has failed to fulfil its obligation to

---

[638] See eg Rhonda Copelon, 'Intimate Terror: Understanding Domestic Violence as Torture' in Cook (n 383) 116, 117. See also UNICEF, *Domestic Violence against Women and Girls* (n 111) 10.

[639] See Celina Romany, 'Women as Aliens: A Feminist Critique of the Public/Private Distinction in International Human Rights Law' (1993) 6 *Harvard Human Rights Journal* 87, 98–99 (identifying 'the diverse layers of coercion embedded in legal discourse'). See also John M Eekelaar and Sanford N Katz, 'Preface' in John M Eekelaar and Sanford N Katz (eds), *Family Violence: An International and Interdisciplinary Study* (Toronto, Butterworths, 1978) iii (observing that, unlike racial conflict, family violence does not take place in public, and the silent suffering of its victims has only recently been recognised). See Copelon (n 638) 117, 122–39.

[640] See Elizabeth M Schneider, 'The Violence of Privacy' in Martha A Fineman and Roxanne Mykitiuk (eds), *The Public Nature of Private Violence: The Discovery of Domestic Abuse* (New York, Routledge, 1994) 36, 41 (describing the progress of the battered women's movement and demonstrating how it has been retarded by the powerful denial by jurors, politicians and courts in general). Some have criticised this movement's labelling as being counter-productive. See eg Martha R Mahoney, 'Victimization or Oppression? Women's Lives, Violence, and Agency' in Fineman and Mykitiuk, ibid, 59, 65.

[641] See eg Copelon (n 638) 117. See also UNICEF, *Domestic Violence against Women and Girls* (n 111) 10.

[642] See Copelon (n 638) 117.

[643] See Andrea Dworkin, *Life and Death* (New York, Free Press, 1997) 153–55.

[644] See generally Schneider (n 100).

[645] See generally Copelon (n 638).

provide effective protection.[646] Awareness of the struggle for international recognition of violence against women was further heightened through a range of literature focusing on FGC, harmful practices against women, and rape as a weapon of war and genocide.[647]

However, criticism continues to be levelled against the inclusion of domestic violence in international human rights law.[648] Therefore, while authors have highlighted the similarities between frequent forms of intimate violence and the acts contemplated by the drafters of the Torture Convention and other international instruments, the explicit legal consequences of this analogy still need to be explored.[649]

Several themes have developed in the realm of women's rights jurisprudence which help to advance the argument that domestic violence is an international human rights violation.

The Distinction between Public and Private

For many years, feminists have noted the failure of legal systems to protect women from harm committed in private—the dominant nature of violence against women.[650] This inflexibility inherent in legal systems is compounded by a communal tendency to shun victims of domestic violence.[651] Cultural conditioning can both trivialise and justify violence against women, with the result that victims of violence become 'the targets of unpunishable and therefore, implicitly endorsed violence'.[652]

As a result, feminist theorists extracted the theory of violence against women from the realm of family law and placed it within the ambit of public law, discussing private violence against women with reference to the nation state. A

---

[646] See Amnesty International, *Broken Bodies, Shattered Minds* (n 527). See also Amnesty International (n 3) 4, 10 (describing how torture is a 'predetermined attack on a person's psyche, body and dignity').

[647] See Rahman and Tubia (n 100). See generally Askin (n 100) (discussing the jurisprudence on rape as a weapon of war/genocide or as a crime against humanity).

[648] See Richard B Felson, *Violence and Gender Reexamined* (American Psychological Association, 2002) 3–5.

[649] See eg Schneider (n 100) 48; Dworkin (n 643) 115 (referring to Amnesty International in the context of domestic violence). See Copelon (n 638) 120–39.

[650] See Fineman and Mykitiuk (n 640) xi–xviii (describing the development of feminist theory, which identified the need to bring the state into the private realm to curb the level of violence, thereby changing the boundaries of the public/private distinction). See also Mahoney (n 640) 78–81 (showing how much violence against abused women takes place at work, underscoring the public nature of the violence and the almost complete absence of free will to exit the relationship).

[651] See Isabel Marcus, 'Reframing "Domestic Violence": Terrorism in the Home' in Fineman and Mykitiuk (n 640) 11, 12–16 (describing the consistent patterns of domestic violence in a range of countries from India to Pakistan, China to Poland. She demonstrates that notwithstanding the extensive and fraught nature of the violence, there is general silence and abstention when action is required).

[652] ibid, 17.

plethora of new and intellectually astute formulations of violence against women arose.[653] The recasting of violence against women from the personal to the political, with a concomitant change in language, clarified the way in which legal systems bypass the specific needs of women. Labels such as 'terrorism', 'patriarchal terrorism', 'torture' and 'private torture' were used to describe the public dimension of domestic violence and to import the state as a figure responsible for the perpetuation of the violence.[654]

The suggestion that the state plays a greater role in the affairs of the family than previously recognised triggered concern that the constitutionally protected right to privacy would be compromised.[655] Schneider discusses the United States Supreme Court case of *Griswold v Connecticut*. The case, which legalised contraception, was both a coup and a blow for women's rights. It was decided on the basis that the right to privacy prevented the state from interfering in the affairs and choices of women but it also entrenched the view that the state was prevented from entering the home and family realm, even where the home was the location of the violence.[656] It became necessary to 'develop both a more nuanced theory of where to draw the boundaries between public and private, and a theory of privacy that is empowering'.[657] To this end, it was argued that 'privacy' is a right that includes 'autonomy, equality, liberty, and freedom of bodily integrity, that are central to women's independence and well-being'.[658] For victims of domestic violence, so the argument develops, these aspects of privacy are absent.

So the private world is the locus of the violence and the violence in turn denies victims their own constitutionally protected right to privacy. Privacy is understood to comprise the 'dimension of autonomy over the development and expression of one's intellect, interests, tastes, and personality'.[659] It is the 'decisional dimension—"freedom of choice in the basic decisions of one's life respecting marriage, divorce, procreation [and] contraception"',[660] and the

---

[653] ibid, 17, 19–21 (arguing that domestic violence is a form of coveture since the woman's identity is subsumed into that of her husband).

[654] ibid, 31 (adopting the terminology of 'terrorism' to replace 'domestic violence', arguing that ultimately, they both create psychological and physical harm through a series of 'seemingly random but actually calculated attacks of violence', creating 'an atmosphere of intimidation in which there is no safe place of escape'). See also Michael P Johnson, 'Patriarchal Terrorism and Common Couple Violence: Two Forms of Violence against Women' (1995) 57 *Journal of Marriage and the Family* 283, 286 (describing extreme forms of domestic violence as patriarchal terrorism); Copelon (n 638) 117 (describing domestic violence as torture); Bonita C Meyersfeld, 'Reconceptualizing Domestic Violence in International Law' (2003) 67 *Albany Law Review* 371 (distinguishing between domestic violence and private torture). See also Dworkin (n 643).

[655] For a discussion of this issue see Schneider (n 640) 36.

[656] ibid, 50. *Griswold v Connecticut* US Supreme Court, 381 US 479 (1965).

[657] ibid.

[658] ibid.

[659] ibid, 51 (citing Justice Douglas' jurisprudence on privacy as gleaned from the United States Supreme Court cases of *Griswold* and *Roe v Wade*, where Justice Douglas distilled three components to privacy, namely, autonomy, decision-making capacity and freedom from intrusion).

[660] ibid.

right to privacy means 'freedom from intrusion, restraint, and compulsion, and freedom to care for oneself and express oneself'.[661]

This description recognises that the true value of privacy is the freedom to flourish as an individual; it is not an impermeable barrier between the state and the individual. Justice Sachs of the South African Constitutional Court describes how 'the concept of autonomy has been used to protect the abusive husband from the actions of the state, but not the abused wife from the actions of the husband [with the result that] all too often the privacy and intimacy end up providing both the opportunity for violence and the justification for non-interference'.[662]

This was confirmed by the ECtHR in the case of *Bevacqua and S v Bulgaria*, where it was held that[663] 'Women's human rights to life and to physical and mental integrity cannot be superseded by other rights, including the right to property and the right to privacy'.[664] The feminist analysis concludes that privacy cannot be understood merely as the right to be left alone; rather, it is linked affirmatively to liberty, the right to autonomy and self-determination. Privacy is not in opposition to, but is an affirmation of, women's safety in the home. And in protecting the right to privacy, it is the state's duty to balance the negative—non-intervention in the affairs of individuals—and positive steps—protection of individuals from intimate harm.

The State's Role

Authors and scholars have started to unravel the perception that domestic violence is a behavioural deviation between private individuals and a pathological exception to the norm.[665] Research and statistics show that domestic violence is not a rare occurrence perpetrated by deviant members of society, as is the case, for example, with serial killers, and today the regular occurrence of domestic violence globally is mostly undisputed. Legal scholars and authors have looked at this research and concluded that the state—and its failure to really understand domestic violence and protect its victims—is in fact one of the driving forces behind its continued, uniform perpetuation.[666] The terrorisation of individual victims is thus compounded by a sense that domestic violence is inevitable. Patterns of systemic sexist behaviour are normalised rather than combated.[667]

---

[661] ibid.

[662] *S v Godfrey Baloyi*, Case CCT 29/99 (South African Constitutional Court, 1999), per Justice Sachs, para 16.

[663] *Bevacqua and S v Bulgaria* (App No 71127/01) ECtHR (12 June 2008) para 83.

[664] *Ms AT v Hungary* (n 261) para 9.3.

[665] Celina Romany, 'Killing "The Angel in the House": Digging for the Political Vortex of Male Violence against Women' in Fineman and Mykitiuk (n 640) 285, 287–88 (maintaining that this perception eroded the politicisation of domestic violence).

[666] See Subedi (n 63) 591.

[667] *S v Baloyi* (n 662) para 12.

Scholars have moved the wide-angle lens away from the narrow criminal-justice focus on the individual perpetrator, to the larger structure of state-sanctioned violence.[668] Most legal theorists today agree that if a state's officials do nothing to help the victims of domestic violence, this sends an unmistakable message to the whole of society that the daily trauma of vast numbers of women counts for little.

Cultural Relativism

International human rights law faces the challenge of prescribing and implementing a set of uniform norms for the protection of individuals in very diverse contexts and cultures. At the same time, it protects the rights of groups to practise and enjoy their cultural autonomy.[669] The result is that some norms may conflict with the practices of groups, the autonomy of which is also protected in international human rights law.

Some autonomous groups have claimed that their cultural heritage includes differentiation between men and women and that this practice of gender distinction trumps international standards of sex equality.[670] They argue that the status of women (and men) is framed by cultural, religious, political or social imperatives which may preclude certain individual rights of women for the benefit of family order, discipline or other communal imperatives. In some instances, even where a practice is harmful, there are those who insist on its role as an essential part of a larger communal practice, the abolition of which 'will destroy the tribal system'.[671]

Theorists have had to refute this argument without subscribing to the cultural imperialism of the so-called western powers that have wreaked havoc among

[668] ibid. See also White J in *United States v Dixon* 509 US 688 (1993) at 730.

[669] ICCPR (n 61) Art 27 (providing that in states 'in which ethnic, religious or linguistic minorities exist, persons belonging to such minorities shall not be denied the right, in community with the other members of their group, to enjoy their own culture, to profess and practise their own religion, or to use their own language').

[670] See Merry (n 130) 946 (discussing the obstacle of culture in implementing human rights). See also Charlesworth et al (n 84) 636 (describing the CEDAW Committee's decision requesting the UN and specialised agencies to review the status of women under Islamic law). The representatives of the Islamic nations objected to the decision as a threat to their freedom of religion and the CEDAW Committee's recommendation was rejected.

[671] See Bowman (n 618) 3 (citing the late president of Kenya and his view of FGC). See also Elaine Pagels, 'The Roots and Origins of Human Rights' in Alice Henkin (ed), *Human Dignity: The Internationalization of Human Rights* (Washington, DC, Aspen Institute for Humanistic Studies, 1979) 1. The issue of cultural relativism and Shari'a law came before the CEDAW Committee in 1984 during Egypt's country report. See *Report of the Third Session of the Committee on the Elimination of Discrimination against Women* (27 June 1984) UN Doc A/39/45, pp 10–17, paras 69–124 (hereinafter CEDAW Third Session Report) p 25, para 183; p 28, para 209; p 28, para 211; p 29, para 215; p 29, para 216. A similar issue arose in respect of Bangladesh. See *Report of the Sixth Session of the Committee on the Elimination of Discrimination against Women* (15 May 1987) UN Doc A/42/38, paras 503–72, pp 69–76 (hereinafter CEDAW Committee Sixth Session Report). See, finally, the remarks of the Philippine representative in respect of that country's initial report: CEDAW Third Session Report, p 14, paras 100 and 105.

thousands of cultures and groups throughout the world. Scholars' responses have become more sensitive and sophisticated, balancing the importance of culture against the need to protect the individual. Calling for the liberation of women from violence, oppression and marginalisation is not necessarily the plea of the righteous to the regressive (nor is it the plea of the regressive to the righteous). One approach is the reconsideration of the narrow definition of culture.[672] Traditionally, academics have perceived culture as petrified in a snapshot moment in time. While this may be the view of westerners encountering certain cultures for the first time, it is shortsighted to believe that a culture has not evolved, influenced to greater or lesser degrees by externalities. This is not to say that because a culture has transmogrified in the past it is therefore legitimate to compel it to change in the future. What is becoming clear, however, is that integrating human rights norms into certain cultures is not necessarily antithetical to the perpetuation of, or respect for, the integrity of those cultures.[673]

One cannot ignore the claim of cultural preservation.[674] Taking an unfiltered, pejorative view of certain cultural practices is dangerous, not only because the value of tradition deserves respect, but also because disregarding the cultural context of practices feeds a rift between such communities and the international human rights system, potentially alienating victims from international assistance.[675] But at the same time, culture or tradition simply cannot excuse or justify harm. Culture, after all, is not a justification for racism, slavery or other prohibited practices, and if the cultural relativism debate continues to oscillate around the hub of gender equality, we need to ask why it is that to hate a black man is a prejudice, but to hate a woman is a custom.

This inconsistency has led scholars to become more robust about the balance that needs to be struck between respecting culture and ousting cruelty. Current scholarship maintains that diversity does not bar the formulation of principles that could be universally adopted within the contours of a group's specific cultural and traditional imperatives.[676] Protecting women from domestic violence is one such principle.

The balanced and sophisticated approach to the cultural relativism debate has resulted in a more finely honed dialogue in international law in relation to violence against women. The protection of women from the violence they experience is a principle of greater universal relevance and less contention than ever

---

[672] See Merry (n 20) 6–10.

[673] ibid.

[674] John Rawls, 'The Law of Peoples' in Stephen Shute and Susan Hurley (eds), *On Human Rights: The Oxford Amnesty Lectures* (New York, Basic Books, 1993) 41, 43.

[675] See Bowman (n 618) 4–5 (summarising the two sides of the cultural relativism debate, and indicating how victims find it difficult to embrace so-called 'universal norms' without being disloyal to their homes, families and communities). For a discussion of the tension between an individual's rights and cultural autonomy see Radhika Coomaraswamy, 'Identity Within: Cultural Relativism, Minority Rights and the Empowerment of Women' (2002) 34 *George Washington International Law Review* 483, 494.

[676] See eg Buchanan (n 55) 76.

before.[677] Academics have also begun to rein in the call for universal solutions to domestic violence, with more emphasis on culturally appropriate tools (discussed in chapter two below).[678] The sameness of the problem, such as the 'difficulty of naming domestic violence', does not mean that inflexible uniform solutions are viable.[679]

While the debate regarding cultural autonomy rages intensely within the context of women's rights, it is still proper and consistent with group rights for international and national governing bodies to develop best methods of protecting women from domestic violence.[680]

Discrimination and Violence

For a long time equality was understood as a formal concept, based on the principle that people in similar situations should be treated similarly.[681] Scholars began to refine this understanding of equality, noting that without taking into account the structural causes of discrimination, formal equality will not end violence against women. Critics argued that the liberal feminism underlying CEDAW is 'unable to deal with situations where men and women are truly not similarly situated'.[682] They questioned the purely gender-neutral approach that there are no differences between men and women and insisted that equality is not necessarily the same as equivalency. A purely gender-neutral state policy, for example, ignores the inherited difficulties women have, inter alia, in accessing the criminal justice system or in earning equal pay for equal work, an inequality which prevents many domestic violence victims from living with their families independently of their male partners.[683]

[677] For a detailed analysis of the cultural relativism debate and its impact on women's rights throughout the world see Martha C Nussbaum, 'Human Capabilities, Female Beings' in Martha C Nussbaum and Jonathan Glover (eds), *Women, Culture and Development: A Study of Human Capabilities* (Oxford, Oxford University Press, 1995) 274, 279–89.

[678] See Michele E Beasley (1994) 'Introduction to Section III: International and Comparative Perspectives on Domestic Violence' in Fineman and Mykitiuk (n 640) 255 (pointing out that there are both similarities and differences in domestic violence around the world).

[679] ibid. See also Rosemary Ofeibea Ofei-Aboagye, 'Domestic Violence in Ghana: Some International Questions' in Fineman and Mykitiuk (n 640) 260, 273 (noting that Ghanaians 'have a sense of communal well-being of their society' that requires mutual assistance and support, yet they do not intervene in cases of domestic violence. She suggests that this communal structure could be harnessed through education to reduce the level of domestic violence). The claim that there are basic global solutions is strong. See Leni Marin, Helen Zia and Esta Soler, *Ending Domestic Violence: Report from the Global Front Lines* (Family Violence Prevention Fund, 1998) 5 (noting that the 'long range challenge for advocates and activists is to forge an international consensus on how to prevent domestic violence').

[680] Coomaraswamy (n 675) 494.

[681] Southard (n 139) 5–6 (describing the criticism of liberal feminism).

[682] ibid, 8.

[683] See Merry (n 130) 950–51. See also Southard (n 139) 23 (describing the many deficiencies of CEDAW due to its failure to take the structural exigencies into account).

Theorists such as MacKinnon, Charlesworth, Fineman, Coomaraswamy, Johnson-Sirleaf and Sen have argued that the law cannot simply be expanded to apply 'equally' to women; rather, it should be recreated to address specifically the needs women have as a result of past discrimination.[684] They note that the law of many states has been moulded according to a predominantly male experience and culture, with the result that violence against women is perceived to be 'either too particular to be universal or too universal to be particular'.[685]

This has led scholars to examine the intersection between violence against women and discrimination against women. Violence was identified as a manifestation of a male-centric view that posits women on a lower social echelon with less social value. The cultural, economic and political abjection of women was revealed as the foundation on which violence rests. The scholastic outcome, therefore, is an understanding of the link between violence against women and the broader, sometimes invisible, patterns of discrimination and differentiation.[686]

Increasingly, academics are seeking to

> reconceptualize violence against women in intimate relationships as a problem rooted in structural conditions such as political economy, globalisation, the expansion of capitalism and the growing inequality between rich and poor nations as well as the dynamics of interpersonal interactions.[687]

To end this structural cycle, scholars generally agree that states should undergo self-audits and take positive and reformative steps to ensure that women are protected from violence including domestic violence.[688]

CONCLUSION

The combination of instruments, cases and commentaries in international law makes a compelling argument that the right to be free from domestic violence is an international human right for which states can be held liable.[689] At this point

---

[684] See Catharine A MacKinnon, *Toward a Feminist Theory of the State* (Cambridge, Harvard University Press, 1989); Hilary Charlesworth, 'What are "Women's International Human Rights"?' in Cook (n 383) 58–84; Martha A Fineman, *The Neutered Mother, the Sexual Family, and Other Twentieth Century Tragedies* (New York, Routledge, 1995); EJ Sirleaf, 'Liberia's Gender-Based Violence National Action Plan' (2007) 27 *Forced Migration Review* 34; Radhika Coomaraswamy, 'Women, Ethnicity and the Discourse of Rights' in Cook (n 383) 39, 40; Amartya Sen, *Development as Freedom* (New York, Random House, 2000) 3–12, 189.

[685] Catharine A MacKinnon, 'Crimes of War, Crimes of Peace' in Shute and Hurley (n 674) 84–85.

[686] Schneider (n 640) 49 (arguing that 'Without access to these resources, violence against women will endure').

[687] Merry (n 130) 943–44.

[688] See Mahoney (n 640) 67 (explaining the focus on positive rights with reference to the abortion struggle).

[689] See eg Vesa (n 152) 312 (confirming that there is evidence of a prohibition of 'domestic violence' in customary international law).

it is probably impossible to argue that there is no international norm prohibiting domestic violence. But is this part of international *law*? On the one hand, the array of instruments addressing domestic violence indicates that states, albeit through the international and regional bodies of which they are members, may have an obligation to prevent domestic violence and punish those who practice it. On the other hand, these instruments are not conclusive evidence of customary international law if one adopts a black letter, traditional approach to customary international law. However, the increasing precision in many international instruments and the adoption of domestic violence within the rubric of mainstream treaty monitoring bodies indicates a trend towards the internationalisation of domestic violence. The fact that states are responding—at least in their reports to the UN—is undeniably evidence of customary international law in the making.

Clarity, authority and precision are, however, still sorely required. We are in the midst of the amorphous process of norm-crystallisation through custom. Therefore, the more precise, certain and authoritative international instruments are, the more the claim that domestic violence is prohibited in international law will be less contentious. The status of this right in international law needs to be developed and matured. It would benefit from (1) the continued integration of domestic violence as a consideration in the work of non-gender-specific treaty monitoring bodies; (2) greater detail and specification as to the precise laws, policies and judicial and governmental activity that are required in international law; and (3) a more nuanced explanation of *why* something so personal and intimate as domestic violence constitutes a violation of *international* human rights law and how domestic violence survivors would benefit from the international system.

The benefit of this to victims of domestic violence is discussed in chapter four. At this stage the proposal is simply that domestic violence is a violation of international human rights law but there is still more work to be done at the international level. What specifically must be done? I address this question in chapter two.

2

Freedom from Systemic Intimate Violence: The Human Right and Corresponding State Obligation

> We have to be clear on the nature of the 'theory' underlying the practice of extreme inequality, and be prepared to outline what justice may minimally demand.
>
> Amartya Sen[1]

THE SUBSTANCE OF THE RIGHT

AT SOME POINT we are moved to ask: 'But why?' Why concern our-selves with the private lives of individuals at the level of international law? In public life, and especially in poor or politically unstable countries, so many issues compete for attention, including famine, war, environmental decay, politics, commerce, and the challenges of globalisation. It would not be unreasonable to suggest that tensions between intimates simply do not warrant comparable consideration.

International human rights law does not protect all our interests. Only core, fundamental interests are protected as 'human rights'. My claim in this chapter is that the right to be free from domestic violence qualifies as such a right, and thereby triggers the rules of international law.

What makes domestic violence different from other violence or crime in society such that it warrants the application of international law? Why should this form of harm receive international disapprobation and not others, such as theft, armed robbery or murder? The answer is that certain forms of domestic violence have various characteristics or constitutive elements that are not present in other forms of social harm. Extreme forms of domestic violence are *systemic*, in a way that armed robbery or bar fights, for example, are not. This form of violence also predominantly harms a *discrete group*—women, who are particularly vulnerable in part because of the way that group has been treated historically.

---

[1] Amartya Sen, 'Gender Inequality and Theories of Justice' in Martha C Nussbaum and Jonathan Glover (eds), *Women, Culture and Development: A Study of Human Capabilities* (Oxford, Clarendon Press, 1995) 259, 270.

And this harm occurs in almost every society worldwide.[2] For those reasons, I propose that domestic violence is a specific human rights violation which requires states to act proactively.

To some extent, the internationalisation of domestic violence has been recognised by important international actors, including the Special Rapporteur on violence against women, its causes and consequences, the Secretary-General of the UN and the Special Rapporteur on torture.[3] But, as discussed in chapter one, not everyone operating in international law agrees with these statements and the subject of domestic violence is still not automatically understood as a contravention of international law. This is due, in part, to the difficulty involved in understanding exactly what it is about domestic violence that makes it sufficiently serious, essentially public, and an appropriate subject at international law.

Therefore, notwithstanding the acceptance of domestic violence as a human rights violation by some international actors, the subject still requires thorough analysis.

Exploring the Internationalising Elements of Domestic Violence

Many people still balk at the notion that domestic violence, something so intimate, could constitute a human rights violation that requires discussion at the international level. This is because we have not yet analysed what types of violence constitutes domestic violence for which a state is responsible. The term 'domestic violence' is one that applies to a miscellany of harms. Currently, falling within the composite term 'domestic violence' are acts as diverse as a single instance of shoving or pushing on the one hand, and ongoing incidents of battering, breaking bones, burning, rape and torture on the other. While all of these forms of harm constitute domestic violence, this book does not propose that all such forms of violence can or should be addressed at international law. Rather, only a subset of domestic violence which has certain internationalising elements, discussed below—which I refer to as 'systemic intimate violence'— has the elements necessary to trigger international law.[4]

Why is it necessary to segregate harm into these categories? By using a single, undifferentiated notion of domestic violence, current discussions, policies and

---

[2] UN Centre for Social Development and Humanitarian Affairs, 'Violence against Women in the Family' (1989) UN Doc ST/CSDHA/2, 14 ('Violence against women is a problem worldwide, occurring, to a greater or lesser degree, in all regions, countries, societies and cultures, and affecting women irrespective of income, class, race or ethnicity').

[3] UNHRC, *Report of the Special Rapporteur on torture and other cruel, inhuman or degrading treatment or punishment, Manfred Nowak: Promotion and Protection of All Human Rights, Civil, Political, Economic, Social and Cultural Rights, Including the Right to Development* (15 January 2008) UN Doc A/HRC/7/3 (hereinafter Special Rapporteur on torture 2008 Report).

[4] The forms of violence that would fall into the category of systemic intimate violence are not limited to the locus of the home but are defined with reference to the intimacy between the perpetrator and the victim of the harm.

legislation fail to grasp the sheer variety and nature of the harm produced by intimate aggression. This results in laws that are improperly fashioned and therefore ineffective. Conflating all forms of violence is also one of the reasons why many dispute or do not understand why this form of violence constitutes— and ought to be accepted as—an international human rights violation.

It is necessary to make a distinction between harm that is systemic and harm that is not. If there is a pandemic of violence against a specific category of people and state authorities cannot or do not stop that violence, there is clearly a governance gap. International law is one method of identifying the deficiencies in governance and formulating methods to reduce the frequency and harmful effects of systemic violence, be it political or intimate. This may make it easier to identify effective, appropriate and direct tools to reduce the frequency and harmful effects of intimate violence.[5]

Distinguishing between types of violence is objectionable but necessary. Lawyers generally must distinguish between: grievous bodily harm and attempted murder; rape and sexual assault; human rights violations and crimes against humanity; torture and ill-treatment; and mass killing and genocide. In the same manner, not all conflict or violence that takes place within a family or intimate context is necessarily a human rights violation which requires a response at the international level. It would be unreasonable, and I believe inaccurate, to suggest that intimate discord of all types warrants the same legal approach.

Systemic intimate violence has a significant and ever-present negative effect on our society which distinguishes it from other forms of violence.[6] The purpose of this distinction is not to reduce the status or seriousness of a category of harm or to rank harm according to some qualitative hierarchy. All forms of domestic violence constitute a violation of the individual victim's human rights. Rather, the objective is to create laws that best address specific types of conduct, to demarcate human conduct that should receive international attention from human conduct that is not suited to global redress.

---

[5] An example of successful conceptual reformulation is the conceptualisation of sexual harassment as an actionable offence. However, it is noted that the reformulation of domestic violence is but one part of a much larger multi-disciplinary approach to this phenomenon. See Ann Scales, 'Law and Feminism: Together in Struggle' (2003) 51 *University of Kansas Law Review* 291, 294. Prior to this relatively new concept, women in the workplace were forced to endure sexually invasive conduct without redress. See Catharine A MacKinnon, *Sexual Harassment of Working Women: A Case of Sex Discrimination* (New Haven, Yale University Press, 1979) 1. See eg *Meritor Savings Bank v Vinson*, 477 US 57, 65 (1986). See Diana EH Russell, 'Introduction: The Politics of Femicide' in Diana EH Russell and Roberta A Harmes (eds), *Femicide in Global Perspective* (New York, Teachers College Press, 2001) 3, 7.

[6] See Justice Sachs' statement in the South African constitutional case of *S v Godfrey Baloyi*, Case CCT 29/99 (South African Constitutional Court, 1999), para 11 ('All crime has harsh effect on society. What distinguishes domestic violence is its hidden, repetitive character and its immeasurable ripple effect on our society and, in particular, on family life'). The Swedish government has stated that domestic violence is 'an extremely difficult area with particular characteristics that could not be compared with those of other acts of violence'. *Report of the Committee on the Elimination of Discrimination against Women* (CEDAW Committee), *Concluding Observations: Sweden* (1993), paras 474–522, www1.umn.edu/humanrts/cedaw/sweden1993.html, provided by the University of Minnesota Human Rights Library (hereinafter CEDAW Concluding Observations: Sweden) para 503.

I therefore distinguish between, on the one hand, forms of domestic violence that can and should be addressed by domestic legal systems in their current form and, on the other hand, systemic intimate violence, which I propose requires a review of national legal systems through the lens of international law. On the basis that categorising forms of violence is uncomfortable but necessary, I now turn to discuss the elements of systemic intimate violence and the particular internationalising characteristics of that harm.

THE ELEMENTS OF SYSTEMIC INTIMATE VIOLENCE

Systemic intimate violence consists of five elements which together constitute an extreme violation of an individual's human rights that ought to trigger the provisions of international law. These elements are as follows: (1) severe emotional or physical harm, or the threat thereof; (2) a continuum of violence rather than a one-off incident; (3) it is committed predominantly by men against women within an intimate relationship; (4) the victim is a member of a group in society which is discriminated against or is inherently more vulnerable to harm—for example, the victim is unable to procure traditional legal assistance due to a societal misunderstanding of the nature of the violence and the victim's isolation or incapacitation; and (5) the violence is 'systemic' in the sense that it occurs in a society in which the state in question has omitted to satisfy the standards that will help to remedy such violence.

The combination of these factors prevents victims of this violence from obtaining protection and, in turn, reinforces the systemic nature of such violence. I deal with each of these elements below.

Severe Acts of Emotional or Physical Harm

Degrees of Severity

In order to trigger international law, physical harm must attain 'a minimum level of severity'.[7] The underlying premise is that every person has an interest in the maintenance of her or his physical autonomy and an essential right to be free from fear.[8] This is reflected in international treaties, declarations, other international

---

[7] *A v The United Kingdom* (App No 100/1997/884/1096) (1998) 27 EHRR 611.

[8] Physical autonomy is a protected right in international law. Universal Declaration of Human Rights (adopted 10 December 1948, UNGA Res 217 A(III)) (UDHR) Art 3 ('Everyone has the right to life, liberty and security of person'); Art 4 (prohibiting slavery: 'No one shall be held in slavery or servitude; slavery and the slave trade shall be prohibited in all their forms'); Art 5 (prohibiting torture: 'No one shall be subjected to torture or to cruel, inhuman or degrading treatment or punishment'); Art 22 (enjoining states to dedicate resources to ensuring the flourishing of individuals' dignity and personality). The principles of safety and equality that are violated by domestic violence are rooted in Arts 2 and 3 of the UDHR. See also Franklin D Roosevelt, 'Four Freedoms' speech (Annual Message to Congress, 6 January 1941), www.fdrlibrary.marist.edu/4free.html ('The fourth is freedom from fear . . .').

instruments and many states' constitutional and legal systems.[9] Legitimate violations of this right take place in very rare circumstances.[10] For the rest, physical harm is prohibited and its perpetrators punished. International law, however, deals only with the sharp end, the most severe forms, of physical and psychological harm. This is the standard, for example, in the Torture Convention, which refers to 'severe pain and suffering',[11] and the Rome Statute of the International Criminal Court, which refers to 'unimaginable atrocities that deeply shock the conscience of humanity'.[12]

The same applies to domestic violence: it is severe forms of domestic violence that ought to trigger international law and which constitute 'systemic intimate violence'. The acts of harm that constitute systemic intimate violence are inhuman, leading to grave consequences, and include serious suffering or humiliation.[13]

Not all acts of domestic violence fulfil the requirement of severity, as they fall along a wide spectrum of ferocity and intensity. A one-off incident of violence, which leaves no lasting physical or emotional damage and does not create a climate of fear, may not require state intervention. A state cannot reasonably be blamed for such an act of violence if there was nothing the state could have done to prevent it. Provided the state addresses the violence or prevents such violence if it is brought to the attention of the state authorities, such act is neither the act of the state nor can it be attributable to the state. By contrast, where a victim suffers lasting physical or emotional damage, and the state fails to provide effective police intervention and basic shelters to help mitigate the consequences thereof, the state reasonably can, and should, be held accountable for its failings.

---

[9] See eg: Convention against Torture and Other Cruel, Inhuman or Degrading Treatment or Punishment (adopted 10 December 1984, entered into force 26 July 1987) 1465 UNTS 85, (1984) 23 ILM 1027 (hereinafter Torture Convention); Convention on the Elimination of All Forms of Discrimination Against Women (adopted 18 December 1979, entered into force 3 September 1981) 1249 UNTS 13, UN Doc A/RES/34/830, (1980) 19 ILM 33 (CEDAW); Declaration on the Elimination of Violence against Women, UNGA Res 48/104 (20 December 1993) UN Doc A/RES/48/104 (DEVAW); International Covenant on Civil and Political Rights (adopted 16 December 1966, entered into force 23 March 1976) 999 UNTS 171 (ICCPR); African Charter on Human and Peoples' Rights (adopted 27 June 1981, entered into force 21 October 1986) (1982) 21 ILM 58 (hereinafter African Charter or Banjul Charter). Physical integrity is an element of crimes against humanity as defined in the Rome Statute. See the United Nations Diplomatic Conference of Plenipotentiaries on the Establishment of an International Criminal Court, Rome Statute of the International Criminal Court (1998) UN Doc A/CONF.183/9, Art 7 (hereinafter Rome Statute).

[10] For example, punitive incarceration and violence in self-defence are considered to be justifiable and proportionate forms of invasive conduct.

[11] Torture Convention (n 9) Art 1.

[12] Rome Statute (n 9) preamble.

[13] *Prosecutor v Kunarac* (Judgment) ICTY-96-23-T (22 February 2001), para 503. The International Criminal Tribunal for the Former Yugoslavia (ICTY) was established by UNSC Res 808 (22 February 1993) UN Doc S/RES/808. The ICTY applied the actus reus requirement of inhumane treatment in common Art 3 of the Geneva Conventions. *Prosecutor v Kunarac*, para 502.

Categorising violence according to degrees of severity is intuitively problematic.[14] How does one begin to grade levels of harm? Social disciplines have engaged in this process, for example by using scales of aggression to assess the extent of physical violence, 'ranging from throwing objects to the use of a weapon',[15] and analysts have relied on tables of abuse which distinguish between 'moderate' and 'severe' violence.[16] The distinction between types of domestic violence is addressed by sociology theorist Michael Johnson.[17] Johnson employs a distinction between 'patriarchal terrorism' on the one hand and 'common couple violence' on the other.[18] He uses the term 'patriarchal terrorism' to refer to 'a product of patriarchal traditions of men's right to control "their" women' that results in 'a form of terroristic control of wives by their husbands that involves the systematic use of not only violence, but economic subordination, threats, isolation, and other control tactics'.[19] His second category, common couple violence, 'is less a product of patriarchy, and more a product of the less-gendered causal process . . . in which conflict occasionally "gets out of hand", leading usually to "minor" forms of violence'.[20]

Assessing Severity in International Law: Objective Test

How does one assess severity for the purposes of international law, especially where the violence is perpetrated in a private context and by private actors and not by the state? According to the European Court of Human Rights (ECtHR), the severity of the harm depends on all the circumstances of the case, such as the nature and context of the treatment, its duration, its physical and mental effects and, in some instances, the sex, age and state of health of the victim.[21] The International Criminal Tribunal for Rwanda (ICTR) confirmed that mass rape

[14] However, this is the very nature of the work conducted by the Committee against Torture, established in terms of Art 17 of the Torture Convention (n 9). See generally UN Office of the High Commissioner for Human Rights (UNCHR), 'Fact Sheet No 17, The Committee against Torture' (January 1990), www.unhcr.org/refworld/docid/4794773d2.html (observing that the Committee monitors compliance with the UN standards of what constitutes torture and other inhuman behaviour).
[15] Mary Ellsberg, Rodolfo Peña, Andrés Herrera, Jerker Liljestrand and Anna Winkvist, 'Candies in Hell: Women's Experience of Violence in Nicaragua' (2000) 51 *Social Science and Medicine* 1595, 1597. The existence and extent of physical violence sometimes is determined with reference to the Conflict Tactics Scale (CTS), which lists eight acts of physical harm in order of severity. Note, though, that there is contention regarding the use of this scale. See eg Michael P Johnson, 'Patriarchal Terrorism and Common Couple Violence: Two Forms of Violence against Women' (1995) 57 *Journal of Marriage and the Family* 283, 285–86.
[16] The most frequent violence includes pushing, punching and kicks, followed by slaps and thrown objects. Ellsberg et al (n 15) 1600.
[17] Johnson (n 15) 283.
[18] ibid, 284.
[19] ibid. Johnson explains that the term '*patriarchal terrorism* has the advantage of keeping the focus on the perpetrator and of keeping our attention on the systematic, intentional nature of this form of violence'. ibid, 284.
[20] ibid.
[21] *A v The United Kingdom* (App No 100/1997/884/1096) (1998) 27 EHRR 611, para 20.

is so severe as to constitute a form of torture;[22] according to the International Tribunal for the Former Yugoslavia (ICTY), a severe act of violence involves serious harm and breaches principles that protect important values, and the breach must involve grave consequences for the victim.[23] The ICTY, in its consideration of acts of mass rape, adopted an objective test to determine whether such acts violate international law. It held that the violence should be deliberate and cause serious mental or physical suffering or injury; it should constitute a serious attack on human dignity; and 'the humiliation to the victim must be so intense that the reasonable person would be outraged'.[24]

The assessment of this minimum is objective. In the *Aleksovski* case the ICTY confirmed that a purely subjective assessment of the existence of humiliation or degradation would be unfair to the accused 'because the accused's culpability would be made to depend not on the gravity of the act but on the sensitivity of the victim. Therefore it was concluded that 'an objective component to the *actus reus* is apposite'.[25] According to the ICTY, the intensity of harm is not a question of inconvenience or discomfort but rather consists of 'physical and psychological abuse and outrages *that any human being would have experienced as such*'.[26]

This also applies to *threats* of harm, as recognised by the ICTR. In the context of sexual violence specifically, the ICTR held that the act of harm is not 'limited to physical invasion of the human body and may include acts which do not involve penetration or even physical contact'.[27]

Moreover, it was recognised that coercion need not manifest itself in physical force but includes threats, intimidation, extortion and 'other forms of duress which prey on fear or desperation'.[28] Severe emotional violence comprising a combination of intense and persistent verbal abuse, insults, derision, threats of harm and intimidation is sufficient to result in a violation of physical integrity.

---

[22] UN Secretary-General, 'In-depth Study on All Forms of Violence against Women' (2006) UN Doc A/61/122/Add.1, para 258 (hereinafter Study of the Secretary-General). See also *Prosecutor v Akayesu* (Judgment) ICTR-96-4-T, T Ch I (2 September 1998), para 597; *Prosecutor v Kunarac* (Judgment) ICTY-96-23-T (22 February 2001), para 597. The International Criminal Tribunal for Rwanda (ICTR) was established by UNSC Res 955 (8 November 1994) UN Doc S/RES/955. The Rome Statute (n 9) Art 8(2)(b), prohibits various forms of sexual violence, such as rape, sexual slavery, enforced prostitution and forced pregnancy, enforced sterilisation and other sexual violence as crimes against humanity when committed as part of a widespread or systematic attack directed at a civilian population.

[23] See *Prosecutor v Kunarac* (Judgment) ICTY-96-23-T (22 February 2001), paras 407(iii), 408 and 597.

[24] ibid, para 502, citing *Prosecutor v Delalic* (Judgment) ICTY-96-21-T (16 November 1998), paras 504, 543; *Prosecutor v Aleksovski* (Judgment) ICTY-95-14/1-T (25 June 1999), para 54.

[25] *Prosecutor v Aleksovski*, ibid, para 54.

[26] *Prosecutor v Kunarac* (Judgment) ICTY-96-23-T (22 February 2001), para 505 (citing *Prosecutor v Aleksovski*, para 838). For a discussion of the mens rea component in respect of criminal liability, see *Kunarac*, paras 508–14. See also Theodor Meron, 'Rape as a Crime under International Law' (1993) 87 *American Journal of International Law* 424, 425.

[27] *Prosecutor v Akayesu* (Judgment) ICTR-96-4-T, T Ch I (2 September 1998), para 688.

[28] ibid.

Applying the Test to Domestic Violence

If we apply this objective test to domestic violence, would the reasonable person be outraged by the mental and physical suffering of women victims of systemic intimate violence? The following is informative:

> I was lying on the floor, two guards held my legs while another kicked me in the testicles. I would lose consciousness and come to, I lost consciousness four times. They hit me around the head, there was blood. They would beat me unconscious and wait until I came round: 'He's woken up,' and they would come in and beat me [again].
>
> Chechnyan survivor of torture by the Russian Army[29]

> From the moment Rodi Adalí Alvorada Peña married a Guatemalan army officer at the age of 16, she was subjected to intensive abuse, and all her efforts to get help were unsuccessful. Her husband raped her repeatedly, attempted to abort their second child by kicking her in the spine, dislocated her jaw, tried to cut off her hands with a machete, kicked her in the vagina and used her head to break windows.
>
> Guatemalan woman[30]

> [F]irst they would beat you and then you would have to lie down on the floor and crawl to them. You would have to say, 'Request permission to crawl.' Me personally, they beat me on the knees, with clubs, and on the kidneys.
>
> Chechnyan survivor of torture by the Russian Army[31]

> He was sittin' on the bed. Had his .357 Magnum. He said, 'June, you get down on this floor right now. You crawl to me'. And when I got to his feet he took that pistol and hit me right alongside of the head. I thought I was gonna die. I still got the knot from it. He said, 'if you even act like you're gonna run I'll blow your brains all over this wall'.
>
> American woman[32]

Acts of systemic intimate violence include various forms of violence, including punching; slapping; shouting; battery; biting; burning; hacking; electrocution; starvation; mutilation; sleep deprivation; forced sexual encounters; non-consensual sexual touching; rape; forced sexual activities with third parties; poisoning; exposure; property destruction; murder; the withholding of medical care; threats of harm; threats of harm to third parties; threats to remove children; threatening to use a lethal weapon; persistent shouting; unrelenting accusations of infidelity; controlling day to day activities; isolation; and threats of suicide. According to Amnesty International, physical violence includes

> assault and battery in the form of blows, kicks, boxes on the ears, shoving, strangleholds and the use of various objects and weapons. Sexual violence includes sexual touching

---

[29] Human Rights Watch, *'Welcome to Hell': Arbitrary Detention, Torture, and Extortion in Chechnya* (New York, Human Rights Watch, 2000) 35.

[30] Amnesty International, *Broken Bodies, Shattered Minds: Torture and Ill-treatment of Women* (6 March 2001) AI-Index ACT 40/001/2001, 23, web.amnesty.org/library/Index/engact400012001.

[31] Human Rights Watch (n 29) 39.

[32] Neil Websdale, *Rural Woman Battering and the Justice System: An Ethnography* (California, Sage Publications, 1998) 10.

and degrading sexual acts and games that a man inflicts upon a woman or forces her to take part in, rape and violence to the breasts and genitals. Psychological violence consists . . . of threats of physical and/or sexual violence, death threats, constant insults and abusive language, controlling behaviour, threats against other persons who are important to the woman (for example, her children or parents), imposed and degrading acts and behaviour, restraining the woman from comforting her crying children or preventing her from seeking help and treatment. Injuries caused by physical assault are most often localised to the head, followed by the arms, the neck and the abdomen.[33]

The severity of acts of domestic violence was recognised by the ECtHR in the case of *Opuz v Turkey*.[34] The Court held that the violence suffered by the applicant in the form of physical injuries, including a knife attack, and the psychological violence she endured, including threats against the applicant, her mother and her children, were sufficiently serious to constitute ill-treatment within the meaning of Article 3 of the European Convention on Human Rights (the prohibition of torture, cruel and inhuman treatment).[35]

As is the case with torture, systemic intimate violence is not only physical and includes emotional violence and threats of violence. Emotional violence comprises a combination of intense and persistent verbal abuse, insults, derision, threats of harm, intimidation, stalking, financial deprivation and/or isolation.[36] Threats of violence which are debilitating also constitute acts of violence. The threat of violence can be as destructive as its execution. Often, one serious physical or sexual attack has the effect of so hurting or degrading the victim that the mere threat of its recurrence is an act of violence whereby the abuser controls the victim.[37] The threat of violence is particularly powerful if there has been past physical injury.[38]

---

[33] Amnesty International, *Men's Violence against Women in Intimate Relationships: An Account of the Situation in Sweden* (19 April 2004) 6, www2.amnesty.se/svaw.nsf/mvaw/$File/mvaw.pdf. See also Elizabeth M Schneider, *Battered Women & Feminist Lawmaking* (New Haven, Yale University Press, 2002) 66; Gun Heimer, Eva Lundgren, Jenny Westerstrand and Anne-Marie Kalliokoski (Julia Mikaelsson and Geoffrey French trans), *Captured Queen: Men's Violence against Women in 'Equal' Sweden—A Prevalence Study* 24 (Sweden, Fritzes Offtliga Publikationer, 2002), www.brottsoffermyndigheten.se/informationsmaterial/Captured%20queen.pdf/Captured%20Que en%20.pdf. Ellsberg et al (n 15) 1595 (identifying 'extreme jealousy and control as constant features of the abusive relationship').

[34] *Opuz v Turkey* (App No 33401/02) ECtHR 9 June 2009. For a discussion of this case see ch 1, p 87–88.

[35] ibid, para 161.

[36] The recognition of emotional abuse is a relatively recent development and most progressive laws refer to the act of violence as both physical and non-physical. For example, the South African Domestic Violence Act (No 116 of 1998) defines domestic violence as physical, sexual, emotional, verbal and psychological abuse, which 'harms, or may cause imminent harm to, the safety, health or wellbeing of the complainant'. See Heimer et al (n 33) (describing controlling behaviour, which does not fall within the purview of a criminal code). See also Ellsberg et al (n 15) 1602 (indicating 'extreme jealousy and control as constant features of the abusive relationship.'). Finally, see Schneider (n 33) 65.

[37] Heimer et al (n 33) 17. The South African Domestic Violence Act recognises the threat of violence and prohibits 'any act or threatened act of physical violence towards a complainant' (s 1).

[38] Because controlling behaviour and threats form a continuum of violence, there is no such thing as 'mere threats'. Heimer et al (n 33) 79. The incremental nature of domestic violence in Sweden was

Physical injury in domestic violence cases may not be external or identifiable, especially in respect of sexual violence.[39] Because the violence is incremental in nature, injuries are normalised, causing victims to 'downplay' the violence or its consequences as insufficiently serious to warrant hospitalisation or police intervention.[40] This makes it difficult for outsiders to understand the severity of the violence and equally difficult to prove in formal judicial proceedings. The important aspect of this element is that serious violence is not addressed by the state, leaving the victims, as a group, repeatedly unprotected. The acts of harm inherent in systemic intimate violence, objectively and relatively, reach this 'minimum level of severity' and we should avoid the incorrect *assumption* that because the violence is committed in private, by a non-state official and often within the context of a relationship, the violence is neither extreme nor severe.

On 15 January 2008 the Special Rapporteur on torture, Manfred Nowak, submitted his second thematic report to the Human Rights Council.[41] The report dealt exclusively with the protection of women from torture, and is one of the most important developments in the internationalisation of the norm against domestic violence. It authoritatively categorises domestic violence as a form of torture. The Special Rapporteur rationalises this categorisation as follows: (1) it is widespread and touches millions of women around the world every year; (2) in many parts of the world domestic violence is still trivialised and the comparison between domestic violence and 'classic' torture will raise awareness with regard to the level of atrocity that it can reach; and (3) the fact that these forms of violence can amount to torture if states fail to act with due diligence illustrates the parallels between torture and other forms of violence against women.[42]

The Special Rapporteur on torture makes the following statement about the severity of domestic violence:

> As with female detainees who experience torture, battered wives may be beaten with hands and objects, kicked, strangled, stabbed or burned. Rape and other forms of sexual abuse are used by intimate partners as well as by prison guards or police officers. In both scenarios, physical violence is usually accompanied by insults, varied forms of humiliation, and threats to kill or harm the victim or her family members (often children). Domestic violence, as well as torture, tends to escalate over time, sometimes resulting in death or leaving women's bodies mutilated or permanently disfigured. Women who experience such violence, whether in their homes or in a prison, suffer depression, anxiety, loss of self-esteem and a feeling of isolation. Indeed, battered women may suffer from the same intense symptoms that comprise the post-traumatic

confirmed in Heimer et al (n 33) 17, 20 and in Nicaragua in Ellsberg et al (n 15) 1596. See also Schneider (n 33) 65 ('What he did wasn't exactly battering but it was the threat. I remember one night I spent the whole night in a state of terror, nothing less than terror all night . . . And that was worse to me than getting whacked').

[39] Amnesty International (n 33) 6.
[40] See Heimer et al (n 33) 65; Amnesty International (n 33) 6.
[41] Special Rapporteur on torture 2008 Report (n 3).
[42] ibid, para 44.

stress disorder identified in victims of official torture as well as by victims of rape. Another parallel between privately battering women and torture, which refers back to the element of powerlessness, is the intention to keep the victim in a permanent state of fear based on unpredictable violence by seeking to reduce the person to submission and destroy his/her capacity for resistance and autonomy with the ultimate aim of achieving total control.[43]

In response to the Special Rapporteur on violence against women, the report also reviews the working principles of the international law of torture to ensure that the state's obligation to prevent and protect against torture includes torturous conduct in private, committed by non-state actors.

The Special Rapporteur on torture authoritatively confirmed that the purpose element is always fulfilled when it comes to gender-specific violence against women, in that such violence is inherently discriminatory and one of the possible purposes enumerated in the Convention is discrimination.[44] He also proposed an additional element, that of 'powerlessness', to underline that,

> whereas detention contexts are classic situations of powerlessness, it can also arise outside of detention or direct state control. Situations constituting of de facto deprivation of liberty may occur in different 'private' settings. There are also contexts, where fear can create a situation of total control: battered wives, victims of trafficking, as well as women prisoners who have been abused are likely to experience a permanent state of fear based on the unpredictable behaviour of the perpetrator.[45]

Both factually and according to the international law authorities, we can conclude that certain acts of domestic violence qualitatively constitute severe acts of harm, which trigger the responsibility of states under international law. The definition of systemic intimate violence envisages severe forms of violence only on the basis that a degree of proportionality is required before a type of harm appropriately triggers international intervention. It encompasses violence which is invasive of the victim's mental and physical autonomy in a way that is particularly destructive of the individual's dignity.[46] The level of severity in such cases, albeit in a context of love, intimacy and domesticity, is such that it shocks human conscience.

Continuum of Harm

Acts of violence that are not in and of themselves severe may become severe and debilitating if they induce an ongoing environment of fear and control from which the victim is unable to escape. Prolonged, tolerated bouts of violence should fall within the definition of systemic intimate violence even if individu-

---

[43] ibid, para 45.

[44] ibid, para 68.

[45] ibid.

[46] The author gathered the instances of abuse cited above from legal consultations with domestic violence clients at the South African NGO, People Opposing Woman Abuse (POWA) over a period of one year. Many abused women experience some form of sexual aggression. See eg Schneider (n 33) 66; Heimer et al (n 33) 24; Ellsberg et al (n 15) 1595; Amnesty International (n 33) 6.

ally they are not severe or alarming. This is because the severity of the violence may be in its repetition, and the frequency of an act of harm compounds its effect and increases its severity.[47]

International law has also recognised that intense and serious harm may occur over a period of time and that the exigency of harm is not in the individual incident. For example, in the case of enforced disappearances, the period of time involved in the detention of the disappeared is a seminal component of the crime.[48] Trafficking is another example of a continuum of harm, involving abduction, recurring abuse and forced transfer from one place to another. The harm manifests itself in a continuum and not only in a single act of abduction. In the case of female genital cutting (FGC) there are long-term impacts on the victim's life, such as absence of sexual enjoyment and normal urinary and menstrual activity for the rest of her life; increased danger in relation to childbirth and sexual intercourse; and, over a period of time, the one act of cutting can lead to a range of infections, tetanus, extreme blood loss, depression, loss of sexuality, infection of the internal organs and death due to haemorrhaging, and other severe infections.[49] The original act of harm is not the only reason why FGC is an international human rights violation. It is this continuum that violates the right to physical integrity.

The notion of a continuum is also evident in the context of mass rape.[50] The ICTY confirmed that it was 'sufficient to show that the act took place in the context of an accumulation of acts of violence which, individually, may vary greatly in nature and gravity'.[51]

---

[47] The *Candies in Hell* report confirms that acts of physical violence do not represent isolated events but rather a relationship based on domination. Ellsberg et al (n 15) 1604.

[48] Juan E Mendez and Jose Miguel, 'Disappearances and the Inter-American Court: Reflections on a Litigation Experience' (1990) 13 *Hamline Law Review* 507, 552–53 (discussing disappearances as a crime 'that involves multiple and continuous violations of rights . . . the effects of which are prolonged over time'). Cases on disappearances include *Kurt v Turkey* (App No 24276/94) ECtHR 25 May 1998 (the ECtHR found that the mother of the deceased, who had brought the application, was a victim of the authorities' complacency and the anguish and distress that she endured over a prolonged period of time constituted ill-treatment within the scope of Art 3 of the Convention for the Protection of Human Rights and Fundamental Freedoms (as amended) (ECHR) (adopted 4 November 1950, entered into force 3 September 1953) 213 UNTS 222, Art 14; *Velásquez Rodríguez v Honduras*, Inter-American Court of Human Rights Series C No 2, (1989) 28 ILM 291 (the Inter-American Court of Human Rights found the government of Honduras responsible for the disappearance of Velásquez Rodríguez, a Honduran student activist); *Hector Perez Salazar v Peru*, Inter-American Commission on Human Rights (Case 10.562, Report No 43/97, OEA/Ser.L/V/II.95 Doc 7 rev, 771) (1998) para 19 (the disappeared individual had been missing for eight years).

[49] See Catherine L Annas, 'Irreversible Error: The Power and Prejudice of Female Genital Mutilation' (1996) 12 *Journal of Contemporary Health Law and Policy* 325, 327–32. FGC entails both physical and emotional harm, which continue over time. See John Tochukwu Okwubanego, 'Female Circumcision and the Girl Child in Africa and the Middle East: The Eyes of the World are Blind to the Conquered' (1999) 33 *International Law* 159, 169–71. For a detailed description of the various forms of FGC/FGM and its health implications see Anika Rahman and Nahid Tubia, *Female Genital Mutilation: A Guide to Laws & Policies Worldwide* (London, Zed Books, 2000).

[50] *Prosecutor v Kunarac* (Judgment) ICTY-96-23-T (22 February 2001), para 415 (indicating that a crime against humanity is not 'one particular act but, instead, a course of conduct').

[51] ibid, para 419.

Not every rape committed during the conflicts in the former Yugoslavia or Rwanda had to fulfil a standard of extremity.[52] It was the unbridled commission of rape, over an extended period of time, and the creation of an environment of terror that distinguished mass rape from random instances of rape.[53] There are of course differences between systemic intimate violence and mass rape, but for the purpose of satisfying the 'minimum severity' element for international intervention it is, to use the phraseology of the ICTY, sufficient to show that the act took place in the context of an accumulation of acts of violence which, while individually may vary greatly in nature and gravity, in aggregate are sufficiently severe to constitute a human rights violation.

Systemic intimate violence too may manifest in a continuum of harm; it is a hybrid of physical, emotional and sexual harm, the effects of which are often invisible. Not only can various incidences of violence against women be extreme, but it is also clear that different acts, perpetrated by one's intimate partner, while individually not alarming, may accumulate to make a cycle of harm that is impenetrable and debilitating.[54] This was acknowledged by the Special Rapporteur on torture, who, in order to ensure a gender-inclusive approach to torture, underlined the need to 'perceive [domestic violence] as a process. Mental trauma does not happen at one point in time, but needs to be put in context.'[55]

The notion of a continuum of harm is necessary in examining domestic violence because it is difficult to determine the extent of the violence based on one incident alone.[56] Often a bout of violence may appear erratic or less serious in a vacuum, but if it is brought into the context of a continuum, it takes on a far more pernicious character. Emotional and physical harm may operate separately, but generally are combined to spin a web of abuse in which the exigency of violence escalates.[57] Threats, violence and sexual abuse are 'impossible to

---

[52] Mass rape, in order to constitute a crime against humanity, must be widespread or systematic (ibid, para 417). According to the ICTY, the adjective 'widespread' 'connotes the large-scale nature of the attack and the number of its victims' (para 428) (citing the Commentary of the International Law Commission in its Draft Code of Crimes against Peace and Security of Mankind). The adjective 'systematic' 'signifies the organised nature of the acts of violence and the improbability of their random occurrence' (para 429).

[53] The ICTY went further and stated that the attack must be 'either "widespread" or "systematic", thereby excluding isolated and random acts' (ibid, para 427).

[54] See Heimer et al (n 33) 17 (discussing the notion of a continuum of violence, which 'is not to be used as a method of creating hierarchies of more or less serious abuse').

[55] Special Rapporteur on torture 2008 Report (n 3) para 70.

[56] See Johnson (n 15) 286 (describing the same difference between patriarchal terrorism and common couple violence, the former evidencing an escalation in frequency and intensity over time). See also Schneider (n 33) 65–66; Rhonda Copelon, 'Intimate Terror: Understanding Domestic Violence as Torture' in Rebecca J Cook (ed), *Human Rights of Women: National and International Perspectives* (Philadelphia, University of Pennsylvania Press, 1994) 116 and 121.

[57] For example, in Nicaragua, 94% of physically abused women reported that verbal abuse and insults usually accompanied the physical violence (Ellsberg et al (n 15) 1600–01). The same report indicated a significant overlap between physical and emotional violence and 21% of abused women reported all three kinds of abuse (ie physical, emotional and sexual). 36% of abused women reported that they were forced to have sex while being beaten and 'physical abuse is so often

isolate from one another; characteristically the boundaries between them are fluid and actions merge into one another'.[58]

This is referred to as a cycle of abuse. Theorists first identified such cycles as consisting of instances of violence followed by apologies, gifts and expressions of remorse.[59] Slowly, the tension intensifies and rebuilds itself; first in the form of verbal denigration and ultimately resulting in another episode of anger and physical violence.[60] As the cycle repeats itself, the severity of the violence intensifies and there are fewer and shorter periods of remorse.[61] The emotional stress caused by this cycle results in dependency, depression, sleeplessness and symptoms of post-traumatic stress disorder.[62] And it is often the case that the violence increases in severity the longer it progresses.

The continual nature of systemic intimate violence has been recognised to varying degrees in the 'domestic violence' legislation of foreign jurisdictions. Mexico and Nicaragua have defined domestic violence with reference to acts that are recurring, intentional and cyclical.[63] The South African Constitutional Court has stated that what distinguishes domestic violence from other crime 'is its hidden, repetitive character and its immeasurable ripple effects on our society and, in particular, on family life'.[64] In Sweden too, domestic violence legislation recognises that 'Gross physical violence is a part of a pattern, a notch on a sliding scale, a continuum, rather than an isolated and inexplicable

---

intertwined with acts of psychological and sexual degradation as to be virtually indistinguishable' (pp 1601–02). 94% of the abused women in Nicaragua reported that physical violence had been accompanied by verbal humiliation and control of daily activities. See also Luisa Pérez-Landa, *Violence against Women in Nicaragua* (Geneva, World Organization against Torture (OMCT), 2001) (Report prepared for the Committee on the Elimination of Discrimination against Women twenty-fifth session, 2–20 July 2001) 12 (hereinafter OMCT CEDAW Report on Nicaragua); Schneider (n 33) 65–66; Heimer et al (n 33) 17.

[58] Heimer et al (n 33) 17.

[59] The cycle is described as having three components, namely, tension-building, followed by an incident of violence, and then seduction, which ultimately leads to a renewed period of tension. See Lenore E Walker, *Terrifying Love: Why Battered Women Kill and How Society Responds* (London, HarperCollins, 1989) 42–47 (providing a detailed analysis of the 'cycle of violence'). See also Heimer et al (n 33) 17 (describing how 'actions which the law defines as minor may signify an explicit or implicit threat to an abused woman').

[60] ibid, 42–45.

[61] ibid, 46.

[62] Copelon (n 56) 124–25 (noting that domestic violence 'often produces anxiety, depression, and sleeplesness). See also Karrisha Pillay, 'Battered Women Who Kill: Avenues for Legal/Political Recourse' (Legal opinion commissioned by the Centre for the Study of Violence and Reconciliation 2005), para 26, www.csvr.org.za/docs/gender/battered.pdf.

[63] Art 1 of the Law of Assistance and Prevention of Domestic Violence, Decree of the Assembly of Representatives of the Federal District, promulgated 26 April 1996, cited by the Center for Reproductive Rights (formerly the Center for Reproductive Law and Policy), *Women's Reproductive Rights in Mexico: A Shadow Report* (1997) 23, www.crlp.org/pdf/sr_mex_1297_eng.pdf. In Mexico, the Law of Assistance and Prevention of Domestic Violence defines the violence as 'an act of power or omission that is recurring, intentional and cyclical, and is aimed at dominating, subordinating, controlling or harming any member of the family through physical, verbal, psycho-emotional, or sexual violence'. See also Ellsberg et al (n 15) 1596.

[64] *S v Godfrey Baloyi*, Case CCT 29/99 (South African Constitutional Court, 1999), para 11.

incident'.[65] The legislation targets not only physical violence but the full fabric of harm which results in the 'gross violation of a woman's integrity'.[66] The objective of the legislation was to mitigate the 'effects of the normalization process and the impact of repeated violations on women subjected to them'.[67] The legislation takes account of 'the changes which a woman gradually experiences while being subjected to violence'.[68] It also takes the position that 'violations which may seem fairly minor when viewed separately have a grave negative effect on a woman when they are part of a process, thus meriting severe punishment'.[69] The continuum was also recognised by the ECtHR in the case of *Opuz v Turkey*, where it stated that although 'there were intervals between the impugned events . . . the overall violence to which the applicant and her mother were subjected over a long period of time cannot be seen as individual and separate episodes and must therefore be considered together as a chain of connected events'.[70]

The continuum of violence inherent in systemic intimate violence demonstrates the seriousness of the harm in question and reveals the infrastructural component and the failure to understand the fluid and cyclical pattern of systemic intimate violence.

Between Intimates

Systemic intimate violence is characterised by the dichotomy between love and pain. For most people it is an incomprehensible notion that within the boundaries of an ostensibly loving relationship an extremely acute manifestation of violence can exist. Yet the reality is that the highest rate of violence against women occurs in private relationships.[71] It is this element that distinguishes domestic violence from other forms of violence in society.

The intimacy complicates the victim's understanding of the violence, her ability to escape it and the approach of society to her experience.[72] The pattern of

---

[65] Amnesty International (n 33) 6 (violence in abusive relationships 'is often recurrent and has almost always been preceded by a pattern of increasing dominance and control over the woman by the man').

[66] See Heimer et al (n 33) 13.

[67] ibid.

[68] ibid.

[69] ibid.

[70] *Opuz v Turkey* (App No 33401/02) ECtHR 9 June 2009, para 111.

[71] It has been argued that 'the family is "naturally" a realm of hierarchy and even injustice'. Susan Moller Okin, 'Inequalities between the Sexes in Different Cultural Contexts' in Nussbaum and Glover (n 1) 274, 279. Another argument is that states and the international community have a dearth of female representatives and that this is the reason for the lack of consensus as regards women's rights. See Margareth Etienne, 'Addressing Gender-based Violence in an International Context' (1995) 18 *Harvard Women's Law Journal* 139.

[72] Amnesty International (n 33) 12 (noting that domestic violence is different from other forms of violent crime because 'the woman has an emotional relationship with the perpetrator and . . . because the violence is generally planned, controlled and carried out in the home, out of sight of other people').

systemic intimate violence may be clear to experts, but rarely will it be discernable by laypeople, least of all by the victim herself. Beginning with imperceptible degradation, the abuser, at times unknowingly, primes his partner for the first onslaught of violence. The shock is debilitating. The abuser's subsequent remorse may be genuine, but it is temporary; it dissipates, making way once more for the subtle, but increasingly more perceptible, disdain that precedes the next attack. As the cycle evolves, the chapters of harm intensify until the abused is imprisoned in a combination of physical immobility and mental despair.[73] Encapsulated within the relationship, the recurrent violence becomes normalised, preventing the abused from reporting the violence and the authorities from recognising it.[74]

A further complication is the principle of privacy and the constitutional injunction against state interference in one's personal affairs. It is difficult to draw a line between improper state interference on the one hand and necessary state protection on the other. This sensitivity also arises in other contexts, such as the regulation of child pornography or dangerous political dissidents. It is crucial that proper procedural guidelines are employed when it comes to asking for state intervention, albeit for protective purposes. But state intervention remains necessary, especially in light of the fact that the predominant cause of harm to women emanates from their private, and not public, world.[75]

Therefore, not only is the cycle of abuse pernicious because of the almost subliminal intensification of harm; the context of the relationship masks the harm, distorts the victim's and society's view of the violence and divorces the abused in her private world from the remedies that exist in the public one.[76]

Group Vulnerability of Women

The fourth element is the vulnerability of women, as a group, to systemic intimate violence. International human rights law generally applies to people in circumstances which render them vulnerable.[77] For example, the Convention

---

[73] Heimer et al (n 33) 77 ('The violence is committed in the woman's home, in indoor and outdoor public places and at women's places of work. The results seem to show that there are no free zones for women'). Systemic intimate violence 'compels many women to change their ways of life and to limit their freedom of movement in order to avoid or reduce the risk of being subjected to abuse' (Amnesty International (n 33) 23).

[74] For a lengthier discussion of the process of normalisation and its impact on reporting domestic violence, see Amnesty International (n 33) 8.

[75] *S v Godfrey Baloyi*, Case CCT 29/99 (South African Constitutional Court, 1999), para 16 ('Despite the high value set on the privacy of the home and the centrality attributed to intimate relations, all too often the privacy and intimacy end up providing both the opportunity for violence and the justification for non-interference').

[76] Judith Resnik, 'Categorical Federalism: Jurisdiction, Gender, and the Globe' (2001) 111 *Yale Law Journal* 619, 633 ('A locked room denotes a safe space, a home').

[77] Harvey Wallace, *Family Violence Legal, Medical, and Social Perspectives* (New York, Pearson Education, 2007) 180 (indicating that 'men have far greater opportunities to leave the abusive situation than women').

against Torture protects detainees who are subject to the control of the state. The Convention against Racial Discrimination protects racial minorities and, in the same way, the Declaration on the Elimination of All Forms of Intolerance and of Discrimination Based on Religion protects religious groups from persecution.[78] The same concept applies to children who are subject to the control of their parents and to civilians detained as prisoners. People who are uneducated, hungry or homeless benefit from the assistance of international bodies in part because their power to remedy their own situation is limited. In all of these examples there is a particular vulnerability on the part of the right-holder.

The vulnerability of women as a group is caused by a combination of: (1) traditional views about male and female roles and hegemony which may make it difficult for authorities to oppose violence in a relationship. This often results in distance between the abused and the public world; (2) the private nature of systemic intimate violence, which tends to remove the abused, and signs of the abuse, from the purview of society; (3) the concomitant escalation of extreme violence upon separation; (4) economic difficulties restraining women's freedom; and (5) the acquiescence of the victim's community to the violence.

Traditional Views of Male and Female Roles

Systemic intimate violence is coloured by gender delineations and discrimination against women. This is not to say that such violence does not include victims and perpetrators of both genders against both genders, but both the statistics and the limited extent to which women enjoy their fundamental rights and freedoms evidence an indisputable intersection between violence and gender. So the right to be treated equally by the state also requires equality of protection against violence where it occurs most frequently, namely in private.[79] In particular, since women suffer the most (although certainly not exclusively) from systemic intimate violence, and systemic intimate violence is the primary cause of injury to women, women constitute a group that is particularly vulnerable.

The combination of these factors increases women's vulnerability to violence to a greater degree than the reasonably protected or empowered person in society. The Committee responsible for the implementation of the Convention on the Elimination of All Forms of Discrimination against Women (CEDAW) has reiterated that violence against women, including domestic violence, is a form of discrimination against women and is perpetuated by traditional views:

---

[78] See the International Convention on the Elimination of All Forms of Racial Discrimination (adopted 21 December 1965, entered into force 4 January 1969) 660 UNTS 195 and the Declaration on the Elimination of All Forms of Intolerance and of Discrimination Based on Religion or Belief, UNGA Res 36/55 (25 November 1981) UN Doc A/36/684. See also the Declaration on the Rights of Persons Belonging to National or Ethnic, Religious or Linguistic Minorities, UNGA 47/135 (18 December 1992) UN Doc A/47/49.

[79] For a discussion on the lack of law and policy regarding sex inequality in the domestic sphere see Okin (n 71) 279–89.

Traditional attitudes by which women are regarded as subordinate to men or as having stereotyped roles perpetuate widespread practices involving violence or coercion, such as family violence and abuse. Such prejudices and practices may justify gender-based violence as a form of protection or control of women. The effect of such violence on the physical and mental integrity of women is to deprive them of the equal enjoyment, exercise and knowledge of human rights and fundamental freedoms.[80]

Inequality has led to a situation where one in three women worldwide is a victim of domestic violence. The result of this perception is that difference becomes discrimination and today women are

less well nourished than men, less healthy than men, more vulnerable to physical violence and sexual abuse. They are much less likely than men to be literate, and still less likely to have preprofessional or technical education. Should they attempt to enter the workplace, they face greater obstacles, including intimidation from family or spouse, sex-discrimination in hiring, and sexual harassment in the workplace . . .[81]

In identifying this inequality it is essential that we do not call for the emancipation of one group while countenancing the subordination of the other. As I discuss in detail below, the proposals relating to effective state action to respond to systemic intimate violence should not impede or treat unfairly the equally important rights of the men who may be perpetrating this violence.[82] It is also important to note that men can also be victims of domestic violence, perpetrated by both men and women. However, when looking at domestic violence from an international law perspective, one of the key elements is the lack of equality, the otherness and the gendered role allocation that continue to affect women today.

In keeping with this theme, the UN endorsed the worldwide Sixteen Days of Activism against Gender Violence Campaign,[83] emphasising 'the connections between women's human rights, violence against women and women's health, and the detrimental consequences violence against women has on the well-being of the world as a whole'.[84] The fundamental importance of combating gender discrimination, and gender-based violence specifically, was confirmed at Beijing +10 in March 2005, when the Beijing Platform for Action was unequivocally reaffirmed.[85]

---

[80] CEDAW Committee, 'Concluding comments: Turkey' (15 February 2005) CEDAW/C/TUR/CC/4–5, paras 11 and 28.

[81] Allen Buchanan, *Justice, Legitimacy, and Self-Determination* (Oxford, Oxford University Press, 2006) 79. See also Martha C Nussbaum, *Women and Human Development* (Cambridge, Cambridge University Press, 2000) 1.

[82] Myres S McDougal, Harold D Lasswell and Lung-chu Chen, *Human Rights and the World Public Order: The Basic Policies of an International Law of Human Dignity* (New Haven, Yale University Press, 1980) 623–25 ('the most rational general community policy requires the complete emancipation of women, without countenancing the subordination of men').

[83] This is an international campaign that originated at the first Women's Global Leadership Institute in 1991. Since 1991 approximately 1,700 organisations in 130 countries have participated in the campaign. ibid.

[84] ibid.

[85] See UNCHR, '2005 Theme Announcement for the Sixteen Days of Activism against Gender Violence Campaign' (25 November–10 December 2005), www.ohchr.org/english/events/16_days/theme.htm.

The connection between discrimination and violence was confirmed in the case of *Opuz v Turkey*, where the ECtHR held that a state's failure to protect women against domestic violence constitutes a breach of their right to equal protection of the law.[86] The Court referred to its case law on discrimination, holding that a general policy or measure that has disproportionately prejudicial effects on a particular group may be considered discriminatory notwithstanding that it is not specifically aimed at that group.[87] The Court also confirmed that that the failure of the state to grant equal protection to the rights of the victim does not need to be intentional and that the gender-specific impact of the failure can be an unintended consequence.[88]

A large number of states have demonstrated a commitment to the fundamentality of gender equality in articulating the third of the Millennium Development Goals, which is to 'promote gender equality and empower women'.[89] The UN Department of Economic and Social Affairs has confirmed this link, indicating that gender equality is a prerequisite to achieving the other Millennium Development Goals.[90] This lead was taken up by former United Nations (UN) Secretary-General Kofi Annan, who confirmed the importance of combating violence against girls and women to achieving the Millennium Development Goals.

While many perceive gender differentiation to be normal or harmless, the perpetuation of separateness—as is the case with any system of 'separate but equal'—manifests in explicit and implicit social subjugation, limited political power and the submergence of women's individual autonomy.[91] McDougal, Lasswell and Chen confirm that 'the existence and perpetuation of distinct sex roles, as dictated mostly by men, have characteristically resulted in male-dominated societies in which women are regarded as "the subordinate sex", "the second sex", "the weaker sex", or "the Other"'.[92] This perception explains the expression of dominance by male family members over female family members through violence. Therefore, as a result of distinct gender roles, when women are subjected to systemic intimate violence, both their communities and the state may perceive their experience as being less important and less serious than public violence.

[86] *Opuz v Turkey* (App No 33401/02) ECtHR 9 June 2009, paras 183–202.

[87] ibid, para 183, citing *DH v Czech Republic* (App No 57325/00) ECtHR 13 November 2007, paras 175–80.

[88] ibid, para 191.

[89] United Nations Millennium Declaration, UNGA Res 55/2 (18 September 2000) UN Doc A/Res/55/2.

[90] See UN Department of Economic and Social Affairs Statistics Division, 'Progress Towards the Millennium Development Goals 1990–2005' (2005), unstats.un.org/unsd/mi/goals_2005/goal_3.pdf.

[91] Richard Rorty identifies discriminating institutions which use 'simpler ways of excluding [women] from humanity: for example, using "man" as a synonym of "human being" . . . [S]uch usages reinforce the average male's thankfulness that he was not born a woman, as well as his fear of the ultimate degradation: feminization': Richard Rorty, 'Human Rights, Rationality, and Sentimentality' in Stephen Shute and Susan Hurley (eds), *On Human Rights: The Oxford Amnesty Lectures* (New York, Basic Books, 1993) 111, 114.

[92] McDougal et al (n 82) 614, citing Simone de Beauvoir, *The Second Sex* (H Parshley trans & ed) (London, Bantam, 1961) xvi.

Privacy and Isolation

Victims of domestic violence tend to be isolated. This is compounded for women, who often operate within a private and, by extension, disconnected environment. A significant cause of their vulnerability, therefore, is the normalcy that attaches to women's submergence into private, domestic and non-public activities. Most domestic violence laws do not cater for the withdrawal of victims of domestic violence into an isolated and non-public space.

In the case of law and gender, the distinction between the public and private spheres historically has correlated with the role differentiation between genders—the public sphere being male dominated, the private sphere being allocated to women.[93] Although gender differentiation may be denied in many legal systems today, the public/private distinction endures and thus informs the reconstruction of facts after they have passed through the apparently neutral filtering process of the legal mechanism.[94] In many ways, current state law regulating private affairs stems from a culture in which, for a host of reasons, the parity of male and female citizens is still to be realised.

The intimate context of the violence also produces an almost visceral reaction that what happens within the home is venerable, impervious to the strictures of law and law enforcement. The opposite, however, is true. Women are particularly vulnerable to systemic intimate violence, which, as the main cause of women's ill-health worldwide, is neither harmless nor gender-neutral. It is hardly surprising that one of the prevalent misconceptions is that systemic intimate violence is a private affair that does not warrant state interference.

For example, 30 years ago it was not unusual for women employees to endure acts of intimidation in the workplace, which limited their earning potential, professional development and general well-being. It was only when the conduct was examined through the lens of discrimination between men and women that the harm was identified as sexual harassment. Today almost every major corporation has a sexual harassment policy, based in part on this more sophisticated legal analysis of the phenomenon. Therefore, identifying the vulnerabilities that are peculiar to women is a necessary precondition to formulating applicable legal remedies, not least of all in respect of systemic intimate violence.

Why Doesn't She Just Leave?

While it may appear that abused women are free to leave, this is often a myth. Flight is a fallacy. Some victims of systemic intimate violence are quite literally

---

[93] See also Susan B Boyd, 'Challenging the Public/Private Divide: An Overview' in Susan B Boyd (ed), *Challenging the Public/Private Divide: Feminism, Law, and Public Policy* (Toronto, University of Toronto Press, 1997) 9 and 10.

[94] Resnik (n 76) points out that while 'Boundaries of role are ... shifting, ... [g]ender systems work through assumptions about the intelligibility of the categories of "women" and "men", which in turn depend upon demarcations of "the family" from "the market" and of "the private" from "the public"' (pp 620–21).

imprisoned and held against their will.[95] But an abuser may implement a more
subtle range of isolating factors: he may control the daily activities of the abused
and prevent her from visiting family, friends or neighbours, receiving visitors,
working outside the home, studying, or using contraceptives.[96] Factors other
than direct force may prevent escape.[97] Reasons for finally leaving may vary and
include a fear of being killed or going mad; fear that a child will be killed; and
the revelation of an opportunity to escape. Most often, however, the dynamics
of the violence and infrastructural deficiencies restrict, at times to the point of
eliminating, the victim's ability to leave.[98]

Escape may also precipitate an escalation in violence against the woman or her
children. It is at the point of leaving that many women die at the hands of their
abusive partners.[99] Faced with the reality of a loss of control and seeking to re-
establish dominance, the aggressor tends to use force, either against the abused or
against her children.[100] The abuser may also threaten to take her children away
or harm her family members, companion animals or work colleagues. In the case
of *Opuz v Turkey* the applicant, a Turkish national, had made several complaints
to the authorities regarding her husband, who had been violent towards her and
her mother. The applicant's husband eventually killed her mother, claiming that
she 'had led his wife into an immoral life, like hers, and was taking his wife and
children away from him'.[101] Similarly, in *Kontrová v Slovakia*,[102] the applicant

[95] See Mexico's Law of Assistance and Prevention of Domestic Violence (n 63) 521, Art 1.

[96] Ellsberg et al (n 15) 1597–600; 1603 and 1605. See also *Women's Reproductive Rights in Mexico: A Shadow Report* (n 63) 24 (describing verbal aggression, confinement to the home, being prevented from seeing family members or working, and forced sexual relations as components of domestic violence).

[97] It is an important aspect of systemic intimate violence that the abuser usually is in control of his actions, evidenced by the fact that the violence takes place in private, out of the public eye. See Amnesty International (n 33) 29. See also Ellsberg et al (n 15) 1601 (indicating that much domestic violence in Nicaragua takes place at weekends or in the evening). See also Jane Maslow Cohen, 'Regimes of Private Tyranny: What do they Mean to Morality and for the Criminal Law?' (1996) 57 *University of Pittsburg Law Review* 757.

[98] See eg Amnesty International (n 33) 10.

[99] Some women experience the most intense violence at the point at which they leave their part-ner or seek help. Women who have left the relationship report more serious instances of violence than women who are in relationships. See Amnesty International, *Broken Bodies, Shattered Minds* (n 30) 1; Schneider (n 33) 77 ('Leaving provides battered women no assurance of separation or safety; the stories of battered women who have been hunted down across state lines and harassed or killed are legion'). Heimer et al (n 33) 81 (women in Sweden who were not living with a man at the time of the survey report 'a higher level of experiences of violence on the part of former husbands/cohab-itant partners than do women who are currently living with a man'). Mahoney refers to this as 'sep-aration assault'. Martha R Mahoney, 'Victimization or Oppression? Women's Lives, Violence, and Agency' in Martha A Fineman and Roxanne Mykitiuk (eds), *The Public Nature of Private Violence: The Discovery of Domestic Abuse* (New York, Routledge, 1994) 36, 78–81.

[100] See Amnesty International (n 33) 10 ('the abuser's perception that he risks losing control over the woman is seen as the triggering factor' and is the 'single most frequent motive behind fatal vio-lence against women by men close to them').

[101] *Opuz v Turkey* (App No 33401/02) ECtHR 9 June 2009. For a discussion of this case see ch 1, p 87–88.

[102] *Kontrová v Slovakia* (App No 7510/04) ECtHR 31 May 2007. For a discussion of this case see ch 1, p 88.

had been beaten and subjected to psychological and physical violence by her husband. After the applicant left her husband, he shot their two children and then himself.

Faced with the prospect of such extreme violence, the victim's 'choice' of escape dissipates and, in reality, she is left with only one course of action, which is to stay. The threats of violence form a barrier to liberation that can be equally as restrictive as prison walls.[103]

Even if the outward signs of harm are visible in the form of bruising or broken bones, the abused may still not recognise the abnormality of the abusive behaviour. The abuser may convince her that the violence is somehow acceptable or not serious. She may also believe her abuser's accusations that she is responsible for the violence and that it is a proportionate response to whatever conduct allegedly triggered the act of aggression. Perhaps most obviously, no one will readily believe that an intimate relationship, which connotes warmth, support and love, could be the setting in which such violence takes place.

In the case of immigrant women, fear of deportation may deter them from seeking assistance from any official government body.[104] One substratum of society that experiences the greatest hurdles when attempting to escape violent relationships is women with so-called questionable or uncertain immigration status.[105] Individuals falling into this opaque category are not entitled to receive state benefits, including housing, health care and financial assistance. Women who are willing to risk their and their children's immigration status and do go to the authorities for assistance are told that they cannot access safe houses, they cannot be given food, and they are not allowed to work. The only 'assistance' offered by the state is to take their children into state care and begin deportation proceedings. In such a situation, the abused may decide either to live with the violence to avoid bringing harm to third parties or, in certain cases, to take independent action, such as hurting the abuser or herself.

Women who are sex workers, alcoholics or drug abusers often feel disempowered to engage the law at all.[106] The 'outsider' status of lesbian couples, and the perception that women would not abuse one another (or the reluctance of

---

[103] Telephones are disconnected and windows are often sealed. One of the author's clients could only communicate to her sister through the letterbox in the front door. See also Andrea Dworkin, *Life and Death* (Free Press, 1997) 115–16 ('When you look at what happened to these women, you want to say, "Amnesty International, where are you?"—because the prisons for women are our homes. We live under martial law. We live in a rape culture. Men have to be sent to prison to live in a culture that is as rapist as the normal home in North America').

[104] For example, the abuser may threaten that a '"court is not going to award custody to a lunatic like you" or "Call the police, see if I care—do you think a policeman doesn't beat his wife?"': Joanne Fedler, 'Lawyering Domestic Violence through the Prevention of Family Violence Act 1993—An Evaluation after a Year in Operation' (1995) *South African Law Journal* 231, 235.

[105] Amnesty International and Southall Black Sisters, *No Recourse, No Safety: The Government's Failure to Protect Women from Violence* (London, Amnesty International UK and Southall Black Sisters, March 2008).

[106] ibid.

women to be public about their sexual orientation), makes it particularly difficult for lesbian victims of domestic violence to engage the law. It must be said
that this is equally problematic for male same-sex couples too.

Psychologically, abused women are threatened, shamed and manipulated
into believing that they deserve the violent treatment.[107] Perpetual violence
exhausts the abused, leaving her too tired and depressed to seek official help. If
she is prevented from obtaining hospital treatment her injuries may become
debilitating. It is increasingly difficult, if not indeed impossible, to reason in the
face of violence.[108] The power of self-blame and shame contributes to the
entrapment process.[109]

The onset of depression is one of the side-effects of repeated acts of assault.
This clinical condition reduces an individual's ability to perform ordinary daily
functions, and long term planning becomes a task that is beyond the victim's
capabilities. Merely making a phone call can be an exhausting experience.
Accepting one's situation and not involving the authorities may be the easiest
way of surviving.[110]

The nature of systemic intimate violence often involves the enforced physical
isolation and effective imprisonment of victims. Given the potential severity of
the violence and its isolating effect, the vulnerability of victims of systemic intimate violence is acute.[111] The literal removal of the abused from her community
and her isolating imprisonment are disquietingly synonymous with the classic
characteristics of torture and disappearances, which use isolation both to mask
violence and as a psychological weapon against victims. Even where an abuser
allows his victim to leave their home, the victim is often so scared of subsequent
violence, whether as a result of direct or implied threats of violence against her,
her children, companion animals, personal property or otherwise, that she feels
unable to access outside help.

By cutting a woman off from her personal support system the abuser limits
the victim's sphere of public interaction. The sense of isolation deflates any hope
she might have of intervention, confirming the seemingly omnipotent control of
the abuser.[112] Women may 'survive their situation by avoiding adversarial
encounters and by actively shunning legal assistance'.[113] Shut off from the outside world, the wave of physical abuse intensifies and progresses without the
impediment of social or communal admonishment.

---

[107] ibid. See also Heimer et al (n 33) 18 (explaining that many women do not report incidents of
violence due to their experience of 'fear, guilt and shame').
[108] Kathleen B Jones, *Living Between Danger and Love: The Limits of Choice* (New Jersey,
Rutgers University Press, 2000) 2–3.
[109] Ellsberg et al (n 15) 1605 (research 'suggests that shame and self-blame are powerful mechanisms keeping many women entrapped in violent relationships').
[110] See Amnesty International (n 33) 9 (describing the effort it takes to keep the violence a secret
in order to give the appearance of 'working order . . . Enormous amounts of activity, planning and
strength are required, simply to cope with everyday life').
[111] Ellsberg et al (n 15) 1605.
[112] ibid.
[113] Fedler (n 104) 235.

Economics

Women may be compelled to remain in violent relationships for economic reasons. A victim may simply not be able to survive without the income of her abuser, especially if she is responsible for children. The fact that most women worldwide earn less than men decreases women's earning potential and, therefore, their ability to sustain themselves and dependants.[114] Leaving a relationship, abusive or otherwise, is a costly effort, entailing moving and travel expenses, which may be high if the abused needs to move to another state to escape her abuser.

In addition, women are most often the primary care-giver, and their ability to enter or re-enter the workforce is undermined by the opportunity cost and lack of experience incurred by their non-remunerated work in the private sphere. In many instances a victim may be unable to return to her place of employment for fear of being traced by her abuser.[115]

Social Factors Leading to Isolation

Social support mechanisms play an important role in the escape, recovery and readjustment of abused women.[116] Where there is a lack of social assistance, abused women often do not seek help due to feelings of shame, a fear of reprisals, or because the abuse itself seems disproportionate in their minds to calling the police—that is, it is not sufficiently serious.[117] In this way, part of the harm exists in society's stigma against abused women.

Systemic intimate violence against women is not a one-off peculiarity, and in many ways it is a manifestation of social views, perceptions, priorities, and custom.[118] In some instances an abused woman may fear social disapprobation for the fact that her marriage has failed to meet an ideal standard. The response of the community may condition the way in which she determines her own self-worth and culpability.[119] This is particularly acute in communities where

[114] See Sen (n 1) 264; McDougal et al (n 82) 614–16; generally, Okin (n 71).

[115] Abused women often lack the 'resources, legal and community support and alternative means to survive'. UNCHR, *Report of the Special Rapporteur on violence against women, its causes and consequences: Further Promotion and Encouragement of Human Rights and Fundamental Freedoms, Including the Question of the Programme and Methods of Work of the Commission. Alternative Approaches and Ways and Means within the United Nations System for Improving the Effective Enjoyment of Human Rights and Fundamental Freedoms* (6 February 1996) UN Doc E/CN.4/1996/53, para 13 (hereinafter Special Rapporteur 1996 Report).

[116] Ellsberg et al (n 15) 1604 ('When friends or family are unavailable or indifferent, this may be more distressing than the initial vicitmising experience, because it reinforces the victim's perception of deviance and self-blame').

[117] ibid (describing how 80% of women did not report the abuse if there were no or limited social services and '26% of women who had suffered severe violence felt that they did not need help').

[118] Copelon (n 56) 120.

[119] See eg Carin Benninger-Budel, *Violence Against Women: 10 Reports/Year 2000 for the Protection and Promotion of the Human Rights of Women* (Geneva, World Organization against Torture, 2000) 116 (in South Asia a woman 'is expected to possess the qualities of obedience, patience, endurance and sacrifice—failing which she is liable to reactions amounting to any degree

family authority is vested in men.[120] In Nicaragua, for example, the notions of *machismo* (male strength and dominance) and *marianismo* (female maternity and chastity) are cultural imperatives that often guide women's behaviour in an abusive situation. The allocated role of the demure, submissive and devout wife necessitates subservient behaviour, with a concomitant 'duty to put up with the abuse and keep your family together'.[121] On the other hand, the man's role is one of power, strength and authority. Such cultural imperatives legitimise the expression of these qualities, even in the form of violence.[122]

In other situations, ironically, an emphasis on the empowerment of women may make women reluctant to reveal their own victim status for fear of failing to comply with the perception of equality.[123] The perceived equality of women in Sweden, for example, may deter women from reporting violence since it 'conflicts with strong normative conceptions of what a modern Swedish hetero-sexual partner relationship is supposed to be like'.[124]

Cultural imperatives often discourage discussion of one's private affairs. Sexual abuse, while a common form of systemic intimate violence, is rarely reported.[125] This social abjection of women is very much a component of, for example, mass rape. The rapes in Rwanda, Darfur and the Former Yugoslavia were (and are) intended to 'spoil' the purity of women, to offend the honour of men and to impregnate the victims, resulting in the birth of children of enemy ethnicity.[126] The stereotypical image of rape is non-consensual sex with a stranger, occurring in a strange and unsafe location. Because of this perception, a victim or her society may not recognise the crime of rape when her sexual partner of many years demands sex without her consent. These externalities are oppressive and contribute to the isolation that many women endure.[127]

Over time, the physical and social differences between men and women have on the whole resulted in a very different quality of life for the two genders.[128] In recent times, of course, the social abasement of women has been diluted. As the feminist

of violence'). In Nicaragua, domestic violence is so commonplace that many Nicaraguan women refer to it as 'the cross one must carry' (OMCT CEDAW Report on Nicaragua (n 57) 11–12, 14). See also Ellsberg et al (n 15) 1604.

[120] Social data confirms that abused women in Nicaragua have less interaction with friends, neighbours and relatives (Ellsberg et al (n 15) 1604).

[121] ibid, 1606.

[122] ibid (providing a detailed discussion of this cultural dichotomy).

[123] Amnesty International (n 33) 10 (describing how some women may be embarrassed at how their violent relationship contradicts the perception of Sweden as an equal and ideal society).

[124] Heimer et al (n 33) 84.

[125] Amnesty International (n 33) 10.

[126] See Jonathan MH Short, 'Sexual Violence as Genocide: The Developing Law of the International Criminal Tribunals and the International Criminal Court' (2003) 8 *Michigan Journal of Race and Law* 503; Sherrie L Russell-Brown, 'Rape as an Act of Genocide' (2003) 21 *Berkeley Journal of International Law* 350.

[127] Ellsberg et al (n 15) 1606 ('If a woman leaves her husband, she risks not only economic hardship, but also dealing with the social stigma of having failed as a wife and mother. On the other hand, if she doesn't leave, it may be assumed that she is somehow to blame for provoking her partner's violent behaviour . . .').

[128] This is endorsed by Amartya Sen (n 1) 264.

movement, particularly in the west, developed and grew, women obtained greater civil liberties and individual freedoms. These movements were responsible for women's progression from disenfranchisement and lack of legal competence to access to political processes, economic fora, and public life in general.[129] However, the residue of inequality lingers in the shadows of the home and workplace. Feminists have made great strides but society lags behind, continuing to demarcate the role of women within domesticity and as a satellite to men.[130] In almost every country women continue to be predominantly responsible for childrearing and concomitant household duties, irrespective of whether they have other jobs.[131]

The correlation between violence and sex discrimination is widely acknow-ledged and is 'predicated upon economic dependency, acculturation to sex roles, and legal and political inequality'.[132] Okin maintains that the 'devaluation of women's work, as well as their lesser physical strength and economic depen-dence upon men, in turn allows them to be subject to physical, sexual and/or psychological abuse by their husbands or other male partners'.[133]

Sex discrimination is also evident in the case of FGC, which is mandated for religious or cultural reasons with a view to delineating a norm of sexual appro-priateness for women. Generally, the objective is to control women's sexuality as a way of ensuring both their sexual subservience and the family's honour. The cutting is linked to a girl's gendered identity within her social group and is quite independent of her personal or individual characteristics. Mostly, FGC is

---

[129] See Reva B Siegel, '"The Rule of Love": Wife Beating as Prerogative and Privacy' (1996) 105 *Yale Law Journal* 2117, 2127–30 (discussing the role of the women's movement in the repudiation of the right of chastisement). See also Schneider (n 33) 4–5.

[130] Charlotte Bunch, 'Transforming Human Rights from a Feminist Perspective' in Julie Peters and Andrea Wolper (eds), *Women's Rights, Human Rights: International Feminist Perspectives* (Routledge, 1995) 11, 12 ('The exclusion of any group—whether on the basis of gender, class, sex-ual orientation, religion, or race—involves cultural definitions of the members of that group as less than fully human').

[131] See Gwendolyn Mikell, 'Introduction' in Gwendolyn Mikell (ed), *African Feminism: The Politics of Survival in sub-Saharan Africa* 1, 3 (Philadelphia, University of Pennsylvania Press, 1997). For an examination of the intersection between the discriminatory treatment of women in society and the greater degree of exposure to violence for such women, see also Donna Sullivan, 'The Public/Private Distinction in International Human Rights Law' Peters and Wolper (n 130) 126, 133–34.

[132] Resnik (n 76) 641. See also United Nations Children's Fund, *Domestic Violence against Women and Girls* (Italy, Innocenti Research Centre, 2000) 7–8, www.unicef-icdc.org/publica-tions/pdf/digest6e.pdf. See also Stanley G French, Wanda Teays and Laura M Purdy, 'Introduction' in Stanley G French, Wanda Teays and Laura M Purdy (eds), *Violence against Women: Philosophical Perspectives* (New York, Cornell University Press, 1998) 1–2. See generally Julie Peters and Andrea Wolper, 'Introduction' in Peters and Wolper (n 130) 1, 2; Benninger-Budel (n 119); Jennifer M Mason, 'Buying Time for Survivors of Domestic Violence: A Proposal for Implementing an Exception to Welfare Time Limits' (1998) 73 *New York University Law Review* 621, 640 fn 117 (over 95% of reported spousal abuse cases involve men attacking women); Jo Dixon, 'The Nexus of Sex, Spousal Violence, and the State' (1995) 29 *Law and Society Review* 359, 367. In the context of post-conflict or transitional regions with high levels of crime and desensitisation to violence in gen-eral, women 'are disproportionately likely to be victims of [domestic] violence'. See Human Rights Watch, *Violence against Women in South Africa—State Response to Domestic Violence and Rape* (New York, Human Rights Watch, 1995) para 1.2; South African Law Commission, 'Research Paper on Domestic Violence' (April 1999) 44, www.doj.gov.za/salrc/rpapers/violence.pdf.

[133] Okin (n 71) 284.

practised on girls in order to prepare them for marriage. A woman who has not undergone the procedure may be deemed impure or unsuitable for marriage. Since marriage provides a livelihood for many women, remaining unmarried is neither economically nor socially viable. The fact that the procedure is a necessary precondition to marriage confirms the role of society in enforcing the harm and reveals the vulnerability of girls to this harm.[134]

Even in egalitarian, progressive societies, the inheritance of historic discrimination is one of the reasons why women suffer systemic intimate violence disproportionately to men. Sex discrimination, at some point and in some way, has infiltrated, affected and, at times, corrupted many national laws vis-a-vis women.[135] It is not my objective here to delve into the well-documented evidence of the effects of inequality. For the purpose of understanding women's particular exposure to systemic intimate violence, it is sufficient to adopt the conclusion of well respected scholars that 'inequality between men and women afflicts—and sometimes prematurely ends—the lives of millions of women, and, in different ways, severely restricts the substantive freedoms that women enjoy'.[136] Therefore, while the social, political and economic equality and equivalency of women has been achieved to varying degrees throughout the world, true choice regarding personal priorities and life ambition, unfettered equality, and de-gendered expectations remain an objective and not an achievement, thus perpetuating the social and legal abjection, and vulnerability, of women.[137]

The Failure of the State to Help

The failure of states to intervene in cases of systemic intimate violence is the fifth element and a key ingredient in the perpetuation of violence against women.[138]

---

[134] See OMCT CEDAW Report on Nicaragua (n 57) 15 (if a man kills a woman after surprising her in illicit intimate relations, he may be sentenced to 2–5 years' imprisonment, while the standard punishment for homicide is 6–14 years). See also United Nations Children's Fund, *Early Marriage: Child Spouses* (Italy, Innocenti Research Centre, 2001), www.unicef-irc.org/publications/pdf/digest7e.pdf.

[135] See eg Peters and Wolper (n 132) 2.

[136] Amartya Sen, *Development as Freedom* (New York, Random House, 2000) 15 (it is 'in the continued inequality in the division of food—and (perhaps even more) that of health care—that gender inequality manifests itself most blatantly and persistently in poor societies with strong anti-female bias' (p 194)). This view is echoed by other theorists. McDougal et al (n 82) refer to many manifestations of discrimination against women, including disproportionate wealth, noting that 'Sex bias takes a greater economic toll than racial bias' (p 619). Okin (n 71) also describes the economic costs of domestic violence, demonstrating that the 'power differential extends beyond the abuse and overwork of women to deprivation in terms of feeding, healthcare, and education of female children' (p 284).

[137] Carin Benninger-Budel (n 119) 279. See generally Susan Faludi, *Backlash: The Undeclared War against American Women,* 15th edn (New York, Three Rivers Press, 1991).

[138] See Special Rapporteur 1996 Report (n 115) 16–18; UNICEF, *Domestic Violence against Women and Girls* (n 132) x; Celina Romany, 'Killing "The Angel in the House": Digging for the Political Vortex of Male Violence against Women' in Martha A Fineman and Roxanne Mykitiuk (eds), *The Public Nature of Private Violence: The Discovery of Domestic Abuse* (New York, Routledge, 1994) 285, 293 (describing the deficiencies in Puerto Rico's domestic violence legislation).

State omission, the theory of which I discuss in chapter three, is usually manifested in deficient police services, inaccessible or inefficient court processes, poor health services and a lack of economic assistance in the form of either welfare systems or protective labour laws. In many countries the courtroom is no friend to women, let alone women who are survivors of systemic intimate violence.[139]

Often national laws are neither the result nor the reflection of needs; they are the result and reflection of a culture, an order, a way of life.[140] This is true of legislative, judicial and policing protection too.[141] In 2003 in Sweden, for example, only three in ten acts of violence against women led to prosecution or other legal proceedings, in part because such crimes are hard to prove due to a lack of witnesses.[142] In 2003, of the 14,802 processed suspicions of acts of violence against women handled by a prosecutor, only 32 per cent (4,808) resulted in some sort of legal action, including a decision to waive prosecution.[143] Of the requests for restraining orders lodged with the public prosecution authorities in 2003,[144] more than half were dismissed, mostly due to a lack of evidence.[145]

Case Study: Opuz v Turkey

The seriousness of the element of state failure is clearly explained in the the case of *Opuz v Turkey*, in which the European Court of Human Rights held that Turkey had violated its obligations under Articles 2 (right to life), 3 (right to be free from torture and cruel, inhuman or degrading treatment) and 14 (right to equal enjoyment of the Convention rights) by failing to assist the applicant and

---

[139] Amnesty International (n 33) 10. It has been noted that in 'extreme cases, women who have survived violence become refugees in their own countries' (ibid, 28). It is also interesting to note that most women in Sweden who are able to turn to a shelter for assistance have not in fact reported the perpetrator to the police or been in contact with the authorities. ibid. Section 55 of the Nigerian Penal Code allows a husband to beat his wife for the purpose of 'correcting her'. See Oby Nwankwo, 'Effectiveness of Legislation Enacted to Address Violence against Women in Nigeria' (Expert Paper prepared for the United Nations Division for the Advancement of Women, Expert Group Meeting on good practices in legislation on violence against women) (19 May 2008 (updated 30 May 2008)) UN Doc EGM/GPLVAW/2008/EP.08, www.un.org/womenwatch/daw/egm/vaw_legislation_2008/expertpapers/EGMGPLVAW%20Paper%20_Oby%20Nwankwo_.pdf (hereinafter Nigeria Expert Paper).

[140] See Anthony V Alfieri, 'Retrying Race' (2003) 101 *Michigan Law Review* 1141, 1145 (demonstrating that race, as a social factor, 'colors law, crime, and community . . . And it stains the operating norms of institutions').

[141] See Vicki Jackson, 'What Judges can Learn from Gender Bias Task Force Studies' (1997) 81 *Judicature* 15, 16 (describing sexist conduct in the courtroom, such as addressing female witnesses and attorneys by their first names or as 'pretty', 'young', or 'girls'). See also Romany (n 138) 289.

[142] ibid, 40.

[143] ibid.

[144] ibid, 36.

[145] ibid. Of the protection orders granted, nearly 30% were violated within one year of the date of issue. ibid. In Sweden in 2003, 22,400 cases of domestic violence were reported to the police, although it is recognised that this figure is probably conservative since many women do not report violence—'Sweden Debates Hitting Men with Domestic Violence Tax' *Sydney Morning Herald*, 6 October 2004, www.smh.com.au/articles/2004/10/05/1096949511735.html.

mother when, over more than a decade, they had sought the assistance of the state to prevent abuse by the applicant's husband.[146] This case exemplifies how the state can be responsible for continued acts of violence between intimate family members.

Over a period of 12 years the applicant's husband, HO, repeatedly threatened to kill the applicant and her mother (and on occasion the applicant's children) and committed acts of physical violence against the applicant and her mother, including beatings sufficient to endanger life; attacks with a knife; damage to property; driving a car into the applicant and her mother; grievous bodily harm; stabbing (including seven knife injuries on one occasion); and brandishing knives and guns while threatening to kill the applicant, her mother and her children.[147] The applicant and her mother had been declared unfit to work for a combined period of 50 days as a result of physical violence committed by HO. This excludes the number of days the applicant was unable to work because she had to attend court, protect her mother or children from HO, provide evidence to the police or deal with any other of the physical or psychological consequences of continued exposure to violence and threats thereof. Even when the case went before the ECtHR, the applicant had to change address frequently to avoid being found by HO. On 11 March 2002 HO shot and killed the applicant's mother.[148]

On at least five occasions the applicant and/or her mother had asked the police, the prosecutor or some other form of state authority for protection. On the first occasion (10 April 1995), the applicant and her mother withdrew their complaint, which removed the jurisdictional basis for the continuation of a criminal assault case under Turkish law.[149] On the second occasion (11 April 1996), HO was remanded in custody after beating the applicant and causing life-threatening injuries.[150] HO asked to be released pending his trial, arguing that he had slapped his wife two or three times. This was denied initially but one month after the incident HO was released.[151] At the hearing a month later the applicant withdrew her complaint and the case was discontinued.[152] After the third assault (5 February 1998), during which HO pulled a knife on the applicant and her mother, the prosecutor decided not to prosecute HO because of a lack of evidence in connection with the knife assault and because the offences of battery and destruction of property could be subject to private law suits. The prosecutor was of the view that there was no public interest in pursuing the case, notwithstanding that the fourth major incident took place two days *before* the prosecutor made this decision.[153] On 4 March 1998, HO drove a car into the

[146] *Opuz v Turkey* (App No 33401/02) ECtHR 9 June 2009.
[147] ibid, paras 10, 12, 20, 21, 23, 27, 30, 34, 37, 45, 47, 49, 51.
[148] ibid, para 54.
[149] ibid, paras 10–12.
[150] ibid, para 13.
[151] ibid, paras 15–17.
[152] ibid, paras 18–19.
[153] ibid, paras 20–22.

applicant and her mother, causing life-threatening injuries.[154] On 5 March he was remanded in custody[155] and on 6 March the prosecutor decided *not* to prosecute HO in respect of the third major assault (where HO had pulled a knife on the applicant and her mother).[156] Later that same month, on 19 March 1998, the public prosecutor initiated criminal proceedings against HO. The next day the applicant brought divorce proceedings, which she later dropped due to threats and pressure from HO.[157]

On 2 April 1998 the applicant and her mother filed a court petition asking for protective measures from the authorities in light of death threats issued by HO (and his father).[158] Police officials took statements from the applicant, her mother, her brother and his wife, and HO and his father. HO claimed that he was trying to bring his family together and that his mother-in-law was preventing this.[159]

The next day one of the government authorities (the Director of Law and Order Department for the Diyarbakir Security Directorate) informed the Chief Public Prosecutor's Office that he had investigated the allegations made by the applicant and her mother and concluded that the 'slanderous' allegations were a waste of the security forces' time.[160] The report maintains that the applicant's mother had insulted HO; HO had already spent 25 days in prison for running into his wife and her mother; and HO had asked mediators to convince his wife to return to him but her mother would 'not allow the applicant to go back to HO'.[161] The report suggests that the affront to HO's honour and his attempts to reunite with his wife excused his abusive behaviour. Notwithstanding the report, the Chief Prosecutor indicted HO (and his father, who had been married to the applicant's mother) and charged them with issuing death threats against the applicant and her mother. HO was released pending trial (which was moved to a different jurisdiction).[162] HO was acquitted of the charges of issuing death threats and the applicant resumed living with HO.[163]

Meanwhile, during the court proceedings regarding the car attack, HO claimed that the incident had been an accident: the open door had accidentally hit the applicant and her mother. The applicant and her mother confirmed this, claimed that they had made the allegations in anger and stated that they no longer wished to continue the proceedings.[164] The court did not consider that HO, who was not in prison and was not subject to a restraining order, might have intimidated the applicant and her mother into withdrawing the charges. The court concluded that

[154] ibid, para 23.
[155] ibid, para 24.
[156] ibid, paras 21–24.
[157] ibid, paras 25–26.
[158] ibid, para 28.
[159] ibid.
[160] ibid, para 29.
[161] ibid.
[162] ibid, paras 30–31.
[163] ibid, para 33.
[164] ibid, paras 32, 36.

the case in respect of the applicant should be discontinued because she had withdrawn her complaint but, even though the mother had also withdrawn her case, the court held that HO should be convicted of that offence because her injuries were more serious. HO's conviction resulted in a fine.[165]

On 29 October 2001 HO stabbed the applicant seven times. He claimed that his wife had attacked him with a fork and that, because his wife was bigger than him, he had responded by stabbing her.[166] HO again blamed the applicant's mother for their difficulties and his violence. HO was released after his statement had been taken.[167]

Two days later, the lawyer for the applicant's mother petitioned the Public Prosecutor's Office, stating, inter alia, that the applicant and her mother had been forced to withdraw their complaints against HO due to continuing death threats and pressure from HO.[168] The applicant then filed a petition complaining that she had been stabbed by HO. HO was charged on 12 December 2001, almost six weeks after the stabbing.[169]

In the meantime, shortly after the stabbing (14 November 2001) the applicant lodged a criminal complaint against HO alleging that HO had been threatening her. Several days later (19 November 2001) the applicant's mother also filed a complaint that HO and his father had been threatening to kill her and the applicant and had carried knives and guns around her property.[170] HO denied the allegations and claimed that his mother-in-law was interfering with his marriage and had influenced his wife to lead an immoral life.

On 10 January 2002 HO was charged with making death threats. Over a month later, on 27 February 2002, the applicant's mother submitted a further petition to the Public Prosecutor's Office maintaining that the threats had intensified and that her life was in immediate danger.[171] When HO was questioned by the authorities he claimed that (1) his wife was being immoral; (2) his mother-in-law was influencing his wife and interfering with his marriage; and (3) his mother-in-law was leading an immoral life.

On 11 March 2002, the court held that there was no concrete evidence to prosecute HO for making threats against the applicant.[172] On the same date, 11 March 2002, HO shot and killed the applicant's mother.[173]

Two days later, on 13 March 2002, the Public Prosecutor filed an indictment accusing HO of intentional murder. In his statement to the police, HO claimed that he had been defending his honour and protecting his family.[174] On

165 ibid, para 36.
166 ibid, paras 37–38.
167 ibid, para 38.
168 ibid, para 39.
169 ibid, para 41.
170 ibid, para 47.
171 ibid, para 51.
172 ibid, para 46.
173 ibid, para 54.
174 ibid, paras 55–56.

26 March 2002, HO was convicted of murder and illegal possession of a firearm and sentenced to life imprisonment. However, because of the defence of provocation, the sentence was reduced to 15 years (and a fine). Because of time he had spent in pre-trial detention and because the matter was being appealed, HO was released.[175]

On 23 May 2002, the court imposed a fine of 839,957,040 Turkish liras on HO, which he could pay in eight instalments, for the knife attack against the applicant.[176]

On 15 April 2008, the applicant, who had now divorced HO, filed yet another criminal complaint regarding threats to her life and asked the authorities to take measures to protect her life. The applicant indicated that she had been changing her address constantly so that HO could not find her, and asked that her address indicated on the petition remain confidential.[177] A month later, on 14 May 2008, the applicant's representative again informed the court about HO's threats and complained that no measures had been taken to protect the applicant.[178] By this stage the applicant had submitted her case to the ECtHR.

On 14 November 2008, the applicant's representative informed the Court that the applicant's life was in immediate danger because the authorities had still not taken any measures to protect her. On 21 November 2008 the Government informed the Court that the police authorities had taken steps to protect the applicant, specifically by distributing a photograph and fingerprints of the applicant's husband to police stations.[179]

The Court analysed the events leading to the death of applicant's mother, the incidences of violence perpetrated by HO against the applicant and the state's response to the years of abuse. It concluded that, as regards the right to life, there had been a violation of both the substantive and the procedural components of Article 2, and held that the state has 'positive obligations to take preventive operational measures to protect an individual whose life is at risk' and that, in light of this obligation, the authorities should have taken 'special measures consonant with the gravity of the situation with a view to protecting the applicant's mother'.[180] The Court concluded that the national authorities had not displayed due diligence and therefore had 'failed in their positive obligation to protect the right to life of the applicant's mother within the meaning of Article 2 of the Convention'.[181]

As regards the effectiveness of the criminal investigation into the killing of the applicant's mother, the Court held that the criminal justice system was deficient and the state had not fulfilled the procedural component of its Article 2

[175] ibid, para 57.
[176] ibid, para 44.
[177] ibid, para 59.
[178] ibid, para 60.
[179] ibid, paras 68–69.
[180] ibid, para 148.
[181] ibid, para 149.

obligations.[182] Specifically, the Court held that the criminal justice system did not have an adequate deterrent effect capable of ensuring the effective prevention of the unlawful acts by HO (HO spent a limited period in prison for the murder of the applicant's mother). The second main deficiency, according to the Court, was that the authorities relied on the victim's attitude for their failure to take adequate measures to prevent the aggressor carrying out his threats against the physical integrity of the victim.[183] The relevant criminal law was too dependent on the applicant's complaint, without being sensitive to the common phenomenon in domestic violence cases that a complaint is withdrawn for fear of recrimination and increased violence by the abuser. This is especially so in the case of HO, who was rarely imprisoned for his acts of violence, even the most extreme of killing the applicant's mother. The ECtHR noted that this was inconsistent with the practice of 11 Member States of the Council of Europe, where the authorities are required to continue criminal proceedings even where the victim has withdrawn her complaint in domestic violence cases.[184]

The state's responses to HO's violence had been deficient in several respects. The state institutions had not considered the cumulative nature of the violence against the applicant and her mother. The ECtHR confirmed this, noting that although

> there were intervals between the impugned events . . . the overall violence to which the applicant and her mother were subjected over a long period of time cannot be seen as individual and separate episodes and must therefore be considered together as a chain of connected events.[185]

The state had not acknowledged the seriousness of the incidences of violence committed by HO against the applicant and her mother. The value placed by the courts on HO's sense of honour and marital entitlements was disproportionate (if at all relevant) to the seriousness of the harm he perpetrated against the applicant and her mother.

Justice had not been done in respect of the death of the applicant's mother. The state had failed to respond to the requests for protection and the notice of HO's threats. Where the state had responded, there had been improper delays, which did not take account of the urgent nature of the aggression.[186] The state had either delayed the implementation of injunctions or had failed to implement them altogether, and the state institutions had displayed attitudes which tend to regard the problem of domestic violence as a private family matter in which the police are reluctant to interfere.[187]

The Court confirmed that Article 3 'requires States to take measures designed to ensure that individuals within their jurisdiction are not subjected to torture

---

[182] ibid, para 153.
[183] ibid.
[184] ibid, para 87.
[185] ibid, para 111.
[186] ibid, paras 91–93.
[187] ibid, paras 95–96.

or inhuman or degrading treatment or punishment, including such ill-treatment administered by private individuals'.[188] It held that there had been a violation of Article 3 of the Convention as a result of the authorities' failure to take protective measures in the form of effective deterrence against serious breaches of the applicant's personal integrity by her husband.[189] In particular, the Court held that the state should have been proactive because the applicant fell within the category of 'vulnerable individuals' entitled to state protection;[190] the violence suffered by the applicant had been sufficiently serious to amount to ill-treatment within the meaning of Article 3;[191] and the authorities had not exercised sufficient due diligence to protect the victim's needs or the public's interest in non-violence, either by deterring HO or by providing shelter to the applicant.[192]

As regards Article 3 of the Convention, the Court upheld the applicant's claim that the ongoing violence and the state's failure to protect her, notwithstanding her repeated requests for help, made the applicant feel 'as though the violence had been inflicted under state supervision'.[193] This was endorsed by the intervening third party Interights, which maintained that states are required

> to take reasonable steps to act immediately to stop ill-treatment, whether by public or private actors, of which they have known or ought to have known. Given the opaque nature of domestic violence and the particular vulnerability of women who are too often frightened to report such violence, it is submitted that a heightened degree of vigilance is required of the State.[194]

In an extraordinary extension of the Court's jurisprudence on Article 14 (that all the rights in the Convention must be applied without discrimination), the Court held that there had been a violation of Article 14 by virtue of the state's failure to implement domestic violence legislation and to provide protection to domestic violence victims, the majority of whom are women. The Court noted that the applicant had provided prima facie evidence that 'domestic violence affected mainly women and that the general and discriminatory judicial passivity in Turkey created a climate that was conducive to domestic violence', and held that there had been a violation of Article 14 in conjunction with Articles 2 and 3 of the Convention.[195] By analysing international and regional law on violence against women and women's rights, the Court held that the state's failure to protect women against domestic violence 'breaches their right to equal protection of the law and that this failure does not need to be intentional'—in other words, it could be an unintended but factual consequence.[196] In this case, the discrimination was not in the absence of legislation but rather in its implementation

---

[188] ibid, para 159, citing *HLR v France* (Case No 11/1996/630/813) ECtHR 22 April 1997, para 40.
[189] ibid, para 176.
[190] ibid, para 160.
[191] ibid, para 161.
[192] ibid, paras 167–72.
[193] ibid, para 155.
[194] ibid, para 157.
[195] ibid, paras 198, 201.
[196] ibid, para 191.

and 'the general attitude of the local authorities, such as the manner in which the women were treated at police stations when they reported domestic violence and judicial passivity in providing effective protection to victims'.[197]

Understanding the intricacies of systemic intimate violence reveals how an abused woman has little, if any, access to traditional legal mechanisms. Simply escaping the physical control of an abuser is a challenge. The fact that something so nebulous occurs in private serves to increase the difficulty involved in harnessing systemic intimate violence within current legal structures.[198] Therefore, procuring help from public structures such as the police, courts or hospitals is not the automatic remedy we would like it to be. It is the exception.[199]

In the darkness and detachment of this isolation, acts of violence are executed in silence. This silence effectively removes the existence of the harm from the realm of reality. As far as the state is concerned, the abuse disappears. The systemic failure of the state to protect victims of severe intimate violence and punish its perpetrators constitutes an endorsement of the harm, implicit or otherwise. The conduct of the state, therefore, by virtue of its failure to act, perpetuates the violence, creating an atmosphere of impunity.

It is in this way that the state's role is triggered in international law.

MOVING FROM AN EMERGING NORM TO A RIGHT IN INTERNATIONAL LAW

While chapter one outlined the history of domestic violence in international law and proposed that increasingly states are recognising a developing principle of international law condemning domestic violence, I now explore what additional steps should be taken in international law to confirm an authoritative and binding obligation on states to protect against and prevent such violence.

Steps Needed in International Law

As discussed in chapter one, there is significant activity in international and regional law regarding domestic violence and violence against women. Depending on one's approach to the sources of international law, the international instruments discussed in the preceding chapter may or may not constitute—or be

---

[197] ibid, para 192.

[198] Amnesty International (n 33) 6.

[199] In 1995, statistics indicated that every second woman in Nicaragua had been physically mistreated at some point by her husband or companion, and one in four women had suffered physical violence within the preceding year. In 1997, '70% of all women had experienced physical violence some time in their lives'. UNIFEM-UNDP-UNFPA-UNICEF-UNAIDS-UNHCR-UNHCHR-ECLAC, 'A Life Free of Violence: It's Our Right. United Nations Inter-Agency Campaign on Women's Human Rights in Latin America and the Caribbean' (1998), freeofviolence.org, specifically, Carmen Clavel and Verónica Gutiérrez, *Nicaragua* (1998), freeofviolence.org/nicaragua.htm.

evidence of—an international legal prohibition of domestic violence. The difficulty arises if one takes a purely traditional approach to the creation of international law. Generally, the easiest way of identifying international law is through treaties or conventions. While there is a treaty prohibiting *discrimination* against women, there is no international treaty prohibiting violence against women or domestic violence. The next question is whether customary international law prohibits domestic violence. This very much depends on one's interpretation of customary international law. If one takes a traditional approach and looks purely at state practice and *opinio juris*, it is unclear whether there is an international principle relating to domestic violence because so many states do not protect victims of systemic intimate violence. On the other hand, if one looks to international instruments, statements and decisions, together with the actions of certain states, there is compelling evidence of a serious and authoritative principle that states may be held responsible for domestic violence.

In order to concretise this position, what more needs to be done to achieve the effective delineation of domestic violence as an international human rights violation? I propose that three steps should be taken in international law.

First, a specific, express and authoritative prohibition of systemic intimate violence, as defined above, should be adopted and developed in international law. Despite the significant developments that have taken place in the last five to ten years whereby UN instruments, regional instruments and UN and regional jurisprudence have increasingly referred to and prohibited domestic violence, there are still many who would question whether this is a serious principle of international law. There should be no uncertainty about the precise right to be free from domestic violence, with all its nuances. The accurate specification of a right to be free from domestic violence (or, more accurately, systemic intimate violence) in international law should be adopted by treaty law or, more simply, by way of a detailed Security Council resolution or an equivalent.

The second step is the general politicisation of domestic violence, with concomitant economic empowerment. This is more a process of acculturation whereby the ramifications of domestic violence are incorporated into the political, economic and health-related components of political dialogues.[200]

The third missing element is the incorporation of domestic violence into the work of mainstream international bodies. The Committee against Torture and the World Health Organization have considered domestic violence to be a human rights violation within their remit.[201] This has aided the development of a precise theory and set of instructions as to what states should be doing to comply with their international obligation to prevent and protect against domestic violence.[202]

---

[200] See Marijke Velzeboer, Mary Ellsberg, Carmen Clavel Arcas and Claudia Garciá-Moreno, *Violence against Women: The Health Sector Responds* (Pan American Health Organization, 2003) 7.

[201] Special Rapporteur on torture 2008 Report (n 3). See also Etienne G Krug, *World Report on Violence and Health* (World Health Organization, 2002) 99.

[202] See eg Elizabeth M Schneider, 'The Violence of Privacy' in Martha A Fineman and Roxanne Mykitiuk (eds), *The Public Nature of Private Violence: The Discovery of Domestic Abuse* (New York, Routledge, 1994) 36, 47 (arguing for the necessity of resources such as trained free legal counsel).

The proposed development of international law should be considered within the context of the transnational legal process, which I discuss in chapter four. I do not maintain that change will come about at the hands of an international policing authority. This is historically inaccurate and conceptually improbable. Rather, the enunciation of a specific legal right to be free from systemic intimate violence may advance the infiltration of effective protection into national legal systems. This, in turn, would help to improve state-sponsored infrastructural support and help to generate the social reform that is necessary to prevent domestic violence and protect its victims.

The First Step: The Enunciation of a Specific Legal Right

As discussed in chapter one, international law provides general overarching principles regarding violence against women, but there is still uncertainty as to whether domestic violence is recognised as a human rights violation under international law and, if it is, what states ought to be doing to protect that right. There needs to be an explicit legal statement in a form such as a legally and universally binding treaty or Security Council resolution which describes the precise contours of the right of women to be free from domestic violence and the conjoint obligation of states to ensure safety in intimate, as well as public, settings.

There are several examples of this type of specification of human rights violations in international law. CEDAW is itself an example of a binding treaty which is a distillation of general international law principles of equality.[203] Its creation was not merely a repetition of the right to equality. It recreated and refined equality in respect of women's lives in a way that was absent from the Universal Declaration of Human Rights (UDHR) and the principles of international law at the time. CEDAW, in other words, filled a gap. This is confirmed in its preamble, which acknowledges that, notwithstanding the commitment to sex equality in the UN Charter, the UDHR and other international instruments, sex discrimination continued to exist, and a more specific understanding of the right to sex equality was needed.[204] I propose the same rationale in respect of domestic violence. The international law statements regarding violence against women have pointed us in the right direction, but the analytical lens still needs to focus in more on the detail of this extremely nuanced and often misunderstood form of violence.

Another example of the international process of specification is the obligation on states to protect women from trafficking. There are roughly 14 international

---

[203] CEDAW (n 9) preamble.
[204] ibid. While the Charter of the United Nations (adopted 26 June 1945, entered into force 24 October 1945) (1945) UNTS 993 and the Universal Declaration of Human Rights (adopted 10 December 1948) UNGA Res 217 A(III) (UDHR) and other international legal instruments confirm the international legal principle of equality between the sexes, sex discrimination continues to exist and something more is needed.

instruments on trafficking, most of them binding treaties. In 1904 the League of Nations adopted the International Agreement for the Suppression of the 'White Slave Traffic'.[205] This was followed in 1910 by the International Convention for the Suppression of the 'White Slave Traffic'.[206] In 1927, the Slavery Convention obliged states to prevent and suppress the slave trade, which included forced labour.[207] This was entrenched in 1930 by the Forced Labour Convention regarding the use of forced or compulsory labour in all its forms.[208]

In 1934, the International Convention for the Suppression of the Traffic in Women of Full Age introduced the obligation to punish

> Whoever, in order to gratify the passions of another person, has procured, enticed or led away even with her consent, a woman or girl of full age for immoral purposes to be carried out in another country . . ., notwithstanding that the various acts constituting the offence may have been committed in different countries.[209]

Almost 20 years later, in 1951, the International Convention for the Suppression of the 'White Slave Traffic' was updated, expanding on the obligations of states vis-a-vis various acts that constitute trafficking.[210] In 1957 the Supplementary Convention on the Abolition of Slavery, the Slave Trade, and Institutions and Practices Similar to Slavery was adopted to 'intensify national as well as international efforts' towards the abolition of slavery and the slave trade.[211] Although the word 'trafficking' was not included in this Convention, the list of prohibited acts includes practices which amount to trafficking.[212]

In 1979, states agreed that trafficking of women is a human rights violation. Trafficking was included in Article 6 of CEDAW, which obliges state parties to take all appropriate measures, including legislation, to suppress all forms of traffic in women. Still further, in 1990, Article 35 of the Convention on the Rights of the Child specifically obliged states to take all appropriate national,

---

[205] International Agreement for the Suppression of the 'White Slave Traffic' (adopted 18 May 1904, entered into force 18 July 1905) 1 LNTS 83.

[206] International Convention for the Suppression of the 'White Slave Traffic' (4 May 1910) 211 CTS 45, as amended by Protocol Amending the International Agreement for the Suppression of the 'White Slave Traffic', and Amending the International Convention for the Suppression of the 'White Slave Traffic' (adopted 4 May 1949, entered into force 21 June 1951) 30 UNTS 23.

[207] Slavery, Servitude, Forced Labour and Similar Institutions and Practices Convention of 1926 (Slavery Convention of 1926) (entered into force 9 March 1927) 60 LNTS 253; Protocol amending the Slavery Convention (entered into force 7 December 1953) 182 UNTS 51.

[208] Forced Labour Convention: Convention (No 29) concerning Forced Labour (adopted 28 June 1930, entered into force 1 May 1932) 39 UNTS 55.

[209] International Convention for the Suppression of the Traffic in Women of Full Age, Art 1 (adopted 11 October 1933, entered into force 24 August 1934) 150 LNTS.

[210] Protocol Amending the International Agreement for the Suppression of the 'White Slave Traffic', and Amending the International Convention for the Suppression of the 'White Slave Traffic' (adopted 4 May 1949, entered into force 21 June 1951) 30 UNTS 23.

[211] Supplementary Convention on the Abolition of Slavery, the Slave Trade, and Institutions and Practices Similar to Slavery (adopted 7 September 1956, entered into force 30 April 1957) 226 UNTS 3, preamble.

[212] ibid, s I and Art 7(c).

bilateral and multilateral measures to prevent the trafficking of children.[213] In 2000 the Optional Protocol to the Convention on the Rights of the Child on the sale of children, child prostitution and child pornography was adopted, which details states' obligations to prevent and protect against the trafficking of children specifically.[214]

In the same year the Protocol to Prevent, Suppress and Punish Trafficking in Persons Especially Women and Children, supplementing the United Nations Convention against Transnational Organized Crime (the Palermo Protocol), was adopted.[215] This Convention aims specifically at combating trafficking, particularly in respect of women and children.[216] The Convention addresses the nuances that make trafficking a discrete form of slavery and recognises that the existing international instruments against slavery in general did not reflect the reality of this particular rights abuse. The Convention's definition of trafficking includes 'the recruitment, transportation, transfer, harbouring or receipt of persons' not only by force, but also as a result of 'deception, of the abuse of power or of a position of vulnerability or of the giving or receiving of payments or benefits to achieve the consent of a person having control over another person, for the purpose of exploitation'.[217]

The Convention also challenges the traditional understanding of consent, noting that the consent of a trafficking victim to certain acts is irrelevant because often they are misled or their vulnerability and/or poverty is exploited.[218] It is also very specific about states' obligations, which include the criminalisation of those who participate in trafficking and those who organise or direct trafficking operations.[219]

All of these treaties and conventions are clearly binding on states and result in a framework of legal obligations that has led to a more sophisticated response to the perpetrators of trafficking and the protection of its victims. Of course it was the trans-border nature of this crime that triggered the plethora of international agreements, and, at first blush, domestic violence is not an international issue. International human rights law, however, embraces not only trans-border violations, such as trafficking, but also purely national violations, such as child abuse. There is also evidence of domestic violence victims seeking asylum for fear that their country's legal system will not protect them from

---

[213] Convention on the Rights of the Child (adopted 20 November 1989, entered into force 2 September 1990) 1577 UNTS 3, (1989) 28 ILM 1456.

[214] Optional Protocol to the Convention on the Rights of the Child on the sale of children, child prostitution and child pornography, UNGA Res A/RES/54/263 (adopted and opened for signature 25 May 2000, entered into force 18 January 2002) UN Doc A/RES/54/263.

[215] Protocol to Prevent, Suppress and Punish Trafficking in Persons, Especially Women and Children, Supplementing the United Nations Convention against Transnational Organized Crime, UNGA Res 55/25 (adopted 15 November 2000, entered into force 9 September 2003) UN Doc A/45/49 (Vol I) (hereinafter Palermo Protocol).

[216] ibid, Art 2.

[217] ibid, Art 3(a).

[218] ibid, Art 3(b).

[219] ibid, Art 5(2).

spousal or family violence, which gives this form of domestic violence a cross-border dimension.

The Convention against Torture is another example of a convention specifically addressing an area of law already covered in the UDHR. It is also based on the UN Charter's commitment to universal human rights and the prohibition of torture contained in the UDHR.[220] The Convention confirms the desire to 'make more effective the struggle against torture . . . throughout the world', thereby justifying the specific articulation and entrenchment of the torture prohibition in the UDHR through this Convention.

We can conclude that the increasing specification and detailed prohibition of certain types of human rights violation has occurred in international law. Whether this specification of certain rights has been successful and could be valuable for domestic violence victims is discussed in chapter four. At the very least, however, there is a precedent for the argument that the loose collection of often non-binding international instruments dealing with domestic violence discussed in chapter one needs to be augmented by a more specific, detailed and authoritative international instrument. This could be achieved by creating a treaty in international law that prohibits domestic violence. Alternatively, I would propose an enunciation by the UN Security Council that domestic violence is a function of government conduct, by virtue of state omission, and that states have a concomitant right to assuage it, through the adoption of specified steps.

The enunciation of a right to be free from domestic violence in international law would translate into better formulated and better implemented legislation in national legal systems. This could be effected through a process of norm infiltration; the potential for national reform through impact litigation; and the granting of asylum to victims of extreme and systemic forms of domestic violence, factors which I discuss in chapter four.[221]

The Second Step: Political Consequences of Domestic Violence

Domestic violence is not a traditional campaign topic for aspiring politicians, but perhaps it should be. It certainly has an impact on more mainstream concerns, such as immigration policies, employment, economic development, and health indicators.

The economic cost of domestic violence is substantial and involves both implicit and explicit costs. Implicit costs include missed work days, poor work performance and the loss of potential labour. Explicit costs include the expense

---

[220] Torture Convention (n 9) preamble.
[221] Jessica Neuwirth, 'Inequality before the Law: Holding States Accountable for Sex Discriminatory Laws under the Convention on the Elimination of All Forms of Discrimination against Women and Through the Beijing Platform for Action' (2005) 18 *Harvard Human Rights Journal* 19, 21 and 47 fn 177 (recommending that treaty bodies should travel more and that their meetings should be held outside of Geneva and New York).

of hospitalisation, police and criminal institutions, homelessness and child welfare. This was confirmed by the Secretary-General in his 2006 report on violence against women when he stated that the costs 'go beyond lowered economic production and reduced human capital formation but also include the costs associated with political and social instability through intergenerational transmission of violence, as well as the funds required for programmes for victims/survivors of violence'.[222] They include the loss of the individual's contribution to society;[223] the drain on the resources of social services, the justice system, healthcare agencies and employers;[224] and the impact on businesses, the state, community groups and individuals. As the primary cause of harm to women, systemic intimate violence is also a significant health hazard. It is a cause of child mortality, high rates of HIV/AIDS and mental diseases.

We know that worldwide, 'one in three women has been beaten, coerced into unwanted sexual relations, or abused—often by a family member or acquaintance'.[225] This violence has economic consequences in the form of health costs, legal proceedings and the loss of productivity on the part of the victim, who may be unable to work as a result of the abuse. We also know that since the beginning of 2000, violence has killed and harmed as many women and girls between the ages of 15 and 44 as cancer, and that the 'costs to countries—in increased health care expenditures, demands on courts, police and schools and losses in educational achievement and productivity—are enormous. In the United States, the figure adds up to some $12.6 billion each year'.[226]

Given this global cost, it is interesting that political candidates do not engage domestic violence in the same way that they approach terrorism, financial markets, trade, employment and crime on their campaign platforms and in party manifestos. For example, a South African non-governmental organisation. The Tshwaranang Legal Advocacy Centre, reviewed the manifestos of political parties in South Africa around the time of the recent elections and found that their approach to domestic violence was deficient.[227] This is probably because politicians inherit a panoply of issues from preceding ruling authorities which they have to address and, in democracies at least, a politician's stand on these issues will determine whether or not s/he is elected. It is probably also because domestic violence is so intimate, belonging ostensibly to the private realm. And just maybe, it could be because it is more likely that the perpetrators of domestic violence rather than their victims will be empowered to vote.

---

[222] Study of the Secretary-General (n 22) para 107.

[223] ibid, para 171.

[224] ibid, para 171.

[225] United Nations Population Fund, *State of World Population 2005: The Promise of Equality: Gender Equity, Reproductive Health and the Millennium Development Goals* (New York, UNFPA, 2005).

[226] ibid.

[227] See Tshwaranang Legal Advocacy Centre, 'How do Political Parties Address the Problem of Violence against Women? A Review of Party Manifestos' (April 2009), www.tlac.org.za/images/documents/political_parties_address_violence_against_woman.pdf.

Linking domestic violence to so-called 'mainstream' issues such as health and economics would help to bring it within the political discourse and demonstrate the seriousness of what traditionally has been perceived solely as a familial aberration.

How can international law achieve this politicisation? One of the ways in which international human rights law operates, as discussed further in chapter four, is by setting standards for countries wishing to form part of the so-called community of nations. For example, compliance with human rights standards is a precondition for membership of the European Union. States must comply with EU standards of human rights, good governance and the rule of law in order to gain membership and take advantage of the concomitant beneficial trade arrangements. By necessity, human rights then become part of the language and content of states' foreign policy dialogues.

A further example is the reference to violence against women and women's rights in post-conflict political dialogue, mostly as a result of UN Resolution 1325 and, more recently, UN Resolution 1820. In 2007, again partly in response to Resolution 1325, India sent the first ever all-female police unit to participate in the UN peacekeeping operations in Liberia. In a country where more than 90 per cent of women have survived some form of sexual violence, the all-female police force was an important manifestation of the empowerment of women, greatly strengthening the transitional justice process.[228] This was unprecedented.

Also for the first time in a post-conflict country, the UN, the government of Liberia, civil society organisations and several heads of state have produced a National Action Plan on women, peace and security in Liberia. The plan incorporates components of UN Security Council Resolution 1820 on sexual violence against civilians in times of conflict.[229] Of course there is a profound gap between the content of these instruments and the extent to which women continue to suffer during and after conflicts. There is little doubt, though, that the internationalisation of the role, needs and experiences of women in post-conflict settings is now on the agenda of many peace talks and transitional justice programmes. In little over a decade this intimate act of violence has become a discussion point among thousands of politicians around the world. The same potential exists in respect of domestic violence.

---

[228] See 'Indian Women Police Inspire Liberian Women to Join Liberia's Police Force' *New Liberian* (Liberia, 14 November 2008), newliberian.com/?p=470.

[229] UNSC Res 1820 on sexual violence in conflict (19 June 2008) UN Doc S/RES/1820 (addressing previously neglected areas such as equal protection under the law for survivors of sexual violence). See 'Liberia Launches UN-backed National Action Plan on Women, Peace and Security' UN News Centre (8 March 2009), www.un.org/apps/news/story.asp?NewsID=30117&Cr=Liberia&Cr1=women. See also 'UN-INSTRAW: Liberia Breaks New Ground for Women, Peace and Security' UN International Research and Training Institute for the Advancement of Women (UN-INSTRAW) (Liberia, 8 March 2009), www.awid.org/eng/Issues-and-Analysis/Library/UN-INSTRAW-Liberia-breaks-new-ground-for-women-peace-and-security.

The Third Step: Bringing Domestic Violence into the Remit of Non-Gender-Specific Human Rights Bodies

Until recently, 'mainstream' human rights bodies had not addressed women's rights per se. Notwithstanding the framing of domestic violence as a form of torture and terror, the Committee against Torture only recently addressed such violence as a form of ill-treatment and torture, and there have been very few successful asylum claims based on domestic violence.[230]

This is changing, and increasingly mainstream international bodies (ie bodies other than CEDAW and women's rights institutions) are taking violence against women into account in their activities.[231] The augmentation of this process could yield fruitful developments both nationally and internationally. Specifically, the framing of violence against women as torture, terrorism and a basis for asylum is a feature of claims currently being pursued by activists, and international bodies should be challenged to incorporate domestic violence into their investigations.

The politicisation of domestic violence is necessary to propel the incorporation of this gender-specific harm into the decision-making processes of 'mainstream' international bodies, such as the Refugee Committee and the Torture Committee. The importance of this is evident from the case of *A v The United Kingdom*.[232] The ECtHR held that abuse of the victim had reached the level of severity prohibited by Article 3 of the European Convention on Human Rights, which prohibits torture and cruel, inhuman and degrading treatment.[233] The extrapolation of the definition of torture to circumstances of unrestrained child abuse enabled the ECtHR to place positive obligations on the state to take steps to protect children in accordance with the state's international obligation to prevent torture. In the case of *Opuz v Turkey*, the Court authoritatively confirmed that acts of domestic violence can amount to ill-treatment, and if the state fails to prevent or punish this violence it will violate its obligations under Article 3 (the prohibition of torture and ill-treatment).[234]

Similarly, by accepting that mass rape and sexual violence may constitute the actus reus of the crimes of torture, genocide and crimes against humanity, the ICTR and ICTY brought gender-specific harm into the jurisprudence of international criminal law and the law of war. This had never been done before. Prior to the *Akayesu* case there was no meaningful jurisprudence on violence committed against women as an unlawful act of war (the traditional view being that violence against women is an unhappy side-effect of war). In fact, *Akayesu* would not have included a conviction for mass rape but for the fact that Judge Pillay, president of the ICTR, insisted that the indictment include sexual

---

[230] See Laura S Adams, 'Beyond Gender: State Failure to Protect Domestic Violence Victims as a Basis for Granting Refugee Status' (2002) 24 *Thomas Jefferson Law Review* 239, 240.

[231] See Amnesty International, *Broken Bodies, Shattered Minds* (n 30).

[232] *A v The United Kingdom* (App No 100/1997/884/1096) (1998) 27 EHRR 611.

[233] ibid, para 21.

[234] *Opuz v Turkey* (App No 33401/02) ECtHR 9 June 2009.

violence. This was contentious, partly because technically it is not the domain of a judge to determine the substance of an indictment and also because prosecutors were reluctant to bring cases on which there was no precedent and in relation to which there were no clear legal principles. Without this jurisprudence, however, it is unlikely that the Rome Statute would have included such robust provisions regarding the criminal elements of mass rape and sexual slavery, amongst others. The inclusion of women in the institutions of transitional justice, such as Louise Arbour, Carla del Ponte, Judges Elizabeth Odio Benito, Gabrielle Kirk McDonald, Navanethem Pillay and Dorothee de Sampayo, has resulted in an expansion of the laws of war and international criminal law that will be felt for generations.

I now turn to discuss the steps that states individually ought to take to mitigate systemic intimate violence.

GOOD GOVERNANCE PRACTICES: WHAT STATES SHOULD DO TO PROTECT AGAINST SYSTEMIC INTIMATE VIOLENCE

If we accept that systemic intimate violence is a human rights violation, what should states do to prevent such a violation? And once we have identified these steps, at what point can we say that a state has fulfilled its obligation to protect women from systemic intimate violence?

In general terms, states are supposed to be diligent in their efforts to protect human rights. The 'due diligence' test is the standard increasingly used in international human rights law, and particularly in respect of violence against women, to describe a state's duty to protect human rights. In her final report to the UN, Radhika Coomaraswamy the former UN Special Rapporteur on violence against women, noted that states must 'demonstrate due diligence by taking active measures to protect, prosecute and punish private actors who commit abuses'.[235] Typically, these measures include drafting legislation, implementing the law and resource allocation.[236]

The barometer used to determine whether a state has complied with the obligation to be duly diligent is whether 'a more active and more efficient course of procedure might have been pursued'.[237] In 2009 the UN collated and

---

[235] ibid. This echoes the Special Rapporteur on state responsibility, James Crawford, who stated that 'the state has a positive duty not to authorize or allow torture'. James Crawford, 'Revising the Draft Articles on State Responsibility' (1999) 10 *European Journal of International Law* 435, 440. For a brief discussion of the due diligence standard within the context of systemic intimate violence see Amnesty International (n 33) 13 (describing it as obliging the state 'to take all the necessary measures to combat violence against women, whoever the perpetrator may be').

[236] I base these steps in part on the discussions that arose during the CEDAW Committee meetings in respect of domestic violence. CEDAW, *Report of the Committee on the Elimination of Discrimination against Women, Eighteenth and Nineteenth Sessions* (14 May 1998) UN Doc A/53/38/Rev.1, para 412, p 35.

[237] Alwyn V Freeman, *The International Responsibility of States for Denial of Justice* (London, Longmans, Green and Co, 1938) 380.

compared material from around the world to extract 'active' and 'efficient' responses, legislative and otherwise, that are necessary to protect women from systemic intimate violence. I discuss these below and highlight some of the debates and proposals regarding ideal practice. As the UN Secretary-General has stated,

> There is no blanket approach to fighting violence against women. What works in one country may not lead to desired results in another. Each nation must devise its own strategy . . . But there is one universal truth, applicable to all countries, cultures and communities: violence against women is never acceptable, never excusable, never tolerable.[238]

States, however, still need guidance.

LEGISLATIVE STEPS

In most instances, the enactment or amendment of legislation is the first necessary step towards achieving compliance with any international obligation.[239] This is required in many international instruments, including the International Covenant on Civil and Political Rights (ICCPR), the International Covenant on Economic, Social, and Cultural Rights (ICESCR) and the Inter-American Convention on Forced Disappearances.[240] As regards the obligation to protect women from violence specifically, the CEDAW Committee has required state parties to enact federal and state laws to criminalise and punish violence against women and the perpetrators thereof, and to 'take steps to ensure that women victims of such violence can obtain reparation and immediate protection'.[241] The 1993 Declaration on the Elimination of Violence against Women (DEVAW) also requires Member States to develop penal, civil, labour and administrative sanctions in domestic legislation, to provide mechanisms of justice and to avoid re-victimisation.[242] The Protocol to Prevent, Suppress and

---

[238] UN Secretary-General Ban Ki-moon, 'Violence against Women Cannot be Tolerated' (remarks on International Women's Day, New York) (5 March 2009), www.un.org/News/Press/docs/2009/sgsm12127.doc.htm.

[239] The international obligation to enact enabling legislation exists in several international instruments. See eg, DEVAW (n 9) Art 2 and Torture Convention (n 9) Art 4(1). *cf* Dinah Shelton, *Remedies in International Human Rights Law* (Oxford, Oxford University Press, 1999) 27, fns 97 and 31.

[240] International Covenant on Economic, Social and Cultural Rights (adopted 16 December 1966, entered into force 3 January 1976) 993 UNTS 3 (ICESCR), Art 2(1); ICCPR (n 9) Art 2(2); and the Inter-American Convention on Forced Disappearances of Persons, Art 1(d) (adopted 1994, entered into force 28 March 1996) (1994) 33 ILM 1429.

[241] The CEDAW Committee referred to 'establishing 24-hour telephone hotlines, increasing the number of shelters and conducting zero-tolerance campaigns on violence against women'. *Report of the Twenty-Seventh Session of the Committee on the Elimination of Discrimination against Women* (6 August 2002) UN Doc A/57/38/Rev.1, para 432, p 209 (hereinafter CEDAW Twenty-Seventh Session Report).

[242] DEVAW (n 9) Art 4.

Punish Trafficking in Persons, Especially Women and Children, supplementing the UN Convention against Transnational Organized Crime (the Palermo Protocol), makes similar demands regarding legislation and its implementation.[243] Non-gender-specific bodies have also called on states to enact or amend legislation to cater specifically for domestic violence.[244]

At a regional level, the Convention of Belem do Para is the only Convention directed solely at eliminating violence against women.[245] The Inter-American Commission on Human Rights addressed the need to review and revise existing laws and policy to eliminate discrimination against women in the case of *Maria Mamerita Mestanza Chávez v Peru*, regarding forced sterilisation.[246]

On several occasions the ECtHR has compelled states to adopt protective legislation in the context of sexual violence. In the case of *X and Y v The Netherlands*, the Court held that the government of the Netherlands had failed to provide 'practical and effective protection' for mentally handicapped women (females over the age of 16) who had been sexually abused.[247] The ECtHR held that 'in such cases, this system meets a procedural obstacle which the Netherlands legislature had apparently not foreseen'. Similarly, in *A v The United Kingdom*, the ECtHR recalled the international law of torture to compel states to amend laws which currently failed 'to provide adequate protection to children' who have been severely abused.[248] This was confirmed by the CEDAW Committee in *Ms AT v Hungary*, where it was found that a lack of specific legislation combating domestic violence and sexual harassment amounted to a violation of the right to security of person.[249]

---

[243] Palermo Protocol (n 215) Arts 5, 6, 7 and 9.

[244] UN Division for the Advancement of Women, 'Background Paper for the Expert Group Meeting on Good Practices in Legislation on Violence against Women' (7 May 2008) UN Doc EGM/GPLVAW/2008/BP.01, www.un.org/womenwatch/daw/egm/vaw_legislation_2008/Background %20Paper%20vaw%20legislation.pdf (hereinafter UNDAW, Background Expert Paper) 3 (noting that the Human Rights Committee requested state parties to provide information on national laws and practice regarding domestic violence, including rape in their reports under the ICCPR). See also General Assembly resolutions calling on Member States to strengthen their legal frameworks in respect of violence against women: UNGA Res 59/166 (10 February 2005) UN Doc A/RES/59/166, on trafficking in women and girls; UNGA Res 58/147 (19 February 2004) UN Doc A/RES/58/147, on the elimination of domestic violence against women; and UNGA Res 56/128 (30 January 2002) UN Doc A/RES/56/128, on traditional or customary practices affecting the health of women and girls.

[245] Inter-American Convention on the Prevention, Punishment and Eradication of Violence against Women (Convention of Belem Do Para) (adopted 9 June 1994, entered into force 5 March 1995) (1994) 33 ILM 1534, Art 7. See also UNDAW, Background Expert Paper (n 244).

[246] Inter-American Commission on Human Rights, *Maria Mamerita Mestanza Chavez v Peru* (friendly settlement) (22 October 2003) Report No 71/03, Petition 12.191, www1.umn.edu/humanrts/research/Peru-REPORT%20No.%2071%20Mestanza.pdf.

[247] *X and Y v The Netherlands* (App No 8978/80) (1985) 8 EHRR 235, para 30.

[248] *A v The United Kingdom* (App No 100/1997/884/1096) (1998) 27 EHRR 611, para 24.

[249] *Ms AT v Hungary* (Decision) CEDAW Committee (views adopted 26 January 2005) Communication No 2/2003 UN Doc CEDAW/C/32/D/2/2003. For a detailed discussion of this case see ch 1, pp 43–45. See also *The Vienna Intervention Centre against Domestic Violence and the Association for Women's Access to Justice on behalf of Hakan Goekce, Handan Goekce, and Guelue Goekce (descendants of the deceased) v Austria* (Decision) CEDAW Committee (views adopted 6 August 2007) Communication No 5/2005 UN Doc CEDAW/C/39/D/5/2005 (*Goekce v Austria*) and *The Vienna Intervention Centre against Domestic Violence and the Association for*

It is logical that enacting legislation would be a state's first port of call in addressing systemic intimate violence. The question, however, is—what legislation? The former Special Rapporteur on violence against women, Radhika Coomaraswamy, prioritised the creation of model legislation regarding violence against women.[250] The model legislation includes draft definitions, complaint mechanisms, civil and criminal provisions, a description of judicial responsibilities, and sentencing guidelines.[251]

It is not necessarily appropriate to have uniform legislation. Different legal systems and different communities will require different approaches. However, states should adopt comprehensive domestic violence legislation and there are fundamentals that should inhere in all such legislation. Some of these are discussed below.

Anti-discrimination Provisions

States should adopt basic anti-discrimination legislation or incorporate the equality principle into their legal systems by abolishing discriminatory laws and adopting appropriate ones that prevent and punish unfair discrimination against women.[252] In his study on violence against women, the Secretary-General identifies the intersection between violence against women and discrimination, defining gender-based violence as 'Any act of gender-based violence that is directed against a woman because she is a woman or that affects women disproportionately'.[253]

South Africa, for example, has injected the notion of equality between men and women into its Constitution, which, as supreme law, requires the incorporation of equality considerations into other national and provincial legislation.[254] This was followed by, for example, the Alteration of Sex Description and Sex Status Act,[255] which seeks to dismantle gender stereotypes; the Promotion of Equality and Prevention of Unfair Discrimination Act, which aims to prevent and prohibit unfair discrimination and harassment, to promote

---

Women's Access to Justice on behalf of Banu Akbak, Gülen Khan, and Melissa Özdemir (descendants of the deceased), alleged victim: Fatma Yildirim (deceased) v Austria (Decision) CEDAW Committee (views adopted 1 October 2007) Communication No 6/2005 UN Doc CEDAW/C/39/D/6/2005 (*Yildirim v Austria*).

[250] See Special Rapporteur 1996 Report (n 115). Coomaraswamy submitted a framework for model legislation on domestic violence. See UNCHR, *Report of the Special Rapporteur on violence against women, its causes and consequences, Ms Radhika Coomaraswamy: A Framework for Model Legislation on Domestic Violence* (2 February 1996) UN Doc E/CN.4/1996/53/Add.2 (hereinafter Special Rapporteur, Framework for Model Legislation).
[251] Special Rapporteur, Framework for Model Legislation (n 250).
[252] CEDAW (n 9) Arts 2(a), (b), (c), (f), (d), 3, 6, 11(3), 15(1) and (4), 16(1)(f) and (2), 18. *cf* Shelton (n 239) 27.
[253] UNDAW, Background Expert Paper (n 244) 2.
[254] See the South African Constitution, 108 of 1996, Art 5.
[255] Act No 49 of 2003.

equality and to prohibit hate speech;[256] and the Promotion of Equality and Prevention of Unfair Discrimination Amendment Act, which provides for the inculcation of gender and sex equality within governmental and other institutions, including the establishment of the Commission for Gender Equality.[257]

The UK has an extensive and complex array of anti-discrimination laws, including the Equal Pay Act 1970; the Equal Pay (Northern Ireland) Act 1970; the Sex Discrimination Act 1975; the Sex Discrimination (Northern Ireland) Orders 1976 and 1988; the Sex Discrimination Act 1975 (Amendment) Regulations 2008 (SI 2008/656) (which implement Council Directive 2002/73/EC concerning the principle of equal treatment of men and women as regards access to employment, vocational training and promotion and working conditions); the Sex Discrimination (Amendment of Legislation) Regulations 2008 (SI 2008/963) (which implement EU Gender Directive (2004/113/EC) concerning equal treatment between men and women with regard to access to and supply of goods and services which are available to the public); the Sexual Offences Act 2003 (which strengthened and modernised the law on sexual offences, including a statutory definition of consent, a test of reasonable belief in consent and a set of evidential and conclusive presumptions about consent and the defendant's belief in consent);[258] the Equality Act 2006 (which established the Commission for Equality and Human Rights); and the Forced Marriage (Civil Protection) Act 2007 (Forced Marriage Act).

This web of legislation is complicated but necessary. It identifies the various manifestations of gender inequality, which are in turn causes of the continued exposure of women to domestic violence. Equality legislation imposes an obligation on state authorities to implement the law equally, regardless of, inter alia, sex and gender.

Anti-discrimination legislation can be approached in many different ways, particularly in relation to the extent to which a state should be 'colour-blind', that is, treat all people as the same, or take 'positive steps' to assist those who have been disadvantaged by past discrimination. Justice Albie Sachs of the South African Constitutional Court noted that 'Equality should not be confused with uniformity; in fact uniformity can be the enemy of equality. Equality means equal concern and respect across difference. It does not presuppose the elimination or suppression of difference.'[259] Violence against women is an area of discrimination which usually requires some kind of proactive policy to prevent its occurrence and remedy its effects. Equality legislation is the point of departure. It encapsulates the broad principles of equality before the law, equal treatment by the law and equal enjoyment of human rights.

---

[256] Act No 4 of 2000.
[257] Act No 52 of 2002.
[258] Sexual Offences Act 2003 (c 42), ss 74–76.
[259] See eg *National Coalition for Gay and Lesbian Equality v Minister of Justice* (1999) (1) SA 6 (CC), para 32, per Justice Sachs.

As well as legislating on equality, states should be responsible for inculcating a norm of equality within their society. This can be achieved by educating legal, police and other officials to ensure that the re-victimisation of women does not occur because of laws insensitive to gender considerations, enforcement practices or other interventions.[260] This applies equally to judges, who should have a basic understanding of gender theory, gender discrimination and society's gender power structure.[261]

Acts of Violence

Domestic violence legislation requires a clear, specific and encompassing definition of domestic violence. The definition should be precise about what types of acts constitute domestic violence, and should reflect the nuances of systemic intimate violence as described above. Acts can be broken down into five general categories of harm: physical violence, sexual violence or harassment, threats of violence, extreme verbal abuse, and controlling behaviour, which would include economic abuse.[262]

Physical abuse includes actual acts of violence and can range in levels of severity. This range of violence *should* be included in national domestic violence legislation, so that violence includes, for example, slapping, shoving and pushing, on the one hand, and burning, raping and breaking on the other. This is not to be confused with the requirement of severity necessary to trigger international law. As far as national law is concerned, all violence is unacceptable and should trigger a proportionate response. The Special Rapporteur's model legislation includes the following definition of acts of domestic violence:

> All acts of gender-based physical, psychological and sexual abuse by a family member against women in the family, ranging from simple assaults to aggravated physical battery, kidnapping, threats, intimidation, coercion, stalking, humiliating verbal abuse, forcible or unlawful entry, arson, destruction of property, sexual violence, marital rape, dowry or bride-price related violence, female genital mutilation, violence related to exploitation through prostitution, violence against household workers and attempts to commit such acts shall be termed 'domestic violence'.[263]

---

[260] ibid, 14. See also DEVAW (n 9) Art 4(j).

[261] See eg Liliana Silva Miguez, 'The Efficiency of Legislation Enacted to Face Harmful Acts against Women in Latin America and the Caribbean' (Expert Paper prepared for the United Nations Division for the Advancement of Women, Expert Group Meeting on good practices in legislation to address harmful practices against women) (11 May 2009) UN Doc EGM/GPLHP/2009/EP.13, 7 (hereinafter Latin America and the Caribbean Expert Paper), www.un.org/womenwatch/daw/egm/vaw_legislation_2009/Expert%20Paper%20EGMGPLHP%20_Liliana%20Silva%20Miguez_.pdf. See also the UN Committee for the Elimination of All Forms of Discrimination against Women, 'General Recommendation 19: Violence against Women' (1992) UN Doc A/47/38, Art 24(f) (states should take 'effective measures' to mitigate attitudes and practices that discriminate against women); Art 24(t)(ii) (educational programmes 'to change attitudes concerning the roles and status of men and women'). See also Amnesty International (n 33) 40.

[262] See eg Heimer et al (n 33) 17, 20.

[263] See Special Rapporteur, Framework for Model Legislation (n 250) para 11.

The definition of sexual abuse should reflect the broad definition that is developing in international law. International jurisprudence recognises that rape is a 'form of aggression' and that 'the central elements of the crime of rape cannot be captured in a mechanical description of objects and body parts'.[264] The ICTR and ICTY jurisprudence established that sexual violence is not 'limited to physical invasion of the human body and may include acts which do not involve penetration or even physical contact'.[265] Moreover, it was recognised that coercion need not manifest in physical force but includes threats, intimidation, extortion and 'other forms of duress which prey on fear or desperation'.[266]

Sexual violence should not be limited to penetration, and should include penetration by non-body parts. The definition should encapsulate the idea that the sexual act 'abuses, humiliates, degrades or otherwise violates the sexual integrity of the complainant'.[267] The concept of sexual violence should encompass 'any physical, visual, verbal or sexual act that is experienced by the woman or girl, at that time or later, as a threat, invasion or assault, that has the effect of hurting her or degrading her and/or takes away her ability to control intimate contact'.[268]

The link between sexual violence and the violation of male honour continues to be an impediment to justice for victims.[269] We have seen developments in this regard in Argentina, Bolivia, Brazil and Ecuador, which, for example, have revised their penal codes to reflect sexual violence as a violation of the survivor rather than a threat to the honour or morality of third persons.[270] The Turkish Penal Code 2004 and the Swedish Penal Code 1998 have eliminated all references to morality, chastity and honour defences to sexual violence, which is now categorised as a 'crime against the individual'.[271] It is also important that evidence of a victim's previous sexual conduct should not as a rule be admissible in criminal or civil proceedings relating to domestic violence.[272]

Legislative approaches to domestic violence should also include forced marriage and marital rape.[273] The concept of rape in intimate relationships remains highly problematic,[274] but increasing numbers of countries are removing

---

[264] *Prosecutor v Akayesu* (Judgment) ICTR-96-4-T, T Ch I (2 September 1998), para 687.

[265] ibid, para 688.

[266] ibid.

[267] South African Domestic Violence Act, s 1.

[268] Heimer et al (n 33) 17.

[269] See UNDAW, Background Expert Paper (n 244) 28 (defining sexual assault as a 'violation of bodily integrity and sexual autonomy').

[270] ibid, 28. See also Latin America and the Caribbean Expert Paper (n 261) 4 (describing amendments to Puerto Rico's penal code regarding sexual violence).

[271] UNDAW, Background Expert Paper (n 244) 28.

[272] Latin America and the Caribbean Expert Paper (n 261) 4 (prohibiting evidence of the previous sexual conduct of rape victims. However, some countries in the region, such as Brazil, Nicaragua, Panama and Guatemala, still allow the aggressor to escape criminal sanctions if he marries the victim).

[273] See eg the UK Forced Marriage (Civil Protection) Act 2007. See also UNDAW, Background Expert Paper (n 244) 29.

[274] Nigeria Expert Paper (n 139) 3–4, 15.

exemptions for rape within an intimate relationship from their penal codes.[275] In 2002, for example, in the case of *Forum for Women, Law and Development (FWLD) v His Majesty's Government/Nepal (HMG/N)*, the Supreme Court of Nepal found that the marital rape exemption was unconstitutional and contrary to the ICCPR and CEDAW.[276] In 2003, the Criminal Code (Sexual Offences and Crimes against Children) Act 2002 of Papua New Guinea also abolished marital immunity in relation to rape.[277]

Ultimately, the definition of sexual violence must incorporate gender-neutral definitions, stranger, non-stranger and family sexual violence and a wide range of invasive acts that constitute sexual violence, and must ensure that the element of non-consent neither re-victimises the victim nor presents a prohibitive barrier to prosecution of the perpetraror.[278]

The definition should also include threats of physical violence towards a complainant and threats to harm third parties.[279] For a person who has been harmed, the threat of further violence is very real and may be as frightening as the violence itself. Threats to kill may be expressed at the same time as earlier threats of abuse are carried out, making the threat particularly real. The threat of violence and actual violence become similar instruments of control, oppression and harm.[280]

Non-physical abuse is much harder to identify and prove. Legislative definitions should be clear about the characteristics that make certain forms of non-physical abuse as harmful as physical violence. Non-physical abuse includes economic abuse, which is the 'unreasonable deprivation of economic or financial resources to which a complainant is entitled under law or which the complainant requires out of necessity'.[281] It is generally accepted that good practice domestic violence legislation should include financial abuse.[282] A number of countries have included this within their legislation, such as India (Protection of Women

[275] See UNDAW, Background Expert Paper (n 244) 29 (regarding the criminalisation of marital rape in Lesotho, Namibia, South Africa and Swaziland).
[276] UNDAW, Background Expert Paper (n 244) 29.
[277] Karen Stefiszyn, 'A Brief Overview of Recent Developments in Sexual Offences Legislation in Southern Africa' (Expert Paper prepared for the United Nations Division for the Advancement of Women, Expert Group Meeting on good practices in legislation on violence against women) (12 May 2008) UN Doc EGM/GPLVAW/2008/EP.04, 4, www.un.org/womenwatch/daw/egm/vaw_legislation_2008/expertpapers/EGMGPLVAW%20Paper%20(Karen%20Stefiszyn).pdf (states which have not criminalised marital rape include Tanzania, Botswana, Zambia and Malawi. In Zimbabwe, although marital rape is prohibited, prosecutions cannot be instituted without the authorisation of the Attorney General).
[278] ibid, 3 (noting the Namibian Combating of Rape Act 2000 as an example of a model statutory definition of rape which is gender neutral and includes a range of sexual acts, without the element of consent. This is contrasted with Tanzania's Sexual Offences Special Provisions Act, which limits rape to non-consensual sexual intercourse by men with women).
[279] South African Domestic Violence Act, s 1 (defining physical abuse as 'any act or threatened act of physical violence towards a complainant').
[280] Heimer et al (n 33) 17.
[281] South African Domestic Violence Act, s 1.
[282] UNDAW, Background Expert Paper (n 244) 26.

from Domestic Violence Act 2005) and Brazil (Maria da Penha Law 2006, which includes patrimonial damage).

Extreme jealousy is another element of non-physical violence and is a common component of domestic violence.[283] This is manifested in controlling behaviour that may prevent the abused having contact with third parties, including relatives and friends.[284] Constant insults and derision may also constitute acts of domestic violence. Psychological violence is difficult to prove and the procedural and evidentiary rules proscribing this element should take into account both due process concerns and victim-sensitive considerations. This may include, for example, the support of professionals or expert service providers.[285]

Continuum of Harm

One of the most important elements of domestic violence that should be reflected in national legislation is the continuing nature of acts of violence that, independently, may not seem severe, but cumulatively are serious.[286] The South African Domestic Violence Act, for example, defines domestic violence as physical, sexual, emotional, verbal or psychological abuse which 'harms, or may cause imminent harm to, the safety, health or wellbeing of the complainant'.[287] The reference to 'imminent harm' is not necessarily correct. The act of domestic violence may not cause imminent harm but it may cause and contribute to long-term harm.

The key is to understand that discrete acts of violence or abuse are actually part of one ongoing assault. The assault comprises a sequence of psychological, physical or sexual violations, which often occur within a context of controlling behaviour, threats, restriction on freedom of movement and sexual harassment. Legislation should guide judicial and enforcement authorities to identify such a continuum of harm. This is particularly important because victims are often the least able to identify the continuum.[288]

In Sweden, for example, the Law on Gross Violation of Integrity and Gross Violation of a Woman's Integrity applies where an abuser commits 'repeated acts of harassment or abuse against a woman with whom he is, or has been, in an intimate relationship'.[289] The provision applies to offences such as assault,

---

[283] See Ellsberg et al (n 15) 1602. See also Schneider (n 33) 65.

[284] See Heimer et al (n 33) 30.

[285] UNDAW, Background Expert Paper (n 244) 26 (describing the difficulty of proving psychological and economic violence and the importance of experts in assessing this form of harm).

[286] The notion of a continuum of violence, which includes the threat of violence, is discussed in analyses of domestic violence in Nicaragua. See Ellsberg et al (n 15) 1596.

[287] See South African Domestic Violence Act, s 1.

[288] See Amnesty International (n 33) 6. See also Heimer et al (n 33) 17 (indicating that the continuum approach to gender-related violence 'views threats, violence and sexual abuse as actions impossible to isolate from one another; characteristically the boundaries between them are fluid and actions merge into one another').

[289] Amnesty International (n 33) 19 (citing ch 4, s 4a of the Swedish Penal Code).

molestation, violation of the privacy of the home and sexual coercion, all with the aim of filling a vacuum where ordinary assault offences may not apply.[290] The original objective of this law was to take into account repeated violations of a woman's integrity jointly. This gives a context to seemingly 'minor' incidents of harm, revealing the continuum of danger, and results in a more stringent sentence than would be the case if the acts were considered separately.[291]

Relationship

While the discussion of domestic violence in international law focuses on violence against women, it is an undisputed fact that similar forms of violence are perpetrated by men and women against children; by women against women; by men against men; by women against men; by carers against the elderly; by carers against the disabled or people with learning difficulties; and between siblings. Domestic violence legislation should embrace as wide an array of relationships as possible and provide remedies for violence committed in all types of intimate or private relationship. It is also important to note that violence against non-human animals is often a sign of violence against women or other family members.

Specific reference should therefore be made to same-sex relationships, relationships between carers and dependants, such as the elderly and disabled people, and intimate relationships among people belonging to specific religious or cultural groups.[292] The legislation should also specifically cover—and make provision for—protection of women who are non-citizens.[293]

The legislation should also cover both formal relationships recognised by the state, such as marriage or same-sex cohabitation, and informal relationships, such as boyfriends/girlfriends. But it is important to note that the abuse may also occur once the relationship has expired. In general, legislation should cover the following relationships: spouses, live-in partners, former spouses or partners, girlfriends and boyfriends (including those not living in the same house), relatives and household workers.[294]

Criminal v Civil Sanctions

Many states have established both civil and criminal measures to address domestic violence. While each has its place and role in addressing domestic violence, there are benefits and disadvantages to both systems.

---

[290] ibid.
[291] ibid, 20.
[292] ibid, para 8.
[293] ibid, para 9.
[294] See Special Rapporteur, Framework for Model Legislation (n 250) para 7.

Sweden's Law on Gross Violation of Integrity and Gross Violation of a Woman's Integrity includes a combination of criminal and civil provisions that take into account many of the elements of systemic intimate violence.[295] The legislation recognises that intimate violence

> is often systematic and it may be difficult for the victim to keep track of the events and dates when the crimes were committed. The law on violation of a woman's integrity takes into consideration all aspects of the abused woman's life, characterised by threats, assault and mental stress, and has been drawn up so as to facilitate prosecution of perpetrators who repeatedly have violated the integrity of a woman with whom they are in an intimate relationship.[296]

Prior to the development of international jurisprudence regarding women's rights in international law, most jurisdictions did not have specific legislation— and certainly not criminal sanctions—addressing domestic violence. Of course, spousal violence technically constitutes assault and battery, but, for the reasons described above, this generic legal categorisation was inappropriate and inadequate. Domestic violence advocates began to call for criminal sanctions for domestic violence.[297] They argued correctly that creating a specific crime (independent of assault and battery) demonstrates the state's serious approach to preventing and punishing domestic violence. This sends a signal of approbation which changes society's perception of domestic violence as a 'family' matter and places it firmly within the realm of objectionable criminal conduct.

Criminal sanctions may also provide better protection for victims if the abuser is imprisoned. It was thought that criminal sanctions would improve protection for victims, who often would not pursue complaints, either because the couple had reconciled or because the victim feared the repercussions of involving the authorities. In 1993, the CEDAW Committee endorsed the notion of criminalising intimate violence on the basis that if such cases

> were treated as other criminal offences were, with the police being obliged to arrest and prosecute the perpetrators regardless of whether the women wished to prosecute or not, and with therapy provided for the perpetrator, the positive outcome would be a changed social attitude towards domestic violence.[298]

The ECtHR supported the criminalisation of intimate violence on the basis that the need for protection exists '*erga omnes*, whilst an injunction could only be directed to a limited circle of persons'.[299] The decision of the ECtHR in *X and Y v The Netherlands* that 'civil law lacked the deterrent effect that was inherent in the criminal law' is appealing.[300] As with sexual abuse, systemic intimate

---

[295] Amnesty International (n 33) 19 (citing ch 4, s 4a of the Swedish Penal Code). See also ibid, 35 fn 45 ('Gross violation of a woman's integrity accounted for 1,840 cases of suspected crime').

[296] ibid.

[297] General Recommendation 19 (n 261) Arts 24(g), (h) (j) (k), (l), (m), (o), (p), (q) and 24(t)(iii).

[298] CEDAW Concluding Observations: Sweden (n 6) para 502.

[299] These were statements made by the Commission, which were adopted by the ECtHR in *X and Y v The Netherlands,* paras 26–27.

[300] ibid.

violence is 'a case where fundamental values and essential aspects of private life are at stake. Effective deterrence is indispensable in this area and it can be achieved only by criminal law provisions; indeed, it is by such provisions that the matter is normally regulated'.[301]

However, the criminalisation of intimate violence is not necessarily appropriate for all jurisdictions and there are disadvantages to activating the criminal system. Given the complexity of intimate violence, the victim's emotional commitment to her abuser may deter her from taking such a drastic step as having him arrested. She may want the violence to stop but may not necessarily want her partner to be imprisoned. This is exacerbated if the abuser is the primary or only earner in the home. The abused, therefore, may be reluctant to report the abuse for fear of losing the financial support her partner provides, particularly if that support includes financial care for her children.

In addition, the standard of proof in criminal matters is much higher than in civil cases. Ensuring a successful claim is difficult. Criminal matters are time-consuming and do not provide the urgent response that victims often need. Experts in the USA indicate that, despite criminalisation, few domestic violence cases actually result in substantial prison sentences.[302]

If a prosecutor is responsible for running the case against the abuser, all power is taken out of the hands of the abused. This has advantages because, as has been discussed, the psychological damage caused by the violence may inhibit an individual's ability to engage in legal action. Therefore, placing the decision to prosecute in the hands of the prosecutor (or having a system of mandatory prosecution or arrest) may better facilitate the safety of the abused. On the other hand, if a victim knows that by calling the police she will trigger an unstoppable series of legal events, which could culminate in the long-term imprisonment of her intimate partner, she may be daunted by the prospect and refrain from contacting the police at all.

A balance needs to be struck, and it makes sense to have an interactive process between the abused and the official legal services.

Some states require the victim to consent to criminal proceedings. For example, in Norway, violence against women is a criminal offence but the abuser may

---

[301] It is important to note that the ECtHR did not base its decision on a violation of Art 13 of the Convention, which enjoins states to provide effective remedies for a violation of a right in the Convention. Rather, it found that because there was a clear violation of the victim's right to family integrity for which no remedy was available, it did not have to pursue a similar analysis in terms of Art 13.

[302] See Sally F Goldfarb, 'The Legal Response to Violence against Women in the United States of America: Recent Reforms and Continuing Challenges' (Expert Paper prepared for the United Nations Division for the Advancement of Women, Expert Group Meeting on good practices in legislation on violence against women) (30 July 2008) UN Doc EGM/GPLVAW/2008/EP.06, www.un.org/womenwatch/daw/egm/vaw_legislation_2008/expertpapers/EGMGPLVAW%20Pap er%20(Sally%20Goldfarb).pdf (hereinafter USA Expert Paper) 3 (despite the criminalisation of domestic violence, few cases result in substantial prison sentences. Empirical research conducted to date has failed to demonstrate that batterer intervention programmes are effective in reducing recidivism).

be prosecuted only at the instigation of the injured party. Norway also facilitates the appointment of an intermediary to advise the abused of her options, which enhances the sense of choice that she may experience.[303]

However, this approach was criticised in the recent case of *Opuz v Turkey*. The ECtHR analysed the provisions of Turkish domestic violence legislation which provided that criminal proceedings in domestic violence cases could not continue if the victim withdrew her complaint.[304] The ECtHR took a most reasonable approach to the criminalisation of domestic violence. It held that the decision whether or not to proceed with a criminal trial where the victim withdraws her/his complaint should lie within the discretion of the prosecuting authority, which will primarily take into account the public interest in continuing with the criminal proceedings.[305] The Court identified 11 Member States of the Council of Europe which require the authorities to continue criminal proceedings despite the victim withdrawing her complaint in domestic violence cases.[306] These countries are Albania, Austria, Bosnia and Herzegovina, Estonia, Greece, Italy, Poland, Portugal, San Marino, Spain and Switzerland. Romania is the only state that bases the continuance of criminal proceedings entirely, and in all circumstances, on the wishes of the victim.[307]

Ideally, the prosecution authorities should only pursue a complaint with the support and consent of the victim. However, the prosecutor should retain a discretionary power to continue with or instigate criminal proceedings even if the complaint is withdrawn where certain factors pertain, including the following:

- How serious was the offence?
- Are the victim's injuries physical or psychological?
- Has the defendant made threats of violence previously, particularly if the threats were repeated to or in the presence of third parties?
- Did the defendant use a weapon (including the brandishing of a weapon)?
- Has the defendant made any attacks or threats since the attack in question?
- Did the defendant plan the attack?
- What has been the effect (including psychological) on any children living in the household?
- What are the chances of the defendant offending again?
- What is the extent of the continuing threat to the health and safety of the victim or anyone else who was, or could become, involved?
- What is the current state of the victim's relationship with the defendant?
- What would be the effect on that relationship of continuing with the prosecution against the victim's wishes?

[303] See *Report of the Third Session of the Committee on the Elimination of Discrimination against Women* (27 June 1984) UN Doc A/39/45, pp 37–45, paras 277–338.
[304] *Opuz v Turkey* (App No 33401/02) ECtHR 9 June 2009.
[305] ibid, para 89.
[306] ibid, para 87.
[307] ibid, paras 87, 90.

- What is the history of the relationship? In particular, has there been any violence in the past?
- Is the victim dependent on the defendant for immigration status?
- What is the extent of the economic dependence of the victim on the defendant and what is the extent of his ability to exploit that dependence?
- What is the defendant's criminal history?[308]

Discretion is important and, as the ECtHR noted, the more serious the offence or the greater the risk of further offences, the more likely it is that the prosecution should continue in the public interest, even if the victim withdraws her complaint.[309] The prosecution certainly should not be dependent solely on the victim's complaint. However, the safety and long-term interests of the victim must always be a consideration that runs alongside the public interest test.

Ultimately, criminal sanctions should be applied effectively and with sensitivity to the safety of the victim and the fact that she might be coerced or manipulated into withdrawing her complaint. Criminal sanctions and their implementation must provide a prompt and effective deterrent, capable of ensuring the prevention of further unlawful acts of violence.

Balancing Civil and Criminal Sanctions: The Protection Order

Domestic violence legislation must provide victims with immediate, easily obtainable legal remedies. For the most part, civil remedies for domestic violence cases include some form of protection order. Protection orders, also known as restraining orders, are legally binding court orders that prohibit an individual who has committed an act of domestic violence from further abusing the victim.

Many states have enacted some form of protection or restraining order facility, falling within the realm of civil law.[310] Ideally this facility should enable an individual to seek an urgent restraining order, which does not require the presence of the abuser or the rigorous evidentiary burdens of criminal law. The urgent restraining order should be temporary and include a return date, on which the judicial officer will make a further determination. The defendant should be given due and proper notice of the return date and regular standards of proof, rules of evidence and principles of justice should apply. This allows an individual to seek immediate redress without having to incur the cost or emotional strain of proving the abuse beyond reasonable doubt or having to secure the presence of the defendant.

---

[308] Some of these considerations are listed by the ECtHR. ibid, para 138.

[309] ibid, para 139.

[310] One of the most progressive definitions is in the South African Domestic Violence Act. The US also enacted civil legislation, but it was struck down by the Supreme Court in the case of *United States v Morrison*, 529 US 598 (2000) (holding that Congress exceeded its powers under the Commerce Clause and s5 of the Fourteenth Amendment when it enacted the VAWA civil rights provision). See also USA Expert Paper (n 302) 2.

Granting a protection order without the presence of the defendant is a form of ex parte proceedings (that is, only one party is involved). These are exceptional proceedings as they breach the natural law principle of *audi alteram partem* (that both parties to a legal claim should be heard), but they are essential as a temporary stopgap in domestic violence cases. The UK's Forced Marriage Act, for example, provides that an ex parte order can be used when it is just and convenient to do so.[311] Ex parte orders are used in emergencies when the usual notice periods informing the defendant of the proceedings cannot be complied with. The UK Family Law Act 1996 contains similar provisions.[312] The Act requires the court to have regard to the risk of significant harm to the person to be protected or another person if the order is not made immediately.

At the same time, the temporary nature of the restraining order with a return date ensures that procedural fairness is maintained, thereby respecting the demands of fairness inherent in the rules of procedure and evidence. For example, in 1998, as part of the country's progress towards gender equality, South Africa enacted the Domestic Violence Act, which includes a two-part protection order process.[313] Victims may apply for an urgent temporary retraining order, which may be heard as soon as is reasonably possible.[314] This is designed to be a simple process, with few evidentiary requirements, and may be granted in the absence of the defendant.[315] At this hearing a return date is set. The interim protection order must then be served on the respondent.[316] On balance, emergency orders should prioritise survivor safety over property rights and other considerations, such as the reconciliation of families or communities.[317]

At the second court date the claimant may obtain a final protection order.[318] The defendant must be present and there is greater scope as to the types of maintenance order that the judges may make.[319] The court is required (ie, there is no discretion), if it finds on a balance of probabilities that the respondent is committing or has committed an act of domestic violence, to issue a final

---

[311] Forced Marriage (Civil Protection) Act 2007, s 63D(1).

[312] UK Family Law Act 1996, s 45 deals with ex parte occupation and non-molestation orders.

[313] See n 36.

[314] South African Domestic Violence Act, s 5(1).

[315] ibid, s 5. The South African Domestic Violence Act replaced the Prevention of Family Violence Act 133 of 1993. The new Act is a considerable improvement on its predecessor, which was criticised as being an 'electioneering strategy undertaken in haste': Elsje Bonthuys, 'The Solution? Project 100— Domestic Violence' (1997) 114 *South African Law Journal* 371, 372. One of the most problematic aspects of the 1993 Act was the lack of provision for interim protection orders, with the result that the rules of procedure and evidence surrounding the issuing of a protection order were necessarily more restrictive. To some extent, many of the problems that existed in the 1993 Act have been alleviated.

[316] South African Domestic Violence Act, s (5)(6).

[317] UNDAW, Background Expert Paper (n 244) 53 (under the UK Family Law Act 1996, a complainant may apply for an occupation order in addition to a protection order to bar the offender from the home or restrict him to a particular part of the home. Similar orders are provided for in s 20 of the Ghanian Domestic Violence Act 2007 and s 19 of the Indian Protection of Women from Domestic Violence Act 2005).

[318] South African Domestic Violence Act, s 6.

[319] The court's power in respect of a protection order is outlined in s 7 of the South African Domestic Violence Act.

protection order.[320] The protection order can consist of an order regarding no further abuse;[321] no further contact;[322] seizure of weapons;[323] police assistance;[324] confidentiality;[325] monetary orders;[326] or eviction orders.[327]

An interesting aspect of the final hearing is that unless he is represented by legal counsel, the respondent 'is not entitled to cross-examine directly a person who is in a domestic relationship with the respondent and shall put any question to such witness by stating the question to the court, and the court is to repeat the question accurately to the respondent'.[328] This recognises the unusual form of fear that is involved in intimate violence and that direct interaction between the accused and the applicant would undermine the victim's security and her faith in the judicial process.

This two-part process strikes a balance between the need for an urgent remedy, on the one hand, and the *audi alteram partem* principle, on the other. By providing for a return date when the respondent can plead his case, the Act provides the immediate and necessary relief without impinging too greatly on the procedural rights of the respondent. Therefore, although an application for a protection order can be made ex parte, only an interim protection order should be granted so that the respondent has an opportunity to contest the provisional order on a return date.[329]

In legislation of this type, the duration of both interim and final orders should be appropriate given the type of harm experienced and other factors, such as the complexity of the judicial system.[330]

In respect of certain types of domestic violence, it should also be possible for third parties to request an urgent protection order on behalf of the victim. This has to be approached with caution and should only be used where the victim's situation prevents her from accessing the court.[331]

---

[320] ibid, s 6(4).

[321] ibid, s (1)(a), (b), (g), (h).

[322] Or restraining orders. ibid, s (1)(c), (d), (e), (f).

[323] ibid, s 2(a).

[324] ibid, s 2(b).

[325] ibid, s 5(a) and (b).

[326] ibid, ss 3, 4.

[327] ibid, s 1(c).

[328] ibid, s 6(3).

[329] ibid, s 5(6). For a discussion of this issue see Brigitte Clerk and Lirieka Meintjies-Van Der Walt, 'The New Domestic Violence Bill: Rhetoric or Reality?' (1998) 115 *South African Law Journal* 760.

[330] See Cheryl A Thomas, 'Legal Reform on Domestic Violence in Central and Eastern Europe and the Former Soviet Union' (Expert Paper prepared for the United Nations Division for the Advancement of Women, Expert Group Meeting on good practices in legislation on violence against women) (12 May 2008 (as revised 17 June 2008)) UN EGM/GPLVAW/2008/EP.01, www.un.org/womenwatch/daw/egm/vaw_legislation_2008/expertpapers/EGMGPLVAW%20Paper%20(Cheryl%20Thomas).pdf (hereinafter CEE/FSU Expert Paper) (discussing the duration of protection orders) 5.

[331] See Rosa Logar, 'Good Practices and Challenges in Legislation on Violence against Women' (Expert Paper prepared for the United Nations Division for the Advancement of Women, Expert Group Meeting on good practices in legislation on violence against women) (20 May 2008) UN Doc EGM/GPLVAW/2008/EP.10, www.un.org/womenwatch/daw/egm/vaw_legislation_2008/expertpapers/EGMGPLVAW%20Paper%20_Rosa%20Logar_.pdf (hereinafter Europe Expert Paper) 13.

This innovative mechanism was used in the UK's Forced Marriage Act, which seeks to protect individuals from being forced to enter into marriage without their free and full consent as well as those who have already been forced to enter into marriage without such consent. The Forced Marriage Act allows applications for a forced marriage protection order to be made by a relevant third party or any person with the leave of the court.[332] The court will decide whether or not a third party may bring the claim and will take into account the third party's connection with the person to be protected; the third party's knowledge of the circumstances of the person to be protected; and the wishes and feelings of the person to be protected so far as they are reasonably ascertainable and so far as the court considers it appropriate, in light of the person's age and understanding, to have regard to them.[333]

This type of representative claim allows NGOs, relatives and other duly authorised persons to bring claims on behalf of victims in circumstances where the victim has been imprisoned by the abuser, is physically unable to be present in the court, or, in order to escape the abuser, has had to move away from the immediate jurisdiction of the court. The Special Rapporteur on violence against women has also argued for greater involvement on the part of the community, comprising the victim's neighbours, friends and health professionals, who may be able to contact the authorities on the victim's behalf.[334] However, the involvement of parties other than the victim and perpetrator is a delicate matter and should not constitute an inappropriate amount of intervention into the choices or rights of the parties.[335]

Although a final protection order may be issued imposing the most rigid constraints on the abuser, there is the very real possibility that the abuser will simply ignore the order.[336] While the law does have remedies for such an event, namely arrest for violating a court order, it is not unusual for the enforcement process to be lengthy, not taken seriously and, often, too late.

Furthermore, the issuing of an order might not serve to intimidate the abuser. Instead, by disempowering him, it might enrage him to such an extent that a new cycle of violence begins.[337] Violence in fact escalates upon separation or when the victim seeks external help.

It is at this point that criminal sanctions are necessary. Non-compliance with a protection order should be a criminal offence and/or carry with it severe financial penalties, depending on the nature of the violation.[338] The accused

---

[332] UK Forced Marriage (Civil Protection) Act 2007, s 63C(2)(b), (3).

[333] ibid, s 63C(4).

[334] Special Rapporteur, Framework for Model Legislation (n 250) 3 (discussing community participation in eradicating domestic violence and third party protection orders, which may empower the community to participate in coming forward to corroborate/support victims).

[335] See eg CEE/FSU Expert Paper (n 330) 8. See also this discussion in *Opuz v Turkey* (App No 33401/02) ECtHR 9 June 2009, para 138.

[336] See eg *Goekce v Austria* (n 249) para 3.

[337] Fedler (n 104) 246.

[338] Nigeria Expert Paper (n 139) 17 (describing the Violence (Prohibition) Bill 2003, which carries a penalty of N50,000 fine or five years' imprisonment or both for a breach of a protection or interim order).

must be detained and should be released on bail only upon the order of a specially designated official (such as a senior ranking officer, prosecuting authority or a member of the judiciary) who is trained and has expertise in the field of domestic violence.

Legislation should require the state's legal authorities to develop and put into effect written procedures for officials policing and prosecuting crimes of domestic violence.[339] The Committee of Ministers of the Council of Europe has recommended that Member States should make provisions to ensure that criminal proceedings can be initiated by the public prosecutor and that prosecutors should consider CEDAW in deciding whether or not to prosecute in the public interest.[340] As regards violence in the family, the Committee of Ministers recommended that Member States should classify all forms of violence within the family as criminal offences, while at the same time enabling the judiciary to adopt interim measures to protect victims during the (often lengthy) criminal process. During the period of the criminal trial, the defendant should not be released if the violence was physical and, in the opinion of an independent expert, there is a reasonable risk that the defendant might harm the complainant or her family.

All complaints made against the victim and all acts of violence (as defined above, to include threats of violence) must as far as possible be included in the indictment. And this information process must be speedy. The crucial moment for a successful prosecution is at the initial stage of the investigation, immediately after the complaint has been lodged, when evidence and testimonies are most reliable.[341] If too much time passes, the recollection of the violence may be dulled, and police and victim interviews may be insubstantial.[342] There may also be a lack of documentation regarding the injuries sustained by the abused.

The victim's testimony should be sufficient to launch criminal proceedings and no corroboration should be required.[343] If the court dismisses criminal charges, specific reasons for the dismissal should be recorded in the court file.[344] Past incidences of abuse must also be admissible evidence during the trial. In the context of an accumulation of violence, physical, emotional and threats thereof, the seriousness is more obvious. It is important, therefore, to charge the accuser with the multiple acts of violence, which, as described above, create a continuum of harm.[345]

---

[339] Special Rapporteur, Framework for Model Legislation (n 250) para 44.

[340] Council of Europe, 'The Protection of Women against Violence, Recommendation Rec (2002) 5 of the Committee of Ministers to member states on the protection of women against violence adopted on 30 April 2002 and Explanatory memorandum' (30 April 2002).

[341] Amnesty International (n 33) 39.

[342] ibid.

[343] Special Rapporteur, Framework for Model Legislation (n 250) para 47. See also UNDAW, Background Expert Paper (n 244) 49 (regarding the removal of the cautionary warning/corroboration rule in regard to cases of sexual violence).

[344] Special Rapporteur, Framework for Model Legislation (n 250) para 45.

[345] See Mahoney (n 99) 83 (referring to the 'Power and Control Wheel' developed by Ellen Pence and the Daluth Abuse Intervention Project. The Power and Control Wheel also shows how each incident forms part of a process that culminates in a 'state of siege').

Both parties should also be able to request in camera or non-public proceedings. This will prevent reputational damage to the accused in cases of false claims. Although this is rare indeed, it makes sense to have this safeguard.

The decision whether to grant bail would fall within each state's discretion according to its approach to criminal procedure. During the trial phase, the accused should be prevented from contacting the complainant.[346] Clear sentencing guidelines should be established,[347] but the guidelines should be sufficiently flexible and subject to review to ensure that they are appropriate, proportionate and effective. Upon conviction of a defendant for a serious crime of domestic violence, the court may order a term of incarceration and counselling.[348] Enhanced penalties are recommended in cases of domestic violence involving repeat offences, aggravated assault and the use of weapons, and counselling should not be recommended in lieu of a sentence in cases of aggravated assault.[349]

The criminal process should also recognise the victim's role, her needs, including economic needs, and the needs of her children. For example, the Spanish Act Regulating the Protection Order for Victims of Domestic Violence 2003 provides a range of remedies, including payment of child support and basic living expenses such as rent and insurance.[350] India, South Africa and Albania have similar provisions.[351]

Compensation and Damages

It has long been argued that women should be able to obtain compensation and damages from their abusers. In the United States, the Violence against Women Act enabled women to obtain compensation in rape cases, although this was later struck down by the Supreme Court.[352] Sweden has proposed the notion of a 'domestic violence' tax, imposed on men who have committed acts of violence against women.[353] This would help to internalise in abusers the external costs borne by society that have been caused by their violence.

---

[346] Special Rapporteur, Framework for Model Legislation (n 250) para 49.

[347] ibid, para 55. See also ch 4, s 4a of the Swedish Penal Code, cited in Amnesty International (n 33) 19.

[348] Special Rapporteur, Framework for Model Legislation (n 250) para 52.

[349] ibid, paras 53–54.

[350] UNDAW, Background Expert Paper (n 244) 52.

[351] ibid, 53 (describing Art 20 of the Indian Protection of Women from Domestic Violence Act 2005: a magistrate may direct the respondent to pay monetary relief to meet expenses incurred and losses suffered. Art 10(1) of Albania's Law on Measures against Violence in Family Relations 2006: a magistrate may direct the respondent to leave the shared dwelling and/or pay rent to the complainant). See also CEE/FSU Expert Paper (n 330) 6–7 (legislation must grant courts the authority to include various forms of relief in the protection order, including relief relating to the needs of the victim, child support, living expenses, or the costs of disposal of property. Albania's new law has multiple forms of relief, including payment of rent, financial maintenance and child support).

[352] See Bonita C Meyersfeld, 'Reconceptualizing Domestic Violence in International Law' (2003) 67 *Albany Law Review* 371, 420.

[353] See 'Sweden Debates Hitting Men with Domestic Violence Tax' (n 145) (describing a proposal to impose a tax on abusive men to cover the cost of domestic violence against women in Sweden).

Evidence and Burden of Proof

There is an appropriate level of proof for each stage of the legal process. The initial hearing for an urgent and temporary protection order should require the lowest standard of proof. The low standard of proof is proportionate to the temporary nature of the order and the potential for escalated violence. The complainant should satisfy the court that there is prima facie or superficial evidence of domestic violence perpetrated by the respondent and that undue hardship will result if the order is not issued immediately.[354] The objective of the interim order is to ensure ease of access and swiftness in implementing the order. The interim order allows for fast and efficient relief which can later be tested in a hearing for a final protection order.

Because of the nuanced nature of domestic violence and the tendency for the violence to escalate when the authorities are involved, legislators should adopt a rebuttable presumption: that if the claimant presents prima facie evidence of abuse, such as telephone calls to the police, police reports, medical reports or affidavits of friends, employers and relatives regarding the abuse, there is then a presumption that the respondent committed acts of domestic violence against the claimant and a final protection order should be granted unless the respondent rebuts that presumption. The standard of proof required for a final protection order should be based on a balance of probabilities: in order to rebut the presumption, the accused must show that it is more likely than not that the claimant will not be harmed if the order is not granted.

Labour Laws

Domestic violence is the primary cause of women's ill-health. As a result, domestic violence victims often have poor work attendance records and the medical consequences of domestic violence, including depression, may limit performance quality. Employment laws should recognise domestic violence as a valid reason for absenteeism, taking into account, of course, the employer's size (that is, smaller businesses may not be able to continue to employ individuals who are not able to work).

Employers should be required by legislation to give employees (both men and women) reasonable time off to attend court. To facilitate this process, for example, the claim forms for both temporary and permanent protection orders may include a simple form, to be signed by the clerk of the court, confirming the fact that the individual in question was required to be in court. The Spanish Organic

---

[354] The onus of proof is another characteristic of the South African Domestic Violence Act that is worthy of mention. The complainant must satisfy the court that there is prima facie evidence of domestic violence perpetrated by the respondent and that 'undue hardship may be suffered by the complainant as a result of such domestic violence if a protection order is not issued immediately' (s 5(2)(a)–(b)).

Act 2004 acknowledges the need for employment protection and social security provisions for survivors, including the right to reduce and/or reorganise working hours.[355] According to the Philippines Anti-Violence against Women and their Children Act 2004, survivors are entitled to 10 days' paid leave in addition to their contractual and statutory leave provisions.[356] The Honduras Domestic Violence Act 2006 also requires both public and private sector employers to allow employees to attend violence-related programmes, support groups and re-education sessions.[357]

Abusers might target women at their place of work, which could compromise the victim's employment.[358] The presence of an abusive partner at a place of work should not be a valid ground for dismissal. Furthermore, a history of abuse should not be used as a basis for denying employment.

There are some very deep structural problems in the employment context that exacerbate women's experience of domestic violence. In almost every country in the world, women are paid less than men for equal work.[359] There also tends to be a pay gap between sectors dominated by men, such as construction, and those dominated by women, such as nursing. As a result, compensation for women's work is often too low to support a family. Families may be dependent on the income of an abuser, and this will be a factor influencing a woman's decision whether to leave the abusive home and/or to contact the authorities.

Studies show that one third of women who are killed by their husbands have already left them and that the danger of homicide increases once a woman has ended an abusive relationship.[360] Where the authorities are unable to provide protection, many domestic violence survivors have to move regularly to avoid detection by their abusers. This prevents them from continuing with their employment and from accepting long-term positions, and clearly impedes their career development. Employment is most precarious.[361] The victim is prevented from gaining experience, her résumé may become disjointed, and a reference from a previous employer or any contact with a past life is simply not a viable option.[362]

---

[355] See legislation to support this. UNDAW, Background Expert Paper (n 244) 36 (the Spanish Organic Act 2004 provides for support for the survivor in her employment).

[356] ibid.

[357] ibid.

[358] See eg *Yildirim v Austria* (n 249).

[359] According to the International Trade Union Confederation, there is a worldwide gender gap of 16%. See International Trade Union Confederation, 'The Global Gender Pay Gap' (February 2008), www.ituc-csi.org/IMG/pdf/gap–1.pdf. According to the UN, the majority of women earn on average about three-quarters of the pay of men for the same work, outside of the agricultural sector, in both developed and developing countries. See UN Department of Public Information, 'Women at a Glance' (factsheet) (May 1997 DPI/1862/Rev.2), www.un.org/ecosocdev/geninfo/women/women96.htm.

[360] Catherine Humphreys, 'Judicial Alienation Syndrome—Failures to Respond to Post-Separation Violence' (1999) 29 *Family Law* 313.

[361] Mason (n 132) 642.

[362] ibid.

The impact that this would have on a person's career is evident, and the integration of labour and welfare laws in respect of systemic intimate violence could help to mitigate the economic complications of systemic intimate violence. It is also important that domestic violence victims are able to ask their employers to keep their personal data confidential and have a right of recourse if such information is released.

Murder by Victims

In cases of domestic homicide committed by battered women, the context of abuse must be available as a defence to murder where appropriate. While criminal justice systems differ, the usual defences to murder that might apply to abused women who kill their abusers are mental illness, temporary non-pathological incapacity, provocation and self-defence. In the case of mental illness, the accused would have to prove that by reason of mental disease or mental defect she was unable to know the nature and quality of her act or unable to realise that it was wrong and, as such, lacked criminal capacity. The key element of this defence is that the accused lacked the cognitive functions that enable her to perceive, think, reason and remember, or the cognitive functions that enable her to control her behaviour by voluntary exercise of free will.[363] Often this defence will not be available to an accused person who kills her abusive partner. Generally, such accused persons are well aware of what they are doing when they kill their abuser and are able to appreciate the legal wrongfulness of their act. It is also not an ideal defence as it may exculpate the accused of murder but could lead to internment in a mental health facility.

The defence of temporary non-pathological incapacity excludes criminal capacity by reason of mental illness, youth, intoxication, provocation or any other factor affecting the accused's mental ability at the time of the murder which made it impossible for the accused to appreciate the wrongfulness of her conduct. The exigencies of domestic violence may fall within this defence, provided that the prosecutorial and judicial authorities are trained and, where necessary, provided with expert testimony as to the impact of extreme domestic abuse.[364]

Many legal systems accept a defence of provocation where the murder is immediately preceded by provocative conduct on the part of the deceased which so angered the accused that she lacked the criminal capacity or mental element for the crime of murder. This defence will not apply where there is a time lapse between the violent actions of the deceased and the murder itself. In the case of domestic violence, an abused woman will often wait for her abuser to be vulnerable, inert or asleep before killing him, often because she lacks the physical

---

[363] Pillay (n 62) para 40.
[364] ibid.

strength to overpower him and must therefore wait for the 'right' moment to take 'defensive' action. The defence of provocation usually requires one major triggering event, whereas abused women may commit murder after a seemingly minor incident but which took place in the context of an extreme cycle of violence.

Self-defence entails the use of reasonable and proportionate force against the deceased where there was a threat of imminent and unlawful bodily harm (to the accused or another person) and the force used was necessary to prevent that harm. This defence, as with the previous defences, is based on a single confrontational encounter that warrants the use of deadly force. This defence does not take into account the fact that there may be a prolonged history of violence and unsuccessful attempts to obtain help that left the accused with limited choice in terms of ensuring her safety.

The difficulty with these defences is that, for the most part, the act of killing must be performed to prevent *immediate* or *imminent* harm. In the case of domestic violence murders, however, as already mentioned, the abused will often wait until the abuser is docile, asleep or unsuspecting before carrying out the murder. The murder, to a certain extent, is planned and *must* be planned, especially where there are no alternatives open to the accused. For example, in the case of *S v Ferreira*,[365] the South African Supreme Court of Appeal considered the personal history of the accused in determining the extent of her criminal culpability for contracting two men to kill her abusive partner. The accused had endured several years of physical and emotional abuse by the deceased: he had prevented her from having contact with family and friends;[366] she was subjected to constant criticism and verbal denigration, often in public, as well as physical violence;[367] and the deceased raped her and threatened to procure others to rape her (after attempting to compel her to remove her clothes in front of a group of farm labourers who worked for the deceased).[368] The accused attempted to leave the deceased on four occasions, without success,[369] and on three occasions she had called for police assistance.[370] The police came only once and advised her to take responsibility for her husband's sobriety.[371]

According to the Court, these factors revealed the accused's subjective state of mind and were relevant to the question of her moral blameworthiness in procuring his murder.[372] The Court considered whether the threat from which the accused sought to escape was, subjectively, perceived to be a real and present danger at the time of the offence, but only in respect of her sentencing,

---

[365] *S v Ferreira* (245/03) [2004] ZASCA 29 (1 April 2004).
[366] ibid, paras 18–19.
[367] ibid, para 23.
[368] ibid, para 26.
[369] ibid, para 24.
[370] ibid, para 25.
[371] ibid.
[372] ibid, para 33.

noting in parenthesis that the threat was 'not imminent enough to escape criminal liability altogether'.[373]

This situation engages two sets of competing rights. On the one hand, the deceased's right to life, the most fundamental of all international human rights, is violated. On the other, the accused's rights to equality, a fair trial and freedom from all forms of violence from public and private sources are engaged. There is also the public policy consideration of sending a strong message of approbation with regard to premeditated murder. However, a thorough understanding of systemic intimate violence reveals that there will be circumstances in which it is neither fair nor reasonable to punish a person for self-preservation when the state has not been able to ensure her safety.

States should adopt and legislate for a specific defence to murder for women who have killed their violent partners which reflects the characteristics of systemic intimate violence and the circumstances in which abused women kill. There are certain common elements that are present where abused women kill their abusers:

- The majority of spousal killings take place where women have been subjected to a long history of physical, sexual, emotional, verbal and financial abuse as opposed to isolated instances of abuse.[374] This so-called 'battered woman syndrome' is employed by experts to demonstrate how the cycle of abuse (tension building; acute battering; extreme contrition) triggers extreme acts of violence on the part of the abused. It refers to the psychological conditioning of victims to explain why women kill their abusers in the face of extreme domestic violence.[375]
- Very often, abused women who kill have sought some recourse through the criminal justice system without success.[376]
- Women may kill their abusers after they have separated or attempted to separate from the abused. The assumption that leaving the abuser will end the violence is incorrect. Research indicates that a third of women who leave violent relationships suffer violence after separation.[377] Women who kill their abusers are often aware that neither separation nor the criminal justice system will be able to protect them, or their dependants, from the abused.
- Abused women who kill their abusers may suffer from depression and/or low self-esteem.

---

[373] ibid, para 45.
[374] Pillay (n 62) para 20.
[375] See Schneider (n 33) 41 (describing the progress of the battered women's movement and demonstrating how it has been retarded by the powerful denial by jurors, politicians and courts in general). Some have criticised this movement's labelling as being counter-productive. See also Mahoney (n 99) 41.
[376] Pillay (n 62) para 21.
[377] L Radford, 'Pleading for Time: Justice for Battered Women who Kill' (1991) 18 *Journal of Law and Society* 219, 235.

- The murder may be premeditated or planned and take place when the abuser is vulnerable and unable to use force. For example, the abused may wait until the abuser is asleep or hire others to murder the abuser.[378]
- Many abused women who kill do so because they see no other way of protecting themselves or their children.

Factors to be considered in deciding on the validity of the domestic violence defence include the following:

- Is there a history of abuse of the accused or her children by the deceased?
- Did the abused seek but receive no protection from the state? It should not be necessary to show that the accused took all legal steps available to abused women. For many of the reasons cited above, including psychological weariness, physical entrapment and hostility from the state, an accused should not be expected to repeatedly procure the assistance of the state.[379]
- Does the accused have a criminal record?
- What was the status of the relationship between the accused and the deceased at the time of the killing? If the accused was in the process of obtaining a divorce or separating from the deceased, the deceased may have become more dangerous.
- Does the accused have children?
- Would the accused be a threat to society if released?
- What are the personal circumstances of the accused, including her financial circumstances?

A history of domestic violence should be a compelling reason for the courts not to apply mandatory sentencing, especially in respect of premeditated murder.

Fair Procedure and Rules of Justice

Whatever the structure of the legislation, the rights of a respondent or accused must be protected. The rules of procedure and evidence must be refined so that the judicial process meets victims' needs and addresses the nuanced process of domestic violence. This must not, however, dilute the integrity of the *audi alterem partem* rule, the presumption of innocence, the right to remain silent and the principles of fairness.

The need to balance the state obligation to protect women from domestic violence and its obligation to protect the fair trial rights of the accused was confirmed in the South African case of *S v Baloyi*. The South African Constitutional Court had to consider whether the legislative provisions regarding an alleged breach of a protection order violated the constitutional right to a fair trial.[380]

---

[378] ibid.
[379] See *S v Ferreira* (245/03) [2004] ZASCA 29 (1 April 2004).
[380] *S v Godfrey Baloyi*, Case CCT 29/99 (South African Constitutional Court, 1999), para 11.

The domestic violence legislation under review empowered the court to convict a person of the offence of violating a protection order. If, on a balance of probabilities, it was satisfied that the respondent had breached a protection order, he would be guilty of an offence, unless the respondent could satisfy the court that his failure had not been due to fault on his part.[381] The legislation was challenged on the ground that it violated the respondent's right to be presumed innocent and to have his guilt proved beyond a reasonable doubt. The Constitutional Court held that there was no violation of the right to be presumed innocent and to have guilt proved beyond a reasonable doubt; rather the legislation in question might engage the right to silence—that is, the respondent would have to provide some response to the allegations against him.[382] The Court held that in the particular circumstances of a domestic violence enquiry, 'where the danger of continuing violence is acute and the immediate issue at stake is upholding respect for the court's interdict, invasion of the right to silence may well be justified under section 36 [of the Constitution]'.[383]

Naturally it is within the margin of appreciation of each state to determine its rules of evidence and standard of proof. In order to meet the exigencies of domestic violence, however, states must ensure that victims of domestic violence are not unfairly prejudiced by seemingly neutral rules of procedure.

Remedies and the Provision of Services

The provision of emergency relief services, hospital services, police protection, counselling, trained judicial officers and shelters must be provided for in legislation. Each of these remedies is discussed below.

POLICE PROTECTION AND IMPLEMENTATION OF THE LAW

One of the most important requirements of any victim is protection. Ideally, a victim of domestic violence should know that the harm is a violation of her rights[384] and, if she deems it necessary, she ought to be able to call for assistance and protection. However, this is not the norm. Due to ignorance and prejudice, police apathy may lead to the breakdown of the protection order and other aspects of a protective system.[385] Ignorant and uneducated officers, who

---

[381] ibid, para 4. The case dealt with s 3(5) of the Prevention of Family Violence Act 133 of 1993, which was replaced by the Domestic Violence Act 116 of 1998.

[382] ibid, para 31.

[383] ibid, para 32.

[384] This could be effected through a state-run educational campaign.

[385] Heimer et al (n 33) 51. One third of the women who reported being in or having been in a violent relationship said that they had sought help from some service or agency other than the police (p 54).

perfunctorily intervene and give ineffectual and inappropriate advice, reinforce the normalcy of the conduct and tacitly condone the violence.[386]

There have been several striking cases where police functionaries either have evidenced actionable neglect or, through prejudicial and accusatory conduct, have alienated the victim from the state and the protection it theoretically provides. In one alarming case, an American woman was partially paralysed and permanently disfigured, sustaining her worst injuries in the yard of her home, while the police, reluctant to interfere, waited in their vehicle on the street.[387] Police aversion to domestic violence also stems from a common social perception that the family is a hallowed realm, surrounded by a barrier of privacy that warrants respect and distance. In Russia, reports indicate that police share the widely held view that spousal abuse is a private matter in which the police should not or need not intervene. Police officers often fail to respond to reports of domestic violence and take no action against the abuser.[388]

This perception may be shared by the victim herself. Many women will make a conscious decision not to ask for help due to a sense of shame and fear of being judged.[389] When a victim calls for help, the perception that she has broken a rule of sanctity feeds the reticence of many police officials to respond to calls for help.[390]

Police acquiescence arises from more than just perception; ironically, domestic violence calls are among the most dangerous and volatile police cases. Because violence within an intimate context is so incongruous, many victims will call the police only in the most exigent and unstable of circumstances, when they fear extreme danger.[391] The violence in these cases is indeed extreme and presents a threat not only to the victim but to anyone who intervenes. And, as discussed previously, the most dangerous time for the abused is when she makes contact with or asks for the help of the authorities.[392] One further possible explanation for the inaction of the police is that in many states there is a great deal of uncertainty about the steps that they may or may not take in protecting

---

[386] Eve Buzawa and Carl Buzawa, *Domestic Violence: The Criminal Justice Response*, 3rd edn (California, Sage Publications, 2002) 71–88. See also David Hirschel and Ira W Hutchison, III, 'Female Spouse Abuse and the Police Response: The Charlotte, North Carolina Experiment' (1992) 83 *Journal of Criminal Law and Criminology* 73, 81.

[387] Raoul Felder and Barbara Victor, *Getting Away with Murder: Weapons for the War against Domestic Violence* (New York, Touchstone, 1996) 13–17 (describing the abuse inflicted upon a victim, Tracey Thurman, by her estranged husband Charles while the police remained outside the house).

[388] See Human Rights Watch Women's Rights Project, *Human Rights Watch Global Report on Women's Human Rights* (New Haven, Yale University Press, August 1995) 341.

[389] See eg Benninger-Budel (n 119) 116.

[390] CEE/FSU Expert Paper (n 330) 11 (prevalent police and prosecutor attitude that domestic violence is not a crime). See also Benninger-Budel (n 119) 279.

[391] ibid, 77. See also *S v Ferreira* (245/03) [2004] ZASCA 29 (1 April 2004), para 25 ('The appellant called for police assistance on three occasions. Only once did they arrive. They said the deceased was drunk and that the appellant should get him to sober up').

[392] CEE/FSU Expert Paper (n 330) 8 (women are at a higher risk of homicide when the abuser is ordered to leave the home).

the abused, and often it is not clear which party is the abused and which is the abuser. Therefore it is often easier to do nothing.

The absence of intervention, however, can be lethal. In the case of *Town of Castle Rock v Gonzales*, the abused killed his three children (and himself) after violating a protection order. The police had refused to seek an arrest warrant for the offender, notwithstanding a state statute obliging them to seek an arrest warrant in such circumstances.[393]

It is disquieting how often calls for police assistance in such circumstances are not answered.[394] This is so even in jurisdictions where the police are legally required to assist victims of domestic violence and inform them of their rights. In South Africa, for example, while the Domestic Violence Act penalises police officials for failing to comply with the Act by refusing to intervene in cases of domestic violence, the perception that intervention in domestic violence does not 'constitute real police work' perpetuates police apathy.[395] The police are pivotal to the success of restraining orders,[396] and yet they have been described as the weakest link in South Africa's interdict structure. This is so notwithstanding s 8(4)(a) of the Domestic Violence Act, which penalises the failure by a police officer to comply with her/his obligations under the Act. Awareness raising and education within the police force are not provided for in this Act.[397]

The same phenomenon exists in Sweden, where 'women do not consider it to be of any use to seek help from the police by reporting the violence to which they have been subjected'.[398] As a result, Sweden has a particularly low reporting rate for domestic violence.[399] There are further reasons for this low rate of reporting, including: the victim's fear that the police will not believe the complaint; the victim's intuition that the police will not be able to do anything; feelings of shame or guilt; fear of revenge from the abuser; general resistance to involving the police; and fear that triggering the legal process will result in the incarceration of the abuser.[400] In Nicaragua, only two out of every ten abused women contact the police.[401] Reasons for this under-reporting include: fear of further violence; shame; feelings of isolation; difficulties in attending hearings (especially for women living in rural areas); difficulties in preparing evidentiary documents; a

---

[393] USA Expert Paper (n 302) 4.

[394] See eg Amnesty International (n 33) 36. See also James Ptacek, *Battered Women in the Courtroom: The Power of Judicial Responses* (Boston, Northastern University Press, 1999) 143 ('78 percent [of women seeking assistance] had called the police before seeking orders.'). See also Special Rapporteur 1996 Report (n 115) 33.

[395] South African Domestic Violence Act, s 18(4)(a). Awareness raising and education within the police are not provided for in this Act.

[396] Practice indicates that most police departments are reluctant to adopt arrest policies (Hirschel and Hutchison (n 384) 85).

[397] Fedler (n 104) 246.

[398] Heimer et al (n 33) 54 (only 5% of women who experienced abuse reported the most recent incident of abuse to the police). See also Amnesty International (n 33) 23.

[399] It is estimated that only 20–25% of violent crimes in Sweden are actually reported, especially where the violence is perpetrated between intimates. Amnesty International (n 33) 24.

[400] Heimer et al (n 33) 52.

[401] OMCT CEDAW Report on Nicaragua (n 57) 13.

lack of economic resources to pay for legal representation; and the failure of the Nicaraguan government to protect victims and to prosecute perpetrators.[402]

Ineffective policing is particularly acute in immigrant and minority communities. Minority communities often view the police and prison system as external to their world. For example, members of enclosed religious groups such as Mormons, Mennonites and Amish in the United States, and Muslim and Turkish communities in Germany and France, view police services as alien to their society.[403] Much of their survival as a homogenous group is dependent on a sense of group loyalty. Calling the police may constitute an infraction of their survival code, which is far worse for many religious groups than any individual, personal violation that a person may endure.

Immigrant women may also fear deportation if they contact the authorities. Even if they are legally present in a country, they may be dependent on their partners for financial support and linguistic and cultural guidance.[404] Often the fear of deportation is well founded. The UK's immigration laws require foreign spouses to remain in their marriage to the spouse with legal status for a period of two years before the foreign spouse is awarded an independent right to remain.[405] As at the date of writing (January 2010), the UK government is reviewing this approach.[406] In the USA, where spouses and children are dependent on an abusive family member for their legal status in the country, they may be able to self-petition for their own immigration status, independently of the abuser.[407]

Women from religious, ethnic or national minorities tend to endure so-called double discrimination, making the services and support offered by the state

[402] ibid, 13. See also Melinda Leonard, 'Post-Conflict Situation in Nicaragua: A Desk Study Overview' in Jeanne Ward (Reproductive Health Response in Conflict Consortium) (ed), *If Not Now, When? Addressing Gender-based Violence in Refugee, Internally Displaced, and Post-Conflict Settings: A Global Overview* (New York, Reproductive Health for Refugees Consortium, 2002) 117, 118–19.

[403] See Maria Rosa Pinedo and Ana Maria Santinoli, 'Immigrant Women and Wife Assault' in Fauzia Rafiq (ed), *Towards Equal Access: A Handbook for Service Providers Working with Immigrant Women Survivors of Wife Assault* (Ottawa, Immigrant and Visible Minority Women Against Abuse, 1991). See generally Amnesty International and Southall Black Sisters (n 105).

[404] Amnesty International (n 33) 32 (Sweden has implemented a new reform in terms of which 'women who have been abused by men may be allowed to stay in Sweden, even if the relationship has lasted less than two years').

[405] Amnesty International and Southall Black Sisters (n 105).

[406] Funmi Johnson, 'The Struggle for Justice: The State's Response to Violence against Women' (Expert Paper prepared for the United Nations Division for the Advancement of Women, Expert Group Meeting on good practices in legislation on violence against women) (12 May 2008) UN Doc EGM/GPLVAW/2008/EP.02, www.un.org/womenwatch/daw/egm/vaw_legislation_2008/expertpapers/EGMGPLVAW%20Paper%20(Funmi%20Johnson).pdf 7 (the Home Office incorporated the 'Domestic Violence Rule' into the Immigration Rules, which allows anyone who experiences domestic violence during the probationary period of two years to apply for indefinite leave to remain in the UK. The applicant will have to show that the relationship has broken down permanently as a result of the violence and will also have to produce evidence of the violence).

[407] USA Expert Paper (n 302) 2–3 (the Violence against Women Act of 1994 reformed immigration law to help battered immigrant women escape their abusers. The Act was amended in 2000 and 2005 to expand safeguards and restore rights to immigrant abused women).

inappropriate to their specific needs. Immigrants who are survivors of domestic violence should be able to apply confidentially for legal immigration status independently of the perpetrator.[408]

The state's obligation to protect women from domestic violence through an effective police force should include the following specific elements.

Statutory Obligation to Protect

Police authorities must be obliged by legislation to respond to domestic violence calls, secure the victim's safety, advise the victim of her rights and the law, and offer to transport or provide transport for the victim and her children to a place of safety.[409] A failure by the police authorities to provide the services required should constitute misconduct for which they and the relevant government department responsible for the administration of justice can be held accountable.

For example, in Sweden and South Africa, the police have a legal obligation to assist victims of domestic violence.[410] In Sweden, the police are 'legally bound to investigate reports of assault and rape, even when the injured party objects to the investigation. Nor can the injured party withdraw a police report that he or she has filed. In most cases, it is the woman herself who reports the assault to the police.'[411]

However, because there are no witnesses to the abuse, if the woman withdraws the complaint, the case is almost always closed.[412] In South Africa there is a common sentiment among police officers that 'domestic violence and other "private misconduct" should not be subject to public intervention'.[413] To remedy this, the South African Domestic Violence Act imposes extensive obligations on police officers.[414]

Training

Police officers cannot be expected to deal with domestic violence properly without the requisite specialist training. Lack of funds or resources should not

---

[408] UNDAW, Background Expert Paper (n 244) 38 (regarding independent and favourable immigration status for survivors of violence against women. The Canadian Immigration and Refugee Protection Act 2002 and the Swedish Aliens Act 2005 allow survivors to apply for permanent residence irrespective of whether their spouse supports the application).

[409] South African Domestic Violence Act, s 8(6).

[410] See eg ibid, s (4)(a): 'Failure by a member of the South African Police Service to comply with an obligation imposed in terms of this Act or the national instructions referred to in subsection (3), constitutes misconduct as contemplated in the South African Police Service Act, 1995, and the Independent Complaints Directorate, established in terms of that Act, must forthwith be informed of any such failure reported to the South African Police Service.'

[411] Amnesty International (n 33) 38.

[412] ibid, 38.

[413] Buzawa (n 386) 31.

[414] South African Domestic Violence Act, s 18.

justify a lack of training, as such services can be obtained at minimal or no cost through academic institutions, international and regional bodies and NGOs.

Specialised Units

Ideally there should be trained officers who specialise in domestic violence. These units should be available at every police station. In certain parts of Sweden, for example, the police have established specialised 'domestic violence' units.[415] These units consist of specially trained officers and have enhanced methods of communication with the prosecutor and other relevant authorities.[416] Investigators in these units attend two-week training sessions on male violence against women.[417] Nigeria has proposed the establishment of a government-funded commission on violence, comprising representatives of the police, government and NGOs, to ensure that victims have effective access to accredited service providers and transport to a shelter or hospital if required.[418]

Female Officers

Ideally, a domestic violence call should trigger a response from at least two officers, one female and one male. This helps to redress the gendered-power disparity that may exist between the abused and the abuser. It is also important that a female police officer accompanies the abused to a place of safety. The abused may be reluctant to accompany male officers.

Data and Inter-departmental Communication

Another vital requirement is effective cooperation and communication among the various state authorities, including the police, prosecutors, and health and social services. Police authorities should be required to record every report of domestic violence. The reporting procedure should be brief in order to minimise the administrative burden, detailing only the names of the parties, the date and the nature of the abuse. Ideally there should be an electronic database which holds details of all domestic violence calls. If there are repeat calls, all relevant information should be relayed to the prosecuting authorities. All such information should be subject to the highest standards of confidentiality.

---

[415] Amnesty International (n 33) 40.
[416] ibid.
[417] ibid. According to Amnesty International, the highest prosecution rates are registered where prosecutor districts introduce family violence units.
[418] Nigeria Expert Paper (n 139) 18 (citing the Violence (Prohibition) Bill 2003).

Police authorities should have access to (1) counselling resources and (2) legal advice for victims and perpetrators. The police should also be able to access the assistance of child and animal welfare specialists to take care of dependants and companion animals if the perpetrator and/or victim are removed from the home.

The aspiration to achieve a cooperative relationship among the judiciary, welfare departments, health care bodies and the police is evident, for example, in section 2 of the South African Domestic Violence Act. This section imposes a duty on the police to inform the victim of her rights in terms of the Act and to help her to access a place of safety where reasonably possible to do so. Section 2(a) requires the police to make 'arrangements for the complainant to find a suitable shelter and to obtain medical treatment'. Failure to comply with the terms of the Act 'constitutes misconduct as contemplated in the South African Police Service Act, 1995'.[419]

Police Powers

The powers of the police should be clear and easily verifiable. Police authorities should have the power to use reasonable and proportionate force to protect the victim and other vulnerable persons. Officers should be able to arrest the abuser for allegedly committing an offence and, in cases of a breach of a protection order, there should be a presumption of arrest, but the decision should be made by the officers present. An arrest should be effected where there are reasonable grounds to suspect that the complainant will suffer imminent harm as a result of the breach of a protection order.[420]

Failure to fulfil this function should result in some form of accountability and/or penalty.[421] Ongoing preventative government involvement, particularly in the form of monitoring and enforcing compliance with protection orders, could be one of the missing links in implementing effective legislation.[422]

JUDICIARY AND JUDICIAL AGENTS

Like the police force, judicial bodies have prejudices, misconceptions of domestic violence and limited legislative mechanisms. The result traditionally is a very poor judicial response to domestic violence. For example, in the case of *Maria da Penha v Brazil*, the Commission found the Brazilian Government to be in

---

[419] South African Domestic Violence Act, s 18(4)(a).
[420] ibid, s 8(4)(b).
[421] See DEVAW (n 9) Art 4(i). See also *MC v Bulgaria* (App No 39272/98) ECtHR 4 March 2004, para 152.
[422] Harvard Law Review, 'Developments in the Law: Legal Responses to Domestic Violence' (1993) 106 *Harvard Law Review* 1498, 1512.

breach of its human rights obligations due to significant judicial delay and incompetence in the investigation of domestic violence.[423]

International instruments repeatedly urge states to provide effective prosecutors, judges and legal procedures that understand and meet the unique needs of female victims of domestic violence.[424] These include special family courts, specialised training for members of the judiciary who handle more complex cases,[425] and systems to expedite domestic violence cases.[426]

The judiciary is involved in both civil and criminal sanctions. Prosecutors are generally involved only in criminal procedures, but their responsibility and involvement really ought to begin at the civil stage of domestic violence proceedings. They should be informed of repeat offences of domestic violence. Ideally, the victim's wishes should be followed as closely as possible but there should be a margin of appreciation where the prosecutor can exercise his or her discretion to prosecute the abuser for repeated acts of violence.

An effective prosecution and judicial process can only work if prosecutors, judges and the law recognise and understand the cumulative nature of domestic violence. Any legal procedure, be it civil, criminal or a hybrid, must be designed to identify the continuum of violence. Prosecutors, like police officers, should be trained to specialise in domestic violence cases so that they are able to identify what evidence is required in the investigative process to prove the continuum of violence when the case does proceed to court.

Once again, almost every gender-specific international instrument requires states to provide gender-specific training to judges, investigators and prosecutors. Notwithstanding this, there is a persistent failure to do so. The level of ignorance and prejudice regarding women's rights and intimate violence is alarmingly high, even in the most progressive societies. Until proper judicial training is implemented there really will be no improvement in a country's judicial response to domestic violence.[427]

In South Africa, for example, enforcement is the 'principal weakness' of the law.[428] If a judge is not sympathetic and is instead hostile, or even merely insensitive, to the dynamics of intimate violence, the attempt that the Domestic Violence Act makes to reduce the inequality and fear characteristic of an abusive relationship may be rendered nugatory. The attitude of a judge may influence a

---

[423] Inter-American Commission on Human Rights, *Maria da Penha Maia Fernandes (Brazil)* (16 April 2001) Report No 54/01, Case 12.051, para 704. See also UNDAW, Background Expert Paper (n 244) 8.

[424] CEDAW Twenty-Seventh Session Report (n 241) para 432, p 209). Art 4(d) of DEVAW (n 9) provides that 'women who are subjected to violence should be provided with access to the mechanisms of justice and, as provided for by national legislation, to just and effective remedies for the harm that they have suffered'.

[425] Special Rapporteur, Framework for Model Legislation (n 250) 12.

[426] See UNDAW, Background Expert Paper (n 244) 21 (Specialised Courts exist in a number of countries, including Brazil (Maria Da Penha Law 2006), Spain (Title V Organic Act on Integrated Measures against Gender Violence 2004), Uruguay, Venezuela, the UK and the USA.

[427] Latin America and the Caribbean Expert Paper (n 261) 6.

[428] Harvard Law Review, 'Legal Responses to Domestic Violence' (n 422) 1511.

victim's decision to use or reject the law in future cases of abuse. The courtroom must aspire to neutralise gender inequality and understand that the family nucleus may be one of the more dangerous locations for women.[429]

KNOWLEDGE OF RIGHTS

It is impossible to use the law and legal apparatus to confront gender-based hegemony without concurrent social change, spearheaded by public governmental support.[430] It makes little sense to have an array of legal, health and social services if women are unaware of their existence. States are responsible for making women aware of two things. First, they should know what their rights are: they should know that physical, psychological or sexual violence, albeit in the context of an intimate relationship, is against the law and an actionable violation of their being. Secondly, they should know what their remedies are.

Such awareness could be achieved through any number of mechanisms, ranging in efficacy and cost. A state may, for example, require all hospitals to display information on domestic violence; require all health officials, especially emergency, dental and gynaecological professionals, to screen high-risk patients for abuse and be required by law to advise the patient on her rights and options; and compel the police, court clerks and judges to advise women of their rights regarding systemic intimate violence whenever they have such cases before them.

This is a necessary step in the reform of social and cultural structures because it is within the context of ignorance and apathy that violations are made possible and carried out. The ways in which these institutions react to abused women 'affect the criminal evidence and the legal proceedings, including the interpretation of the legal prerequisites, the evaluation of evidence and the possibility of treating victims of sex-related crimes with greater respect'.[431] For example, when one abused Nicaraguan woman sought assistance from the police, she discovered that the abuser and the police knew each other, and since 'he was in the military they let him go right away and gave him a ride back to

---

[429] See UNDAW, Background Expert Paper (n 244) 18–19 (regarding gender sensitive training and capacity building to ensure that the police, prosecutors and judges have an in-depth understanding of such legislation and implement it in a gender sensitive manner, with reference to the Spanish Organic Act on Integrated Protection Measures against Gender Violence 2004; the Albanian Law on Measures against Violence in Family Relations 2006; and the Philippines Anti-Violence against Women and their Children Act 2004).

[430] See Harvard Law Review, 'Legal Responses to Domestic Violence' (n 422) 1503. In the 1997 South African Draft Discussion Paper for Public Consultation on Gender Policy Considerations, an undertaking was made, in recognition of the fact that 'women have largely been rendered invisible in the legal system'. Gender Policy Considerations June 1997 Draft Discussion Paper for Public Consultation 3, developed by the South African Gender Unit, in consultation with the Department of Justice. Published by Dr ME Tshabalala-Msimang, the then Deputy Minister of Justice of South Africa, www.polity.org.za/html/govdocs/discuss/gender.html?rebookmark=1. See also the Latin America and the Caribbean Expert Paper (n 261) 7 (regarding ignorance of one's rights as a barrier to the implementation of legal reforms).

[431] Amnesty International (n 33) 38.

my house. That time he kicked down my door . . . After that I didn't know what to do. I felt trapped, a prisoner and I couldn't escape'.[432] The fact that both officials and abusers are predominantly male reinforces the mantra of the abuser that the law will never help the abused.[433]

Many states' judicial officers, police forces, health services and other relevant agents are immersed in the pool of misconceptions surrounding domestic violence. International instruments are replete with provisions that require policy amendments to ensure that governments endorse the principle of equality and equivalency between men and women, which includes the reduction of violence perpetrated by one gender against the other.[434] For example, CEDAW binds states to implement policy changes that take effect not only in the political sphere but also in the more intimate compartments of private life.[435] DEVAW also provides that all appropriate measures, including education, should be taken by states to abolish existing prejudicial customs and practices that mitigate women's safety.[436] General Recommendation 19 requires states to undertake research to 'identify the nature and extent of attitudes, customs and practices that perpetuate violence against women and the kinds of violence that result'.[437] This includes the 'compilation of statistics and research on the extent, causes and effects of violence, and on the effectiveness of measures to prevent and deal with violence'.[438] Educating service providers is not a new recommendation but it cannot be stressed strongly enough.[439]

Education also includes cultural reform and emphasising the approbation of violence against women. For example, countries such as South Africa have encouraged daytime television shows and soap operas to address issues of domestic violence and gender discrimination. In India, the Protection of Women from Domestic Violence Act 2005 requires the state to take measures to publicise the Act regularly through television, radio and the print media.[440] Nigeria

[432] Ellsberg et al (n 15) 1604–05.

[433] See Schneider (n 33) 91. See also Benninger-Budel (n 119) 123; OMCT CEDAW Report on Nicaragua (n 57) 14.

[434] See eg CEDAW (n 9): Art 7, regarding political equality; Art 8, dealing with the role of women in international organisations; Art 10, dealing with equality in education; Art 11, prescribing equality in the workplace; Art 13, protecting economic, family and recreational equality; Art 14, regarding the peculiar difficulties for rural women; and Art 16, dealing with equality within marriage. The analogous provisions in DEVAW (n 9) are: Art 4 (political equality); Art 8 (women in international organisations); Art 9 (equality in education); Art 10 (equality in the workplace); and Art 6 (equality within marriage).

[435] This is clear from CEDAW (n 9) Art 5(a).

[436] DEVAW (n 9) Arts 2–3.

[437] General Recommendation 19 (n 261) Art 24(e).

[438] ibid, Art 24(c).

[439] Celina Romany, 'Women as Aliens: A Feminist Critique of the Public/Private Distinction in International Human Rights Law' (1993) 6 *Harvard Human Rights Journal* 87, 98–99. See also Romany (n 138) 298.

[440] UNDAW, Background Expert Paper (n 244) 32. See also *Report of the Thirty-Sixth Session of the Committee on the Elimination of Discrimination against Women* (25 August 2006) UN Doc CEDAW/C/MEX/CO/6, para 15 (hereinafter CEDAW Thirty-Sixth Session: Sixth Periodic Report on Mexico).

adopted the format of a mock tribunal in 2001 to raise awareness of violence against women, which encouraged several legislators to pledge their support for a Violence against Women Bill.[441]

SHELTERS

Often, the victim's first port of call is a shelter.[442] An examination of the role of the shelter in conjunction with protection orders is necessary as the victim or the abuser may have to be removed from particularly volatile environments. Unlike any other violent crime, the victim of systemic intimate violence has no place of refuge. Her home is the locus of the crime.

Shelters generally offer effective protection to women, and almost everywhere they are run by not-for-profit NGOs. Non-profit women's shelters 'are still the most important actors in providing help, support and protection to women who survive violence—even though the municipal authorities and the social services bear the ultimate responsibility'.[443] For example, women in Sweden reportedly receive more satisfactory assistance when they approach hospitals, lawyers, women's shelters or crime-victim centres than when they have recourse to state facilities.[444] In Sweden, government agencies actually refer abused women to non-government-run women's shelters.[445]

However, the number and resources of shelters are too often inadequate. There are non-profit women's shelters in only 150 of Sweden's 290 municipalities.[446] Most of them have no paid or professionally qualified staff, and are run entirely by volunteer staff.[447] In 2001, a particular shelter received 3,000 incoming calls (from both individual women and government agencies); they were only able to assist 15 women, 10 children and nine girls in that year.[448] In 2002, one group of shelters recorded 12,630 requests for assistance from abused women. The shelters managed to provide only 367 women and 316 children with sheltered accommodation. Another group of shelters received 54,675 requests for assistance and they were able to assist 48,467 of these calls. They referred 1,216 women to other places due to a lack of vacancies.[449]

---

[441]　Nigeria Expert Paper (n 139) 12.

[442]　Harvard Law Review, 'Legal Responses to Domestic Violence' (n 422) 1506 (noting that the shelter has been identified as 'the battered woman's first encounter with the legal system after she flees her assailant').

[443]　Amnesty International (n 33) 43.

[444]　In Sweden, one third of women who have suffered systemic intimate violence turn to agencies other than the police for assistance, including hospitals, psychiatric clinics, non-governmental women's shelters, crime-victim centres and emergency social services (ibid).

[445]　ibid, 44.

[446]　ibid, 47.

[447]　ibid.

[448]　In the year 2000 the municipalities contributed a total of SEK24 million to women's shelters, although the amounts provided by individual municipalities varied and as many as '68 municipalities did not contribute at all' (ibid, 47).

[449]　ibid.

Shelters may be run by private organisations or non-governmental groups, but governments cannot abrogate their financial and infrastructural responsibility. Ideally, governments should be required to allocate a percentage of their annual budget to aid victims of domestic violence.[450] General Recommendation No 19 requires states to establish or support bodies that provide protection or safe haven for women who have been abused (including assistance to refugees).[451]

Shelters are important not only because they provide immediate safety but also because they help the victim to break the cycle of violence. This is necessary both to secure her physical safety and to allow her sufficient distance from the violence to adjust to the fact that what has happened to her is not 'normal' or acceptable.[452] Shelters also provide an important haven to accumulate evidence for legal proceedings. [453]

Ideally, there should be enough shelters so that victims of abuse are able to seek confidential and temporary safety without having to travel excessive distances. But this is rarely the case. In the UK, for example, studies show that many thousands of women receive no protection from gender-specific violence because of where they live. The 'Map of Gaps' report reveals the uneven and random distribution of specialist services in Britain. Women's protection becomes dependent on this so-called 'postcode lottery'.[454] On the other side of the coin, in rural areas comprised of small communities, shelters may be easily identifiable and might therefore not provide the necessary protection. Specific remedies need to be created to meet the needs of different communities and societies. It is also important that shelters are able to accommodate women with children, including disabled children and, ideally, companion animals; that they have medical and psychological facilities; and that they function as well as any government-run hospital.

The ultimate goal would be to develop a support system in which the shelter would act as a central point for accessing 'tangible physical services, such as child care, housing access, job referral, food and clothing, transportation and case monitoring'.[455] For example, the Philippines' Rape Victims Assistance Act 1998

[450] UNDAW, Background Expert Paper (n 244) 18 (in the USA the Violence Against Women Act 1994 and its reauthorisations provide a significant source of funding for NGOs working on violence against women).

[451] See Amnesty International (n 33) 43.

[452] Heimer et al (n 33) 18 (referring to this as the 'denormalization process'). See also Amnesty International (n 33) 43.

[453] States should also be encouraged to provide rape crisis centres, which are one-stop centres servicing the variety of needs of survivors of rape and domestic violence. UNDAW, Background Expert Paper (n 244) 35 (Recommendation for immediate access to comprehensive and integrated services at the expense of the state, with reference to rape crisis centres in the United States and Germany; one-stop centres in Malaysia; and women-friendly centres attached to hospitals in India).

[454] See Maddy Coy, Liz Kelly and Jo Foord, *Map of Gaps 2: The Postcode Lottery of Violence against Women Support Services in Britain,* Report for End Violence against Women and the Equality and Human Rights Commission (January 2009).

[455] Harvard Law Review, (n 422) 1507. While an overriding problem is obviously lack of funds, it is interesting to note that a solution has been found by some American states which use marriage license fees and fines for violations of protection orders to fund such structures (ibid).

requires the establishment of crisis centres in every province and city, although the failure to allocate funds has made this impossible to achieve.[456] While an overriding problem is obviously a lack of funds, it is interesting to note that one solution implemented by some states in the USA is to use marriage license fees and fines for violations of protection orders to fund such structures.[457]

A remaining problem is that when a woman is abused it is she who must leave the home and not the abuser. The South African Domestic Violence Act, however, empowers the court, when making a protection order, 'to prohibit the respondent from . . . entering a residence shared by the complainant and the respondent'.[458]

It is also important to remember that shelters offer only a temporary solution. This was noted by the ECtHR in the case of *Opuz v Turkey*[459] and by the UK Law Lords in *Birmingham City Council v Ali*.[460] In the latter case, the Lords held that the obligation of the state to provide housing for victims fleeing domestic violence is not obviated when a victim seeks refuge in a shelter for domestic violence victims.

Shelters require resources. In countries where the necessary money and/or interest is scarce, lobbyists could challenge international organisations and the private sector to contribute towards developing a network of shelters. Bringing women together in shelters enables both formal and informal education to take place, and facilitates a link between the abused and the public world, which is especially important given the isolating nature of domestic violence. Moreover, a victim should be allowed to return to, and escape from, her abuser as many times as is necessary until she decides to leave for good, if that is in fact what she decides to do.

EMERGENCY AND LONG-TERM HEALTH AND ECONOMIC WELL-BEING

One of the main reasons why victims of domestic violence do not leave abusive situations is because they cannot afford to do so. The Council of Europe has recommended that victims of systemic intimate violence should have the right to adequate financial assistance, free childcare centres, education and training, including free language courses for immigrants, assistance in finding a job, and affordable housing; all immigrant women subject to systemic intimate violence should further have an individual right of residence.[461] Austria, for example, has

---

[456] UNDAW, *Report of the Expert Group Meeting on good practices in legislation on violence against women* (26–28 May 2008) 36, www.un.org/womenwatch/daw/egm/vaw_legislation_2008/Report%20EGMGPLVAW%20(final%2011.11.08).pdf.

[457] Harvard Law Review, 'Legal Responses to Domestic Violence' (n 422) 1507.

[458] South African Domestic Violence Act, s 7(1)(c).

[459] *Opuz v Turkey* (App No 33401/02) ECtHR 9 June 2009, para 172.

[460] *Birmingham City Council v Ali* [2009] UKHL 36; [2009] WLR (D) 221.

[461] Europe Expert Paper (n 331) 5.

recommended the creation of resources for victims of domestic violence, including fast-track access to financial support and easy access to affordable housing.[462] In Nigeria, the Violence (Prohibition) Bill 2003 established a trust fund for victims of violence which provides help and assistance in the form of rehabilitation, shelters, legal aid, and payment of medical expenses.[463]

One of the first state agents a victim may encounter is the health sector. Health care professionals will come into contact with abused women regularly, either to provide urgent medical assistance or in relation to other health-related issues, such as gynaecological and dental, pre- or post-natal or psychological needs.[464] The Special Rapporteur on violence against women has recommended that states provide emergency services including crisis intervention services, counselling and long-term rehabilitation.[465] Austria, for example, has pursued this to a certain extent and guarantees free psychological and legal aid in criminal proceedings.[466]

Health professionals can be very useful in the process of protecting victims of domestic violence. They should be trained to identify, understand and provide advice in respect of domestic violence. Such education is 'decisive for the early detection of acts of aggression and for handling these women with competence and referring them on for further help and care'.[467]

It should not be the responsibility of health providers to advise on the law, and they should certainly not be expected to enforce it. However, it is reasonable to engage health professionals in monitoring incidences of abuse and repeated abuse, and providing broad-based advice regarding state protection, shelters and legal rights to domestic violence victims.[468] Sweden, for example, has proposed the inclusion of compulsory training programmes regarding violence against women in the education of professionals who are likely to come into contact with abused women, including lawyers, physicians, midwives, nurses, psychologists, psychotherapists, dentists, social workers and others employed in the social services, teachers and educational staff.[469]

STATISTICS, INDICATORS AND BUDGET

Statistics on the prevalence, causes and effects of gender-based violence are valuable for determining which steps are required and what differences may apply in different states or regions.[470] Research should include compiling data

---

[462] ibid, 6.
[463] Nigeria Expert Paper (n 139) 14–15.
[464] South African Domestic Violence Act, s 7(1)(c).
[465] Special Rapporteur, Framework for Model Legislation (n 250) 11.
[466] Europe Expert Paper (n 331) 18.
[467] Amnesty International (n 33) 43.
[468] See ibid, 14.
[469] Amnesty International endorses the notion of a decree ordinance (ibid, 49, 56).
[470] UNDAW, Background Expert Paper (n 244) 24 (collection of statistical data).

on whether abusers re-offend and, if so, whether they target the same or different victims.[471] States should devote resources towards generating, compiling and using statistics and social surveys aimed at combating systemic intimate violence in the context of their unique social settings and infrastructures. This is a practical requirement and will determine the meaningful and effective implementation of legislation and policies.

In Italy, for example, the Financial Law 2007 created a national observatory for violence against women, to which 3 million euros per year were allocated for the following three years. The Guatemalan Law against Femicide and other Forms of Violence against Women 2008 obliges the national statistical office to compile data and develop indicators on violence against women.[472] The Albanian Law on Measures against Violence in Family Relations 2006 obliges the Ministry of Labour to maintain statistical data on domestic violence, and the Polish Law on Domestic Violence 2005 requires the Minister for Social Affairs to direct and fund research and analysis on domestic violence.[473] Mexico's Law on Access of Women to a Life Free of Violence 2007 mandates the creation of a national databank to record cases of domestic violence.[474]

Increasingly, international bodies are calling on governments to provide an adequate budget to ensure that domestic violence legislation is implemented effectively. Funding should be allocated to specialist family courts and prosecutors, NGOs and police training.[475] It is important that any budgetary allocation be based on a full analysis of the funding required to implement all measures contained in the legislation. The specific allocation of part of the national budget to address violence against women had an enormously positive impact in the United States in 1994, when the Violence against Women Act 1994 authorised the appropriation of 1.62 billion dollars in federal funds to support a broad range of programmes, including the creation of a national toll-free domestic violence telephone hotline.[476]

NATIONAL ACTION PLANS

International standards repeatedly call on states to develop national action plans to target domestic violence. This has the benefit both of ensuring that the state response to systemic intimate violence is coordinated and of allocating sufficient funds at a national level to preserve women's right to be free from systemic intimate violence.[477]

---

[471] ibid.
[472] ibid.
[473] ibid.
[474] ibid.
[475] ibid, 17.
[476] For a discussion of funding see USA Expert Paper (n 302) 2; CEE/FSU Expert Paper (n 330) 13; Latin America and the Caribbean Expert Paper (n 261) 6; Europe Expert Paper (n 331) 20, 22.
[477] See UNDAW, Background Expert Paper (n 244) 17.

In 2006, for example, Mexico reported to the CEDAW Committee on steps it had taken to strengthen the National Programme against Domestic Violence (PRONAVI), including the preparation of the National Programme for a Life without Violence 2002–2006.[478] This programme reportedly promotes the creation of a national system of public policies for prevention, treatment, information and evaluation with a gender perspective, implemented through eight strategy lines: prevention; services; detection; regulations; communication and institutional linkage; coordination and linkage with civil society; information and evaluation; and monitoring of compliance with the Inter-American the Belem do Para Convention. Each strategy has specific objectives and detailed lines of action.[479]

The Uruguayan Law for the Prevention, Early Detection, Attention to and Eradication of Domestic Violence 2002 mandates the design of a national action plan regarding domestic violence.[480] The Kenyan Sexual Offences Act 2006 requires the relevant minister to prepare a policy framework to guide implementation of the Act and review the framework at least every five years. Mexico's 2007 General Law on Women's Access to a Life Free of Violence prioritises the inclusion of measures and policies to address domestic violence in a national action plan and obliges the government to formulate and implement such a plan.[481] In Spain, the Organic Act 2004 provides for the launch of a National Sensitisation and Prevention Plan regarding domestic violence.[482] This targets both women and men in order to raise awareness of values based on respect for human rights and the equality of men and women.

CONCLUSION

While some international authorities and institutions have recognised that domestic violence is a human rights violation, there is no universal or detailed understanding of precisely why such violence should be prohibited. This has led to a continued state of uncertainty as regards the internationalisation of domestic violence. In this chapter I have sought to distil the constitutive elements that make extreme, severe and systemic forms of domestic violence against women an international human rights violation.

Systemic intimate violence comprises severe acts of harm between intimates, which operate on a continuum and to which women are especially vulnerable. Due to inappropriate state responses, and often the complete inertia of state officials, the violence becomes systemic, normalised and condoned. While there is little the law can do to change individual human behaviour, it can require states to create better facilities to respond to pain when it is caused.

---

[478] CEDAW Thirty-Sixth Session: Sixth Periodic Report on Mexico (n 440) para 53.
[479] ibid, para 54.
[480] UNDAW, Background Expert Paper (n 244) 17.
[481] ibid.
[482] ibid, 32.

In order to entrench the principle that systemic intimate violence is an international human rights violation, there needs to be a thorough and detailed enunciation of the right to be free from systemic intimate violence; the political and public nature of systemic intimate violence must be recognised; and systemic intimate violence should continue to fall within the ambit of non-gender-specific human rights bodies and institutions, such as the Committee against Torture, the Human Rights Council and the Security Council.

As a human rights violation, systemic intimate violence must be prohibited by states and its victims protected. The elements of systemic intimate violence must be specifically and authoritatively addressed in international law. A state's failure to take these practical steps ought to be recognised as an internationally wrongful act. The theory underpinning this notion of state responsibility and the benefits of internationalising systemic intimate violence are discussed in the following chapters.

3

State Responsibility in Relation to Systemic Intimate Violence

PRINCIPLES OF STATE RESPONSIBILITY

I F WE ACCEPT that systemic intimate violence, as defined in chapter two, is a human rights violation for which the state is responsible, then it is necessary to identify the rules that apply in international law when a state breaches an international obligation.

Under international law states are responsible for the protection of human rights. If the substance of systemic intimate violence is such that the harm factually falls within international human rights law, a failure by governments to assist abused women ought to fall within the rules of state responsibility.[1] This means that if states fail to protect women from systemic intimate violence they technically are in breach of international law and the principles of state responsibility apply.

In this chapter I discuss the theoretical application of the principles of state responsibility, as codified in the Draft Articles on Responsibility of States for Internationally Wrongful Acts (ILC Articles) adopted by the International Law Commission (ILC), in respect of states' duty to protect women from systemic intimate violence. A number of questions arise. Some of them are quite general: Do the principles of state responsibility apply in respect of human rights violations? Can states be held responsible for human rights violations where the violator is not a state actor but a private individual? Are individual women subjects under international law? And, if the answer to these questions is yes, at what stage can we conclude that a state has committed an internationally wrongful act—that is, when has a state *not* done enough to protect women from systemic intimate violence? The final question, that of whether there is value in pursuing the international principles of state responsibility in respect of systemic intimate violence, is addressed in chapter four.

---

[1] Christian Tomuschat, 'Individual Reparation Claims in Instances of Grave Human Rights Violations: The Position under General International Law' in Albrecht Randelzhofer and Christian Tomuschat (eds), *State Responsibility and the Individual: Reparations in Instances of Grave Violations of Human Rights* (Leiden, Martinus Nijhoff, 1999) 4. See also James Crawford, *The International Law Commission's Articles on State Responsibility* (Cambridge, Cambridge University Press, 2002) 126.

Background

The study of state responsibility deals with the principle that states have an obligation to make good any violation of international law that produces an injury.[2] In 2001, the International Law Commission adopted the ILC Articles, which are an attempt to codify and develop basic rules concerning the responsibility of states for their internationally wrongful acts.[3] The ILC's work on state responsibility is widely invoked as evidence of general international law,[4] and the ILC Articles represent nearly 40 years of work by the ILC, guided by five special rapporteurs.[5] It provides a comprehensive description of the circumstances in which a state is responsible for internationally wrongful acts, the obligation of states to remedy such acts, and applicable reparations.

The ILC Articles identify two elements that are necessary to establish state responsibility. These are 'conduct' and 'wrongfulness'. The conduct element requires some kind of act or omission which is done by or can be attributed to the state. The wrongfulness element requires that the conduct breaches an international obligation. As regards state conduct, international law recognises both positive acts and omissions as constituting the conduct element of an internationally wrongful act. Such conduct must either be carried out by the state *directly* or the conduct in question must be *attributable* to the state. As regards the second element, wrongfulness, one asks whether the state's conduct is in conformity with what is required of it by the applicable international obligation.

The principles of state responsibility distinguish between primary and secondary obligations. Primary obligations relate to the substance of the particular duty with which the state must comply.[6] This focuses on the substance of the conduct required, the standard to be observed, and the result to be achieved.[7] Primary rules are codified and/or enunciated in the various sources of international law, including treaties, tribunal and court decisions, customary international law and scholarly works.[8]

Secondary obligations are the generic rules with which states must comply whenever they breach an international obligation, irrespective of what that specific obligation is. Secondary obligations apply when a state, either in the form of an omission or commission, violates, or causes the violation of, an identified human right. Therefore, while primary-rule analysis looks to specific aspects of the obligation in question (such as the obligation not to torture a prisoner),

[2] Clyde Eagleton, *The Responsibility of States in International Law* (New York University Press, 1928) 22.

[3] International Law Commission, *Report of the International Law Commission on the work of its fifty-third session: Draft Articles of Responsibility of States for Internationally Wrongful Acts, with commentaries* (2001) UN Doc A/56/10, 43 (hereinafter ILC Articles).

[4] O Schachter, 'United Nations Law' (1994) 88 *American Journal of International Law* 5.

[5] Crawford (n 1) ix. See also Ian Brownlie, *Principles of Public International Law*, 7th edn (Oxford, Oxford University Press, 2008) 3, 436.

[6] Crawford (n 1) 74 (primary obligations relate to the content of a right).

[7] ibid, 124.

[8] Statute of the International Court of Justice (ICJ Statute), Art 38.

secondary-rule analysis refers to generic state conduct, applicable in all instances of a breach of international law.

This begs the question: Do states have a primary obligation in international law to protect women from systemic intimate violence? As discussed in chapter one, the answer to this depends on how one interprets the rules of customary international law; that is, whether one takes a 'traditional' or 'new' approach to establishing and interpreting customary international law. However, for the reasons discussed in that chapter, it is reasonable to proceed on the basis that there is an increasingly authoritative rule in international law that states are responsible for the protection of women from systemic intimate violence. Moreover, the elements of the primary obligation, that is, which steps a state should take to protect women from systemic intimate violence, are addressed in chapter two, where I discuss these steps in detail.

This takes us to the next step of the analysis, and the focus of this chapter, namely the secondary obligations of states and the 'general conditions under international law for the state to be considered responsible for wrongful actions or omissions, and the legal consequences which flow therefrom'.[9] Before I engage the elements of this analysis, however, I address several preliminary questions that may seem obvious to some, but they do need to be addressed. These questions all relate to the role of the individual in international law and the duties states owe, not to each other, but to individuals.

Who are the Subjects of International Law?

Article 1 of the ILC Articles provides that the commission of an internationally wrongful act by a state 'entails the international responsibility of that State'.[10] To whom is that responsibility owed? Originally, the international community was concerned only with the conduct of states vis-a-vis other states and the obligations owed by one state to another.[11] International law was premised on the need for states to regulate their behaviour inter se, benefiting from mutual compliance with rules and regulations.[12] This global regulation of states was limited by the notion of sovereign immunity: that what happens within the boundaries of a state is the exclusive concern of that state. However, in very narrow circumstances, mostly in the context of diplomatic relations, states could and would intervene to protect the interests (economic and otherwise) of their own nationals who were living and operating in another state.[13] States were also

[9] Crawford (n 1) 74.
[10] ILC Articles (n 3) Art 1.
[11] Crawford (n 1) 14–15.
[12] Mark W Janis, *An Introduction to International Law*, 3rd edn (Washington, DC, Aspen Publishers, 1999) 2 ('That nations ought to do to one another in peace, the most good, and in war, the least evil possible').
[13] Alwyn V Freeman, *The International Responsibility of States for Denial of Justice* (London, Longmans, Green and Co, 1938); Eagleton (n 2).

bound to protect foreign nationals living in their jurisdiction and a failure to do so constituted a denial of justice.[14]

The principles of denial of justice, which originally applied to aliens living in foreign states, were one of the first areas of law to impose obligations on states in respect of individuals. Freeman defines denial of justice as 'a concept designating some failure on the part of authorities charged with administering justice to comply with the State's general, very fundamental obligation of providing an adequate legal protection for the rights of aliens'.[15] These were the first real incursions into the doctrinal stronghold of sovereign immunity, but, for the most part, it was rare that the international community would intervene in the internal affairs of another state.[16] Even in cases of diplomatic protection, states were the dominant actors and, until 1945 and the Charter of the United Nations, the individual was at best the object—and not the subject—of international law.[17]

In the mid-1940s, this trend began to change with the rise of international humanitarian and human rights law.[18] The law of humanitarian intervention was one of the first areas of international law to recognise the rights of the individual, especially in cases 'in which a State maltreats its subjects in a manner which shocks the conscience of mankind'.[19] According to these doctrines, a state is liable in international law not only for conduct committed against other states, but also for conduct committed against its own citizens. This shift led to the question whether an individual possesses, or can possess, rights given to her or him directly by customary international law or by treaties.[20] Underlying this movement was the issue of the so-called 'fundamental rights' of the individual; rights that could be protected by international law as against the sovereign power of the state.[21] John Locke articulated this duty as the government's obligation not to act capriciously towards its citizens.[22]

This change reached its pinnacle after the Holocaust. The culmination of World War Two and the revelation of the full extent of the Holocaust placed renewed and serious focus on human rights, or the so-called 'rights of man'.[23] Having taken humankind to the brink of inhumanity and beyond, the events of

[14] For a thorough examination of this notion, see Freeman (n 13); Eagleton (n 2).
[15] Freeman (n 13) 41.
[16] Eagleton (n 2) 27.
[17] Tomuschat (n 1) 2.
[18] Janis (n 12) provides an important introduction to the notion of individuals as rights-bearers in international law (p 253).
[19] H Lauterpacht, *International Law and Human Rights* (New Haven, Shoe String Pr Inc, June 1968) 32.
[20] ibid, 5. See also Freeman (n 13) 18.
[21] ibid.
[22] John Locke, *Questions Concerning the Law of Nature with an Introduction* (text and translation by Robert Horwitz, Jenny Strauss Clay and Diskin Clay) (Ithaca, Cornell University Press, 1990) 213 (noting that, 'while all [divine] law must be obeyed, it is not necessary to obey 'a king out of fear, because he is more powerful and can compel us. For this would be to establish the power of tyrants, thieves, and pirates').
[23] The application of public international law to individuals authoritatively began with the Nuremburg Trials (Janis (n 12) 259).

the Holocaust inculcated a fresh need to articulate the rights of individuals and groups and identify corresponding obligations. This development coincided with the establishment of the United Nations (UN), charged with the creation of a supra-standard of order, a standard to which states could aspire and on which individuals could rely.[24] The reverberation of 'never again' resulted in the tapestry of the Universal Declaration of Human Rights (UDHR) in 1948[25] and, in 1956, the two rights covenants, namely the International Covenant on Civil and Political Rights (ICCPR)[26] and the International Covenant on Economic, Social and Cultural Rights (ICESCR).[27] These binding instruments placed a duty on states to protect their citizens and all people from denials of their rights.

As the application of rights broadened, so did the question of duties. If individuals could be the subjects of international rights, could they also be the holders of international duties?[28] Increasingly the question arose as to whether non-state actors, such as international institutions, corporations, private death squads and rebel groups, are subjects under international law. Some argued that unless legal duties are accepted as resting upon the individual, they do not in practice or in law oblige anyone.[29]

Certainly, by the late nineteenth century it was recognised that there are acts or omissions for which international law imposes criminal responsibility on individuals and for which punishment may be applied.[30] In 1949 the International Court of Justice authoritatively accepted 'instances of action upon the international plane by certain entities which are not States', in particular the UN.[31] This confirmed that states are not the only subjects of international law and that individuals can directly acquire international rights under treaties.[32] In 1961 in the case of *Van Gend en Loos*, the Court of Justice of the European Communities ruled that a European Community citizen has the right to see the law protecting her/his status respected by Community institutions as well as Community states.[33] This was reinforced in the case of *Francovich and Bonifaci v Italian Republic*, where the Court held that the subjects of the European Community's legal system are

---

[24] Lauterpacht (n 19) 38 ('It is in the Charter of the United Nations that the individual human being first appears as entitled to fundamental human rights and freedoms' and 'the recognition of fundamental human rights superior to the law of the sovereign State').

[25] Universal Declaration of Human Rights (UDHR) (adopted 10 December 1948) UNGA Res 217 A(III).

[26] International Covenant on Civil and Political Rights (ICCPR) (adopted 16 December 1966, entered into force 23 March 1976) 999 UNTS 171.

[27] International Covenant on Economic, Social and Cultural Rights (ICESCR) (adopted 16 December 1966, entered into force 3 January 1976) 993 UNTS 3.

[28] See ibid, preamble ('that the individual, having duties to other individuals and to the community to which he belongs, is under a responsibility to strive for the promotion and observance of the rights recognized in the present Covenant'). See also Lauterpacht (n 19) 5.

[29] Lauterpacht (n 19) 5.

[30] Brownlie (n 5) 565.

[31] *Reparations for Injuries Suffered in the Service of the United Nations* (Advisory Opinion) [1949] ICJ Rep 174 (discussing whether the UN constitutes a legal subject in international law).

[32] Lauterpacht (n 19) 23.

[33] Tomuschat (n 1) 8.

not only 'Member States but also their nationals'.[34] In this case, Italy had failed to implement an EC directive which required Member States to compensate workers who suffered damage when their employer went insolvent. Individual workers brought a claim before their national courts for compensation for the damage they had suffered due to the state's failure to implement the directive. The responsibility of states for the implementation of EU law vis-a-vis the individual became known as the *Francovich* principle of state liability. This led to the establishment of the principle that 'since the individual is deemed to be placed at the same level as the States which have created the Community legal order, no differentiation seems justifiable, provided that the rules in issue are clearly intended to benefit the Community citizen'.[35] The elements of the *Francovich* principle include: (i) a breach of EC law; (ii) attributable to the Member State; (iii) which causes damage to an individual. If these elements are established, compensation may be claimed in a legal action before a national court.

In 1980 the Vienna Convention on the Law of Treaties came into force,[36] compelling states to comply with treaties, including human rights treaties that focus on individuals.[37] In 1988, the Inter-American Court of Human Rights, in the foundational case of *Velásquez Rodríguez v Honduras*,[38] articulated the responsibility of states to 'investigate every situation involving a violation of the rights protected by the [Inter-American] Convention'. The Court noted that it was not the objective of international human rights law to punish the individual who commits violations, 'but rather to protect the victims and to provide for the reparation of damages resulting from the acts of the States responsible'.[39] If the state apparatus acts in such a way that 'the violation goes unpunished and the victim's full enjoyment of such rights is not restored as soon as possible, the State has failed to comply with its duty to ensure the free and full exercise of those rights to the persons within its jurisdiction'.[40]

In principle, the international community was now able to compel a delinquent state to treat its own citizens according to the tenets of international law.

Some argue that the individual is not only a subject of international law, but also the de facto actor in international law, deserving of protection notwithstanding the source of harm.[41] Lauterpacht, a leading scholar in the theory of

---

[34] See Case C-6/90 *Andrea Francovich and Danila Bonifaci v Italian Republic* [1991] ECR I-5357, 31.

[35] Tomuschat (n 1) 8.

[36] Vienna Convention on the Law of Treaties (adopted 23 May 1969, entered into force 27 January 1980) 1155 UNTS 331, (1969) 8 ILM 679.

[37] ibid, Art 18 ('a State is obliged to refrain from acts which would defeat the object and purpose of a treaty').

[38] *Velásquez Rodríguez v Honduras*, Inter-American Court of Human Rights Series C No 2, (1989) 28 ILM 291 (the Inter-American Court of Human Rights found the government of Honduras responsible for the disappearance of Velásquez Rodríguez, a Honduran student activist).

[39] ibid, 134.

[40] ibid, 176.

[41] Support for this position can be found in proponents of both positive and natural law. See Hans Kelsen, *Principles of International Law* (Clark, Law Book Exchange, 2003) 217–21, 151; Lauterpacht (n 19) 74.

natural law, argued that the doctrine that only states are subjects of international law has been largely rejected by the majority of international law theorists and practitioners.[42] His argument is that since international law incorporates obligations to respect fundamental human rights and freedoms 'it amounts to recognition of individuals as subjects of international law'.[43] Renowned critical legal positivist Hans Kelsen argues that international law constitutes the regulation of human conduct:

> It is to men [*sic*] that the norms of international law apply; it is against men that they provide sanctions; it is to men that they entrust the competence of creating the norms of the order. If international law lays down duties, responsibilities, and rights (it must do so if it is a legal order), these duties, responsibilities, and rights can have only human conduct for content . . . If duty, responsibility, and right do not refer to the conduct of men, duty, responsibility, and right would be only empty formulas, meaningless words.[44]

Ronald Dworkin and John Rawls, two leading theorists of political philosophy, agree that states have obligations to their citizens, and both theorists, spawning a range of subsequent ideas, have developed theories to identify the most pressing needs and how states should operate to ensure the fulfilment of such needs.[45] In determining the extent of a state's responsibility to its citizens, Rawls looks to justice and famously suggests that what is just is that which is fair.[46] For Rawls, social justice (or justice as fairness) is achieved by 'the way in which the major social institutions distribute fundamental rights and duties'.[47]

The ILC Articles do not make an express link between states and individuals, but the Commentaries to them make it clear that states can hold each other responsible for internationally wrongful acts that affect individuals.[48] By virtue of its membership in the international community, each and every state 'has a legal interest in the protection of certain basic rights and the fulfilment of certain essential obligations'.[49] Special Rapporteur Professor James Crawford points out that

---

[42] See Lauterpacht (n 19) 6 fn 2, 9 ('Like various other tenets of the positivist creed, the doctrine that only State are subjects of international law is unable to stand the test of actual practice').

[43] Lauterpacht (n 19) 35.

[44] Kelsen (n 41) 97.

[45] Any satisfactory discussion of these theorists exceeds the ambit of this book. For an initial study of these authors' theories, see Ronald Dworkin, 'What is Equality? Part I: Equality of Welfare' (1981) 10 *Philosophy and Public Affairs* 3, 185–246 and 191–92; John Rawls, *A Theory of Justice* (Cambridge, Belknap Press, rev edn 1971). See also Allen Buchanan, *Justice, Legitimacy, and Self-Determination* (Oxford, Oxford University Press, 2006) 77 (confirming Dworkin's point that the State's 'correlative obligation "trumps" appeals to what would maximize utility').

[46] Rawls, ibid, 3–6.

[47] ibid, 6.

[48] Crawford (n 1) ix. Art 33 is one of the few articles confirming the application of international law to the individual.

[49] Crawford (n 1) 66. See generally Gareth J Evans, *The Responsibility to Protect: Ending Mass Atrocity Crimes for Once and for All* (Washington, DC, Brookings Institution Press, 2008).

a State's responsibility for the breach of an obligation under a treaty concerning the protection of human rights may exist towards all the other parties to the treaty, but the individuals concerned should be regarded as the ultimate beneficiaries and in that sense as the holders of the relevant rights.[50]

Although not without contention,[51] it is now largely accepted that an individual may be a subject of international law, bearing both rights and responsibilities.[52] It is equally clear that international human rights law applies to women and their rights to equality, safety, dignity and life. We can accept, therefore, that women are subjects for the purpose of international law and the principles of state responsibility. But does this obligation apply where the state is not the perpetrator of the harm?

Doctrine of Denial of Justice

According to the doctrine of denial of justice, international law will impose responsibility on a state where there is 'a failure to provide adequate police protection before a crime has been committed, as well as by proven deficiencies in connection with apprehending and punishing the culprits'.[53] Denial of justice focuses on a state's failure to institute adequate measures to apprehend, prosecute and punish persons guilty of crimes against aliens. The requirement is not that the state agents are flawless in their execution of the law; this would be impossible.[54] Rather, the discussion focuses on reasonable and basic remedies, the absence of which is unsustainable in light of the social, political and economic circumstances of the state in question. The justification for, and the principles embedded in, the notion of denial of justice may be extrapolated equally to instances where *citizens*, and not aliens, are unable to access legal assistance in the event of egregious physical violation.

The standard demanded of states is high but it does not include ad hoc or incidental incidences of maladministration of justice. Professor Freeman, an authority on the theory of denial of justice, points out that, assuming

> proper measures of police protection have been taken, there is clearly no duty incumbent upon members of the family of nations to answer for the injuries which resident

---

[50] Crawford (n 1) 209.

[51] See Lauterpacht (n 19) 5 (describing the debate as to whether not only states but also individuals are subjects of the law of nations). See generally John H Currie, *Public International Law*, 2nd rev edn (Toronto, Irwin Law, 2008) 18 (arguing in favour of the status of an individual as a subject in international law). See also Albrecht Randelzhofer, 'The Legal Position of the Individual under Present International Law' in Albrecht Randelzhofer and Christian Tomuschat (eds), *State Responsibility and the Individual: Reparations in Instances of Grave Violations of Human Rights* (Leiden, Martinus Nijhoff, 1999) 231, 235; UN High-Level Panel on Threats, Challenges and Change, *A More Secure World: Our Shared Responsibility* (2003) UN Doc A/59/565, 23, www.un.org/secureworld/report.pdf.

[52] Crawford (n 1) 5. See also Buchanan (n 45) 77.

[53] Freeman (n 13) 368.

[54] ibid, 367.

aliens may suffer at the hands of individuals unconnected with the State or acting in a purely private capacity.[55]

His initial assumption, however, is crucial, and it is only *if* proper measures of police protection have been taken that a state can discharge its duty in international law. If not, even if the suffering is induced by an individual in a purely private capacity, such as in the context of systemic intimate violence, arguably the state would fail to fulfil its duty and it would be responsible for a breach of its international obligation.

Of course, effective police protection is nugatory without concomitant judicial enforcement. As Freeman points out, the state has an 'irrefutable duty' to take adequate steps to apprehend and punish guilty parties. 'It may have been unable to prevent commission of the crime complained of . . . Its duty subsists none the less.'[56] Freeman acknowledges that the state is not, in principle, under an obligation to prevent harm occurring to aliens, but it is under a duty to punish harm where it occurs.

It is interesting to note that this obligation pertains irrespective of the political makeup of the state in question. In the case of a federal system such as the United States, the federal government will remain answerable in international law for the actions of its constituent states.[57] Moreover, not only should unlawful activity trigger the judicial mechanism, but the penalty imposed by the judiciary must be reasonable (in that it is proportionate to the misconduct)[58] and it must be implemented in full (in that the sentence is served).[59]

Denial of justice theory can be used as a point of reference to determine the extent of a state's obligations under international law, and I refer to the principles of denial of justice in the following discussion where appropriate. But there is a pertinent question: the principles of denial of justice envisage a contentious claim between two states. Can an individual hold her or his own state to account either at an international tribunal or in national courts for a failure to comply with an international obligation?

According to the ILC Articles, a state is responsible to one or more states or to the international community as a whole.[60] However, this is 'without prejudice to any right, arising from the international responsibility of a state, which may accrue directly to any person or entity other than a State'.[61] Therefore, where a state's international obligation is owed to its citizens, those citizens may invoke the principles of state responsibility to compel states to remedy their breach of the duties in question.

---

[55] ibid, 368.
[56] ibid, 369.
[57] ibid, 370.
[58] There is also a requirement that adequate penalties be imposed (ibid, 383–84).
[59] ibid, 374–75.
[60] Crawford (n 1) Art 33(1).
[61] ibid, Art 33(2).

In *Steiner and Gross v Polish State*, a Czechoslovakian citizen brought an action against the Polish State before the Upper Silesian Arbitral Tribunal under the German-Polish Convention of 15 May 1922.[62] The tribunal allowed the claim, in part on the basis that a guiding aspect of the Convention was respect for private rights. Therefore, it would be incompatible with the tenor of the Convention to exclude a claim solely because of the nationality of the claimant.[63] In 1926, in the case of *Menge v Polish Railway Administration*,[64] the High Court of Danzig held that, in order to give effect to the purpose of the treaty concluded between Poland and the Free City of Danzig (concerning railways within the City of Danzig), it was necessary 'to construe the provisions of a treaty regulating private rights of individuals in such a manner as to recognize claims grounded directly in the treaty and put forward by private persons without interposition on the part of their State'.[65]

Following World War Two, the Convention on the Settlement of Matters arising out of the War and the Occupation, signed on 26 May 1952, incorporated a Charter giving nationals or residents of the states or territorial entities referred to in the Charter direct access to the decision-making authorities.[66] This was a phenomenon repeated by the Iran–US Claims Tribunal, which allowed claims by nationals of both the United States and Iran.[67]

These principles have continued to be upheld. In 1991, in the *Francovich* case, the European Court of Justice posed the question whether an individual citizen can bring a claim in international law against his or her own state for a failure to implement European Community law.[68] The Court asked whether, under the system of Community law, a private individual who has been adversely affected by the failure of a Member State to implement Directive 80/897—a failure confirmed by a judgment of the Court of Justice—is 'entitled to require the State itself to give effect to those provisions of that directive which are sufficiently precise and unconditional, by directly invoking the Community legislation against the Member State in default so as to obtain the guarantees which that State itself should have provided'.[69] The European Court of Justice held that, based on broad principles of state responsibility, the plaintiffs were entitled to redress, since

> the possibility of obtaining redress from the Member State is particularly indispensable where . . . the full effectiveness of Community rules is subject to prior action on the part of the State . . . It follows that the principle whereby a State must be liable for

---

[62] *Steiner and Gross v Polish State* (1927–28) 4 Annual Digest of Public International Law 291.
[63] See Kelsen (n 41) 142 fn 31, citing *Steiner and Gross,* ibid.
[64] *Menge v Polish Railway Administration* (1925–26) Annual Digest of Public International Law 258. See Kelsen (n 41) 143 fn 32.
[65] See Kelsen (n 41) 143 fn 32.
[66] See Brownlie (n 5) 589 fn 136.
[67] ibid.
[68] *Francovich* (n 34) 7.
[69] ibid.

loss and damage caused to individuals as a result of breaches of Community law for which the State can be held responsible is inherent in the system of the Treaty.[70]

I now turn to discuss whether the principles of state responsibility apply where the state is not the perpetrator of the harm.

Is a State Responsible for the Actions of Non-State Actors?

When the fundamental and universal rights of a vulnerable individual or group are violated, states have a duty to take positive steps to help remedy such violations. States do not merely have a duty not to violare rights directly. They must also, when charged with knowledge of such violations, positively act to help protect the rights of their citizens. When a state fails to satisfy that duty, it commits an internationally wrongful act.

Theorists have long argued that the concept of human rights in international law requires the state 'not only to respect but to ensure rights, that is, ensure respect for them by private persons'.[71] The result is that

> Every legal right of the individual is by definition an interest which in greater or lesser degree has the protection of the law. The protection is in the first instance against the violation of his rights by other individuals.[72]

In other words, individuals are subjects under international law and are entitled to state protection following a violation of their rights, irrespective of whether that violation is committed by public or private actors.

This is borne out in the proliferation of treaties and international statements that deal with violence against women (and other groups) in intimate circumstances. State responsibility for a failure 'to take reasonable steps to prevent or respond to an abuse' has been framed as a 'failure to exercise due diligence and to provide equal protection in preventing and punishing such abuses by private individuals'.[73] The Declaration on the Elimination of Violence against Women (DEVAW) places an obligation on states to condemn violence against women and to exercise 'due diligence to prevent, investigate and, in accordance with national legislation, punish acts of violence against women, whether those acts are perpetrated by the State or by private actors'.[74]

---

[70] ibid, 34. While the thrust of this decision targets the ability of a citizen to sue its own state in the European Court of Justice specifically (as opposed to in her/his own national courts), it nonetheless provides stable authority for the principle that a citizen can in fact hold its own state liable for non-compliance with European Union law.

[71] Louis Henkin, *The Age of Rights* (New York, Columbia University Press, 1990) 8.

[72] Humphrey Waldock, 'The Legal Protection of Human Rights—National and International' in Francis Vallat (ed), *An Introduction to the Study of Human Rights* (London, Europa Publications, 1970) 83.

[73] Amnesty International, *Broken Bodies, Shattered Minds: Torture and Ill-treatment of Women* (6 March 2001) AI-Index ACT 40/001/2001, 6, web.amnesty.org/library/Index/engact400012001.

[74] Declaration on the Elimination of Violence against Women (DEVAW), UNGA Res 48/104 (20 December 1993) UN Doc A/RES/48/104, Art 4(c).

The former UN Special Rapporteur on violence against women, Radhika Coomaraswamy, concluded in her report to the UN that the Convention on the Elimination of All Forms of Discrimination against Women (CEDAW), DEVAW and General Recommendation 19 of the CEDAW Committee impose legal obligations on states and that 'at the beginning of the twenty-first century, the action of State parties may be measured against international standards that clearly articulate a strategy for the elimination of violence against women in the family'.[75] The former Secretary-General of the UN, Kofi Annan, confirmed this position, noting that it is now well established under international law that 'violence against women is a form of discrimination against women and a violation of human rights'.[76] In January 2009 the UN General Assembly passed Resolution 63/155 on the intensification of efforts to eliminate all forms of violence against women, which reaffirms 'the obligation of all States to promote and protect all human rights and fundamental freedoms'.[77] Freeman summarises the position neatly:

> Finally, insofar as responsibility growing out of the uncontrollable, independent acts of private individuals is concerned, the rule may be thus stated: Although such acts cannot be imputed to the state, the latter is not free to regard them with utter indifference.[78]

How does this responsibility operate in respect of systemic intimate violence? At what point has a state committed an international wrongful act by failing to protect women when the violence takes place in private, in the home and in the intimacy of a relationship, places where the state ought not to be present? And is it intellectually sound to apply the principles of state responsibility to systemic intimate violence? These answers can only really be addressed by analysing the elements of state responsibility as they apply generally and then applying them to systemic intimate violence. The following sections discuss these elements, proposing that a state's omission to take certain minimum positive steps to protect individuals from systemic intimate violence is 'conduct' which is 'wrongful' in that it breaches that state's primary international obligation to help remedy such violence.

---

[75] UNCHR, *Report of the Special Rapporteur on violence against women, its causes and consequences, Ms Radhika Coomaraswamy, Cultural practices in the family that are violent towards women* (31 January 2002) UN Doc E/CN.4/2002/83, 31, with reference to the Convention on the Elimination of All Forms of Discrimination against Women (CEDAW) (adopted 18 December 1979, entered into force 3 September 1981) 1249 UNTS 13, UN Doc A/RES/34/830, (1980) 19 ILM 33; DEVAW (n 74) and the UN Committee for the Elimination of All Forms of Discrimination against Women, 'General Recommendation 19: Violence against Women' (1992) UN Doc A/47/38.

[76] Secretary-General, 'In-depth Study on All Forms of Violence against Women' (2006) UN Doc A/61/122/Add.1, para 254 (hereinafter Study of the Secretary-General).

[77] UNGA Res 63/55 (30 January 2009) UN Doc A/RES/63/155, Intensification of efforts to eliminate all forms of violence against women.

[78] Freeman (n 13) 27.

ELEMENTS OF STATE RESPONSIBILITY AND THEIR APPLICATION TO SYSTEMIC INTIMATE VIOLENCE

In order to establish state responsibility for systemic intimate violence in international law, the following elements must exist. First, there must *be state conduct*, either in the form of an omission or a commission.[79] The conduct must be carried out by the state or the conduct in question must be *attributable* to the state.[80] Second, the conduct must be *wrongful* in that it breaches a primary obligation of the state.[81] It is important to note that, subject to the content of the primary obligation, fault and harm are not necessary to trigger state responsibility.[82]

Conduct Element

State responsibility is triggered when a state commits an internationally wrongful act.[83] 'Act' can include both actions and omissions.[84] For the purposes of assessing state responsibility for systemic intimate violence, it is necessary to demonstrate that (1) a state can commit an internationally wrongful act through a failure to protect citizens from non-state violence, that is, from the harmful acts of other citizens; (2) states therefore have to be proactive and take steps to enforce both negative (freedom from) and positive (freedom to) rights; and (3) where state officials and agents fail to act, they may trigger an internationally wrongful act. I discuss each factor below.

Conduct by virtue of an Omission

According to the ILC Articles, state conduct can consist of actions or omissions. In the case of systemic intimate violence, it is the state's inaction in the face of

---

[79] Art 2 refers to 'conduct consisting of an action or omission'; Art 15(1) allows for a breach through a series of omissions 'defined in the aggregate as wrongful'. See Crawford (n 1).

[80] ILC Articles, Art 2(a). The notion of attribution is detailed in Chapter III of the ILC Articles. For a criticism of 'imputability' see Brownlie (n 5) 438. See also Crawford (n 1) 4 (confirming the notion that the conduct of persons can be attributed to the state).

[81] ILC Articles, Arts 1 and 2(b). See Crawford (n 1) 68. See also *United States Diplomatic and Consular Staff in Tehran (United States of America v Iran)* (Judgment) General List No 64 [1980] ICJ 3: in order to establish the responsibility of Iran 'First, it must determine how far, legally, the acts in question may be regarded as imputable to the Iranian State. Secondly, it must consider their compatibility or incompatibility with the obligations of Iran under treaties in force or under any other rules of international law that may be applicable.' See also *Dickson Car Wheel Company Claim (US v Mexico)* (1931) 4 RIAA 669, 678. As regards wrongfulness, see Crawford (n 1) 71; *Case Concerning the Factory at Chorzów (Germany v Poland)* (Merits) PCIJ Rep Series A No 17, 29; *Rainbow Warrior (New Zealand v France)* (Arbitration Tribunal) (1990) 82 ILR 499, para 75.

[82] See Malcolm N Shaw, *International Law*, 5th edn (Cambridge, Cambridge University Press, 2003) 696–98. See also Brownlie (n 5) 436; Crawford (n 1) 73.

[83] ILC Articles, Art 1.

[84] ibid, Art 2.

recurring and systemic violence that constitutes 'conduct' for the purposes of state responsibility. The responsibility arises before the moment of the attack (the responsibility to prevent violence) and in the state's reaction to the attack (the responsibility to punish and protect).[85] Where the state fails to prevent, protect or punish, it has committed an act for the purposes of state responsibility. This omission constitutes an internationally wrongful act.

Complicity

Increasingly, a failure to comply with an international obligation is being framed as complicity with those who perform the original act of harm. Former UN Special Rapporteur on violence against women, Radhika Coomaraswamy, claims that states are obliged to take basic steps to stop domestic violence and 'a State can be held complicit where it fails systematically to provide protection from private actors who deprive any person of his/her human rights'.[86] However, not all commentators agree with this. Freeman, for example, disagrees that state inertia constitutes *complicity*, referring to it as the 'utterly fictitious theory of implied State *complicity*' in what seems 'clearly a politico-legal effort to render more palatable the postulate of State responsibility in these cases'.[87] According to Freeman, in the context of 'denial of justice', foreigners

> may fall victim to an initial wrong, perpetrated by a private person against whom they subsequently seek relief in the courts. For the act itself, the state is not answerable; but if the conduct of the proceedings in this private litigation is deficient, a duty to make reparation for the denial of justice will arise under the law of nations.[88]

As far as systemic intimate violence is concerned, the responsibility of the state does not need to be grounded in a legal fiction or in a notion such as complicity. There is a closer, more direct and more logically sustainable basis from which state responsibility arises, namely the state's *omission*. It is its failure to take steps to help remedy systemic intimate violence that is itself unlawful; there is no need to attribute the original act of violence to the state.[89] The state's own, independent conduct is what amounts to an internationally wrongful act; the element of conduct is not grounded in the individual abuser's behaviour, but

---

[85] General Recommendation 19 (n 75) calls on states to prevent violations of rights and to investigate and punish acts of violence (Art 9).

[86] UNCHR, *Report of the Special Rapporteur on violence against women, its causes and consequences: Further Promotion and Encouragement of Human Rights and Fundamental Freedoms, Including the Question of the Programme and Methods of Work of the Commission Alternative Approaches and Ways and Means within the United Nations System for Improving the Effective Enjoyment of Human Rights and Fundamental Freedoms* (6 February 1996) UN Doc E/CN.4/1996/53 (hereinafter Special Rapporteur 1996 Report).

[87] Freeman (n 13) 20.

[88] ibid, 372. See also Eagleton (n 2) 24. In his view it is the failure to take basic steps and act with due diligence that leads to an independent internationally wrongful act.

[89] This is confirmed by Freeman (n 13) 372 ('The act itself can never charge the State; only the latter's independent failure to observe its repressive duties is capable of so doing').

rather in the conduct, by way of omission, of the state itself to take appropriate steps, along the lines of those discussed in chapter two.[90]

Precedent in International Law

There is now extensive precedent in international law for the principle that a failure of the state to prevent predictable and extreme harm being caused to an identifiable portion of the population constitutes an internationally wrongful act.[91] There are several examples in international law where government omission constitutes an internationally wrongful act. These include: failure to intervene in cases of persecution of racial minorities;[92] failure to apply the law equally to all citizens;[93] failure to prevent acts of torture;[94] failure to provide a transparent criminal justice system;[95] failure to prevent child abuse;[96] failure to prevent the trafficking of human beings;[97] and failure to prevent mass rape.[98]

Recently, this principle was confirmed in the groundbreaking case of *Opuz v Turkey*, where the European Court of Human Rights (ECtHR) held that the state had violated Article 2 (right to life), Article 3 (prohibition against torture) and Article 14 (equal enjoyment of Convention rights) of the European Convention on Human Rights by virtue of its failure to exercise due diligence in

---

[90] Eagleton (n 2) 77 (arguing that 'the State is never responsible for the act of an individual as such: the act of the individual merely occasions the responsibility of the State in an illegality of its own—an omission to prevent or punish, or positive encouragement of, the act of the individual').

[91] This approach has been used in respect of trafficking. See eg Joan Fitzpatrick, 'Trafficking as a Human Rights Violation: The Complex Intersection of Legal Frameworks for Conceptualizing and Combating Trafficking' (2003) 24 *Michigan Journal of International Law* 1143, 1157–58.

[92] International Convention on the Elimination of All Forms of Racial Discrimination (adopted 21 December 1965, entered into force 4 January 1969) 660 UNTS 195 (hereinafter Convention against Racial Discrimination), Art 2(1).

[93] UDHR (n 25) Art 6. Art 14(1) of the ICCPR (n 26) provides that 'All persons shall be equal before the courts and tribunals'.

[94] Convention against Torture and Other Cruel, Inhuman or Degrading Treatment or Punishment (adopted 10 December 1984, entered into force 26 July 1987) 1465 UNTS 85, (1984) 23 ILM 1027 (hereinafter Torture Convention), Art 2(1).

[95] ICCPR (n 26) Art 14(1) and (2).

[96] Convention on the Rights of the Child (adopted 20 November 1989, entered into force 2 September 1990) 1577 UNTS 3, (1989) 28 ILM 1456 (hereinafter Children's Convention). Art 2(2) requires states to 'take all appropriate measures to ensure that the child is protected against all forms of discrimination or punishment'.

[97] Protocol to Prevent, Suppress and Punish Trafficking in Persons, Especially Women and Children, Supplementing the United Nations Convention Against Transnational Organized Crime, UNGA Res 55/25 (adopted 15 November 2000, entered into force 9 September 2003) UN Doc A/45/49 (Vol I) Art 1: states are required to 'punish any person who, to gratify the passions of another: (1) Procures, entices or leads away, for purposes of prostitution, another person, even with the consent of that person; (2) Exploits the prostitution of another person, even with the consent of that person'.

[98] See United Nations Diplomatic Conference of Plenipotentiaries on the Establishment of an International Criminal Court, Rome Statute of the International Criminal Court (1998) UN Doc A/CONF.183/9, Art 7(1)(g); *Prosecutor v Akayesu* (Judgment) ICTR-96-4-T, T Ch I (2 September 1998) para 597.

protecting women from domestic violence.[99] It is informative to consider the precedent in international and regional law that substantiates this judgment.

Several international treaties have identified the need for proactive state conduct in order to fulfil its various human rights obligations. In 1969, the UN adopted the International Convention on the Elimination of All Forms of Racial Discrimination, which prohibits prejudicial conduct on the part of states, and also requires them to 'prohibit and bring to an end . . . racial discrimination by any persons, group or organization'.[100] The state is obliged to provide 'effective protection and remedies, through the competent national tribunals and other state institutions, against any acts of racial discrimination which violate his [*sic*] human rights and fundamental freedoms contrary to this Convention'.[101] The definition of torture in the Convention against Torture and Other Cruel, Inhuman or Degrading Treatment or Punishment includes conduct in the form of 'consent or acquiescence of a public official or other person acting in an official capacity'.[102] It further requires states to criminalise 'all acts of torture' including 'an act by any person which constitutes complicity or participation in torture'.[103]

CEDAW, which was adopted in 1979, provides that a government's duty to prevent discriminatory conduct extends to discriminatory conduct on the part of individuals, organisations and enterprises, and each state must take steps to prevent this.[104] General Recommendation 19 stipulates that CEDAW 'applies to violence perpetrated by public authorities'[105] and emphasises that state conduct 'is not restricted to action by or on behalf of governments'; a state may also be responsible for private acts if it fails 'to act with due diligence to prevent violations of rights or to investigate and punish acts of violence'.[106] This definition undoubtedly extends the obligation of states to address the conduct of its officials, either in the form of harmful action or pernicious inaction.

In 1989, the Children's Convention was adopted, in terms of which governments undertook

> to ensure the child such protection and care as is necessary for his or her well-being, taking into account the rights and duties of his or her parents, legal guardians, or other individuals legally responsible for him or her, and, to this end, shall take all appropriate legislative and administrative measures.[107]

---

[99] *Opuz v Turkey* (App No 33401/02) ECtHR 9 June 2009, paras 149, 176, 201.
[100] Convention against Racial Discrimination (n 92) Art 2(1)(d).
[101] ibid, Art 6.
[102] Torture Convention (n 94) Art 1.
[103] ibid, Art 4(1).
[104] CEDAW (n 75) Art 2(e).
[105] General Recommendation 19 (n 75) para 19.
[106] ibid.
[107] Children's Convention (n 96) Art 3(2).

The Children's Convention requires state parties to

take all appropriate measures to ensure that the child is protected against all forms of discrimination or punishment on the basis of the status, activities, expressed opinions, or beliefs of the child's parents, legal guardians, or family members.[108]

A similar obligation exists in European regional arrangements. In Europe, the 1992 Treaty Establishing the European Economic Community enjoins Member States to 'take all appropriate measures, whether general or particular, to ensure fulfilment of the obligations arising out of this Treaty or resulting from action taken by the institutions of the Community'. There have also been several cases on state responsibility before the International Court of Justice (ICJ) and regional courts. Cases in which the international responsibility of a state has been invoked on the basis of an omission are at least as numerous as those based on positive acts and, in principle, there is no difference between the two.[109] As early as 1923, in the *Tellini* case, the Permanent Court of Justice acknowledged the importance of attributing responsibility to a state 'if the State has neglected to take all reasonable measures for the prevention of the crime and the pursuit, arrest and bringing to justice of the criminal'.[110] In the *Corfu Channel* case the ICJ held that Albania had committed an internationally wrongful act because it knew, or must have known, that there were unexploded mines in its territorial waters and yet did nothing to warn third states of their presence.[111] Although Albania did not itself lay the mines, it was held responsible on the basis of 'knowledge possessed by that State as to the presence of such mines, even though there was no finding as to who had actually laid the mines'.[112] Albania's responsibility was premised not on its *actions* but rather on its failure to advise third party states of the presence of mines in its territorial waters.

In the *United States Diplomatic and Consular Staff in Tehran* case, the ICJ concluded that the responsibility of Iran was entailed by the 'inaction' of its authorities, which had 'failed to take appropriate steps' in circumstances where such steps were evidently necessary.[113]

In 1982 the UN Human Rights Committee interpreted Article 7 of the ICCPR, which prohibits torture or cruel, inhuman, or degrading treatment or punishment,[114] and stated that

The scope of protection required goes far beyond torture as normally understood . . . [T]he prohibition must extend to corporal punishment, including excessive chastisement as an educational or disciplinary measure . . . Finally, it is also the duty of public

---

[108] ibid, Art 2(2).
[109] Crawford (n 1) 70.
[110] *Tellini* case (1923) 4 League of Nations Official Journal 11.
[111] *Corfu Channel* case (*United Kingdom v Albania*) (Merits) [1949] ICJ Rep 4.
[112] ibid, 155: See also Shaw (n 82) 701; Lauterpacht, *International Law Reports* (Cambridge, Cambridge University Press, 1949) 155–70.
[113] *United States Diplomatic and Consular Staff in Tehran* case (n 81) 31–32. See also Crawford (n 1) 70.
[114] ICCPR (n 26) 52.

authorities to ensure protection by the law against such treatment even when committed by persons acting outside or without any official authority.[115]

The Human Rights Committee also developed the positive duty of states vis-a-vis their citizens in the context of the ICCPR:

> It is the duty of the State party to afford everyone protection through legislative and other measures as may be necessary against the acts prohibited by article 7, whether inflicted by people acting in their official capacity, outside their official capacity or in a private capacity. The prohibition in article 7 is complemented by the positive requirements of article 10, paragraph 1, of the Covenant, which stipulates that 'All persons deprived of their liberty shall be treated with humanity and with respect for the inherent dignity of the human person'.[116]

The CEDAW Committee has reviewed the question of whether state parties can be held accountable for the conduct of non-state actors in stating that 'discrimination under the Convention is not restricted to action by or on behalf of Governments' and that

> under general international law and specific human rights covenants, States may also be responsible for private acts if they fail to act with due diligence to prevent violations of rights or to investigate and punish acts of violence, and for providing compensation.[117]

Scholars have noted that states may be responsible for the harmful conduct of their citizens where they have been complicit, acquiesced or remained passive in the face of private conduct.[118] Freeman maintains that a state can be responsible for conduct 'where the original source of the injury was the act of some individual acting in a private capacity and where the State subsequently failed in the duties incumbent upon it as a consequence of an earlier wrong'.[119] Philip Alston includes in states' human rights obligations

> the positive organization of the social and economic conditions within which men can participate to a maximum as active members of the community at the highest level permitted by the material development of the society.[120]

---

[115]   ibid.

[116]   Human Rights Committee, 'CCPR General Comment No 20: Replaces general comment 7 concerning prohibition of torture and cruel treatment or punishment (Art 7)' (10 March 1992) (hereinafter General Comment 20).

[117]   *The Vienna Intervention Centre against Domestic Violence and the Association for Women's Access to Justice on behalf of Banu Akbak, Gülen Khan, and Melissa Özdemir (descendants of the deceased), alleged victim: Fatma Yildirim (deceased) v Austria* (Decision) CEDAW Committee (views adopted 1 October 2007) Communication No 6/2005 UN Doc CEDAW/C/39/D/6/2005, para 12.1.1 (hereinafter *Yildirim v Austria*). See also Inter-American Commission on Human Rights, Organization of American States, *The Situation of the Rights of Women in Ciudad Juárez, Mexico: The Right to be Free from Violence and Discrimination* (7 March 2003) EA/Ser.L/V/II.117 Doc 44, para 34.

[118]   This is confirmed by Crawford (n 1) 80.

[119]   Freeman (n 13) 19.

[120]   Philip Alston, 'Conjuring Up New Human Rights: A Proposal For Quality Control' (1984) 78 *American Journal of International Law* 607, 614.

Nozick, whose theory is characterised by the notion of least possible state intervention, identifies the role of the state as minimal, mostly abstaining, and intervening only to protect citizens against 'force, fraud, theft, and breach of contracts, to settle disputes, and to punish violations'.[121] Even at this minimalist level, Nozick recognises that the state has a duty to intervene to protect its citizens against force. The duty applies a fortiori where a particularly vulnerable subset of society requires protection. Henkin also proposes that the fundamental rights include not only freedoms that governments must respect, but also 'rights to what is essential for human well-being, which government must actively provide or promote'.[122]

The precedent is clear: a failure of the state to prevent predictable and extreme harm to an identifiable portion of the population constitutes an internationally wrongful act. There appears to be no reason why this should not apply in respect of systemic intimate violence. But what precisely does the theory of state responsibility require governments to do?

Positive Steps to Prevent a Negative Right

Chapter two described the steps that states should take to protect women from systemic intimate violence. What is the theoretical substantiation for the claim that states must take these steps, and is it appropriate that the international legal system imposes an obligation on states to be proactive?

Traditionally, human rights have been grouped into so-called negative rights (freedoms *from*) and positive rights (freedoms *to*). Negative rights are associated with civil and political rights, for example freedom of speech, which often is described as a negative right to communicate ideas independently of the state and *free from* state limitation. Positive rights are generally associated with economic, social and cultural rights, and include, for example, the right *to* food, shelter and education.

This distinction is more a product of historical politics than sound legal reasoning. It developed as a result of the existence of competing legal and ideological considerations. The categorisation of socio-economic rights and civil and political rights is largely a product of the Cold War. Socio-economic rights were associated with non-democratic communist regimes while the West committed itself to the ideology of civil and political liberties. This stark legal distinction was never intended. In the UDHR, the rights to social security, health, housing and education stand alongside the rights to vote, to speak freely, to be free from torture and to equality. The official position was that these rights are universal, indivisible,

---

[121] Jerome J Shestack, 'The Jurisprudence of Human Rights' in Theodor Meron (ed), *Human Rights in International Law: Legal and Policy Issues* (Oxford, Clarendon Press, 1984) 69, 94.

[122] Louis Henkin, 'International Human Rights and Rights in the United States' in Theodor Meron (ed), *Human Rights in International Law: Legal and Policy Issues* (Oxford, Clarendon Press, 1984) 25, 33–34.

interdependent and interrelated.[123] In the build-up to the Universal Declaration, Franklin D Roosevelt (influenced by Eleanor Roosevelt) identified four essential human freedoms:[124] freedom of speech, freedom to worship God in one's own way, freedom from want, and freedom from fear. As the foundations of the well-known Bangalore Principles of Judicial Conduct confirm, both 'civil and political rights and economic, social and cultural rights are integral, indivisible and complementary parts of one coherent system of global human rights'.[125]

The impact of this ideological categorisation is that historically, negative rights such as civil and political rights have been better enforced in democratic nations. Such rights require the state to *abstain* from invasive action. In the case of positive rights, however, enforcement requires positive state action, which usually translates into providing funds and resources to meet socio-economic needs, such as health, education and welfare.

Clearly the categorisation of positive and negative rights is not ideal. In reality, both civil-political and socio-economic rights may require governments to act positively or negatively. As a matter of normative desirability, there is no difference between social and economic rights and civil and political rights. As Justice Kate O'Regan (of the South African Constitutional Court) points out:

> The desirability of ensuring that all citizens receive basic education, are properly housed, have access to food, clean water and health care is not, I think, a controversial one. Indeed, social and economic rights are in some sense anterior to civil and political rights. The basic needs of human beings to shelter, nutrition and clothing need to be met before a lively interest in freedom of expression and association arises. It is for this reason that many international documents acknowledge the indivisibility and interdependence of social and economic rights on the one hand and civil and political rights on the other.[126]

In 1982 the UN Human Rights Committee interpreted Article 7 of the ICCPR, which prohibits torture, as including the duty on public authorities 'to ensure protection by the law against such treatment even when committed by persons acting outside or without any official authority'. The same committee enunciated the positive duty of states vis-a-vis their citizens, instructing states that complaints must be 'investigated promptly and impartially by competent authorities so as to make the remedy effective'.[127] Even in respect of the less obviously enforceable socio-economic rights, Henkin reminds us that the ICESCR

[123] 'Vienna Declaration and Programme of Action', World Conference on Human Rights (Vienna, 14–25 June 1993) UN Doc A/CONF.157/24 (12 July 1993) para 5.
[124] Franklin D Roosevelt, 'Four Freedoms' speech (Annual Message to Congress, 6 January 1941), www.fdrlibrary.marist.edu/4free.html.
[125] 'Bangalore Principles of Judicial Conduct 2002' (Bangalore Draft Code of Judicial Conduct 2001), adopted by the Judicial Group on Strengthening Judicial Integrity, as revised at the Round Table Meeting of Chief Justices (The Hague, 25–26 November 2002) para 4.
[126] Kate O'Regan, 'The Challenge of Change: Thirteen Years of Constitutional Democracy in South Africa' (John Foster and Miriam Rothschild Memorial Lecture 2007), www.rothschildfostertrust.com/trust/lectures.
[127] General Comment 20 (n 116) para 14.

uses the language of right, not merely of hope; of undertaking and commitment by governments, not merely of aspiration and goal . . . the language of rights is increasingly used and the sense of entitlement to such benefits is becoming pervasive.[128]

The European Social Charter, which contains a list of objectives and provisions, and the EU Charter of Fundamental Rights also reflect this indivisibility.[129]

Most rights consist of a cross-section of economic, social, civil and political elements. For example, the right to participate in elections—a political right—includes a right to vote, which is an uncontroversial but nevertheless positive enunciation of a right. The right to a fair trial, including the right to legal representation at public expense, is commonly considered to be a civil-political right which contains clear positive obligations. On the other hand, the right to freedom of movement—a civil-political right—is rarely considered to impose an obligation of free air or train travel upon a state. In this sense the enforcement of this right is 'negative'. And the right to education could well be applied to prevent a law which stipulated that a person suffering from Down's Syndrome should be denied education.[130] This is a negative enforcement of a social right in that government must not prevent that child from attending school.

Systemic intimate violence is a further example of the overlap that exists between economic, social and cultural rights and political and civil rights. It compromises the right to life,[131] the right to equality,[132] the right to be free from torture,[133] the right to liberty and security of the person,[134] the right to privacy[135] and the right to marriage.[136] These are all civil and political rights enumerated in the ICCPR. Systemic intimate violence also breaches the victim's right to health[137] and right to work.[138] Even though systemic intimate violence straddles socio-economic and civil and political rights, it is still necessary to finesse the question of how states should protect these rights, especially where they must do something active.

There is a wealth of debate and dialogue about the enforcement of rights 'to'. The UDHR identified the obligation of states to respect and to *ensure respect* for human rights.[139] The Maastricht Guidelines on Violations of Economic, Social and Cultural Rights identify obligations to respect, protect and fulfil rights

---

[128] Henkin (n 122) 43.
[129] European Social Charter (open for signature 18 October 1961, entered into force 26 February 1965) CETS No 035, ETS No 35; Convention for the Protection of Human Rights and Fundamental Freedoms (European Convention on Human Rights, as amended) (ECHR).
[130] O'Regan (n 126).
[131] ICCPR (n 26) Art 6.
[132] ibid, Arts 2, 3, 26.
[133] ibid, Art 7.
[134] ibid, Art 9.
[135] ibid, Art 17.
[136] ibid, Art 23.
[137] ICESCR (n 27) Art 12.
[138] ibid, Art 6.
[139] UDHR (n 25) preamble.

(Guideline 6)[140] and governments must take action reasonably calculated to realise the enjoyment of a particular right (Guideline 7).

Some of the more useful guidance comes from the ECtHR and its interpretation of the various rights enunciated in the ECHR. It has interpreted Article 2 of the Convention, the right to life, as imposing a duty on the state not only to refrain from taking life but also to take positive steps to protect the lives of those in their jurisdiction.[141] Article 2(1) places on the state both a positive duty to safeguard the lives of those within its jurisdiction and a negative duty to refrain from the intentional and unlawful taking of life.[142] As with all positive duties to ensure rights, states have a broad discretion as to how to fulfil their positive duty to protect life given the political and operational choices that must be made in terms of priorities and resources. A state is obliged by Article 2 to put in place effective criminal law provisions to deter the commission of offences against the person, backed up by law enforcement machinery for the prevention, suppression and punishment of breaches of such provisions.[143] It may also, in appropriate circumstances, be under a positive obligation to take preventive operational measures to protect an individual or individuals whose life is at risk from the criminal acts of another individual.[144] The scope of this positive obligation must be interpreted in a way which does not impose an impossible or disproportionate burden on the authorities, 'bearing in mind the difficulties in policing modern societies, the unpredictability of human conduct and the operational choices which must be made in terms of priorities and resources'.[145] Criminal proceedings are not always necessary. Civil, administrative or even disciplinary remedies may satisfy this part of Article 2.[146]

Of course, not every claimed risk to life can entail for the authorities an obligation to take operational measures to prevent that risk from materialising. As established in *Osman v The United Kingdom*,[147] and successfully invoked in *Kiliç v Turkey*,[148] for a violation of the positive obligation to protect the right to life to arise,

> it must be established that the authorities knew or ought to have known at the time of the existence of a real and immediate risk to the life of an identified individual or indi-

---

[140] International Commission of Jurists, 'Maastricht Guidelines on Violations of Economic, Social and Cultural Rights' (26 January 1997), reprinted in (1998) 20 *Human Rights Quarterly* 691.

[141] *Osman v The United Kingdom* (1998) 29 EHRR 245, para 115. See also *Savage v South Essex Partnership NHS Foundation Trust* [2008] UKHL 74, [2009] 2 WLR 115.

[142] *LCB v The United Kingdom* (1998) 27 EHRR 212, para 36.

[143] *Kiliç v Turkey* (2001) 33 EHRR 1357, para 62; *Mahmut Kaya v Turkey* (App No 22535/93) ECtHR 28 March 2000, para 85, citing *Osman v The United Kingdom,* para 115.

[144] *Kiliç v Turkey*, ibid, para 62; *Osman v The United Kingdom* (n 141) para 115. See also *Keenan v The United Kingdom* (2001) 33 EHRR 913, para 88.

[145] *Osman* (n 141) para 116. See also *Kiliç v Turkey* (n 143) para 63; *Mahmut Kaya v Turkey* (n 143) para 86; *Keenan v The United Kingdom* (n 144) para 89; *Isayeva v Russia* (2005) 41 EHRR 791, paras 172, 176.

[146] *Vo v France* (2005) 40 EHRR 259 (ECtHR, Grand Chamber), para 90.

[147] *Osman v The United Kingdom* (n 141) para 116.

[148] *Kiliç v Turkey* (n 143) para 87; see in general *Mahmut Kaya v Turkey* (n 143).

viduals from the criminal acts of a third party and that they failed to take measures within the scope of their powers which, judged reasonably, might have been expected to avoid that risk.

This is essentially a two-part test, with the first part concerning the extent of the state's knowledge and the second concerning the reasonableness of the steps taken. According to the ECtHR in *Osman,*

> it is sufficient for an applicant to show that the authorities did not do all that could reasonably be expected of them to avoid a real and immediate risk to life of which they have or ought to have knowledge.[149]

As for the risk, it can be considered 'real and immediate' when the authorities are aware of a significant number of incidents involving the killing of persons similar to the individual concerned, who appear to have been targeted because of their political views by either the security forces or other non-state actors acting with the state's knowledge and acquiescence.[150]

A request to the authorities for protective measures may also support a finding of a 'real and immediate' risk.[151] In *Osman,* the ECtHR was concerned with the alleged failure of the police to take the steps necessary to protect a family who had been repeatedly threatened and intimidated by the mentally disturbed teacher of one of their children. The teacher fatally shot the father and seriously wounded the child. The Court recognised the potential application of Article 2 and applied the two-part test. On the facts, the ECtHR found no violation of Article 2 because the applicants had failed to point to any decisive stage in the sequence of events leading to the shooting when it could be said that the police knew or ought to have known that the lives of the Osman family were at a real and immediate risk from the criminal acts of a third party.[152] Nor could it be said that the missed opportunities to intervene would have saved the life of the deceased. The high threshold of the state's obligations under this test was further illustrated in *Mastromatteo v Italy,* where the applicant's son was murdered by three criminals during the course of an armed robbery; one of them had been released from prison on leave and another was subject to a semi-custodial regime.[153] The ECtHR held that the state was not in breach of its duty to protect the life of the applicant's son because there was nothing to make the authorities fear that the release of the two men might pose a real and immediate threat to life or alert the authorities to the need to take additional measures against them.

---

[149] *Osman v The United Kingdom* (n 141) para 116.
[150] *Kiliç v Turkey* (n 143) para 66; *Mahmut Kaya v Turkey* (n 143) paras 89–91. See also *Akkoç v Turkey* (2002) 34 EHRR 1173, paras 77–78.
[151] *Kiliç v Turkey* (n 143) para 67.
[152] *Osman v The United Kingdom* (n 141) para 121.
[153] *Mastromatteo v Italy* (App No 37703/97) ECtHR 24 October 2002. See also *Keenan v The United Kingdom* (n 144) para 89 (where the ECtHR found that the authorities were not aware of a 'real and immediate risk to life' before a mentally ill prisoner committed suicide); *Carmichelle v Minister of Safety and Security* 2001(4) SA 938 (CC).

However, the Court's approach began to change. In *Kontrová v Slovakia*, the ECtHR applied the two-part test and found a violation of Article 2.[154] The applicant had been beaten and subjected to psychological and physical violence by her husband. Despite reports of the violence, the police failed to bring criminal charges or investigate the complaints. Eventually, the applicant's husband shot their two children and then himself. The ECtHR held that the state had a positive obligation to take preventive operational measures to protect the applicant's children from severe beatings and psychological abuse in the applicant's family, which behaviour was known to the local police department. The police had an array of specific obligations with which they had failed to comply.[155] The direct consequence of these failures was the death of the applicant's children and a violation of Article 2. In *Medova v Russia*, the ECtHR held that the authorities' decision to release six men from detention, which resulted in the disappearance of Mr Medov, constituted a breach of the positive obligation to take preventive measures to protect those whose life is at risk from the criminal acts of other individuals.[156]

It is not always necessary that death should actually occur in order for Article 2 to be engaged. In exceptional circumstances, a threat or attempt may be sufficient. Arguments involving a potential breach of Article 2 were successfully invoked in the UK in *Venables v News Group Newspapers Ltd*, where lifetime anonymity was granted to Robert Thompson and Jon Venables, the juveniles found guilty of murdering toddler James Bulger, following 'specific and serious' threats to their lives on their release from detention.[157] In *Family Planning Association of Northern Ireland v Minister of Health*, the Northern Ireland Court of Appeal referred to a general 'target' duty to secure the efficient provision of health services and healthcare facilities in the context of reproductive rights.[158] The court held that the state is obliged to investigate what was happening on the ground and to give guidance regarding the lawful procurement of abortion facilities.[159] Although the case was decided on common law grounds and not under the Human Rights Act 1998 (which incorporates the European Convention into UK law), it provides important guidance regarding the state's positive obligation to provide proper healthcare, particularly in the context of abortion.

The ECtHR has also addressed the positive steps that a state is obliged to take to prevent an environmental hazard which leads to death. In *Öneryildiz v Turkey*, nine members of the applicant's family were killed when a landslide from a rubbish tip in an Istanbul shantytown buried their house.[160] The court

---

[154] *Kontrová v Slovakia* (App No 7510/04) ECtHR 31 May 2007, para 49.
[155] ibid, paras 52–54.
[156] *Medova v Russia* (App No 25385/04) ECtHR 15 January 2009, para 99.
[157] *Venables v News Group Newspapers Ltd* [2001] Fam 430.
[158] *Family Planning Association of Northern Ireland v Minister of Health* [2004] NICA 39 (CA), paras 6–9 per Nicholson LJ.
[159] ibid, paras 38–44 per Nicholson LJ; para 11 per Sheil LJ; paras 45–49 per Campbell LJ.
[160] *Öneryildiz v Turkey* (2005) 41 EHRR 20.

found a violation of Article 2 on the basis that the local authorities had failed to implement existing protective regulations and that they had known, or should have known, of a real threat to the inhabitants and had failed to do all that could reasonably be expected of them to avoid the risks.[161] The state had reliable information that the inhabitants of certain slum areas were in danger because of technical shortcomings of the municipal rubbish tip.[162] Because of the reality and immediacy of the danger, the state had a positive obligation under Article 2 to take preventative operational measures, especially as the state had set up the site and authorised its operation, which gave rise to the risk in question.[163]

The Court also made important comments about its role in determining socio-economic cases. It acknowledged that it is not its task to substitute for the views of the local authorities its own view of the best policy to adopt in dealing with social, economic and urban problems. However, it found that the regulatory framework in this case was defective and not properly implemented, leading directly to the loss of life.[164] In this case the state's *omission* was the conduct for which it was responsible in international law.

In *Budayeva v Russia*, the ECtHR considered whether the state was responsible for the death of eight people in the town of Tyrnauz as a result of a series of mudslides.[165] There was documentary evidence that the town was threatened by mudslides and the Prime Minister had been warned that the only way to avoid casualties was to establish observation posts to warn civilians of the threat. This measure was never implemented. Between 18 and 25 July 2000, Tyrnauz was hit by a succession of mudslides, which resulted in loss of life. The ECtHR held that the substantive element of Article 2, particularly in the context of dangerous activities, required that special emphasis be placed on regulations geared to the special features of the activity in question, particularly with regard to the level of the potential risk to human life.[166] It cited several regulatory measures that a state should take and highlighted the public's right to information to find out about the risk.[167] The Court also held that

> in the context of dangerous activities the scope of the positive obligations under Article 2 of the Convention largely overlap with those under Article 8 . . . Consequently, the principles developed in the Court's case-law relating to planning and environmental matters affecting private life and home may also be relied on for the protection of the right to life.[168]

The choice of a particular practical measure remains within the discretion of the state,[169] and

[161] ibid, paras 81–82.
[162] ibid, para 90.
[163] ibid, paras 92–93.
[164] ibid, paras 99–102.
[165] *Budayeva v Russia* (App No 15339/02) ECtHR 20 March 2008.
[166] ibid, para 132.
[167] ibid.
[168] ibid, para 133.
[169] ibid, para 134.

an impossible or disproportionate burden must not be imposed on the authorities without consideration being given, in particular, to the operational choices which they must make in terms of priorities and resources.[170]

On the facts, the ECtHR held that the state had omitted to implement emergency relief policies and that there was a causal link between the omission and the consequent death and injuries. As such, the state had failed to discharge the positive obligation to establish a legislative and administrative framework designed to provide effective deterrence against threats to the right to life as required by Article 2.[171]

This authority, although in the context of environmental degradation, is precedent for the increasing recognition in international law that states have an obligation to take positive steps to protect the lives and well-being of individuals against all forms of harm, whether due to environmental hazards or intimate violence.

Therefore, the absence of any operational measures of protection undermines the effectiveness of the protection accorded by a state to the right to life. Where there is no evidence of the authorities taking any steps in response to a request for protection, either by applying reasonable measures of protection or by investigating the extent of the alleged risk with a view to instituting any appropriate measures of prevention, ECtHR precedent indicates that the authorities have failed to take reasonable measures available to them to prevent a real and immediate risk to life.[172]

In the case of *X and Y v The Netherlands*, the ECtHR considered Article 8 of the Convention, which guarantees the right to respect for one's private and family life.[173] The Court described the objective of Article 8 as not only protecting the individual against arbitrary interference by public authorities:

> in addition to this primarily negative undertaking, there may be positive obligations inherent in an effective respect for private or family life . . . These obligations may involve the adoption of measures designed to secure respect for private life even in the sphere of the relations of individuals between themselves.[174]

In the case of *MC v Bulgaria* the ECtHR stated that

> Positive obligations on the State are inherent in the right to effective respect for private life under Article 8; these obligations may involve the adoption of measures even in the sphere of the relations of individuals between themselves. While the choice of the means to secure compliance with Article 8 in the sphere of protection against acts of individuals is in principle within the State's margin of appreciation, effective deterrence against grave acts such as rape, where fundamental values and essential aspects

---

[170] ibid, para 135.
[171] ibid, para 159.
[172] *Kiliç v Turkey* (n 143) para 76. See also *Mahmut Kaya v Turkey* (n 143) paras 100–01.
[173] *X and Y v The Netherlands* (App No 8978/80) (1985) 8 EHRR 235, paras 21–30.
[174] ibid, para 23.

of private life are at stake, requires efficient criminal-law provisions. Children and other vulnerable individuals, in particular, are entitled to effective protection.[175]

The Court has also held that the positive obligation to launch an official investigation into accusations of torturous conduct 'cannot be considered in principle to be limited solely to cases of ill-treatment by State agents'.[176] The Court emphasised that

> the obligation of the High Contracting Parties under Article 1 of the Convention to secure to everyone within their jurisdiction the rights and freedoms defined in the Convention, taken together with Article 3, requires States to take measures designed to ensure that individuals within their jurisdiction are not subjected to ill-treatment, including ill-treatment administered by private individuals.[177]

Therefore, the ECtHR held that

> States have a positive obligation inherent in Articles 3 and 8 of the Convention to enact criminal-law provisions effectively punishing rape and to apply them in practice through effective investigation and prosecution.[178]

In the context of domestic violence against women specifically, the Court has held that the state must take positive steps to protect the substance of an individual's rights under Article 8, namely, respect for one's private and family life. In the case of *Bevacqua and S v Bulgaria*[179] the applicant had been 'battered' by her husband, N, on numerous occasions and had petitioned the District Court for an interim custody order and for a divorce order.[180] Several hearings took place and repeatedly the court failed to consider the interim application. In the meantime, N took their child into his care. Whenever the applicant visited her son, she was exposed to more violent abuse. Eventually she fled to a refuge with her son. In response N complained to the local child authorities that the applicant had abducted his son.[181] The applicant's allegations of violence were not believed by the authorities (notwithstanding medical certificates) and, in order to avoid prosecution for abduction, the applicant agreed to a custody sharing arrangement.[182]

Divorce proceedings began in June 2000 and shortly thereafter N once again battered the applicant in front of their son.[183] Only in November 2000, during one of the divorce hearings, did the court consider the interim custody order. N raised objections which led the court to postpone the hearings several times, relating to issues such as the authenticity of an expert's report and the registration status of a non-governmental organisation (NGO), all tangential procedural

---

[175] *MC v Bulgaria* (App No 39272/98) ECtHR 4 March 2004, para 150.
[176] ibid, para 151.
[177] ibid, para 150.
[178] ibid, para 153.
[179] *Bevacqua and S v Bulgaria* (App No 71127/01) ECtHR 12 June 2008, para 83.
[180] ibid, para 7.
[181] ibid, para 16.
[182] ibid, paras 16–18.
[183] ibid, paras 21–22.

matters, peripheral to the actual custody and interests of the child.[184] As a result of these postponements, the applicant withdrew her application for interim custody. The divorce was granted on 23 May 2001.[185] On 18 June 2002, a year after the divorce, the applicant returned to N's apartment to collect her belongings and was 'battered' again by N.[186]

The prosecution authorities refused to institute criminal proceedings against N, noting that the applicant could bring private prosecution proceedings as the alleged injuries fell into the category of light bodily injuries.[187]

The Court stated that,

> while the essential object of art 8 is to protect the individual against arbitrary action by the public authorities, there may in addition be positive obligations inherent in effective 'respect' for private and family life and these obligations may involve the adoption of measures in the sphere of the relations of individuals between themselves. Children and other vulnerable individuals, in particular, are entitled to effective protection.[188]

The Court confirmed that the concept of private life 'includes a person's physical and psychological integrity'.[189] Therefore, the right is not only a negative right, requiring the state to abstain from certain invasive activity, it is also a positive right, imposing positive obligations on the authorities and a duty to maintain and apply in practice an adequate legal framework affording protection against acts of violence by private individuals.[190] In particular, the Court held that the authorities should have examined the interim measures application with due diligence and without delay.[191] The state failed to fulfil this obligation in part because the District Court adjourned the examination of the interim custody application repeatedly for reasons far removed from the substance of the dispute.[192] The Court concluded that the lax judicial response and the absence of protective measures violated the applicant's and her son's right to respect for their private life.[193] The Court confirmed that the state's argument that this was a 'private matter' was 'incompatible with their positive obligations to secure the enjoyment of the applicants' Article 8 rights'.[194]

The most authoritative and recent case on the positive obligation of states to protect women from domestic violence specifically is *Opuz v Turkey*.[195] The

---

[184] ibid, paras 29–31.
[185] ibid, para 34.
[186] ibid, para 38.
[187] ibid, para 38.
[188] ibid, para 64.
[189] ibid, para 65.
[190] ibid, para 65.
[191] ibid, para 73.
[192] ibid, para 74.
[193] ibid, paras 79, 83, 84.
[194] ibid, para 83.
[195] For a detailed discussion of this case see ch 2 p 135. See also Bonita C Meyersfeld, '*Opuz v Turkey*: Confirming the State Obligation to Combat Domestic Violence' (2009) 5 *European Human Rights Law Review* 684.

Court examined the nature of the state's positive obligations under Articles 2, 3 and 14 of the Convention.[196] In this case, the applicant and her mother had endured more than a decade of violence on the part of the applicant's ex-husband, HO, including stabbing and being run over by a car. The applicant and her mother regularly sought the protection of the state but no effective action was taken. On one occasion, the applicant and her mother withdrew their complaint and the authorities halted the criminal proceedings, notwithstanding that HO was free to intimidate and threaten the applicant and her mother and the applicant's children. HO eventually killed the applicant's mother and his punishment effectively was a fine after time served leading up to the trial. HO had also stabbed the applicant seven times and for that too he was fined a small amount that could be paid in instalments.

An examination of the state's responsibility under each article is informative. As regards Article 2, the Court reiterated that this article enjoins the state not only to refrain from the intentional and unlawful taking of life, but also to take appropriate steps to safeguard the lives of those within its jurisdiction.[197] This involves a primary duty on the state to secure the right to life by putting in place effective criminal law provisions to deter the commission of offences against the person backed up by law-enforcement machinery for the prevention, suppression and punishment of breaches of such provisions. Based on its previous decisions on Article 2, the Court confirmed that the obligation also extends in appropriate circumstances to a positive obligation on the authorities to take preventive operational measures to protect an individual whose life is at risk from the criminal acts of another individual.[198]

This obligation must not impose an impossible or disproportionate burden on the authorities and not every claimed risk to life can entail a requirement on the authorities to take operational measures to prevent that risk from materialising.[199] So, when does the obligation arise? According to the Court, it will arise if the authorities knew or ought to have known at the time of the existence of a real and immediate risk to the life of an identified individual from the criminal acts of a third party and that they failed to take measures (subject to the legitimate constraints of due process) within the scope of their powers which, judged reasonably, might have been expected to avoid that risk.[200]

How does this obligation manifest in the case of systemic intimate violence? The issue before the Court was whether the authorities had fulfilled their positive obligation to take preventive operational measures to protect the applicant's mother's right to life. Specifically, had the authorities displayed due diligence to prevent such violence by pursuing criminal or other appropriate preventive

---

[196] *Opuz v Turkey* (n 99) paras 149, 176, 201.
[197] ibid, para 128, citing *LCB v The United Kingdom* (n 142).
[198] ibid, para 128, citing *Osman v The United Kingdom* (n 141) para 115 and *Kontrova v Slovakia* (n 154) para 49.
[199] ibid, para 129.
[200] ibid.

measures, despite the fact that, during the decade of violence, the applicant and her mother had on occasion withdrawn their complaints?[201] In approaching this question the Court noted 'the gravity of the problem' of domestic violence, which affects men, women and children and is a problem which every state has to address.[202]

The Court determined first whether the local authorities could have foreseen a lethal attack; if so, it asked whether the authorities had shown due diligence with regard to preventing the killing of the applicant's mother. As regards knowledge, the Court held that it was obvious that there was an escalating and continuing risk based on the perpetrator's record of domestic violence and the many complaints submitted by the applicant and her mother.[203] In particular, the applicant's mother had submitted a petition to the Chief Public Prosecutor's Office stating that her life was in immediate danger. Two weeks later she was killed by HO.[204]

Having established that the state authorities had knowledge about the dangerous nature of HO, or ought to have foreseen a lethal attack by him, the Court then determined whether the authorities should have taken reasonable measures which could have had a real prospect of altering the outcome or mitigating the harm.[205] It held that the legislative framework in force in Turkey fell short of the requirements inherent in the state's positive obligations to establish and effectively apply a system punishing all forms of domestic violence and providing sufficient safeguards for victims.[206] In the circumstances the state should have pursued criminal proceedings, notwithstanding the fact that the complaints were withdrawn.[207] Taking a rational approach, the Court held that there is no automatic duty to pursue criminal proceedings in domestic violence cases; rather, one should take into account factors such as the history of violence, the use of weapons, the seriousness of the violence and possible threats to the health and safety of the victim and, if relevant, children.[208] The authorities should also consider the possible motive of the victim in withdrawing a complaint.[209] The importance of privacy and family life, protected in Article 8 of the Convention, should be considered, but it should not trump the victim's right to safety.[210]

In addition to the deficient legislative framework, the Court held that the authorities had not acted with due diligence to protect the applicant's mother's right to life.[211] Specifically, the authorities had failed to place HO in detention,

---

[201] ibid, para 131.
[202] ibid, para 132.
[203] ibid, paras 134, 135.
[204] ibid, para 135.
[205] ibid, para 136.
[206] ibid, para 145.
[207] ibid, para 138.
[208] ibid, para 138.
[209] ibid, para 143.
[210] ibid, para 140.
[211] ibid, para 149.

failed to take appropriate action regarding his possession of weapons, and failed to issue an injunction against HO.[212] The Court also found that the state had not complied with its positive obligation to establish and maintain an efficient and independent judicial system which could respond to the killing of the applicant's mother.[213] It held that an effective investigation is one that is prompt and reasonably expeditious.[214] While there may be obstacles to an investigation, in the case of the use of lethal force, a prompt response by the authorities is essential in maintaining public confidence in their adherence to the rule of law and in preventing any appearance of tolerance of unlawful acts.[215] The criminal proceedings, which lasted more than six years, were neither prompt nor did they have an adequate deterrent effect capable of ensuring the effective prevention of the unlawful acts committed by HO. The Court held that:

> The obstacles resulting from the legislation and failure to use the means available undermined the deterrent effect of the judicial system in place and the role it was required to play in preventing a violation of the applicant's mother's right to life as enshrined in Article 2 of the Convention.[216]

The Court's assessment of the violation of Article 3 is similarly informative as regards the scope of the state's responsibility for acts of domestic violence. It confirmed that Article 1 of the Convention, read together with Article 3, requires the state to take measures designed to ensure that individuals within its jurisdiction are not subjected to torture or inhuman or degrading treatment or punishment, including such ill-treatment administered by private individuals.[217] This obligation is particularly relevant in respect of people who fall within a group of 'vulnerable individuals', such as the applicant, who had been subjected to violence and threats by HO in the past and who, as a woman living in southeast Turkey, was particularly vulnerable.[218]

Having established the nature of the state's obligation, the Court found that the violence suffered by the applicant, in the form of physical injuries and psychological pressure, were sufficiently serious to amount to ill-treatment within the meaning of Article 3 of the Convention.[219] It then determined whether the authorities had taken all reasonable measures to prevent a recurrence of this violence.[220] Once again, the Court focused on the deficient legislative framework (which should have enabled the prosecuting authorities to pursue criminal investigations despite the withdrawal of complaints on the basis that the violence was sufficiently serious to warrant prosecution and that there was a constant threat

---

[212] ibid, paras 147–49.
[213] ibid, para 153.
[214] ibid, para 150.
[215] ibid, para 150, citing *Avflar v Turkey* (App No 25657/94) ECtHR 10 July 2001, para 395.
[216] ibid, para 153.
[217] ibid, para 159 (regarding children and other vulnerable groups).
[218] ibid, para 160.
[219] ibid, para 161.
[220] ibid, para 162.

to the applicant's physical integrity).[221] In addition, the authorities had failed to exercise due diligence to prevent the attacks recurring.

The Court substantiated this finding with the fact that, following the first major incident of reported violence, HO again beat the applicant severely, causing her injuries which endangered her life but he was released pending trial 'considering the nature of the offence and the fact that the applicant had regained full health'.[222] With HO free to attack or threaten the applicant, it is not surprising that she withdrew her complaint. HO went on to attack the applicant and her mother with a knife and ran his car into them. He spent 25 days in jail and received a fine. As punishment for stabbing the applicant seven times, HO received another small fine, payable in instalments.[223] The judicial decisions contained a degree of tolerance and had no noticeable preventive or deterrent effect on the conduct of HO.[224] The response of the authorities was therefore 'manifestly inadequate to the gravity of the offences in question'.[225]

Finally, as regards Article 14 and the right to equal enjoyment of Convention rights, the Court held that the state's failure to protect women from domestic violence breached their right to equal protection of the law.[226] Discrimination, which did not have to be intentional, was not based in the legislation but in its implementation, as well as the general attitude of the local authorities, such as the manner in which women were treated at police stations when they reported domestic violence and judicial passivity in providing effective protection to victims;[227] the tendency on the part of police officers not to investigate complaints of domestic violence but rather to act as mediators by trying to convince the complainant to go home and drop the complaint;[228] and unreasonable delays in issuing injunctions and mitigating sentences on the grounds of custom, tradition or honour.[229] The Court concluded as follows:

> Bearing in mind its findings . . . that the general and discriminatory judicial passivity in Turkey, albeit unintentional, mainly affected women, the Court considers that the violence suffered by the applicant and her mother may be regarded as gender-based violence which is a form of discrimination against women . . . [T]he overall unresponsiveness of the judicial system and impunity enjoyed by the aggressors, as found in the instant case, indicated that there was insufficient commitment to take appropriate action to address domestic violence.[230]

Therefore, ignoring a violation of human rights by non-state actors arguably constitutes a failure on the part of states to ensure respect for human rights

---

[221] ibid, para 168.
[222] ibid, para 169.
[223] ibid.
[224] ibid, para 170.
[225] ibid.
[226] ibid, para 191.
[227] ibid, para 193.
[228] ibid, para 195.
[229] ibid, para 196.
[230] ibid, para 200.

within their borders and, as has been stated, any failure to comply with an obligation in international law is an internationally wrongful act and a breach of international law.[231] On this basis, a state's failure to uphold their female citizens' right to be free from systemic intimate violence, in the form of denying the right to life, physical integrity, equality or an amalgamation of these rights, is an internationally wrongful act for which the state is responsible.

The next question to consider, and discussed in the next section, is *who* constitutes the 'state' for the purpose of determining state conduct?

Omission by Whom?

Article 4 of the ILC Articles provides that 'the conduct of a State organ shall be considered an act of that State under international law, whether the organ exercises legislative, executive, judicial or any other functions.'[232] Article 4(2) provides that 'an organ includes any person or entity which has that status in accordance with the internal law of the State'.[233]

State conduct in international law includes omissions on the part of state organs and officials,[234] including conduct of 'its organs of government, or of others who have acted under the direction, instigation or control of those organs, ie, as agents of the State'.[235] The notion of state responsibility is that 'the State may be held responsible for the acts of any of its agents, if such acts violate international law'.[236] Because state agents are empowered by the state, the acts performed by them 'in the discharge of the functions of the office must be attributed to [their] State'.[237] This is premised on the notion that when 'the State invests such an individual [an agent] with its authority, his acts become the acts of the State itself, for which the State must accept responsibility under international law'.[238] The state may not dissociate itself from the conduct of these actors. As far as international law is concerned, 'Externally, the State speaks with one voice, and it does not matter from which agent the voice emanates'.[239]

The principles of state responsibility require state agents not only to refrain from prohibited conduct, but also to take steps to prevent violations of international law. This applies to state agents such as police, state lawyers and prosecutors, court administrative officials such as court clerks and judges, and welfare departments and public hospitals.[240] Freeman argues that a

---

[231] Tomuschat (n 1) 283, discussing the draft basic principles and guidelines for reparations.
[232] ILC Articles, Art 4(1).
[233] ibid, Art 4(2). See also Crawford (n 1) 83: 'In speaking of attribution to the State what is meant is the State as a subject of international law . . . The State is treated as a unity, consistent with its recognition as a single legal person in international law.'
[234] Crawford (n 1) 94.
[235] ibid, 91 and fn 97.
[236] Eagleton (n 2) 45.
[237] ibid, 73–74.
[238] ibid, 45.
[239] ibid, 74.
[240] DEVAW (n 74) Art 11(2) (urging government, non-governmental organisations *and individuals* to implement its provisions). The notion of individual liability is also underscored in the

failure to provide adequate police protection against impending violence, inadequate steps to punish the perpetrators of crimes against aliens, or an infraction of the state's fundamental duty to operate properly its machinery of judicial protection for remedying private wrongs will entail international responsibility.[241]

As far as courts are concerned, Eagleton maintains that 'There can be no doubt that a court, as any other agency of the State, may, through an internationally illegal act, bring responsibility upon its State'.[242]

The tenets of denial of justice apply logically to the obligation on states to protect the rights of women. This is confirmed by Eagleton, who states that, if an organ of state (in particular a court) 'directly collides with international law' or if it is guilty of denial of justice through fraud, excess of jurisdiction, improper process or otherwise, it has committed an internationally illegal act for which the state may be held responsible.[243] So, where a police official fails to respond to a domestic violence call or a prosecutor fails to bring charges against an abusive spouse, or where a court refuses a protection order because it is reluctant to expel an abuser from her/his home, these acts are all deemed to be conduct of the state.

All organs of state are bound by international obligations, irrespective of whether they are 'engaged in enacting, executing, or construing the law'.[244] Article 5 of the ILC Articles provides that where a person or entity is not an organ of state but is empowered to exercise elements of governmental authority, that person's actions may too be attributed to the state.[245] Of course a state is only responsible for the conduct of its agents where they act within their official capacity as state actors.[246]

By definition, in the context of systemic intimate violence, there is a grand failure on the part of government to protect women from intimate violence. Freeman, in writing on the principles of denial of justice, notes that a state is responsible for an internationally wrongful act where there is a 'failure of authorities responsible for law and order to take prompt and necessary steps to apprehend criminals; an inordinate lapse of time without offenders being brought to trial; as well as negligence, laxity, and undue delay in their prosecution'.[247]

The same obligations apply to states in respect of systemic intimate violence against women: where persons empowered to exercise elements of governmental authority—such as police, state lawyers and prosecutors, court administra-

---

preamble to the ICESCR (n 27): 'Realizing that the individual, having duties to other individuals and to the community to which he belongs, is under a responsibility to strive for the promotion and observance of the rights recognized in the present Covenant.'[241] Freeman (n 13) 27.

[242] Eagleton (n 2) 71.
[243] ibid.
[244] Freeman (n 13) 29.
[245] Crawford (n 1) 100.
[246] ibid, point 13. According to Brownlie (n 5) 40, objective tests of responsibility were applied by the General Claims Commission set up by the Convention between Mexico and the United States in 1923.
[247] Freeman (n 13) 378.

tive officials and public hospital staff—ignore incidents of systemic intimate violence and fail to take action to help remedy that violence, their omission constitutes conduct of the state, which is then responsible for an internationally wrong act. Since the rules of international law provide that state agents include organs of government or those who have control over such organs, the officials with whom domestic violence victims interact become responsible for the way the state interacts with, protects and responds to victims of domestic violence.

Wrongfulness Element

Certainly not every unanswered call for help or deficient police action will trigger international responsibility. The absence of police protection must be sustained and systematic, and its repetition must follow a particular pattern; a pattern that remains unaddressed by state authorities. Where, in specific circumstances, police consistently fail to address harm perpetrated against specific members of a society, a failure by the state to compel police protection constitutes an omission the nature of which is sufficiently serious to constitute a breach of its international obligation to protect its citizens.

Definition of Wrongfulness

Having identified what constitutes conduct for the purposes of state responsibility, it is now necessary to identify the circumstances in which that conduct is wrongful. The ILC Articles define a wrongful act as conduct that 'constitutes a breach of an international obligation of the State'.[248] A breach of an international obligation is an act of a state that is 'not in conformity with what is required of it by that obligation'.[249] The former Special Rapporteur on state responsibility, Professor Crawford, explains this as 'the non-conformity of the State's actual conduct with the conduct it ought to have adopted in order to comply with a particular international obligation'.[250]

Several difficulties arise. If we follow a strict and traditional approach to international law (as discussed in chapter one) it is not clear that there is an authoritative and binding legal rule regarding domestic violence in international law. Is it even possible, then, to say that states have an international obligation? And if there is an obligation, at what stage can we say that a state has 'done enough' to fulfil its international obligation to protect women from systemic intimate violence? What level of diligence is required of the state and how do we measure whether the state has conformed to this expectation?

---

[248] ILC Articles, Art 2.
[249] ibid, Art 12.
[250] Crawford (n 1) 100.

Is there an International Obligation with which the State Must Comply?

The origin of the obligation, namely, whether it is a treaty obligation or a principle of customary international law, is irrelevant for the purposes of state responsibility.[251] The principles that pertain to state responsibility

> are equally applicable in the case of breach of treaty obligation, since in the international law field there is no distinction between contractual and tortious responsibility, so that any violation by a State of any obligation, of whatever origin, gives rise to State responsibility.[252]

In fact, the rules of state responsibility apply to all international obligations of states, whether the rule is 'established by a customary rule of international law, by a treaty or by a general principle applicable within the international legal order'.[253] This is said to include 'all possible sources of international obligations, that is to say, to all processes for creating legal obligations recognized by international law'.[254] It is also recognised that these various grounds of obligation interact with each other: treaties, especially multilateral treaties,

> can contribute to the formation of general international law; customary law may assist in the interpretation of treaties; an obligation contained in a treaty may be applicable to a state by reason of its unilateral act, and so on. Thus international courts and tribunals have treated responsibility as arising for a State by reason of any violation of a duty imposed by an international juridical standard.[255]

The Commentaries to the ILC Articles confirm that the decisions of organs of international organisations competent in the matter and judgments given by the ICJ or other tribunals may also create international obligations.[256] Therefore, a state may be responsible for the violation of a right that is articulated in a treaty, founded in customary international law, falls within the range of peremptory norms or has been decided upon by an authoritative international tribunal or court.[257]

On this basis, while the authority for the right to be free from systemic intimate violence does not subsist in a treaty per se, to the extent that it exists in customary international law or by virtue of an extrapolation of the principles of international law, or is subsequently articulated as a specific, authoritative and binding statement in international law, the obligation to protect women from such harm still triggers the principles of state responsibility because the origin of the obligation is irrelevant for the purposes of assessing responsibility.

---

[251] ILC Articles, Art 12.
[252] *Rainbow Warrior* (n 81) 251, para 75.
[253] See also Crawford (n 1) 65, 126–27.
[254] ibid.
[255] ibid.
[256] ibid.
[257] ibid, 550. See also Shaw (n 82) 694–95.

Seriousness of the Breach

While the seriousness of a state's breach may be relevant when determining remedies, it is irrelevant when ascertaining state responsibility.[258] For example, a state will be responsible equally for an internationally wrongful act irrespective of whether that wrongful act involves the violation of a bilateral trade treaty by providing preferential treatment to its own nationals, or the violation of the genocide convention. Both acts result in the state being responsible for non-compliance with an international obligation, notwithstanding their marked difference in gravity. Therefore, in the context of assiduous systemic intimate violence, liability would attach to the violation itself, requiring the state to obviate the effects of the international obligation it has breached.[259]

I am not suggesting that each incident of severe woman abuse means that the state has committed an internationally wrongful act; nor that there should be a state presence in the home to stay the thrust of a violent fist. The state's obligation is to meet basic standards in providing safety and the redemption of dignity for those who endure systemic intimate violence, including taking the positive, *systematic* steps discussed in chapter two.

Due Diligence Standard

If there is an obligation that requires states to protect women against systemic intimate violence, at what point has a state done enough to comply with that international obligation? In the context of denial of justice, Freeman proposes that

> International law, anticipating unlawful acts by private persons, requires the State to fulfil certain duties in relation thereto. These duties are, generally speaking, two: the use of due diligence in the prevention of injury to foreigners; and, proper measures of repressing crime, or remedying wrong, as the case may be, in the event that such acts nevertheless occur.[260]

The standard of 'due diligence' was developed in the context of human rights and a state's obligations not only in respect of foreigners but also in respect of the state's own citizens. In 1988, the Inter-American Court of Human Rights established the due diligence standard for states:

> An illegal act which violates human rights and which is initially not directly imputable to a State (for example, because it is the act of a private person . . .) can lead to international responsibility of the State, not because of the act itself, but because of the lack of due diligence to prevent the violation or to respond to it as required by the [American Convention on Human Rights].[261]

---

[258] Eagleton (n 2) 23.
[259] This is confirmed by Crawford (n 1) 191–92.
[260] Freeman (n 13) 27
[261] *Velásquez Rodríguez v Honduras* (n 38) 172.

In 1993, the UN General Assembly applied the due diligence standard in DEVAW, enjoining states to 'Exercise due diligence to prevent, investigate and, in accordance with national legislation, punish acts of violence against women, whether those acts are perpetrated by the State or by private persons'.[262] This echoes the Special Rapporteur on state responsibility, James Crawford, who stated that 'the State has a positive duty not to authorize or allow torture'.[263]

The due diligence standard was utilised once again in respect of violence against women by the first Special Rapporteur on violence against women, Radhika Coomaraswamy. In her report, she confirmed that domestic violence is an underestimated cause of poor health, continued economic and social hardship and mortality of women. She demonstrated that the harm that is the most serious for women is that which has been the most neglected by states.[264] In her final report to the UN, Dr Coomaraswamy revitalised the due diligence standard as follows:

> [T]he standard for establishing State complicity in violations committed by private actors is more relative. Complicity must be demonstrated by establishing that the State condones a pattern of abuse through pervasive non-action. Where States do not actively engage in acts of systemic intimate violence or routinely disregard evidence of murder, rape or assault of women by their intimate partners, States generally fail to take the minimum steps necessary to protect their female citizens' rights to physical integrity and, in extreme cases, to life. This sends a message that such attacks are justified and will not be punished. To avoid such complicity, States must demonstrate due diligence by taking active measures to protect, prosecute and punish private actors who commit abuses.[265]

Fulfilling the Due Diligence Standard

In general, states are required to be proactive within their society to guarantee and *ensure respect* for human rights.[266] The fulfilment of this objective, though, is amorphous, especially in the case of systemic intimate violence, where it is difficult to measure a state's performance without a precise standard of compliance. The due diligence standard assists in 'quantifying' the fulfilment of

---

[262] DEVAW (n 74) Art 4(c).

[263] James Crawford, 'Revising the Draft Articles on State Responsibility' (1999) 10 *European Journal of International Law* 435, 440.

[264] Special Rapporteur 1996 Report (n 86) 16–18 (presenting statistical data on the battering of women in various countries in accordance with Commission on Human Rights Resolution 1995/85 and detailing the extent of violence against women, the inadequacy of governmental and societal response, and providing recommendations for reform).

[265] ibid. For a brief discussion of the due diligence standard within the context of systemic intimate violence see Amnesty International, *Men's Violence against Women in Intimate Relationships: An Account of the Situation in Sweden* (19 April 2004) 13, www2.amnesty.se/svaw.nsf/mvaw/$File/mvaw.pdf.

[266] Louis Henkin, 'Human Rights and State Sovereignty' (1994) 25 *Georgia Journal of International and Comparative Law* 31, 34–36.

human rights obligations. The circumstances of each state, the nature of the systemic intimate violence involved, and the state's response to such violence will be different in every case. And of course, not every instance of domestic violence, even if lethal, will point to a systemic failure to protect. How then does one assess the different methods used in different states to protect women from systemic intimate violence?

There are a number of factors which, on a case-by-case basis, are usually relevant to determining whether a state has met its due diligence standard or whether it has failed and is thus responsible for an internationally wrongful act. Any failure by a state to take action to meet its international legal obligations is adjudicated with regard to 'the degree of protection required under the particular circumstances; the practical factors going to render such protection possible or impossible; and finally the ensuing neglect to undertake the requisite steps of pursuit prescribed by the law of nations'.[267]

On this basis, I discuss below three factors that can be extrapolated from these considerations to identify the fulfilment or otherwise of the due diligence standard in respect of systemic intimate violence: (1) the nature of the right involved in the particular circumstances; (2) the practical resources and capabilities of the country in question in attenuating something as vague and nebulous as domestic violence; and (3) the repetition of aggregate omissions.

Nature of the Right

What is the nature of the right in question and what degree of protection is needed under the particular circumstances? These questions were raised by the ECtHR, for example, which analyses states' obligations under Articles 2 (to protect life) and 3 (to protect against torture) of the Convention from the perspective that they are two of the most important rights to be found in the Convention. According to the ECtHR, Article 2 is a 'fundamental' right which, together with Article 3, 'enshrines one of the basic values of the democratic societies making up the Council of Europe'.[268] The UN Human Rights Committee, in its General Comment on the equivalent provision in the ICCPR, describes the right as a 'supreme right' and a right 'basic to all human rights'.[269] The UK courts have similarly ranked an individual's right to life as 'the most fundamental of all human

---

[267] Freeman (n 13) 373.

[268] *McCann v The United Kingdom* (App No 18984/91) (1995) 21 EHRR 97, para 147; *Andronicou and Constantinou v Cyprus* (App No 25052/94) (1997) 25 EHRR 491, para 171; *Ertak v Turkey* (App No 20764/92) ECtHR 9 May 2000, para 134; *Çakici v Turkey* (App No 23657/94) (1999) 31 EHRR 133, para 86. Approved in *Jordan v The United Kingdom* (App No 24746/94) (2003) 37 EHRR 52, para 102; *Kelly v The United Kingdom* (App No 30054/96) ECtHR 4 August 2001, para 91; *McKerr v The United Kingdom* (App No 28883/95) (2002) 34 EHRR 553, para 108; and *Shanaghan v The United Kingdom* (App No 37715/97) ECtHR 4 May 2001, para 82.

[269] See ICCPR (n 26) Art 6. On Art 6 generally, see D McGoldrick, *The Human Rights Committee: Its Role in the Development of the International Covenant on Civil and Political Rights* (Oxford, Oxford University Press, 1994) 328–61.

rights'[270] such that when the right to life is engaged, the options available to the reasonable decisionmaker are curtailed.[271]

When the ECtHR determines whether a state has taken the necessary steps to protect the right to life, it will ask whether the state has effective criminal law provisions to deter the commission of lethal offences against individuals and whether this is reinforced by law enforcement machinery for the suppression, prevention and punishment of a breach of a person's right to life.[272]

This was mirrored by the CEDAW Committee in several cases involving domestic violence. In *Ms AT v Hungary*, the Committee considered whether the author of the communication was the victim of a violation of Articles 2(a), (b) and (e), 5(a) and 16 of the CEDAW Convention due to the fact that for four years the state had failed in its duty to provide her with effective protection from the serious risk to her physical integrity, physical and mental health and her life from her former common law husband.[273] The Committee considered the nature of the rights involved in domestic violence, which 'constitute a violation of the author's human rights and fundamental freedoms, particularly her right to security of person', and concluded that 'Women's human rights to life and to physical and mental integrity cannot be superseded by other rights, including the right to property and the right to privacy'.[274]

The Committee considered whether there were legal remedies and noted that the state party had not offered 'information as to the existence of alternative avenues that the author might have pursued that would have provided sufficient protection or security from the danger of continued violence'.[275] As a result, for four years, the author had felt threatened by her former common law husband and had been battered by this same man. She had been unsuccessful, in both civil and criminal proceedings, in her attempt to have her abuser barred temporarily or permanently from the apartment in which she and her children lived. She could not get a restraining or protection order since neither option existed in the country at the time (2003) and she was unable to flee to a shelter because none was equipped to accept her together with her children, one of whom is severely disabled. The CEDAW Committee concluded that considered together, these

---

[270] *Bugdaycay v Secretary of State for the Home Department* [1987] AC 514, 531E per Lord Bridge, cited with approval in *R v Lord Saville of Newdigate, ex p A* [2000] 1 WLR 1855 concerning the risk to life posed by the withdrawal of anonymity from the soldiers appearing before the Saville Inquiry into Bloody Sunday.

[271] See *R v Lord Saville of Newdigate, ex p A* [2000] 1 WLR 1855, paras 34–37, relying on *R v Ministry of Defence, ex p Smith* [1996] QB 517 (CA).

[272] *Kiliç v Turkey* (n 143) para 62; *Mahmut Kaya v Turkey* (n 143) para 85, citing *Osman v The United Kingdom* (n 141) para 115. See also *Keenan v The United Kingdom* (2001) 33 EHRR 913, para 88. But see *Mastromatteo v Italy* (n 153).

[273] *Ms AT v Hungary* (Decision) CEDAW Committee (views adopted 26 January 2005) Communication No 2/2003 UN Doc CEDAW/C/32/D/2/2003, para 9.2. For a detailed discussion of this communication see ch 1, p 43–5.

[274] ibid, para 9.3.

[275] ibid.

facts indicated that the rights of the author under Articles 5(a) and 16 of the Convention had been violated.[276]

The due diligence assessment, therefore, is quite a practical one. But the analysis becomes more complicated where the state has taken a progressive approach to domestic violence and still fails to protect women. In the case of *Şahide Goekce (deceased) v Austria*, the state party had domestic violence laws in place when the deceased was killed by her partner.[277] The police were empowered to—and did—issue an expulsion and prohibition to return order against Mustafa Goekce covering the Goekce apartment, pursuant to section 38a of the Security Police Act (Sicherheitspolizeigesetz).[278] The state could prosecute an accused for domestic violence, but, under section 107, paragraph 4 of the Penal Code (Strafgesetzbuch), a threatened spouse, direct descendant, brother or sister or relative who lives in the same household of the accused must give authorisation in order to prosecute the alleged offender for making a criminally dangerous threat. The deceased did not authorise the Austrian authorities to prosecute Mustafa Goekce for threatening her life. He was therefore charged only with the offence of causing bodily harm, and he was acquitted because Şahide Goekce's injuries were too minor to constitute such harm.[279] The police eventually also informed the Public Prosecutor (on two occasions) that Mustafa Goekce had committed aggravated coercion because of the death threat against the deceased and asked that he be detained.[280] The Vienna District Court of Hernals issued an interim injunction for a period of three months against Mustafa Goekce, under which he was forbidden to return to the family apartment and its immediate environs and to contact Şahide Goekce or the children. The order was to be effective immediately and was entrusted to the police for execution.[281]

So what went wrong? The police request to the Public Prosecutor was denied on both occasions. The state authorities apparently knew that the accused was dangerous and owned a firearm but they ignored warnings, not only from the deceased but also from the deceased's father and brother. The police did not check whether Mustafa Goekce had a handgun, even though a weapons prohibition was in effect against him.[282] The Vienna Public Prosecutor actually stopped the prosecution of Mustafa Goekce for causing bodily harm and making a criminal dangerous threat on grounds that there was insufficient reason to

---

[276] ibid, para 9.4.
[277] For a detailed discussion of this case see ch 1, p 45–47.
[278] *The Vienna Intervention Centre against Domestic Violence and the Association for Women's Access to Justice on behalf of Hakan Goekce, Handan Goekce, and Guelue Goekce (descendants of the deceased) v Austria* (Decision) CEDAW Committee (views adopted 6 August 2007) Communication No 5/2005 UN Doc CEDAW/C/39/D/5/2005, para 2.2 (*Goekce v Austria*).
[279] ibid, para 2.3.
[280] ibid, para 2.4.
[281] ibid, para 2.7.
[282] ibid, para 2.9.

prosecute him.[283] The facts demonstrate that the Federal Act for the Protection against Violence within the Family (Bundesgesetz zum Schutz vor Gewalt in der Familie) did not provide the means to protect women from highly violent persons, especially in cases of repeated, severe violence and death threats. There was poor communication between the police and Public Prosecutor, who should have known about the ongoing violence and death threats and may have found that he had sufficient reason to prosecute Mustafa Goekce.[284]

Was the murder of Şahide Goekce an anomaly, or was it a tragic example of the 'prevailing lack of seriousness with which violence against women is taken by the public and by the Austrian authorities'?[285] Does this case reflect a systemic deficiency, where the criminal justice system, particularly public prosecutors and judges, considers the issue a social or domestic problem, a minor or petty offence that just happens in certain social classes? Do they fail to apply criminal law to such violence because they do not take the danger seriously, and view women's fears and concerns with a lack of gravity?[286] The state authorities had their hands tied, to a certain extent. They could not prosecute the accused without the permission of the abused and the police and judicial officers received mixed signals from the deceased as to the severity of the abuse and the degree of protection she needed from the state.

The key omission is the failure on the part of state agents to understand the nuances and complexities of domestic violence: the fact that an abused may downplay the seriousness of the violence to the authorities, that she may not want the person she loves, or on whom she depends financially, to be imprisoned, and that the relationship may vacillate between safety and violence. The state officials failed to identify, record and act upon the *continuum* of violence, the repetitive acts of harm that led, ultimately, to the death of the deceased.

Similarly, in the case of *Fatma Yildirim (deceased) v Austria*, the CEDAW Committee noted that Austria had established a comprehensive model to address domestic violence that included

> legislation, criminal and civil-law remedies, awareness raising, education and training, shelters, counselling for victims of violence and work with perpetrators. However, in order for the individual woman victim of domestic violence to enjoy the practical realization of the principle of equality of men and women and of her human rights and fundamental freedoms, the political will that is expressed in the aforementioned comprehensive system of Austria must be supported by State actors, who adhere to the State party's due diligence obligations.[287]

---

[283] ibid, para 2.10.
[284] ibid, para 3.1.
[285] ibid, para 3.6.
[286] ibid.
[287] *Yildirim v Austria* (n 117) para 12.1.2. For a detailed discussion of this communication to the CEDAW Committee see ch 1, p 49–52.

The content of the due diligence standard or the standard relating to compliance with international obligations depends on the primary obligation in question.[288] The full nature of the right to be free from systemic intimate violence and the steps that states should take to extenuate such violence are addressed in chapter two above. In sum, states must provide facilities to protect against domestic violence; must take precautions to prevent its occurrence; and must enforce the prohibition of domestic violence through combined legal, political and social mechanisms.[289]

Aggregate Omissions

Given the complexity of systemic intimate violence, how do we carve out the content of an actionable omission? Article 15 of the ILC Articles allows for a breach of an international obligation to fall within a series of acts defined in aggregate as wrongful.[290] In principle, therefore, a continuing failure to undertake the requisite minimum steps prescribed by international law will trigger a state's responsibility.[291] So, for example, 'negligent or dilatory measures in investigating the circumstances of a criminal offence, whereupon the culprits are never brought to justice, will justify the complaint that international law has been affronted'.[292] It is not simply one failure by a state to protect women from abusers but a series of omissions that triggers state responsibility. So long as a state conducts itself contrary to its international obligations, even where such conduct inheres in a series of omissions, it will be in breach.[293]

A state's repeated failure actively to assist women who suffer systemic intimate violence may be construed as implied sanctioning of this behaviour.[294] The isolation of victims of systemic intimate violence demonstrates that, while their abusers may be private individuals, the conduct itself takes place within a structure of hegemony, which both mirrors and incorporates the power disparity between a state and its citizens. When, with knowledge of protracted, generic violence, a state persistently fails to take basic steps, such as providing training to police officials, establishing shelters and prosecuting repeat abusers, the international standards of fundamental human dignity should pertain.

---

[288] Crawford (n 1) 70 (the standard of compliance with international obligations, including the due diligence standard, will vary based on the context and substance of the primary obligation).
[289] ibid, 125–26 (conformity with international obligations has been described as 'the provision of facilities, or the taking of precautions or the enforcement of a prohibition').
[290] ILC Articles, Art 15.
[291] Freeman (n 13) 376.
[292] ibid.
[293] Shaw (n 82) 697–98 (discussing the duration of the breach).
[294] Carin Benninger-Budel, *Violence Against Women: 10 Reports/Year 2000 for the Protection and Promotion of the Human Rights of Women* (Geneva, World Organization against Torture, 2000) 10: 'a State's lack of exercising due diligence in preventing, investigating, prosecuting and punishing violence against women at the hands of private actors can result in finding a State responsible for torture . . .' See also Crawford (n 1) 141 (the essence here is 'a series of acts or omissions defined in aggregate as wrongful').

Often, it is not one organ but a combination of several organs of state that fail to protect women from systemic intimate violence, either by alienating the victim or through negligence.[295] Clearly it would be untenable to hold a state liable if its police, judiciary or politicians are unable to protect individuals in their society from every act of violence. However, it is inveterate and virulent gender-based violence that calls for state consideration.

Practical Resources and Capabilities of the Country

Preventing domestic violence is not inexpensive, although it may be less expensive than the cost of not addressing domestic violence.

We know intuitively that a different standard will apply to countries with strong economies and developed, progressive anti-discrimination laws, on the one hand, and states which are developing, economically dependent and where discrimination occurs with limited, if any, legal redress.[296] Each country will have practical exigencies that may make it difficult to render specific protection. This is recognised by the principles of state responsibility, which take into consideration the inability of a state to prevent all harmful acts. It is possible, therefore, 'that circumstances which might produce responsibility in one State would not do so in another'.[297] This is underscored by Freeman's citation of Huber, who remarks that

> penal and civil proceedings are necessarily dependent on the means at the disposal of the state and on the degree of authority which it is able to exert . . . It is not possible to demand the uniform application in all cases of a system of justice which satisfies the minimum standards, (critères minima), of international law.[298]

The standards of due diligence will fluctuate depending on the circumstances of each state, particularly with reference to the availability of resources and social, political and/or economic exigencies that reasonably mitigate a state's ability to protect women from systemic intimate violence. This is complicated by the standard used to assess responsibility in the context of denial of justice. These principles hold that the mere fact that in a state a high coefficient of criminality may exist is no proof, by itself, that the government of that state has failed in its duty to maintain an adequate police force for the prosecution and punishment of criminals.[299] This contextual caveat is necessary, both intellectually and practically, to delineate the nature of the liability and lend it viability and perpetuity. Each country will have practical exigencies that render specific protection relatively more or less possible.[300] In other words, the obligation must be reasonable.

---

295 Crawford (n 1) 95.
296 Freeman (n 13) 373.
297 Eagleton (n 2) 79. See also Freeman (n 13) 376.
298 See Freeman's citation of Huber in Freeman (n 13) 373.
299 ibid.
300 ibid, 376.

Ultimately, the application of the due diligence standard to systemic intimate violence requires an analysis, on a case-by-case basis, of the resources available to the state in question, the practical factors that are available to protect victims, and the level of neglect. These considerations ought to form part of the test determining when a state has failed to comply with its international obligation to protect women from systemic intimate violence.

Could one envisage a situation, however, where a state's failure to protect women from systemic intimate violence might *not* be wrongful? If so, what are those circumstances?

Circumstances Precluding Wrongfulness

Systemic intimate violence is replete with the strangeness of love, fear and intimacy. These concepts do not fit easily into legal categories. It is even more difficult to attach legal obligations in respect of vague, amorphous and private concepts. States can be particularly proactive and still not motivate victims to seek help or prevent abusers from extreme violence. Is it the state's obligation to arrest abusers, even if the victim retracts her charge? Should states insist on greater intervention in our homes and relationships or should our privacy be absolute? At times it is unclear who is the victim and who is the perpetrator, so should the police arrest both parties? These difficulties must be considered when assessing the wrongfulness of a state's failure to protect.

In determining whether or not there has been an internationally wrongful act, 'there must be taken into account the circumstances, which can limit or even nullify the activity of the State'.[301] Chapter V of the ILC Articles identifies six instances where a state's conduct, while not complying with international law, is not wrongful. These are: (1) consent (Article 20); self-defence (Article 21); countermeasures (Article 22); force majeure (Article 23); distress (Article 24); and necessity (Article 25).[302] These circumstances would not annul or terminate a state's international obligation to take positive steps to prevent and help remedy systemic intimate violence; instead they would provide 'a justification or excuse for non-performance while the circumstance in question subsists'.[303]

Not every category listed in Chapter V is relevant to systemic intimate violence. I discuss below only (1) distress, (2) force majeure, and (3) necessity.[304]

---

[301] ibid, 373.

[302] For a detailed discussion of these circumstances see Crawford (n 1) 169.

[303] ILC Articles, Art 169. See also *Gabčíkovo-Nagymaros Project (Hungary/Slovakia)* (Judgment) [1997] ICJ Rep 7, para 48.

[304] I do not deal with countermeasures, since these are acts which a state takes to ensure the compliance of a third state with its international obligations. Consent is a nullity since a state cannot consent to another state's non-compliance with obligations *erga omnes,* ie owing to everyone. Finally, self-defence is inapplicable since a state could not argue that it allowed the perpetuation of systemic intimate violence because it was defending itself against the victims. If a state is under attack by another state, that will constitute one of the other preclusions, namely, distress, necessity or force majeure.

But is this analysis even suitable for domestic violence? Can one conceive of a situation where a state is held to account for its failure to protect women from systemic intimate violence and raises the defence, for example, of distress? What I think is more realistic is that these principles, including the principles that preclude wrongfulness, help to structure the discussion of what states should do to protect women and also lend greater clarity to the issue of where exactly we want the state's agents to be when a woman's private world becomes unsafe.

Distress

The wrongfulness of a state's failure to comply with its international obligation will be precluded 'if the author of the act in question has no other reasonable way, in a situation of distress, of saving the author's life or the lives of other persons entrusted to the author's care'.[305] The plea of distress is also accepted in many treaties as a circumstance justifying conduct which would otherwise be wrongful, such as the Convention on the Prevention of Marine Pollution by Dumping of Wastes and Other Matter, which provides that the prohibition on dumping of wastes does not apply when it is 'necessary to secure the safety of human life or of vessels, aircraft, platforms or other man-made structures at sea'.[306]

The Commentaries to the ILC Articles describe distress as a 'specific case where an individual whose acts are attributable to the state is in a situation of peril, either personally or in relation to persons under his or her care'.[307] Usually, the peril that would prevent the state's agent from fulfilling the state's obligation is the 'immediate [interest] of saving people's lives', 'where the agent had no other reasonable way of saving life'.[308] In practice, cases of distress have usually involved aircraft or ships wrongfully entering state territory as a result of adverse weather conditions or a mechanical or navigational failure. The Commentaries to the ILC Articles interpret Article 24 as 'limited to cases where human life is at stake'.[309] As opposed to force majeure, the act is not an involuntary one; rather a choice is made, even if 'the choice is effectively nullified by the situation of peril'.[310]

The defence of distress was evaluated in the *Rainbow Warrior* arbitration. France sought to justify its conduct in removing two officers from the island of Hao on the ground of 'circumstances of distress in a case of extreme urgency involving elementary humanitarian considerations affecting the acting organs

---

[305] ILC Articles, Art 24.
[306] Convention on the Prevention of Marine Pollution by Dumping of Wastes and Other Matters (adopted 13 November 1972, entered into force 30 August 1975) 1046 UNTS 138, at Art V(1). See also Crawford (n 1) 192.
[307] Crawford (n 1) 189.
[308] ibid, 189
[309] ibid, 192.
[310] ibid, 189.

of the State'.[311] According to this case, three factors must be shown in order to demonstrate distress: (1) the existence of very exceptional circumstances of extreme urgency involving medical or other considerations of an elementary nature;[312] (2) the re-establishment of the original situation of compliance as soon as the reasons for the emergency had disappeared;[313] and (3) the 'existence of good faith effort' to obtain the consent of the injured state to the non-compliance.[314]

The principle of distress requires very exceptional circumstances of extreme urgency involving medical or other considerations of an elementary nature.[315] This element will apply where a state was unable to implement and enforce a policy of protection against systemic intimate violence because it had to focus on other circumstances of extreme urgency and this absorbed all of its attention and resources. However, in practice, such a situation would likely be rare.

Force Majeure

Wrongfulness may be precluded where the omission is due to force majeure. This is the occurrence of an irresistible force or of an unforeseen event, beyond the control of the state, making it materially impossible in the circumstances to perform the obligation.[316] Force majeure is characterised by the notion of compulsion and the absence of choice. The internationally wrongful act is involuntary and on this basis wrongfulness is precluded.[317] Both distress and force majeure will not apply if the state caused the circumstances or the state assumed the risk of that situation occurring.[318]

Three elements must be met in order to raise a successful plea of force majeure: (1) the force in question must have been brought about by an irresistible force or an unforeseen event, (2) which is beyond the control of the state, (3) making it materially impossible in the circumstances to perform the obligation.[319]

A breach will not be wrongful if a state is prevented from complying by 'a constraint which the State was unable to avoid or oppose by its own means'.[320] This event must have been unforeseen or not of a foreseeable kind and must be linked to the 'situation of material impossibility'.[321] Such material impossibility may be due to natural events, for example earthquakes, floods or drought, or to human acts, or a combination of the two.[322] The essence of this requirement is

---

[311] *Rainbow Warrior* (n 81) 254–55, para 78. See also Crawford (n 1) 191–92.
[312] *Rainbow Warrior* (n 81) 254–55, para 79.
[313] ibid.
[314] ibid.
[315] ibid.
[316] ILC Articles, Art 23(1).
[317] See Crawford (n 1) 183–84.
[318] ILC Articles, Art 23(2). See also Crawford (n 1) 193.
[319] See Crawford (n 1) 183–84.
[320] ibid.
[321] ibid.
[322] ibid, 184.

that the situation preventing the state from satisfying its duty to uphold a woman's right to be free from systemic intimate violence 'must be irresistible, so that the State concerned has no real possibility of escaping its effects'.[323] However, this does not include circumstances where the performance of the obligation has become difficult due to a political or economic crisis.[324]

Any circumstances which would preclude the wrongfulness of a state's failure to prevent systemic intimate violence would have to be unforeseen and beyond the control of the state, making it impossible for it to comply with its obligation. The standard is high and there must be material impossibility of performance.[325]

Necessity

Necessity validly precludes wrongfulness if: (1) non-compliance is the only way for the state 'to safeguard an essential interest against a grave and imminent peril',[326] and (2) the non-compliance does not seriously impair 'an essential interest of the State or States towards which the obligation exists, or of the international community as a whole'.[327] As with force majeure and distress, the state may not rely on necessity where it has contributed to the occurrence of such necessity.[328]

Necessity arises where there is an irreconcilable conflict between an essential interest on the one hand and an obligation of the state on the other.[329] The plea of necessity was raised in the *Caroline* incident of 1837, where the British armed forces entered United States territory and destroyed a vessel owned by US citizens which was carrying recruits and military material to Canadian insurgents.[330] The British defended their actions by citing the 'necessity of self-defence and self-preservation' which, they claimed, trumped the territorial integrity of the United States.[331]

Another example of necessity is the 'Russian Fur Seals' controversy of 1893. In this matter the 'essential interest' of protecting an endangered seal population against the 'grave and imminent peril' of extermination caused the Russian government to prohibit sealing in the high seas, which was not subject to the

---

[323] ibid.

[324] ibid.

[325] One type of claim that might be accepted is attacks by rebels or the collapse of a government (ibid, 186).

[326] ILC Articles, Art 25(1).

[327] ibid. See also Crawford (n 1) 194: 'The term "necessity" ("état de necessité") is used to denote those exceptional cases where the only way a State can safeguard an essential interest threatened by a grave and imminent peril is, for the time being, not to perform some other international obligation of lesser weight or urgency. Under conditions narrowly defined in Art 25, such a plea is recognized as a circumstance precluding wrongfulness.'

[328] ILC Articles, Art 25(2).

[329] Crawford (n 1) 195.

[330] See ibid, 196.

[331] ibid.

jurisdiction of any state.[332] In the *Gabãíkovo-Nagymaros Project* case, the ICJ accepted the principle of necessity.[333] It articulated the following conditions for the case in question, which provide a useful generic guide: the omission must have been occasioned by an 'essential interest' of the state which is the author of the act conflicting with one of its international obligations; the act being challenged must have been the 'only means' of safeguarding that interest; that act must not have 'seriously impair[ed] an essential interest' of the state towards which the obligation existed; and the state which is the author of that act must not have 'contributed to the occurrence of the State of necessity'.[334] As a result of these requirements, the necessity plea is used rarely and is subject to 'strict limitations to safeguard against possible abuse'.[335]

In order for a state to rely on necessity as a preclusion of wrongfulness in the context of systemic intimate violence, the following conditions must be satisfied: (1) there must be an irreconcilable tension between the needs of abused women and another interest of the state; (2) that other interest must be essential; (3) it must have been threatened by a grave and imminent peril; (4) non-compliance with the state's obligation to address systemic intimate violence must have been the only means of safeguarding that other interest; (5) the state must not have impaired an essential interest of another state; and (6) it must not have contributed to the circumstances of necessity. On this basis, I propose that it will be very rare that the principles of 'necessity' will act to justify a state's failure to prevent and help remedy systemic intimate violence. In particular, it is difficult to envisage a competing interest for which non-compliance with the state's obligations in respect of systemic intimate violence will be the *only* way in which the state can protect that other interest.

Application of the Justification Principles to Systemic Intimate Violence

Following the floods caused by Hurricane Katrina in August 2005, the city of New Orleans diverted most of its attention and resources to the urgent matter of rescuing people as quickly as possible. There is no question that the exigency and timing of that situation required the city's authorities to prioritise the saving of lives. However, one of the responsibilities of the state in the aftermath of a disaster (or conflict) is to ensure that restructuring and relief efforts are not shaped by the social constructs preceding the disaster, social constructs that value some people over others.

---

[332] ibid, 197 (facing the danger of extermination of a fur seal population by unrestricted hunting, the Russian Government issued a decree prohibiting sealing in an area of the high seas).

[333] *Gabãíkovo-Nagymaros* case (n 303) 7. See also Crawford (n 1) 199.

[334] Crawford (n 1) 40–41, paras 51–52.

[335] ibid, 195.

In New Orleans, following the hurricane there was a significant increase in domestic violence and sexual assault.[336] Increases in this type of violence are common in post-conflict or post-disaster situations, where female refugees or internally displaced persons are particularly vulnerable to extreme violence.[337] There are several possible reasons for this increase, including the collapse of societal support mechanisms, psychological strain on perpetrators, the collapse of legal and health infrastructures, shortage of affordable housing, and the normalisation of violence.

The question, then, is whether the events following Hurricane Katrina constituted a situation of distress, force majeure or necessity for the purpose of expunging the state's obligation to protect women from domestic violence during that period.

If a state has knowledge of the fact that, following a natural disaster, there is an increase in violence against women, clearly its response to that disaster should include a plan to protect women from such violence. The state is also required to re-establish 'the original situation of compliance' as soon as possible.[338] Therefore, if there is an acceptable degree of urgency preventing the state from protecting victims of systemic intimate violence at the height of a crisis, as soon as the situation is over it must resume compliance with its duties. The state's response to Katrina should have taken into account the fact that domestic violence survivors may need to turn to their abusers for assistance; domestic violence refuges may be destroyed; survivors of domestic violence may be relying on anonymity to escape their abusers and disaster relief projects may compromise this; and generally, women's safety should be a significant consideration in any rescue or rehabilitation plan.[339]

The state's obligation to provide services equally and without discrimination applies in respect of an emergency as much as it does during times of stability. This element also entails a balancing investigation. Inherent in the concept of distress is the notion that certain interests 'clearly outweigh the other interests at stake in the circumstances'.[340] However, according to a strict application

---

[336] See 'As Domestic Violence Rises in New Orleans in Wake of Katrina, Catholic Charities Provides (*sic*) a Refuge for Abused Women' *US Newswire* (10 April 2006), www.ncdsv.org/images/AsDomesticViolenceRisesinNewOrleansWakeKatrina.pdf.

[337] See UNHCR, *Sexual and Gender-based Violence against Refugees, Returnees and Internally Displaced Persons: Guidelines for Prevention and Response* (Geneva, 2003). See also New York City Alliance against Sexual Assault, 'Katrina, Natural Disasters and Sexual Violence', www.nycagainstrape.org/media/factsheets/fsht_111.pdf; UNHCR, 'OPT: UN Tracks Rising Violence against Women in Gaza' (Integrated Regional Information Networks (IRIN), 24 March 2009.

[338] *Rainbow Warrior* (n 81) 254–55, para 79.

[339] See eg UNHCR, *Sexual Violence against Refugees: Guidelines on Prevention and Response* (Geneva, 1995). See also Michelle Hynes and Barbara Lopez Cardozo, 'Observations from the CDC: Sexual Violence against Refugee Women' (2000) 9 *Journal of Women's Health and Gender-Based Medicine* 8; Avis A Jones-DeWeever, 'Women in the Wake of the Storm: Examining the Post-Katrina Realities of the Women of New Orleans and the Gulf Coast' (Institute for Women's Policy Research, 2008).

[340] Crawford (n 1) 194.

of the ILC Articles and Commentaries, it is unlikely that a state could claim economic or political distress as a justification for failing to protect women from systemic intimate violence. This is because the violence in question is *systemic*. It is not a one-off occurrence but a perpetual and repeated form of harm against a distinct group within society. By definition, the time element and urgency connoted with force majeure, distress and necessity really does not apply to systemic intimate violence.

In order for state responsibility to arise, both elements of conduct and wrongfulness must pertain. The next section discusses whether there are any other reasons, other than the factors precluding wrongfulness, that would excuse a state from providing effective protection to women against systemic intimate violence.

Competing Values: Privacy

It is necessary to balance the victim's right to physical safety—and the concomitant state responsibility to protect her from intimate violence—against the abuser's *and the victim's* right to privacy. Whether such a balancing exercise is necessary is debatable. This question often arises in discussions regarding state responsibility, and it is important to understand precisely what is at issue and to determine the appropriate response. The question is not whether the right to privacy trumps the right to bodily integrity, life and liberty. This is simplistic and does not take into account the compelling interests of both sets of rights. Perhaps the more appropriate question is how the state should balance its duty to respect the right to privacy (and the right not to interfere arbitrarily in individuals' family and home lives) whilst at the same time protecting women's right to safety in the home, the realm in which many women are most at risk.

The right to privacy is not absolute. Respect for privacy is recognised in Article 12 of the UN Declaration, which states that 'No-one shall be subjected to arbitrary interference with his privacy, family, home or correspondence . . .'. However, note that only arbitrary interference is prohibited. The tenor of the right is that the state should be reluctant to interfere in activities which occur in private, especially where such interference would compromise the honour and dignity of the individual. Where intervention is not arbitrary but is necessary to protect an individual from harm (as is accepted in the case of child abuse, for example),[341] not only is it justifiable to curtail the abuser's right to privacy, it becomes the responsibility of the state to intervene.

The CEDAW Committee has considered the balancing of these interests. In the communication of *Fatma Yildirim (deceased) v Austria*, the deceased had been abused by her husband, who later killed her. Notwithstanding several incidents of violence reported to the police, the state took the view that it was correct not to detain the deceased's husband:

---

[341] See *A v The United Kingdom* (App No 25599/94) (1999) 27 EHRR 611, para 22.

the imposition of detention constitutes massive interference with a person's fundamental freedoms . . . The proportionality assessment is a forward-looking evaluation
of how dangerous the person concerned is and whether that person will commit an
offence that must be weighed against a suspect's fundamental freedoms and rights
. . . [The husband] had no criminal record, did not use a weapon and appeared quiet
and cooperative to the police officers who intervened . . . [The deceased] had no apparent injuries.[342]

The state argued that on the information available to the investigating judge,
an interim injunction appeared sufficient to protect the deceased and that,
because the husband 'was socially integrated and did not have a criminal
record', his basic rights (such as the presumption of innocence, his right to private and family life, and his right to personal freedom) would have been directly
violated had he been detained.[343]

The police decided not to arrest the husband because from an 'ex ante point
of view . . . this would not have been proportionate'.[344] The test employed by
the state would be appropriate in many incidents of violence, but not in respect
of systemic intimate violence. These cases are typified by an escalation of violence, and the behaviour of the abuser towards the abused is rarely visible in
public. The husband's cooperation with officials is typical behaviour that forms
part of the abusive process. By escaping the authorities, the abuser demonstrates
to the victim his alignment with law enforcement officials, and, in the mind of
the abused, this protects him from legal sanction. In this case, the message was
correct. Notwithstanding myriad complaints and protection orders, the only
action taken by the police was to talk to the husband. The CEDAW Committee
concluded that in cases of domestic violence and violence against women, 'the
perpetrator's rights cannot supersede women's human rights to life and to physical and mental integrity'.[345]

For many years, feminists have noted the failure of legal systems to protect
women from harm committed in private.[346] This call for state protection against
domestic violence, however, triggered concern that the constitutionally protected right to privacy would be compromised.[347] In response, theorists argued
that the right to privacy is not only about the absolute removal of the state from
the private realm; it also entails the ability to live an autonomous life without
interference from third parties.[348]

[342] *Yildirim v Austria* (n 117) para 4.3. For a detailed discussion of this communication to the
CEDAW Committee see ch 1, p 49–51.
[343] ibid, para 8.14.
[344] ibid, para 4.3.
[345] ibid, para 12.1.5. See also *Ms AT v Hungary* (n 273) para 9.3.
[346] See Martha A Fineman and Roxanne Mykitiuk, 'Introduction' in Martha A Fineman and
Roxanne Mykitiuk (eds), *The Public Nature of Private Violence: The Discovery of Domestic Abuse*
(New York, Routledge, 1994) xi–xviii. See also Martha R Mahoney, 'Victimization or Oppression?
Women's Lives, Violence, and Agency' in Fineman and Mykitiuk, 78–81.
[347] For a discussion of this issue see Elizabeth M Schneider, 'The Violence of Privacy' in Fineman
and Mykitiuk, ibid, 36.
[348] For a discussion of this theory see ch 1, p 100–102.

This echoes the thinking of Martha Nussbaum, who posits the state as a facilitating structure, one that develops institutions to draw on the capacity of each individual to achieve her/his potential.[349] According to Nussbaum, 'capability, not actual functioning, should be the goal of public policy'.[350] In the same vein, Amartya Sen raises the standard of the state's obligations to its citizens to facilitate social opportunities. Social opportunities, according to Sen,

> refer to the arrangements that society makes for education, health care and so on, which influence the individual's substantive freedom to live better. These facilities are important not only for the conduct of private lives (such as living a healthy life and avoiding preventable morbidity and premature mortality), but also for more effective participation in economic and political activities.[351]

Without institutional remedies for physical violence, irrespective of whether the violence emanates from a public or private source (that is, without protective security), both individuals and their society will be impeded in their development and attainment of comprehensive and meaningful liberty.[352]

Justice Sachs describes how

> the concept of autonomy has been used to protect the abusive husband from the actions of the state, but not the abused wife from the actions of the husband [with the result that] all too often the privacy and intimacy end up providing both the opportunity for violence and the justification for non-interference.[353]

The South African Constitution recognises that the right to privacy is not a non-derogable right and may be limited to protect the right 'to be free from all forms of violence from either public *or private* sources' (emphasis added).[354]

The approach of the ECtHR to the issue of privacy is informative. In the case of *Bevacqua and S v Bulgaria*,[355] the Court held that the view that the authorities did not have to assist a victim of domestic violence 'as the dispute concerned a "private matter" was incompatible with their positive obligations to secure the enjoyment of the applicant's Article 8 rights'. The Court in this case took the approach that the right to privacy and family, as enshrined in Article 8, entails not only an obligation on the state to refrain from interfering with that right, but also a duty to secure respect for the right to family and private lives of both parties to a domestic violence dispute—not only that of the aggressor. The Court

---

[349] Nussbaum argues expressly for positive state intervention. She proposes that 'human capabilities exert a moral claim that they should be developed'. Martha C Nussbaum, 'Human Capabilities, Female Beings' in Martha C Nussbaum and Jonathan Glover (eds), *Women, Culture and Development: A Study of Human Capabilities* (Oxford, Oxford University Press, 1995) 88 ('thinking of the basic capabilities of human beings as needs for functioning, which give rise to correlated political duties')

[350] ibid, 83.

[351] Amartya Sen, *Development as Freedom* (New York, Random House, 2000) 39.

[352] ibid, 10.

[353] *S v Godfrey Baloyi*, Case CCT 29/99 (South African Constitutional Court, 1999), per Justice Sachs, para 16.

[354] s 12(1)(c).

[355] *Bevacqua and S v Bulgaria* (n 179).

thus recognised that privacy is not only about the insulation of one's life from public scrutiny; it is also about the well-being of an individual and the richness of her/his life. Systemic intimate violence may impede this notion of privacy and itself can constitute a failure on the part of the state to protect a victim's rights under Article 8.

In the case of *Opuz v Turkey*, the applicant alleged that the state had violated her rights under Articles 2, 3 and 14 of the ECHR because, in part, it had failed to take effective steps to prevent the applicant's ex-husband, HO, from causing her harm and killing her mother.[356] The state maintained that it was bound by Article 8 of the Convention not to continue criminal proceedings against HO, especially when the applicant had withdrawn her complaint.[357] The Court held that state authorities must strike a balance between a victim's Article 2, Article 3 and Article 8 rights.[358]

The Court confirmed its findings in *Bevacqua and S v Bulgaria*,[359] holding that the authorities' view that no assistance was required as the dispute concerned a private matter was incompatible with their positive obligation to secure the enjoyment of the applicants' rights.[360] The Court went further and held that, in some instances, 'the national authorities' interference with the private or family life of the individuals might be necessary in order to protect the health and rights of others or to prevent commission of criminal acts'.[361]

Privacy cannot be understood merely as the right to be left alone; rather, it is linked affirmatively to liberty, the right to autonomy and self-determination. Privacy is not in opposition to, but is an affirmation of, women's safety in the home. And in protecting the right to privacy, it is the state's duty to balance negative—non-intervention in the affairs of individuals—and positive steps— protection of individuals from intimate harm.

Fault and Knowledge

In most legal systems, in order for a person to be responsible for a wrongful act they must be at fault. The notion of fault as classically understood in national legal systems—as involving intention or negligence—is notably absent from the text of the ILC Articles. Crawford maintains that it is only the act of wrongfulness that constitutes liability; no fault element is necessary to trigger state responsibility.[362] This is not to say that fault is irrelevant for the purposes of state responsibility; rather the examination of whether or not there is a fault

---

[356] *Opuz v Turkey* (n 99).
[357] ibid, paras 137, 140.
[358] ibid, para 138. The considerations that a state must take into account in balancing these rights are discussed in ch 2, p 123 and 127.
[359] *Bevacqua and S v Bulgaria* (n 179) para 83.
[360] ibid, para 144.
[361] ibid, para 144.
[362] Crawford (n 1) 84.

element occurs at the level of the primary obligation or rule that is breached. Different primary obligations involve differing degrees of responsibility, ranging from 'due diligence' to strict liability.[363]

Fault, in the form of either intent or mental knowledge of the breach, would likely be a requirement of states' primary obligation in respect of systemic intimate violence.[364] Common sense dictates that it would be unreasonable to hold a state responsible for an act of violence which it neither anticipated nor reasonably could have anticipated, especially where the violence is perpetrated by a non-state actor in private. In order to hold a state responsible for an act of systemic intimate violence, it is necessary for the state to have a degree of knowledge, or it reasonably ought to have foreseen that such violence might occur and nonetheless failed to take reasonable steps to prevent and/or alleviate that harm.[365]

In the *Corfu Channel* case the Court held that Albania knew about the existence of mines in its territorial waters (there was sufficient evidence that Albania had a view of and kept a vigil over the relevant waters, which precluded its claim of ignorance).[366] Knowledge on the part of the Albanian government was essential in order to hold it liable for the damage caused when the mines exploded. Based on the admission of so-called 'indirect evidence', the Court held that proof of knowledge may be drawn from an inference of facts, 'provided that they leave *no room* for reasonable doubt'.[367] The ICJ held that it was irrelevant *who* actually laid the mines; all that was applicable was that the Albanian government had failed to act upon that knowledge.

This was emphasised by the CEDAW Committee in the communications of *Goekce (deceased) v Austria* and *Fatima Yildirim (deceased) v Austria*.[368] In both cases the Committee emphasised the state's knowledge of violence against the deceased. In the *Goekce* case, the deceased had contacted the state authorities about the violence around 10 times before she was killed by her husband.[369] The CEDAW Committee found that the state ought to have done more to protect the deceased, even though at various points the deceased had withdrawn her allegations. In the second domestic violence case against Austria, in contrast to the *Goekce* case, the deceased at no point withdrew her complaints against her abuser. He had been physically and psychologically violent and on several occasions threatened to kill the deceased both in the family home and, after she had moved out, at her place of work. On numerous occasions the deceased had

---

[363] ibid, 13.

[364] See Crawford (n 1) 70 (explaining that the standard of fault 'is a matter for the interpretation and application of the primary rules engaged in the given case').

[365] The Commentaries to the text of the ILC Articles expressly allow for either a subjective or objective approach, without stipulating a rule or preference in respect of either. See generally Shaw (n 82) 702–03.

[366] *Corfu Channel* case (n 111) 18.

[367] ibid, 18.

[368] *Goekce v Austria* (n 278); *Yildirim v Austria* (n 117). For a detailed discussion of both cases see ch 1, pp 45–51.

[369] ibid, para 12.1.3.

requested that her husband be detained; she had sought and obtained several expulsion and prohibition to return orders against her husband; she had instituted divorce proceedings; she had applied on her own behalf and on behalf of her minor daughter for an interim injunction against her husband; she had reported her husband to the police; and eventually she engaged the help of an NGO (the author of the complaint). Ten days after yet another interim injunction was ordered against the husband, he killed the deceased.[370] Austria, through various agents of the state, clearly had knowledge of the abuse and failed in both instances to take reasonable steps to prevent the death of the deceased.[371] In the case of domestic violence, 'the perpetrators' rights cannot supersede women's human rights to life and physical and mental integrity'.[372]

In the case of *Opuz v Turkey* the ECtHR held:

> where there is an allegation that the authorities have violated their positive obligations to . . . prevent and suppress offences against the person, it must be established that the authorities knew or ought to have known at the time of the existence of a real and immediate risk to the life of an identified individual or individuals from the criminal acts of a third party and that they failed to take measures within the scope of their powers which, judged reasonably, might have been expected to avoid that risk.[373]

Whether or not the state had knowledge or could have foreseen that a third party would commit a harmful act depends on the circumstances of each case.[374] The Court held that there were sufficient incidences of severe violence committed by HO (the applicant's ex-husband) against the applicant and her mother such that the local authorities could have foreseen a lethal attack by HO:

> it appears that there was an escalating violence against the applicant and her mother by HO. The crimes committed by HO were sufficiently serious to warrant preventive measures and there was a continuing threat to the health and safety of the victims. When examining the history of the relationship, it was obvious that the perpetrator had a record of domestic violence and there was therefore a significant risk of further violence.[375]

Knowledge—together with the practical question of whether there were practical measures that the authorities could have taken to alleviate the harm—is therefore a precursor to determining whether the state has breached its international obligations.

While the position is unclear at international law, even if an element of fault, probably in the form of negligence, is required to trigger the responsibility of states in the context of systemic intimate violence, such a requirement will likely

---

[370] *Yildirim v Austria* (n 117) paras 2.1–2.13.
[371] ibid, The CEDAW Committee took the view that the failure to detain the husband was a breach of the state's due diligence obligation to protect the deceased. ibid, para 12.1.5.
[372] ibid.
[373] *Opuz v Turkey* (n 99) para 130.
[374] ibid.
[375] ibid, para 134.

be satisfied in most cases of systemic intimate violence, as defined, due to the continuum of extreme harm that characterises this form of violence. The evidence pointing to the extreme nature and proliferation of severe forms of systemic intimate violence in almost every country worldwide is staggering.[376] The failure of a government and its agents to take reasonable steps to prevent and help remedy such violence is, at the very least, negligent.

Role of the Judiciary

It is necessary briefly to consider the role of the judiciary in relation to the state's obligation to protect women from systemic intimate violence. If breakdowns in the state's response to domestic violence are the result of poor policy, should the courts be able to hold the executive and legislative branches of government to account? This is a complex question that has dominated the area of socio-economic rights.[377] Primary responsibility for the protection of vulnerable groups rests with the executive and the legislature, and it is proper that policies should be determined by the elected arms of government. For reasons of democratic legitimacy, crucial resource allocation decisions are best left in the hands of the legislature and executive, rather than being determined by an unelected judiciary.

The judiciary, however, does have a role to play where there is a sufficiently gross failure to uphold basic rights. In such cases, the judiciary must question— and hold to account—the government's protection of women from systemic intimate violence. The question of the justiciability of economic, social and related policy rights is fraught and I do not attempt to cover the full range of arguments here. However, where the other two branches of government have comprehensively failed to fulfil their responsibilities, then the 'least dangerous branch' has a duty to intervene, for example when free Nivirapine is available for distribution and the government refuses to provide it to a population with the highest rate of HIV in the world.[378]

In the UK the courts operate according to the so-called '*Wednesbury*' principle, which enables courts to review an administrative decision in circumstances where there has been a special degree of unreasonableness.[379] This principle of judicial review extends across the spectrum of government action, whether in relation to economic or civil or any other policy: the government must not act irrationally (in the legal sense of that word). Equality laws, for example, generally enable courts

---

[376] UN Children's Fund, *Early Marriage: Child Spouses* (Italy, Innocenti Research Centre, 2001) 3, www.unicef-irc.org/publications/pdf/digest7e.pdf.

[377] See Lord Lester of Herne Hill QC and Colm O'Cinneide, 'The Effective Protection of Socio-Economic Rights' in Y Ghai and J Cotterill (eds), *The Role of Judges in Implementing Economic, Social and Cultural Rights* (London, Interights, 2004).

[378] *Minister of Health v Treatment Action Campaign* (2) 2002 (5) SA 721 (CC) para 135.

[379] *Associated Provincial Picture Houses Ltd v Wednesbury Corporation* [1984] 1 KB 223.

to review governmental action and to ensure that there are very good reasons for any action that treats people unequally, be it in the context of labour or health or imprisonment or politics. This is commonly known as a culture of justification for actions which have an adverse impact on basic rights and freedoms.

Even where human rights treaties have not ratified or incorporated into domestic law, they provide important guidance to lawmakers, public officials and, importantly, the courts. As discussed above, one of the key reasons why the international community should establish standards regarding domestic violence is precisely so that governments can be held to account when they fail to do so. The court system is one of the most important mechanisms by which victims, survivors and NGOs can require the executive and legislative arms of government to comply with these standards, not only on a case-by-case basis, but also in respect of the state's overall policy regarding the combating of systemic intimate violence.

Consequences of an Internationally Wrongful Act

If a state commits an internationally wrongful act: (1) it remains obliged to comply with its international obligation;[380] (2) it must cease the conduct that caused the breach and offer assurances of non-repetition;[381] (3) it is obliged to make full reparation for the injury it has caused, be it moral or material;[382] and (4) it may not rely on the provisions of its internal law to justify its omission.[383]

Part II of the ILC Articles addresses the consequences of an internationally wrongful act. I do not address them here because they deal with issues of compensation and reparation. While these consequences certainly would apply to systemic intimate violence, I maintain that the primary purpose of understanding the international right and obligation vis-a-vis systemic intimate violence is its ability to change state laws to address systemic intimate violence or to hold states responsible for an omission to assist victims of domestic violence in national, regional and international courts. There is greater value in this, at least initially, than in determining which remedies would be appropriate.

CONCLUSION

If there is a type of harm that human beings have a right not to experience, states have a corresponding obligation to protect their citizens from violations of such

---

[380] ILC Articles, Art 29.
[381] ibid, Art 30.
[382] ibid, Art 31.
[383] ibid, Art 32. The government of a federal state remains responsible for the activities of its individual Member States in international law and 'the central government is unable to avoid responsibility on the plea of lack of control over its constituent parts' (Eagleton (n 2) 32).

a right, even where a violation is caused directly by private citizens and not by state actors. If a state through its agents knows that a segment of its population is subject to persistent abuse, or reasonably ought to have foreseen such abuse, and fails to prevent harm to this group of people, the state has participated in the violation of those people's human right to physical security and to live free from fear.[384] Therefore, if a state fails to act where it has an international duty to perform, it commits an internationally wrongful act, even if the omission affects private individuals in their intimate relationships.

There is no reason why the full force of international law should not apply to states which fail to protect women from systemic intimate violence. The only real reason why steps towards such enforcement have not been taken is the continued perception that domestic violence is not an extreme act of harm, that it is limited to deviant members of society, and that it is not a human rights violation. Only with constant monitoring of the seriousness of domestic violence, the frequency with which it occurs, and the regular harm it causes to millions of women, and women especially, will the political approach to the violence change. We need a mind shift on the scale of the abolition movement. At the international level that mind shift is slowly coming about, but significant progress is still required.

---

[384] For authority for the notion that states are responsible for their international wrongful acts, see Crawford (n 1) 77–78 point 2.

4

The Benefits of International Law for Victims of Systemic Intimate Violence

NON-COERCIVE COMPLIANCE THEORY

WHY IS IT at all useful to formulate a theory of domestic violence in international law? International law lacks traditional enforcement mechanisms and there is no international policing authority that can compel states to comply with their international obligations. Furthermore, as discussed in chapter three, the principles of state responsibility in respect of systemic intimate violence are unlikely to be invoked in a court of law between two nation states.

I do not turn lightly to international law as a remedy. Many perceive international law as a weak body of law. Some theorists argue that it is either 'soft law' or not law at all but rather a vague and arbitrary alliance of states' interests.[1] Others reject international law on the basis that it comes with no effective enforcement mechanisms. Law without such mechanisms, they maintain, results in neither compliance nor respect.[2] Still others maintain that 'international law' is nothing more than a coincidence of conduct. While it may appear that states act according to various standards, in fact this appearance is nothing more than states acting according to 'relations of physical force'.[3] In addition, a common mistrust of international law stems from the perception that the individual is too far removed from international law to benefit from its

---

[1] See Harold Hongju Koh, 'Why do Nations Obey International Law?' (1997) 106 *Yale Law Journal* 2599, 2610–11.

[2] W Michael Reisman, 'How shall we Conceive International Law?' in W Michael Reisman, Mahnoush H Arsanjani, Siegfried Wiessner and Gayl S Westerman (eds), *International Law in Contemporary Perspective,* 2nd edn (New York, Foundation Press, 2004) (citing John Austin, *The Province of Jurisprudence Determined,* Wilfred E Rumble ed (Cambridge, Cambridge University Press, 1995) and John Basset Moore, 'Fifty Years of International Law' (1937) 50 *Harvard Law Review* 395, 397). See also Martti Koskenniemi, *The Gentle Civilizer of Nations: The Rise and Fall of International Law 1870–1960* (Cambridge, Cambridge University Press, 2001) 515; Oona A Hathaway, 'Do Human Rights Treaties Make a Difference?' (2002) 111 *Yale Law Journal* 1935.

[3] This is discussed by Hersch Lauterpacht in *Function of Law in the International Community* (Oxford, Claredon Press, 1933) 400.

precepts and that international law is unsuitable for national systems charac-terised by diverse cultural values.[4]

I turn to international law as an institution designed to induce states to rem-edy the deficiencies within their own domestic legal systems.[5] The enunciation of a norm in international law acts as a guide to be used by national govern-ments, state institutions, non-governmental organisations (NGOs) and individ-uals to improve legislation and policies in respect of, amongst other phenomena, systemic intimate violence. I do not maintain that international law has the same force as a state's domestic laws,[6] nor do I propose that international human rights law is an additional body of law with which states must comply. Rather, I turn to international law as a standard setting spectrum, an enuncia-tion of norms to which states can aspire and on which individuals can rely in holding their governments to account.

There is evidence that international law influences the behaviour of states and the way they treat their citizens through a cooperative rather than a coercive process.[7] I refer to this process as the theory of non-coercive state compliance or cooperative compliance with international law.[8] This is contentious since many theorists reject international law as a fallacy, based on a spurious interpretation of international affairs as legal rather than political. A fortiori, how is it possible to apply international law to systemic intimate violence, which is less 'political' than many other under-enforced human rights violations? Notwithstanding this skepticism, legal scholars are increasingly explaining how international law operates without central law-making or enforcement agencies. These theories maintain that, through varying processes, international law permeates states' boundaries, influencing their conduct vis-a-vis other states and vis-a-vis their own citizens.[9]

---

[4] For a discussion of this theme see Andrew Guzman, 'A Compliance Based Theory of International Law' in Oona A Hathaway and Harold Hongju Koh (eds), *Foundations of International Law and Politics* (New York, Foundation Press, 2005) 58. This theory is rejected by Hathaway, who engages the 'broader perspective on the role that international law plays in shaping how states actu-ally behave'. Oona A Hathaway, 'The Promise and Limits of the International Law of Torture' in Hathaway and Koh, ibid, 228, 230.

[5] Louis Henkin, *The Age of Rights* (New York, Columbia University Press, 1990) 17.

[6] Hathaway (n 2) 1938.

[7] For a discussion of the various theories in support of and rejecting this notion see Koh (n 1) 2599 fn 2.

[8] I use this phrase to distinguish between compliance as a result of force and compliance as a result of free will or self-interest. For a discussion of the motives driving states to comply with inter-national law, see Koh's discussion of the Chayeses' 'managerial model' versus Franck's fairness theory. Koh (n 1) 2600–03 (describing the Chayeses' view which holds that 'nations obey inter-national rules not because they are threatened with sanctions, but because they are persuaded to comply by the dynamic created by the treaty regimes to which they belong'). Koh describes Franck's view as asserting that 'nations "obey powerless rules" because they are pulled towards compliance by considerations of legitimacy . . . and distributive justice'. *cf* Abram Chayes and Antonia Handler Chayes, *The New Sovereignty: Compliance with International Regulatory Agreements* (Cambridge, Harvard University Press, 1995); Thomas M Franck, *Fairness in International Law and Institutions* (Oxford, Clarendon Press, 1995).

[9] Sidney Tarrow, *Power in Movement: Social Movements in Contentious Politics*, 2nd edn (Cambridge, Cambridge University Press, 1998) 178.

This body of theory is supported by a new phenomenon of powerful non-governmental actors, coupled with the benefits of technology, which has oiled the gears of international law. International and local organisations are working in tandem to apply human rights in local settings. This vertical application of the international to the national effects incremental changes in national legal and policy systems.

Despite the absence of an international legislature, judiciary or policing institution, international law is a legal structure, which regulates state behaviour, albeit through non-traditional mechanisms and by non-traditional agents. These processes and agents are not necessarily beyond criticism, not least of all because of their non-democratic nature; however, their existence demonstrates that using international human rights law to mitigate violence is beneficial and valuable, even in the most intimate of contexts.

In this chapter, I briefly describe the debate about the efficacy of international law, the multi-faceted process through which international law manifests in national legal systems, and the value of this in respect of systemic intimate violence.

THE GREAT DEBATE: IS INTERNATIONAL LAW EFFECTIVE?

Suspicion of International Law in Brief

There is a longstanding dialogue regarding the nature of international law and its authoritative status.[10] While it is true that international law has failed miserably in many instances, it is equally true that it has succeeded in many others. The successes are less high profile and often occur in unexpected or peculiar ways but, nonetheless, international law remains effective. The fact that it is not obeyed some of the time does not mean that it is never obeyed at any time. As Professor Koh points out, our national legal systems are immensely flawed, yet we do not reject the entire concept of national law. The deficiencies of international law—and there are many—do not require us to abandon it as a source of law; rather, we are motivated to work towards its improvement.

The rejection of international law emanates from an assertion that international legal principles neither prevent human rights disasters nor effectively control the conduct of states. To a certain extent, this is accurate. Historically,

---

[10] Koh (n 1) 2603 (explaining that, traditionally, there are two divergent claims regarding international law: 'on the one hand, the realists charge that international law is not really law, because it cannot be enforced; on the other, the rationalistic claim that nations "obey" international law only to the extent that it serves national self-interest'). For a description of the early development of the discussion regarding compliance with international law, see ibid, 2606–07 (concluding that Hugo Grotius was the first to demarcate international law as something other than natural/religious law; instead he saw international law as 'the consequence of volitional acts, generated by independent operation of the human will').

there are few examples of international norms 'successfully socialized into domestic societies without the exercise of agency'.[11]

Support of International Law in Brief

Increasingly, however, theorists are recognising the non-coercive influence of international law. Koh explains this development as being

> characterized by the marked decline of national sovereignty; the concomitant prolif-eration of international regimes, institutions, and nonstate actors; the collapse of the public-private distinction; the rapid development of customary and treaty-based rules; and the increasing interpenetration of domestic and international systems.[12]

Michael Reisman, proponent of the New Haven School of international law (policy oriented jurisprudence), describes the process of international law

> systematically in terms of those who engage in it (the participants), the subject dimen-sions that animate them (their perspectives), the situation in which they interact, the resources upon which they draw, the ways they manipulate those resources and the aggregate outcomes of the process of interaction, which are conceived in terms of a comprehensive set of values.[13]

While these theories vary, the common evaluation is that international law may operate in unexpected ways and that we can best utilise international law if we understand and work with the peculiar ways in which it operates.

It is also important that we do not compare international law to domestic law. According to Lauterpacht, international law is peculiar and its implemen-tation is not analogous to municipal legal orders.[14] Theorists propose that inter-national law comprises norms which filter into national legal systems through a multi-faceted process and that international law in fact calls upon a variety of enforcement mechanisms which are not comparable with the enforcement mechanisms of national legal systems. This body of thought proposes that the absence of traditional enforcement mechanisms does not negate the efficacy of international law. The objective of international law and international bodies is not to impose law on nations but rather to work together with nations to improve their relations inter se and the way they treat their citizens.

---

[11] Tarrow (n 9) 183.

[12] Koh (n 1) 2604.

[13] W Michael Reisman, 'The View from the New Haven School of International Law' (1992) 86 *American Society of International Law and Procedure* 118. See also Kenneth W Abbott, 'International Relations Theory, International Law, and the Regime Governing Atrocities in Internal Conflicts' in Hathaway and Koh (n 4) (maintaining at p 236 that in respect of humanitarian law 'States comply with humanitarian law primarily because of expectations of reciprocity, though other considerations, including concern for their international reputation and domestic political support, also come into play').

[14] Lauterpacht (n 3) 399.

The deficiencies of international law do not negate its efficacy as a legal system. Its method of enforcement, according to such theorists, is by infiltration of international norms through national courts, legal systems and political lobbying.[15] I discuss this in more detail below.

THE MULTI-FACETED PROCESS OF INTERNATIONAL LAW

Norm Infiltration

A multitude of actors within local, regional and international institutions apply and implement international law. According to McDougal, Lasswell and Chen, the literature on international law

> affords little recognition of the comprehensive, interpenetrating constitutive processes (global, regional, national, local) which identify authoritative decision makers, specify basic community policies, establish necessary structures of authority, allocate bases of power, authorize appropriate procedures, and make provision for many different, indispensable types of decision.[16]

This 'interpenetrating' constitutive process of international law is now the subject of debate among theorists. In examining how decisions are made in international law, Reisman identifies a combination of factors, which include: the gathering and dissemination of information regarding an objectionable state of events; the galvanizing of community intervention and regulation; subsequent prescription or lawmaking; the invocation or characterisation of a certain action as inconsistent with a prescription or law; the application of such prescription or law to a set of events (which may occur in formal settings such as courts or informal, unorganised situations); the termination or abrogation of existing norms and the social arrangements based upon them; and appraisal of the decision in relation to the community's needs.[17]

Oscar Schachter identifies a long list of non-traditional enforcement mechanisms used by the United Nations (UN) to implement international law. These are: (1) reporting and supervision procedures, such as periodic reports, and review by treaty monitoring committees, special rapporteur assessments and committee reports noting discrepancies between the requirements of international law and state conduct. This is augmented by the complaints procedure for individual or governmental complaints such as those brought under the Optional Protocol; (2) 'facilitative' mechanisms, for example armed peace-

---

[15] Harold Hongju Koh, 'The 1998 Frankel Lecture: Bringing International Law Home' (1998) 35 *Houston Law Review* 623. For a brief description of the distinction between realists on the one hand and liberal and constructivists on the other, see Abbott (n 13) 329.

[16] Myres S McDougal, Harold D Lasswell and Lung-chu Chen, *Human Rights and the World Public Order: The Basic Policies of an International Law of Human Dignity* (New Haven, Yale University Press, 1980) 66.

[17] Reisman (n 13) 5–6.

keeping forces and election observers; (3) penalising measures in the form of expulsion from the community of nations; (4) non-military enforcement action, such as economic sanctions, severing communications and breaking diplomatic relations; (5) use of armed force pursuant to Chapter VII of the UN Charter; (6) judicial enforcement by national and international courts and tribunals; (7) national courts interpreting and applying international law; and (8) public opinion, expressed through the activities of NGOs.[18]

Schachter goes further and argues that 'in practice, texts that are only recommendatory have as much effect as formal rules in channeling state conduct'.[19] As an example of a 'code' that lays down standards and prescribes action notwithstanding that it is not legally mandatory, Schachter cites the Codex Alimentarius, produced by the Food and Agricultural Organization of the World Health Organization, which prescribes standards 'for all principal foods'. This is an example of a formally non-binding instrument that has become effective law for many countries throughout the world on a matter that is of vital importance to all peoples.[20]

Hathaway too rejects the argument that the absence of enforcement mechanisms renders international law nugatory. While she maintains that states that sign human rights treaties tend to violate human rights more than non-signatory states, she still references the notion of 'self-enforcement'. International law, according to Hathaway, is obeyed primarily because domestic institutions create mechanisms for ensuring that a state abides by its international legal commitments, 'whether or not particular governmental actors wish it to do so'.[21]

Symbiotic Relationship between National and International Law

Proponents of international law argue that it supports and contributes to state laws and policies, thereby providing greater legal redress for victims of human rights violations.[22] Tom Campbell notes that human rights discourse can 'serve both as a potent source for radical critiques of actual social arrangements and also as a powerful basis for working out and presenting alternative institutional practices'.[23]

Henkin summarises this position as follows

The purpose of international law is to influence states to recognize and accept human rights, to reflect these rights in their national constitutions and laws, to respect and

---

[18] O Schachter, 'United Nations Law' (1994) 88 *American Journal of International Law* 1, 10–16.
[19] ibid, 5.
[20] ibid.
[21] Hathaway (n 4) 234.
[22] See Mark W Janis, *An Introduction to International Law*, 3rd edn (Washington, DC, Aspen, 1999) 174.
[23] Tom Campbell, 'Introduction: Realizing Human Rights' in Tom Campbell, David Goldberg, Sheila McClean and Tom Mullen (eds), *Human Rights: From Rhetoric to Reality* (Oxford, Basil Blackwell, 1986) 1.

ensure their enjoyment through national institutions, and to incorporate them into national ways of life.[24]

Anne-Marie Slaughter advances the liberal theory of international law from the point of view of liberal international relations theory. She maintains that an important function of international law is not to create international institutions to perform functions that individual states cannot perform by themselves, 'but rather to influence and improve the functioning of domestic institutions'.[25] This echoes Henkin's view that international human rights law is effective because it operates not independently of national legal systems, but rather in conjunction with them.[26]

Koh explains this interactive process between national and international law in his transnational legal theory. He argues that states obey international human rights law because they 'somehow internalized that rule and made it a part of their internal value system'.[27] According to Koh, the internalisation of international law into domestic law is a

> process whereby an international law rule is interpreted through the interaction of transnational actors in a variety of law-declaring fora, then internalized into a nation's domestic legal system. Through this three-part process of interaction, interpretation, and internalization, international legal rules become integrated into national law and assume the status of internally binding domestic legal obligations.[28]

Through an 'interactive process . . . law helps translate claims of legal authority into national behaviour'.[29]

Deficiency Not Nugatory

Professor Koh explains that although domestic laws may be violated, we do not discard the entire system for its imperfection. Similarly, he maintains, we should accept that international human rights norms are 'underenforced, imperfectly enforced; but they are enforced' nonetheless.[30] Koh refers to this as the complex 'transnational legal process'. This is

---

[24] Louis Henkin, 'International Human Rights and Rights in the United States' in Theodor Meron (ed), *Human Rights in International Law: Legal and Policy Issues* (Oxford, Clarendon Press, 1984) 25.

[25] Anne-Marie Slaughter, 'A Liberal Theory of International Law' in Hathaway and Koh (n 4) 95 (international human rights law is 'precisely about structuring state-society relations to ensure at least minimal individual flourishing', 101).

[26] See Louis Henkin, *How Nations Behave,* 2nd edn (New York, Columbia University Press, 1979) 225–26.

[27] Harold Hongju Koh, 'How is International Human Rights Law Enforced?' (1999) 74 *Indiana Law Journal* 1397, 1400.

[28] Koh (n 15) 626. See also Koh (n 1) 2646.

[29] Koh (n 1) 2618.

[30] Koh (n 27) 1399.

the institutional interaction whereby global norms of international human rights law are debated, interpreted, and ultimately internalized by domestic legal systems. To claim that this complex transnational legal process of enforcing international human rights law . . . exists is not to say that it always works or even that it works very well . . . But the process of enforcing international human rights law also sometimes has its successes, which give us reason not to ignore that process, but to try to develop and nurture it.[31]

If one accepts the approach of the compliance based theory, then our focus can turn to designing social, political and institutional frameworks that help to internalise these norms.[32] An inextricable component of cooperative compliance is the role of state and non-state actors in international law.

Proliferation of Actors Facilitating Compliance with International Law

The multiplicity of actors who are capable of incorporating international law into domestic law helps to illustrate the cooperative compliance theories. According to Reisman, international law is an anthropological process and theorists should take account of the 'range of centralized and decentralized settings in which decisions are made, their varying degree of organization and formality, the extent to which they are specialized and the extent to which they are continuous or episodic'.[33] Reisman includes in this analysis actors 'who, though not endowed with formal competence, may nonetheless play important roles in influencing decisions'.[34] The Special Rapporteur on violence against women also discusses the role of these actors in the protection of women's rights.[35]

Therefore, where international law is effective, often its success is due to the coalescence of various actors, including state agents and NGOs, pressure groups and individuals.[36] It is possible to categorise these international actors as (1) NGOs and transnational social movements, and (2) international bodies. These entities have come to play a prominent role in the creation, implementation and enforcement of international human rights law and I discuss them below.[37]

---

[31] ibid.

[32] See in general Hathaway and Koh (n 4); see also Reisman (n 13).

[33] Reisman (n 13) 5.

[34] ibid, 4.

[35] UNCHR, *The Due Diligence Standard as a Tool for the Elimination of Violence against Women—Report of the Special Rapporteur on violence against women, its causes and consequences, Yakin Ertürk* (30 January 2006) UN Doc E/CN.4/2006/61, para 58 (hereinafter Special Rapporteur 2006 Report).

[36] Reisman (n 13) 4.

[37] Koh (n 1) 2624 (stating that by the 1970s and 1980s 'Multinational enterprises, nongovernmental organisations, and private individuals reemerged as significant actors on the transnational stage'). See in general Margaret E Keck and Kathryn Sikkink, 'Activists Beyond Borders' in Hathaway and Koh (n 4) 217. See also John D McCarthy, 'The Globalization of Social Movement Theory' in Jackie Smith, Charles Chatfield and Ron Pagnucco (eds), *Transnational Social Movements and Global Politics: Solidarity Beyond the State* (New York, Syracuse University Press, 1997) 243. See also Louis Kriesberg, 'Social Movements and Global Transformation' in Smith, Chatfield and Pagnucco, ibid, 3.

Non-governmental and Transnational Organisations

NGOs and transnational organisations have been described as

> the forces which, for the longest time and with the greatest persistence, have taken the lead in reporting this clear violation of human rights and demanding justice. They are also a source of truthful, heartrending testimony, criteria and evidence which are essential to the effort to shed light on many of the circumstances under which the crimes have taken place.[38]

This category of non-state actors includes NGOs, transnational advocacy networks, religious bodies and transnational social movement organisations.[39] While the specificity of these labels differs, for the purposes of understanding the broad role of non-state actors in international law I analyse them as one group and refer to them either as transnational organisations generically or NGOs specifically.

Transnational organisations, together with academics and UN agents, have been responsible for the propulsion of women's rights in international law and have succeeded in establishing effective facilities and legislation for the protection of women's rights in many states. Generally, they achieve this through a process of documenting and publicising information, educating individuals, governments and other organisations, and working with so-called grass-roots organisations to implement the norms for which they or others have lobbied.[40] This process is not always ideal; there are important concerns regarding the power of NGOs, their source of income, the agendas they pursue and the impact all of these factors may have on democratic values and cultural autonomy. However, in the context of systemic intimate violence, there is evidence of successful NGO work, which is a key driver in the argument for the authoritative internationalisation of this violation of women's rights.

Transnational organisations are effective players in the process of implementing international law for a number of reasons. The first is that they operate on the basis of ideological commitment and, as opposed to states, non-governmental advocates plead the causes of others.[41] Ideological commitment to causes has galvanised the implementation of human rights in a range of countries and in respect of a multitude of issues. It has been stated that one of the most successful 'transnational framing efforts in the recent period has been the creation of a common transnational conception of human rights',[42] a code of ideological advocates who

---

[38] CEDAW Committee, *Report on Mexico* (27 January 2005) UN Doc CEDAW/C/2005/OP.8/MEXICO, 40.

[39] Keck and Sikkink (n 37) 220–21 (describing a transnational advocacy network as comprising those relevant 'actors working internationally on an issue, who are bound together by shared values, a common discourse, and dense exchanges of information and services').

[40] Tarrow (n 9) 186–87. See also Kriesberg (n 37) 4 (describing four trends which have caused the growth in the number and potency of NGOs: 'growing democratization, increasing global integration, converging and diffusing values, and proliferating transnational institutions').

[41] Keck and Sikkink (n 37) 220 (noting that 'they often involve individuals advocating policy changes that cannot be easily linked to a rationalist understanding of their "interests"').

[42] McCarthy (n 37) 245.

'are bound together by shared values, a common discourse, and dense exchanges of information and services'.[43] Transnational organisations often represent the needs of those who do not have a political voice or no voice at all, as is the case, for example, in respect of the environment or non-human animals.

As with all ideological commitments, one needs to be cautious. Some NGOs have pursued their own agendas, be they religious or political, under the auspices of protecting vulnerable groups, and have thus contributed to the harm. Notwithstanding that the ideology of some transnational organisations may be questionable and non-democratic, it remains true that these institutions are effective due to a combination of ideological commitment and a seemingly endless supply of ideological causes.[44]

The second reason for the success of transnational organisations is their method of obtaining and disseminating information by utilising the media and information technology. Explosive developments in 'information technology and communications have greatly enhanced the ability of nongovernmental organizations to bring pressure to bear on governments'.[45] The transfer and free flow of information is one of the key activities of transnational organisations.[46] They are able to effect norm implementation by framing and explaining a given set of facts.

> [By] pressuring target actors to adopt new policies, and by monitoring compliance with international standards . . . they contribute to changing perceptions that both state and societal actors may have of their identities, interests, and preferences, to transforming their discursive positions, and ultimately to changing procedures, policies and behaviour.[47]

How does this process of persuasion occur? Transnational organisations frame an issue and show that 'a given state of affairs is neither natural nor accidental, identify the responsible party or parties, and propose credible solutions'.[48] The publication of information has various effects. Government officials and other relevant actors become knowledgeable about the issue and how to prevent it; this creates experts who interact with officials, dignitaries, advocates and politicians; who in turn facilitate agreement in both formal and informal settings, from official meetings to informal discussions and agreements that take place in the corridors of the UN.[49]

---

[43] Keck and Sikkink (n 37) 220–21.
[44] ibid. See also Tarrow (n 9) 186–87 (describing the phenomenon of cross-border diffusion as a form of transnational politics, comprising 'the communication of movement ideas, forms of organization, or challenges to similar targets from one center of contention to another').
[45] Schachter (n 18) 10–16.
[46] See also Kriesberg (n 37) 4.
[47] Margaret E Keck and Kathryn Sikkink, *Activists Beyond Borders: Advocacy Networks in International Politics* (Ithaca, Cornell University Press, 1998) 3. For a discussion of the technique of framing issues for international attention, see ibid, 19.
[48] ibid.
[49] See Chadwick F Alger, 'Transnational Social Movements, World Politics, and Global Governance' in Smith, Chatfield and Pagnucco (n 37) 260, 265–67.

Moreover, transnational organisations have access to the resources and global networks that are necessary to obtain and transmit such information.[50] Resource support for transnational organisations is provided by international and national political authorities, religious organisations, national, regional and international NGOs, foundations, constituent organisations, and individual members and sympathisers,[51] and comes in the form of direct financial aid and in-kind aid, such as office space, temporary grants of personnel, access to communications technology and other equipment, and public support. This allows increasingly large and respected institutions to obtain information about factual scenarios, transmit that information to formal and informal authorities, and lobby for a proportionate reaction from the global powers.[52]

Transnational organisations are the political organisms of the age of globalisation, creating unprecedented support for their causes through the use of the media, and particularly the internet.[53] Effective human rights campaigns by NGOs include the international boycott of Nestlé to prevent the corporation from promoting nutritionally deficient infant formula to poor women in the developing world.[54] The Brent Spar episode saw Greenpeace oppose the scuttling of rigs by Shell in the North Sea, with the result that 'one might doubt that oil companies will dare undertake scuttlings so long as Greenpeace maintains its vigilance on the issue'.[55] Tarrow provides various examples of transnational social movements, including campaigns to stop the construction of dams, the empowerment of environmental and workers' groups through the establishment of the multilateral North American Free Trade Agreement, the organisation of dissident groups under the rubric of the Helsinki Accords, and the impact of Greenpeace on reducing pollution and environmental destruction by multinational corporations.[56]

Clearly, transnational organisations facilitate the implementation of international law through 'forms of organization characterized by voluntary

[50] See McCarthy (n 37) 253. For an example of the impact of media reporting see Lizette Alvarez, 'Sweden Boldly Exposes a Secret Side of Women's Lives' *New York Times*, 6 April 2005. Finally, see Kriesberg (n 37) 5 ('Movies, telephones, television, audio and video tape cassettes, fax, and electronic mail provide multiple sources of information . . . [making] rapid exchange and sustained social interaction possible').

[51] See Alger (n 49) 263.

[52] ibid.

[53] See Keck and Sikkink (n 37) 222. See also the Business and Human Rights website, which hosts information on corporate responsibility for human rights: www.business-humanrights.org/Home.

[54] Keck and Sikkink (n 37) 222.

[55] For criticism of this event see Peter J Spiro, 'New Global Potentates: Nongovernmental Organizations and the "Unregulated" Marketplace' (1996) 18 *Cardozo Law Review* 957, 964–65. For a discussion of the benefits and drawbacks of the role of NGOs in international law generally see Julie Mertus, 'From Legal Transplants to Transformative Justice: Human Rights and the Promise of Transnational Civil Society' (1999) 14 *American University Law Review* 1335, 1366. See also Abbott (n 13) 330 (describing the role Amnesty International played in the campaign against enforced disappearances).

[56] Tarrow (n 9) 178.

reciprocal, and horizontal patterns of communication and exchange'.[57] In the context of human rights, these institutions are seminal in situations where vulnerable individuals have little access to state justice institutions or where those making claims are too weak politically for their voices to be heard.[58] In such cases, international institutions may be the only forum in which claims can be legitimately or safely presented.[59]

The third reason for the success of transnational organisations is that they are generally well connected. Members of leading transnational organisations are politically respected and influential individuals.[60] They have a great deal of interaction with government officials and, if the cause and its advocate are of a sufficiently high profile, a government's attention may be caught and, on occasion, objectionable circumstances will be altered.

Transnational organisations are also connected to, and work with, local organisations. Both entities benefit from this relationship. Transnational organisations provide local organisations with funding, networks, personnel, publicity and, if necessary, protection.[61] In turn, local organisations provide access to local information, local stories and individual witnesses.

Finally, transnational organisations are effective because they take a creative approach to the challenge of changing norms, by developing original methodologies in implementing their campaigns. Typical strategies include education campaigns, conferences, direct aid to victims of injustice, public marches and changing structures directly through lobbying.[62]

One of the more important mechanisms is the practice of naming and shaming states with a view to compelling compliance with international law. Publicising governments' poor human rights records triggers a kind of international shame, especially where states 'aspire to belong to a normative community of nations'.[63] In this sense, transnational organisations provide a watchdog service, vigilantly surveying the activities of governments around the world.[64] And this often works. For example, in 2003 the Center for Reproductive Rights ('CRR') investigated the forced sterilisation of Roma women in Slovakia[65] and publicised its findings, which included racial disparagement, poverty and

---

[57] Keck and Sikkink (n 37) 219. See also Tarrow (n 9) 177 (describing transnational social movements as 'a collective challenge, based on common purposes and social solidarities, in sustained interaction with elites, opponents, and authorities').

[58] Tarrow (n 9) 190, citing Keck and Sikkink.

[59] ibid.

[60] Keck and Sikkink (n 37) 220–21. See also McCarthy (n 37) 245; Tarrow (n 9) 186–87 (describing the phenomenon of cross-border diffusion as a form of transnational politics, comprising 'the communication of movement ideas, forms of organization, or challenges to similar targets from one center of contention to another'); Kriesberg (n 37) 4.

[61] See Alger (n 49) 265–67.

[62] McCarthy (n 37) 257.

[63] Keck and Sikkink (n 47) 29.

[64] See Alger (n 49) 267.

[65] See Center for Reproductive Rights, *Body and Soul: Forced Sterilization and Other Assaults on Roma Reproductive Freedom in Slovakia* (2003), reproductiverights.org/sites/crr.civicactions. net/files/documents/bo_slov_part1_0.pdf.

widespread non-consensual forced sterilisation. This exposure of the health care system's approach to Roma women triggered an international outcry. It also pointed to a violation of the provisions of the European Convention for the Protection of Human Rights and Fundamental Freedoms,[66] which resulted in an investigation into the Slovak government's treatment of the Roma people and a re-evaluation of Slovakia's entry into the European Union.[67]

Similar concerns were raised in respect of Germany in 2004. A CRR shadow report indicated that so-called Roma and Sinti women suffered forms of harm and discrimination which are prohibited by relevant EU regulations, demonstrating that the

> phenomenon of intersectional discrimination, the cumulated effects of both gender and ethnic or racial discrimination, is a particularly important factor for vulnerable minority groups such as Sinti and Roma women. At present, the German legislative framework does not provide adequate protection against intersectional discrimination. Full transposition of European Union anti-discrimination Directives into German law through the adoption of a comprehensive anti-discrimination law would provide important additional protections, which would significantly help this group of women counter discriminatory practices.[68]

These revelations rely on 'public opinion', which is voiced by civil society organisations such as professional bodies, universities, and religious and communal institutions. Such entities, together with international bodies, national and local governments, national, regional and international courts, and powerful individuals, have the potential to effect improved conditions where necessary.[69]

International Bodies

International bodies play a valuable role in developing and implementing international law, not least the law and principles relating to violence against women. Over the last four decades several authoritative international bodies have

---

[66] Convention for the Protection of Human Rights and Fundamental Freedoms (European Convention on Human Rights, as amended) (ECHR) (adopted 4 November 1950, entered into force 3 September 1953) 213 UNTS 222, Art 14.

[67] See Center for Reproductive Rights, 'Council of Europe Finds Evidence of Forced Sterilization of Romani Women in Slovakia' (30 October 2003), reproductiverights.org/en/press-room/council-of-europe-finds-evidence-of-forced-sterilization-of-romani-women-in-slovakia.

[68] EU Monitoring and Advocacy Program and European Roma Rights Center, *Shadow Report* (provided to the CEDAW Committee, commenting on the fifth periodic report of the Federal Republic of Germany, submitted under Art 18 of the United Nations Convention on the Elimination of All Forms of Discrimination against Women) (2004), www.soros.org/initiatives/eu/articles_publications/publications/eumap_roma_20040121/roma_shadow_20040121.pdf, 3–4.

[69] Keck and Sikkink (n 37) 217–18. For a brief discussion of the efficacy of international law from the perspective of NGOs see Amnesty International, *Men's Violence against Women in Intimate Relationships: An Account of the Situation in Sweden* (19 April 2004) 13, www2.amnesty.se/svaw.nsf/mvaw/$File/mvaw.pdf. See also Jessica Neuwirth, 'Inequality before the Law: Holding States Accountable for Sex Discriminatory Laws under the Convention on the Elimination of All Forms of Discrimination against Women and through the Beijing Platform for Action' (2005) 18 *Harvard Human Rights Journal* 19, 38.

emerged, including treaty monitoring bodies, regional political organisations and numerous UN institutions, ranging from committees and commissions to special rapporteurs. As Schachter notes, a large proportion of international regulatory instruments has been developed by these specialised UN agencies.[70]

International treaty bodies monitor states' compliance with various treaties. The most relevant treaty in respect of women's rights is the Convention on the Elimination of All Forms of Discrimination against Women (CEDAW), and states that have signed or acceded to CEDAW are technically bound to implement its provisions.[71] Signing a treaty in no way *guarantees* a state's compliance with its provisions, but while CEDAW has the highest number of reservations as compared with other international treaties and is violated regularly by signatory states, there is strong evidence that it does generate change in its members' national legal systems.[72]

One of the ways in which CEDAW can be said to have reformative effects is through its reporting procedure. State parties are obliged to submit national reports, at least every four years, on measures they have taken to comply with their treaty obligations.[73] Of course many states do not submit reports or do not take the reporting process seriously. There is little the CEDAW Committee can do about this, other than exposing details of the standard of women's rights protection in a particular state and recommending and encouraging reform.[74] This is a weak form of enforcement, if it qualifies as enforcement at all. But these powers are not irrelevant. Exposing problems and accumulating information is usually a necessary starting point for reform. In a way, the CEDAW Committee is a truth seeker, assisted by non-government affiliated institutions producing so-called shadow reports.[75] The effects of this interactive process on women's rights and domestic violence specifically are discussed in further detail below.

---

[70] Schachter (n 18) 5.

[71] Convention on the Elimination of All Forms of Discrimination against Women (CEDAW) (adopted 18 December 1979, entered into force 3 September 1981) 1249 UNTS 13, UN Doc A/RES/34/830, (1980) 19 ILM 33. CEDAW established the Committee 'For the purpose of considering the progress made in the implementation of the present Convention'. I refer to the Convention as 'CEDAW' and its committee as 'CEDAW Committee'. For a list of states that have signed and ratified CEDAW see www.un.org/womenwatch/daw/cedaw/states.htm. For a state-by-state list of reservations see www.un.org/womenwatch/daw/cedaw/reservations-country.htm.

[72] See *Report of the Third Session of the Committee on the Elimination of Discrimination against Women* (27 June 1984) UN Doc A/39/45, p 12 para 70 (hereinafter CEDAW Third Session Report).

[73] CEDAW, Art 18(1).

[74] See eg the CEDAW Committee's reaction to the 1984 Hungary report on the status of women where the representative is praised for his 'sincere and frank exposition of the situation of women in Hungary and for the clear and thought-provoking presentation of his country's initial report'. CEDAW Third Session Report (n 72) 5, para 27. Another example is in China's report to the CEDAW Committee in the same session. CEDAW Third Session Report (n 72) 18, para 134.

[75] For a discussion of the importance of 'naming and shaming' in international law, see Hathaway (n 4) 235 ('reputational concerns often play a more significant role than do the much-studied sanctions imposed by a treaty in states' decisions to commit to international legal limits'). See also Keck and Sikkink (n 47) 23 ('Moral leverage involves what some commentators have called the "mobilization of shame", where the behaviour of target actors is held up to the light of international scrutiny').

FUNCTIONS OF INTERNATIONAL HUMAN RIGHTS LAW IN
RESPECT OF VIOLENCE AGAINST WOMEN

International Law Leading to Change: The Expressive and Implementing Functions

Let us return for a moment to the theory of non-coercive state compliance. It may well be that international law can have an effect on national legal and political systems, but to what end? Why is it desirable from a normative point of view to have international standards, especially in respect of something as intimate and nuanced as domestic violence?

International law can improve the way we understand and respond to domestic violence in two ways. First, international law has an *expressive* value: it gives a name to forms of harm that fall outside the ambit of established legal principles. In this way, international law facilitates the creation of new norms and laws to address harm in respect of which no regulation exists. The expressive function can also be understood as expanding the legal categories of objectionable conduct.

The second function of international law that is useful for combating domestic violence is its *implementing* capability. International law requires states to modify their laws in accordance with international standards. There are countless examples of how international norms and laws have revised state practice, not only through compulsion but also through non-coercive means.

It is these functions of international law that lead to changes in the way certain states address domestic violence. They are evident, for example, in developments in international law relating to enforced disappearances, mass rape and female genital cutting (FGC). Below I discuss each of these forms of violence; the way in which these acts of harm are categorised by international law; and the impact of that categorisation on national laws and policies. The categorisation of domestic violence in international law could have similarly reformative effects.

Expressive Function: Articulation of a Wrong

The expressive function of international law consists in its articulation of norms, the process by which a conceptual boundary is drawn around specific conduct and prohibited. The articulation of norms gives a label to forms of harm and provides a forum for otherwise marginalised groups and individuals. Acting as a voice for the muted, international law is especially effective

> where governments are inaccessible or deaf to groups whose claims may nonetheless resonate elsewhere, international contacts can amplify the demands of domestic groups, pry open space for new issues, and then echo back these demands into the domestic arena.[76]

[76] Keck and Sikkink (n 37) 221.

Perhaps the best known example of this is Raphael Lemkin's formulation of the word 'genocide' to articulate in particular the planned massacre of the Jewish race during the Holocaust.[77]

The articulation of a prohibition changes the nature of a specific type of behaviour from acceptable to unlawful. Certain acts of harm exist for which we have deficient language and law. These types of harm are peculiar and manifest in ways which appear to be remediable by existing law but which in truth are not. They fall outside the purview of existing laws and the harm continues without restraint. International law helps to identify such harm and develop appropriate mechanisms to prevent it. This aspect of international law, together with activism in domestic politics, 'may be [international law's] most important function'. Transnational organisations 'can help resource-poor actors construct new *domestic* movements out of combinations of indigenous and imported materials'.[78] An example of this is the internationalisation of laws relating to the phenomenon of enforced disappearances (discussed in detail below).

The reformative effect of international law is evident when international standards are used successfully by national and international litigators and activists. It is necessary for litigators and activists to have external norms, clearly expressed by international law, to make legal arguments. In certain circumstances,

> When a government violates or refuses to recognize rights, individuals and domestic groups often have no recourse within domestic political or judicial arenas. They may seek international connections finally to express their concerns and even to protect their lives.[79]

A global set of standards has the potential to guide national courts and their assessment of the lawfulness of a state's conduct.

The categorisation of a type of harm in international law often leads to a change in a country's institutional response to that conduct.[80] The express condemnation of certain conduct produces cognitive 'focal points' around which international bodies, transnational organisations, states and individuals can coalesce.[81] The Special Rapporteur on violence against women identified the important strategic and political tool of formulating rights-based claims by women specifically, as this language offers a recognised vocabulary for framing social wrongs.[82] Since the 1980s, women's rights activists have been working within the existing framework to expand the ambit of rights to respond to the violations

---

[77] See Abbott (n 13) 330.
[78] Tarrow (n 9) 177.
[79] Keck and Sikkink (n 37) 221.
[80] Elizabeth Heger Boyle and Sharon E Preves, 'National Politics as International Process: The Case of Anti-Female Genital Cutting Laws' (2000) 34 *Law and Society Review* 703, 704–05 (discussing law's social-construction capabilities and positing law as 'a key ingredient in the social construction of reality').
[81] Abbott (n 13) 330.
[82] Special Rapporteur 2006 Report (n 35) para 29.

specific to women's experiences, thereby transforming the understanding of international human rights law and the doctrine of state responsibility.

In this way, the international condemnation of certain types of behaviour infiltrates national law via local and national politicians, activists, policy makers and citizens. For this to occur, however, the articulation of a norm is necessary. Without such expression by authoritative international institutions this function of international human rights law is impeded.

Implementing Function: Responding to the Wrong

The second function of international law that is relevant to systemic intimate violence is the actualisation or implementation of norms in national legal systems. Usually, international principles are implemented through a political process, which is fed by both internal and external or international influences.[83] The process comprises a progression of factors, such as the revelation of shocking events, which are recognised as a contravention of international law.[84] These organisations propel sentiment and galvanise public reaction and outcries.[85] This may be followed either by a change in state law and policy or litigation in international courts, tribunals or national courts.

Many governments are quite vigilant—or are required to be vigilant—about trends in international law and will adapt their policies and laws accordingly.[86] Where governments are not so robust, litigation may be brought against the government to compel compliance with international law. So, in theory, individuals or organisations can bring claims in national courts to compel their governments to take steps against the proliferation of systemic intimate violence as required by international law. NGOs and transnational organisations are also effective galvanisers of change. Referencing international law lends significant 'legitimacy' to their campaigns and to their engagement with government institutions. This process is facilitated by so-called assimilative means.[87] Assimilative techniques include holding conferences, working with grass roots

---

[83] Boyle and Preves (n 80) 729–30 (demonstrating that 'the ruling elites of countries are playing to a larger global community as much as a local audience').

[84] See Theodor Meron, 'Rape as a Crime under International Law' (1993) 87 *American Journal of International Law* 424, 425 (describing the new role of the media and the benefits of instant reporting from the field).

[85] This was the case in the world's reaction to the genocides in Rwanda and Yugoslavia and the call for 'Gender Justice'. See Jennifer Green, Rhonda Copelon, Patrick Cotter and Beth Stephens, 'Affecting the Rules for the Prosecution of Rape and Other Gender-Based Violence before the International Criminal Tribunal for the Former Yugoslavia: A Feminist Proposal and Critique' (1994) 5 *Hastings Women's Law Journal* 171, 175 ('A pronounced international outcry for action to punish the perpetrators of these brutal abuses placed tremendous pressure on the UN to establish an international tribunal').

[86] See eg Parliamentary Joint Committee on Human Rights, *Monitoring the Government's Response to Human Rights Judgments: Annual Report 2008*, HL Paper 173, HC Paper 1078, para 47; see also the debate in the House of Lords on this issue: Hansard HL vol 705 col GC123 (24 November 2008).

[87] For a discussion of these mechanisms, see Boyle and Preves (n 80) 713–15.

agencies and discussing legislative and political changes with governments. The increasing prohibition of FGC in the world's legal systems is an example of this process.

International condemnation usually occurs when circumstances 'shock the public conscience into focusing on important, but neglected, areas of law'.[88] And indeed, one of the most shocking offences recently condemned in international law is the phenomenon of mass rape of women during conflict.

How International Law Changed the Legal Response to Mass Rape

The mass rape of women in war is not a new phenomenon.[89] While rape in war has long been a prohibited act, it has been 'given license, either as an encouragement for soldiers or as an instrument of policy'.[90] This is largely because, although it was actionable in theory under a broad construction of international law, rape was not covered by the Nuremberg Charter, nor was it prosecuted at Nuremberg (although it received more coverage in Japan).[91] In reality, the rape of women was considered an acceptable or necessary side-effect of war.

The international rules of war prohibit attacks upon civilians and the use of certain 'illegitimate' weapons. The mass rape of civilian women violates both of these principles, but it was not until a wealth of academic and activist lobbying brought this to the attention of the world powers that the International Criminal Tribunal for Rwanda (ICTR) and International Criminal Tribunal for the Former Yugoslavia (ICTY) recognised mass rape as an actionable offence in international criminal law. Primarily, it was the revelation of the number of rapes and their role in ethnic cleansing that 'was needed to shock the international community into rethinking the prohibition of rape as a crime under the laws of war'.[92]

The use of rape as a weapon of war during the genocides in Rwanda and the Former Yugoslavia, with the specific intent of linking sexual violence to social destruction, resulted in the prohibition of mass rape as a crime against humanity,

---

[88] Meron (n 84) 425.

[89] For a detailed discussion of the background, development, elements and application of the crime of mass rape in international law see Kelly D Askin, 'Prosecuting Wartime Rape and other Gender-Related Crimes under International Law: Extraordinary Advances, Enduring Obstacles' (2003) 21 *Berkeley Journal of International Law* 288, 347; Meron (n 84) 425–27; James R Mchenry III, 'The Prosecution of Rape under International Law: Justice that is Long Overdue' (2002) 35 *Vanderbilt Journal of Transnational Law* 1269; Human Rights Watch Women's Rights Project, *Human Rights Watch Global Report on Women's Human Rights* (New Haven, Yale University Press, August 1995); Elizabeth A Kohn, 'Rape as a Weapon of War: Women's Human Rights during the Dissolution of Yugoslavia' (1994) 24 *Golden Gate University Law Review* 199.

[90] See Meron (n 84) 425–27 (describing how rape by soldiers has been prohibited by the law of war for centuries, and 'violators have been subjected to capital punishment under military codes, such as those of Richard II (1385) and Henry V (1419)').

[91] ibid, 425–27.

[92] ibid, 425.

a war crime and an instrument of genocide in the Rome Statute.[93] The ICTY and ICTR generated a number of successful prosecutions for mass rape, not only for acts of rape themselves but also in relation to the incitement thereof.[94] Through a process of publicity, international lobbying and decision-making, the harm of mass rape changed from a non-justiciable form of violence to an international human rights violation, a crime against humanity and a war crime.

As described in chapter one, the ICTR was the first international tribunal to try and convict an accused for genocide and crimes against humanity based on his orchestration and encouragement of mass rape.[95] In fact, this case was almost not heard by the tribunal. ICTY President Judge Pillay, whose wide and nuanced understanding of violence against women gave her an insight into the legal principles applicable to mass rape, directed the prosecution to incorporate charges of sexual violence in the indictment against Rwandan genocidaire Akayesu.

The ICTR's Akayesu judgment 'paved the way for later prosecutions of sexual crimes by international tribunals'.[96] The enunciation of a norm against mass rape in the Akayesu judgment led to the ICTY's judgment in *Prosecutor v Kunarac*, which, cementing the Akayesu precedent, confirmed widespread rape as a war crime and crime against humanity.[97] By combining the provisions of common Article 3 of the Geneva Conventions and Article 3 of the ICTY Statute, the ICTY established the requisite elements for certain conduct to constitute mass rape under international criminal law.[98] The systematic and widespread rape that took place in Yugoslavia was linked to the objective of ethnic cleansing and genocide, which were prohibited in international law at the time, creating an understanding of how the violent rape of enemy women facilitates the destruction of a people. Rapes in Bosnia 'were designed in large part to have the

[93] Both the ICTR and ICTY Statutes define rape as a crime against humanity when it is committed during an armed conflict, or when it forms part of a widespread or systematic attack against a particular segment of a civilian population. See Statute of the International Criminal Tribunal for Rwanda, www.ictr.org/ENGLISH/basicdocs/statute/2007.pdf (hereinafter ICTR Statute); Statute of the International Criminal Tribunal for the Former Yugoslavia, www.icty.org/sid/135 (hereinafter ICTY Statute). Art 3(g) of the ICTR Statute defines rape as a crime against humanity when it is 'committed as part of a widespread or systematic attack against any civilian population on national, political, ethnic, racial or religious grounds'. Art 4(3) of the ICTR Statute makes reference to the violations of Article 3 Common to the Geneva Conventions of 12 August 1949 for the Protection of War Victims, and of Additional Protocol II thereto of 8 June 1977, which include 'Outrages upon personal dignity, in particular humiliating and degrading treatment, rape, enforced prostitution and any form of indecent assault'.
[94] See *Prosecutor v Kunarac* (Judgment) ICTY-96-23-T (22 February 2001), para 597.
[95] *Prosecutor v Akayesu* (Judgment) ICTR-96-4-T, T Ch I (2 September 1998), para 597. See also Mchenry (n 89) 1272; Sherrie L Russell-Brown, 'Rape as an Act of Genocide' (2003) 21 *Berkeley Journal of International Law* 350.
[96] See Mchenry (n 89) 1272.
[97] *Prosecutor v Kunarac* (Judgment) ICTY-96-23-T (22 February 2001). Due to the lack of precedent and patchwork authority regarding mass rape in war, the ICTY was able to develop the principles of this crime based on the precedent of *Prosecutor v Akayesu*. See Mchenry (n 89) 1284.
[98] For an analysis of this process see Mchenry (n 89) 1290–96.

effect of impregnating the victim so that she would have a child that would be identified as being a member of the rapist's/enemy's ethnicity'.[99]

The ICTY also established that widespread rape comprised all the elements necessary to prove the commission of a crime against humanity.[100] The express criminalisation of mass rape led to developments in the law regarding state responsibility and sovereign immunity, confirming that a state does not have the authority to massacre its people under any kind of international legal standard, and that sexual violence is equally prohibited.[101] The decisions expanded the trend of recognising the legal personality and importance of individuals in international law, principles which are sourced in the general norms of the Universal Declaration of Human Rights (UDHR).[102]

This jurisprudence culminated in the historic criminalisation of mass rape in the Rome Statute, which, while it may not prevent the occurrence of mass rape, lays the groundwork for compelling international intervention and prosecution in respect of such crimes.[103]

By expressing a norm against mass rape and identifying its constitutive elements, the ICTY and the ICTR had the legal tool to hold officials responsible for their failure to protect individuals from mass rape, even if the accused had not committed the act her/himself.[104] Today, the express norm against mass rape can lead to criminal responsibility if a commander knowingly allowed the mass rape of hundreds of . . . women'.[105] This may not prevent the crime of mass rape from happening in future, especially because the International Criminal Court has failed to use its full institutional resources to target sexual violence; however, by demarcating a clear boundary between acceptable and intolerable behaviour, the decisions of the tribunals 'suggest that such behaviour is less likely to be tolerated or ignored by the international legal community'.[106]

And this is in fact what happened. On 31 October 2000, Security Council Resolution 1325 was passed unanimously. It the first resolution ever passed by the Security Council to address the impact of war on women and women's contributions to conflict resolution and sustainable peace.[107] On 19 June 2008 the

[99] See ibid, 1271–72. See also Askin (n 89) 355.

[100] Namely, a widespread or systematic attack, directed against a civilian population, within the context of an armed conflict and where the accused knows that his conduct occurs within the context of a broader attack on a civilian population. Mchenry (n 89) 1284–91 (describing the reasoning of the ICTY Trial Chamber in casting widespread rape as a crime against humanity).

[101] ibid, 1297 ('these decisions represent a trade off between domestic state autonomy and the desire of the international community to effect justice following the commission of particularly inhumane crimes', 1296).

[102] ibid, 1299.

[103] A similar sentiment is expressed by Richard Goldstone in respect of the International Criminal Court. See his 'Justice Now, and For Posterity' *International Herald Tribune*, 14 October 2005.

[104] See Mchenry (n 89) 1272.

[105] ibid.

[106] ibid, 1296.

[107] UNSC Res 1325 on women, peace and security (31 October 2000) UN Doc S/RES/1325 (noting, inter alia, the urgent need to mainstream a gender perspective into peacekeeping operations and negotiating and implementing peace agreements).

UN Security Council again voted unanimously to classify rape as a tactic of war and a threat to international security. This became UNSC Resolution 1820, which demands the

> immediate and complete cessation by all parties to armed conflict of all acts of sexual violence against civilians, expressing its deep concern that, despite repeated condemnation, violence and sexual abuse of women and children trapped in war zones was not only continuing, but, in some cases, had become so widespread and systematic as to 'reach appalling levels of brutality'.[108]

It also notes that rape and other forms of sexual violence can constitute war crimes, crimes against humanity or a constitutive act with respect to genocide. It affirms the Council's intention, when establishing and renewing state-specific sanction regimes, to consider imposing targeted and graduated measures against warring factions who commit rape and other forms of violence against women and girls.

The persistent (and admirable) efforts of activists, lawyers and journalists exposed the extent and severity of the mass rape of women in Rwanda and the Former Yugoslavia, leading to this specific harm appearing on the agendas of the judges of the ICTR and ICTY, and receiving final condemnation in the Rome Statute and two UN Resolutions. The result is that 'after Kunarac, there can be no more confusion or uncertainty regarding whether rape is to be tolerated or ignored as an act of war'.[109]

This change was not limited to international law. The express articulation of the norm prohibiting mass rape in international law influenced the rape laws of Member States of the European Union. In the case of *MC v Bulgaria*[110] the European Court of Human Rights (ECtHR) held that Bulgaria's rape laws had to be amended to take into account the silent shock of rape victims who display no signs of physical resistance. In that case, the applicant, who had been raped as a young teenager, had not cried out or struggled during the rape. As a result, the Bulgarian courts dismissed the case on the basis that there was no evidence of resistance and hence no evidence of lack of consent. The applicant took the case to the ECtHR, maintaining that Bulgarian law was deficient because it failed to address certain forms of rape where the victim did not display physical resistance.[111] The Court was persuaded that 'any rigid approach to the prosecution of sexual offences, such as requiring proof of physical resistance in all circumstances, risks leaving certain types of rape unpunished and thus jeopardising the effective protection of the individual's sexual autonomy'.[112] The Court substan-

---

[108] UNSC Res 1820 on sexual violence in conflict (19 June 2008) UN doc S/RES/1820.

[109] ibid, 1304.

[110] *MC v Bulgaria* (App No 39272/98) ECtHR 4 March 2004.

[111] ibid, paras 111–13(i) (according to the applicant, 'the prosecution of rape was only possible if there was evidence of the use of physical force and evidence of physical resistance. Lack of such evidence would lead to the conclusion that sexual intercourse had been consensual'). The applicant argued that she suffered from 'frozen fright' and was therefore unable to resist. ibid, 70.

[112] ibid, para 166.

tiated its decision with reference to international criminal law, in terms of which 'force is not an element of rape and . . . taking advantage of coercive circumstances to proceed with sexual acts is also punishable'.[113]

The Court referred expressly to the decision of the ICTY that 'in international criminal law, any sexual penetration without the victim's consent constitutes rape and . . . consent must be given voluntarily, as a result of the person's free will, assessed in the context of the surrounding circumstances'. The Court also made the point that it was appropriate to extrapolate the law applying to mass rape in circumstances of armed conflict to the individual rape in question since the international norm 'reflects a universal trend towards regarding lack of consent as the essential element of rape and sexual abuse'.[114] Therefore the Court held that, in accordance with 'contemporary standards and trends in that area', the Member States of the European Union were obliged to penalise and prosecute any non-consensual sexual act, including 'in the absence of physical resistance by the victim'.[115]

The case of *MC v Bulgaria* evidences the link between the articulation of a norm on one level and how it infiltrates legal systems on another. The ECtHR drew on the 1993 Declaration on the Elimination of Violence against Women (DEVAW) and the jurisprudence of the ICTY to embrace a broader definition of rape to include 'serious violations of sexual autonomy', which occur 'wherever the person subjected to the act has not freely agreed to it or is otherwise not a voluntary participant'.[116] The ECtHR also held that a state has a positive obligation to conduct effective criminal investigations in cases of rape where there is no physical resistance, noting international precedent and 'the development of law and practice [which] reflects the evolution of societies towards effective equality and respect for each individual's sexual autonomy'.[117] This included the obligation 'to take measures designed to ensure that individuals within their jurisdiction are not subjected to ill-treatment, including ill-treatment administered by private individuals'.[118]

However, without the precedent of an express prohibition on mass rape as an international human rights violation, the doctrine of state responsibility could not have been utilised to advance the rape jurisprudence to include silent victims.

Can we envisage a similar pattern in respect of systemic intimate violence?

---

[113] ibid, para 163.

[114] ibid.

[115] ibid, para 166.

[116] Declaration on the Elimination of Violence against Women, UNGA Res 48/104 (20 December 1993) UN Doc A/RES/48/104 (hereinafter DEVAW). *MC v Bulgaria* (App No 39272/98) ECtHR 4 March 2004, paras 106–08 (citing *Prosecutor v Kunarac* (Judgment) ICTY-96-23-T (22 February 2001)). The Court also made reference to the fact that under international criminal law an element of force was no longer required to make out the crime of rape. ibid, 163.

[117] ibid, 165. The Court also drew on precedent confirming that states have a positive obligation to secure their citizens' rights and freedoms as guaranteed by the European Charter. ibid, para 149.

[118] ibid, para 149.

Part of the value in creating a defensible legal norm prohibiting systemic intimate violence is ending 'the international community's willingness to tolerate sexual abuse against women', which, through the process described earlier in this chapter, leads to changes in states' domestic systems, policies and institutions.[119] The South African Constitutional Court, for example, has referred to South Africa's international obligations which 'require effective measures to deal with the gross denial of human rights resulting from pervasive domestic violence'.[120] The Court determined that the imperatives of constitutional and international law oblige 'the state directly to protect the right of everyone to be free from private or domestic violence. Indeed, the state is under a series of constitutional mandates which include the obligation to deal with domestic violence'.[121]

If there existed a supra-standard prohibiting systemic intimate violence, the tenets of that standard could be applied nationally through legislation and court decisions.[122] In the absence of an express universal standard, national legal systems lose a source of law that has become most pertinent in the human rights context. It is for this reason that I turn to international law as a supplement to domestic law to enhance governments' regulation of, and response to, domestic violence.[123]

The value of expressly prohibiting certain conduct in international law and delineating the state's obligation in respect thereof provides a legal precedent and an authoritative basis for reformative litigation and lobbying. The absence of such precedent is not detrimental to the development of national laws in respect of systemic intimate violence, nor would such a precedent guarantee that nations will comply with the obligation, but a clearly articulated international law norm would fill a void and provide the basic tools necessary for litigation, lobbying and policy reform in respect of protecting individuals from systemic intimate violence.

---

[119] See Mchenry (n 89) 1307 (citing *Global Report on Women's Human Rights*).

[120] *S v Godfrey Baloyi*, Case CCT 29/99 (South African Constitutional Court, 1999), para 21.

[121] ibid.

[122] For the most part, international human rights law is most effectively implemented by and through the domestic courts. See Judge Edward D Re, 'The Universal Declaration of Human Rights: Effective Remedies and the Domestic Courts' (2003) 33 *California Western International Law Journal* 137, 153–56.

[123] Judith Resnik, 'Categorical Federalism: Jurisdiction, Gender, and the Globe' (2001) 111 *Yale Law Journal* 619, 623 ('State, federal, and transnational laws are all likely to be relevant [to pursuing women's rights to safety]'). The question whether international law 'works' is widely debated. See Koh (n 27) 1401 (proposing that the relationship between enforcement and obedience is premised on the notion that 'the most effective form of law-enforcement is not the imposition of external sanction, but the inculcation of internal obedience').

How International Law Changed the Legal Response to Enforced Disappearances

Enforced disappearances are a peculiar harm which for a long time fell outside the protection of national legal mechanisms. While the phenomenon of disappearing political dissidents is not new, it has only recently been addressed by international law, which, through the process discussed below, has expanded both understandings of the rights violated by the crime of enforced disappearances and the concomitant state obligation to prevent and address it.

The expansion of international law to include a prohibition on enforced disappearances was initiated predominantly by events that took place in Argentina after the military coup in 1976.[124] From 1976 to 1983 the so-called 'Dirty War' in Argentina resulted in the disappearance of over 9,000 people (although many claim that the figure is closer to 30,000). At the time, no label existed for the curious events comprising enforced disappearances: individuals were arrested or kidnapped based on allegations of political dissidence; no trials were held; and, when relatives and friends inquired after the detainee, the official state response was ignorance.

No legal remedies existed. The law against summary execution did not apply because there was no evidence that the disappeared individual had been killed. Since a defining element of enforced disappearances is government denial of the abduction, habeas corpus relief and other institutional safeguards designed to protect imprisoned individuals from abuse were rendered ineffective.[125] In addition, often, attempts to obtain information about the disappeared resulted in intimidation, creating an environment of fear for those left behind. Existing laws, therefore, were rendered nugatory.

Over time, however, an equally curious response emerged. The mothers of the disappeared, having received no assistance from the authorities, turned to the world at large and staged what became a weekly parade, held for the first time in the Plaza De Mayo. The women, who became known as the Mothers of Plaza De Mayo, rallied with signs asking the outside world to help because 'Every place is closed to us. Everywhere they shut us out. We beg you to help us. We beg you'.[126] International organisations, individuals and governments responded.[127]

'Framing' the harm from the point of view of those left behind resulted in a greater understanding of the peculiar manifestation of enforced disappearances,

---

[124] Keck and Sikkink (n 37) 223–27 (describing the activities of Amnesty International in demonstrating that 'disappearances were part of a deliberate government policy by which the military and the police kidnapped perceived opponents, took them to secret detention centers where they tortured, interrogated, and killed, then secretly disposed of their bodies').

[125] Juan E Mendez and Jose Miguel, 'Disappearances and the Inter-American Court: Reflections on a Litigation Experience' (1990) 13 *Hamline Law Review* 507, 511.

[126] See Luis Clemens, 'Argentina's Dirty War: An Ugly Episode that Won't Die' CNN (Beunos Aires, 2 March 1998), World News Story Page, www.cnn.com/WORLD/9803/02/argentina.dirty.war.

[127] Keck and Sikkink (n 47) 17.

for which no legal remedy existed.[128] Once the harm was properly framed it was possible for national and international lawyers and activists to respond to its nuances. The internationalisation of this harm resulted in the creation of the label 'enforced disappearances', a previously amorphous and nameless phenomenon. This led to the creation of the Inter-American Convention on Enforced Disappearances, which defined enforced disappearances as:

> the act of depriving a person or persons of his or their freedom, in whatever way, perpetrated by agents of the state or by persons or groups of persons acting with the authorization, support, or acquiescence of the state, followed by an absence of information or a refusal to acknowledge that deprivation of freedom or to give information on the whereabouts of that person, thereby impeding his or her recourse to the applicable legal remedies and procedural guarantees.[129]

One of the seminal changes brought about by the expansion of law was the recognition of the harm caused by the government's *failure* to act, and not only the initial act of abduction. In the landmark case of *Velásquez Rodríguez v Honduras*, the Inter-American Court of Human Rights enunciated the due diligence standard in relation to governments' obligations vis-a-vis their citizens.[130] In response to the claims of enforced disappearances, the Court held that the relevant acts of the public authorities consisted of not the only the state's positive acts:

> An illegal act which violates human rights and which is initially not directly imputable to a State (for example, because it is the act of a private person or because the person responsible has not been identified) can lead to international responsibility of the State, not because of the act itself, but because of the lack of due diligence to prevent the violation or to respond to it as required by the Convention'.[131]

This was confirmed by Inter-American Commission on Human Rights in the case of *Hector Perez Salazar v Peru*:

> This situation of impunity is incompatible with the State's general obligation to respect and protect human rights. The jurisprudence of the Inter-American Court of Human Rights holds in this regard that the State has the legal duty to use the means within its reach to seriously investigate violations committed within its jurisdiction, in order to identify those responsible, impose the appropriate punishment, and ensure the victim adequate compensation.[132]

---

[128] For a discussion of the importance and efficacy of properly 'framing' an issue see Keck and Sikkink (n 47) 17, 27.

[129] Inter-American Convention on Forced Disappearances of Persons, Art II (adopted 1994, entered into force 28 March 1996) (1994) 33 ILM 1429.

[130] *Velásquez Rodríguez v Honduras*, Inter-American Court of Human Rights Series C No 2, (1989) 28 ILM 291, para 79 (indicating that the Honduran government and judicial officers did not act with due diligence).

[131] ibid, para 172.

[132] *Hector Perez Salazar v Pern*, Inter-American Commission on Hman Rights (Case 10.562, Report No 43/97 OEA/Ser.L/V/II.95. Doc 7 rev 771) (1998) para 28.

Velásquez Rodríguez v Honduras began a course of jurisprudence which, while developing slowly, is providing a framework within which litigants, activists and victims can claim relief from at national and international fora.[133]

Lobbying and information sharing in relation to enforced disappearances led the UN to realise that the existing prohibitions on imprisonment, detention and extra-legal, arbitrary and summary executions were deficient. It noted that disappearances occurred in a persistent manner

> in the sense that persons are arrested, detained or abducted against their will or other-
> wise deprived of their liberty by officials of different branches or levels of Government,
> or by organized groups or private individuals acting on behalf of, or with the support,
> direct or indirect, consent or acquiescence of the Government, followed by a refusal to
> disclose the fate or whereabouts of the person concerned or a refusal to acknowledge the
> deprivation of their liberty, which places such persons outside the protection of the
> law.[134]

The UN proclaimed the Declaration on the Protection of All Persons from Enforced Disappearance 'a body of principles for all States'[135] and urged 'that all efforts be made so that the Declaration becomes generally known and respected'.[136] It acknowledged the need to expand the provisions of international law vis-a-vis enforced disappearances because:

> while the acts which comprise enforced disappearance constitute a violation of the
> prohibition found in the [other] international instruments, it is none the less impor-
> tant to devise an instrument which characterizes all acts of enforced disappearance of
> persons as very serious offences and sets forth standards designed to punish and pre-
> vent their commission.[137]

The former UN Human Rights Commission then established the Working Group on Enforced or Involuntary Disappearances.[138] The Working Group has

---

[133] See eg *Trujillo Oroza v Bolivia*, Inter-American Court of Human Rights (Judgment) Series C No 64 (2000). During a public hearing in January 2000, Bolivia formally acknowledged its responsibility for the disappearance in question and apologised to the mother of the victim.

[134] See preamble to the Declaration on the Protection of all Persons from Enforced Disappearance, UNGA Res 47/133 (18 December 1992) UN Doc A/RES/47/133 (hereinafter UN Declaration on Enforced Disappearances). For a discussion of the historical development of the legal prohibition on enforced disappearances see Mendez and Miguel (n 125) 556–57. The Rome Statute includes 'enforced disappearances' as part of a widespread or systematic attack against a civilian population in its definition of crimes against humanity. United Nations Diplomatic Conference of Plenipotentiaries on the Establishment of an International Criminal Court, Rome Statute of the International Criminal Court (1998) UN Doc. A/CONF.183/9, Art 7(1)(i) (hereinafter Rome Statute). These definitions are mirrored in the Inter-American Convention on Forced Disappearances (n 129) 576 (defining enforced disappearances as involving a lack of recourse to the applicable legal remedies and procedural guarantees).

[135] UN Declaration on Enforced Disappearances (n 134) preamble.

[136] ibid.

[137] ibid.

[138] The Working Group on Enforced and Involuntary Disappearances (WGEID) was established in 1980 by UNCHR Res 20 (XXXVI) (29 February 1980).

become a global authority on enforced disappearances and its mandate includes assisting the families of individuals who have been 'disappeared'.[139] In fact, the primary task of the Working Group

> is to assist families in determining the fate or whereabouts of their family members who are reportedly disappeared. In this humanitarian capacity, the Working Group serves as a channel of communication between family members of victims of disappearance and Governments.[140]

The Working Group has transmitted 52,952 cases to governments since its inception and over the past five years it has clarified 1,763 cases.[141] The Working Group clarified 54 of these cases (in Algeria, Argentina, China, Colombia, Ecuador, India, Libyan Arab Jamahiriya, Morocco, Nepal, Philippines, Sri Lanka and Turkey). Of those, 38 cases were clarified based on information provided by the government and 16 cases were clarified based on information provided by alternative sources.[142]

Transnational organisations, international bodies and local organisations expanded international law to include enforced disappearances and established an international watchdog with an enormous infrastructure. The internationalisation of enforced disappearances has not always compelled governments to produce disappeared dissidents; nor will it prevent enforced disappearances from happening. However, by expanding the legal notion of enforced disappearances the structure of remedies increased, resulting in the channelling of resources and extra-state assistance for individuals affected by such violations.

Curing the violation is not necessarily the only objective of international law. It also acts as a forum that can assist individuals who are vulnerable within their state. Therefore, notwithstanding that the Working Group has settled few cases, it is a significant presence in preventing new cases of disappearances and, at times, assisting in saving human lives.[143]

Systemic intimate violence, similarly to enforced disappearances, is a form of harm which has peculiar qualities. These qualitative components, as discussed in chapter two, preclude the effective application of existing national laws. New policy and legislative mechanisms are required to circumvent these difficulties. The expansive nature of international human rights law has benefited states' responses to systemic intimate violence in a manner similar to that achieved in respect of enforced disappearances. This is evident, for example, in the

---

[139] See UNHCR, 'Fact Sheet No 6 (Rev 2), Enforced or Involuntary Disappearances' (May 2004).

[140] UN Human Rights Council, *Report of the Working Group on Enforced or Involuntary Disappearances* (6 February 2009) UN Doc A/HRC/10/9, para 2.

[141] ibid, para 8. From 1 December 2007 to 30 November 2008, the Working Group transmitted 1,203 new cases of enforced disappearance to the Governments of Algeria, Argentina, Bangladesh, Cameroon, Chad, Colombia, India, Indonesia, the Islamic Republic of Iran, Iraq, Japan, Libyan Arab Jamahiriya, Mexico, Morocco, Nepal, Pakistan, Peru, Philippines, the Russian Federation, Sri Lanka, Sudan, Switzerland, Thailand, Turkey, Vietnam, Yemen and Zimbabwe. ibid, para 15.

[142] ibid, para 18.

[143] ibid.

approach of Sweden to systemic intimate violence and the creation of the crime against the integrity of women in Sweden, as discussed below.

How International Law Changed the Legal Response to FGC

Although individual organisations had been working with survivors of FGC for many years, it was only during the UN Decade for Women, from 1975 to 1985, that the issue became global.[144] The procedure of genital cutting captured the attention of the international community and individual nations. Details were revealed of non-remedial surgery, performed without anaesthetic and with the use of non-sterilised, rudimentary instruments. The violence caused to girls' sexual organs and the range of attendant side-effects, including death, shocked the world. Notwithstanding the private nature of the violence, the severity of the practice triggered the attention and disapprobation of international law. The removal of healthy bodily tissue impedes a woman's ability to attain the highest standard of mental and physical health.[145]

International admonishment triggered an intense debate regarding cultural autonomy and individual rights. It exacerbated tensions between so-called 'non-western' states and the international community. Local communities that practised FGC were indignant at the resulting condemnation and outraged when the procedure was framed as child abuse and the parents as child abusers. The volley of debate between international and local players revealed the need to approach the issue with greater respect and understanding for the context in which the cutting takes place. It became clear that in many communities cutting could not be abandoned since an uncut woman is unable to marry, which could lead to a life of exclusion, shame and impoverishment. The consequences of this are severe, both for the individual and for her family. Without a husband, a woman is unable to experience the social and economic normalcy that typifies her community. The practice is linked inextricably to communal life and its absence makes participation in communal life untenable.[146]

Transnational organisations recognised the component of the practice that binds women to the male members of their community for protection, support and respect.[147] They realised that traditional legal responses were inadequate.

---

[144] See Kirsten Bowman, 'Bridging the Gap in the Hopes of Ending Female Genital Cutting' (2005) 3 *Santa Clara Journal of International Law* 132, 147. See also Keck and Sikkink (n 47) 20 (describing the background to the campaign against FGC).

[145] Female genital cutting refers to the practice of cutting away part or all of a girl's external genitalia. See UNICEF, 'Female Genital Mutilation/Cutting' (Fact Sheet) www.unicef.org/protection/index_genitalmutilation.html. See also Catherine L Annas, 'Irreversible Error: The Power and Prejudice of Female Genital Mutilation' (1996) 12 *Journal of Contemporary Health Law and Policy* 325, 327–32. For a detailed description of the various forms of FGC and the attendant health implications see Anika Rahman and Nahid Tubia, *Female Genital Mutilation: A Guide to Laws & Policies Worldwide* (London, Zed Books, 2000).

[146] See Bowman (n 144) 139.

[147] See Annas (n 145) 349–50.

The search for effective mitigation culminated in the implementation of a number of more creative remedies, including discussions among local religious and cultural leaders and local developmental organisations;[148] the creation of alternative and less invasive forms of initiation; and the creation of alternative sustainable sources of income for women who do not want to undergo the procedure and are able to escape it.

One of the key remedies to arise from the internationalisation of FGC is the ability of women who fear circumcision to obtain asylum in foreign jurisdictions.[149] This was not always possible. Notwithstanding the obvious torturous elements of the practice of FGC, the practice does not fall neatly within the grounds of asylum in the Refugee Convention. Article 1A(2) of the Refugee Convention, as amended, defines a 'refugee' as any person who,

> owing to well-founded fear of being persecuted for reasons of race, religion, nationality, membership of a particular social group or political opinion, is outside the country of his nationality and is unable or, owing to such fear, is unwilling to avail himself of the protection of that country.

The Refugee Convention is one of the few international instruments that do not recognise gender as a basis for relief. Of course there is the catch-all category of 'membership of a particular social group'. In cases of gender-based violence, asylum seekers generally need to demonstrate that they have a well-founded fear of being persecuted for reasons of membership of a particular social group. This gives rise to a number of difficulties, not least whether 'women' can be said to comprise a particular social group. A 'particular social group' cannot be defined with reference to the persecution. There have to be other unifying or common characteristics that demarcate a group independently of the persecution that is being carried out against it.

In 1985, the Executive Committee of the United Nations High Commission for Refugees adopted the position that states are 'free to adopt the interpretation that women asylum seekers who face harsh or inhuman treatment due to their having transgressed social mores of the society in which they live may be regarded as a "particular social group" '.[150] For the most part, though, states did not accept that such applicants were being targeted because they belonged to a particular social group.[151]

---

[148]   See Bowman (n 144) 139.

[149]   For a discussion of the relevant case law and legal requirements see generally Patricia A Armstrong, 'Female Genital Mutilation: The Move Toward the Recognition of Violence against Women as a Basis for Asylum in the United States' (1997) 21 *Maryland Journal of International Law and Trade* 95.

[150]   UNHCR EXCOM Conclusion No 39, 'Refugees, Women and International Protection' (1985).

[151]   See *Secretary of State for the Home Department v K (FC) and Fornah (FC) v Secretary of State for the Home Department* [2006] UKHL 46, para 9.

In 1994, a shift in international law occurred when the UNHCR stated the following:

> FGM, which causes severe pain as well as permanent physical harm, amounts to a violation of human rights, including the rights of the child, and can be regarded as persecution. The toleration of these acts by the authorities, or the unwillingness of the authorities to provide protection against them, amounts to official acquiescence. Therefore, a woman can be considered as a refugee if she or her daughters/dependants fear being compelled to undergo FGM against their will; or, she fears persecution for refusing to undergo or to allow her daughters to undergo the practice.[152]

In 1996, in the groundbreaking case of *In Re Kasinga*, the US immigration authorities accepted the practice of FGC as a possible basis for asylum due to the fact that the claimant could not seek protection from her government in an attempt to avoid the procedure, which would result in permanent disfigurement and the 'risk of serious, potentially life-threatening complications'.[153] That same year, Canada issued guidelines on gender-related persecution.[154]

On 20 September 2001 the European Parliament adopted a resolution expressing the hope that the European institutions and Member States would recognise the right to asylum of women and girls at risk of being subjected to FGM.[155] In 2002, the UNHCR issued guidelines confirming that international human rights law and international criminal law have clearly identified certain acts such as sexual violence as serious abuses amounting to persecution and that such treatment constitutes a well-founded fear of persecution. The guidance confirmed that rape and other forms of gender-related violence, such as dowry-related violence, female genital mutilation, domestic violence and trafficking, are acts which inflict severe pain and suffering and which may be used as forms of persecution, whether perpetrated by state or private actors.[156]

In this sense, the guidelines both draw on international law and feed into the formulation of an international norm regarding state responsibility for the acts of private individuals.[157] The guidelines emphasise the analysis of

> forms of discrimination by the State in failing to extend protection to individuals against certain types of harm. If the State, as a matter of policy or practice, does not

---

[152] UNHCR, 'Female Genital Mutilation' (Memorandum) (10 May 1994), cited in *Secretary of State v K and Fornah v Secretary of State* (n 151) para 26, per Lord Bingham.

[153] See *In re Kasinga* (Interim Dec 3278) 1996 WL 379826 (BIA 13 June 1996). The basis of the Board of Immigration's decision was that the claimant could not escape the FGC procedure and could not expect assistance from her government. See also Megan Annitto, 'Asylum for Victims of Domestic Violence: Is Protection Possible After In Re R-A-?' (2000) 49 *Catholic University Law Review* 785, 795.

[154] Immigration and Refugee Board of Canada, 'Guidelines on Women Refugee Claimants Fearing Gender-Related Persecution' (9 March 1993).

[155] European Parliament, Resolution A5-0285/2001, 'Female Genital Mutilation'.

[156] UNHCR 'Guidelines on International Protection: Gender-Related Persecution within the Context of Article 1a(2) of the 1951 Convention and its 1967 Protocol Relating to the Status of Refugees' UN Doc HCR/GIP/02/01 (Geneva, 2002), para 9.

[157] ibid ('In this sense, international law can assist decision-makers to determine the persecutory nature of a particular act').

accord certain rights or protection from serious abuse, then the discrimination in extending protection, which results in serious harm inflicted with impunity, could amount to persecution. Particular cases of domestic violence, or of abuse for reasons of one's differing sexual orientation, could, for example, be analysed in this context.[158]

In 2004 an EU Council Directive was adopted which established that gender-specific harm constitutes acts of persecution for the purposes of the Refugee Convention.[159] As regards membership of a particular social group, the Directive maintains that a group comprises 'a particular social group' where

> members of that group share an innate characteristic, or a common background that cannot be changed, or share a characteristic or belief that is so fundamental to identity or conscience that a person should not be forced to renounce it, and that group has a distinct identity in the relevant country, because it is perceived as being different by the surrounding society.[160]

Finally, depending on the circumstances of the country of origin, a particular social group might include a group differentiated by the common characteristic of sexual orientation, and 'gender related aspects' may also be considered.[161] In 2005 this was interpreted by the UNHCR:

> Gender is a clear example of a social subset of persons who are defined by innate and immutable characteristics and who are frequently subject to differentiated treatment and standards. This does not mean that all women in the society qualify for refugee status. A claimant must demonstrate a well-founded fear of being persecuted based on their membership in the particular social group.[162]

In 2006 the UK House of Lords considered whether fear of FGC constituted a ground for asylum under the Refugee Convention in the case of *Secretary of State for the Home Department v K (FC) and Fornah (FC) v Secretary of State for the Home Department*.[163] The Law Lords unanimously held that the appellant, a woman from Sierra Leone, had a well-founded fear of persecution (manifested in FGC) for reasons of membership of a particular social group, as required by Article 1A(2) of the Refugee Convention.

The Law Lords differed as to the demarcation of the social group (that is, whether the group consisted of women or only women who might be subject to FGC) but all agreed that the threat of FGC constitutes a ground for protection

---

[158] ibid, para 15.

[159] Council Directive (EC) 2004/83/EC concerning minimum standards for the qualification and status of third country nationals or stateless persons as refugees or as persons who otherwise need international protection and the content of the protection granted, Art 9(2)(f).

[160] ibid, Art 10(1)(d).

[161] ibid.

[162] UNHCR, 'Annotated Comments on the EC Council Directive 2004/83/EC of 29 April 2004 on Minimum Standards for the Qualification and Status of Third Country Nationals or Stateless Persons as Refugees or as Persons who Otherwise Need International Protection and the Content of the Protection Granted (OJ L 304/12 of 30.9.2004)' (28 January 2005) 23, www.unhcr.org/refworld/docid/4200d8354.html.

[163] [2006] UKHL 46.

under the Refugee Convention.[164] Lord Bingham held that women in Sierra Leone are a group of persons who share the common characteristic of a position of social inferiority compared with men and that this is a characteristic which would exist even if FGM were not practised.[165] Lord Hope underscored the state-sanctioned inequality between men and women, noting that because of the role of Chiefs, customary law and the way in which many rural communities operate, it was improbable that a victim of FGM could look to the Sierra Leone courts for assistance.[166]

We can also see the effect of the internationalisation of FGC on cultural norms. On 25 November 2006, for instance, a group of distinguished Islamic scholars assembled at Al-Azahr University in Cairo and issued a set of recommendations recognising that female genital mutilation 'is a deplorable, inherited custom, which is practised in some societies and is copied by some Muslims in several countries'.[167] They concluded that 'there are no written grounds for this custom in the Qur'an with regard to an authentic tradition of the Prophet' and acknowledged that 'female genital circumcision practised today harms women psychologically and physically' and should be 'seen as a punishable aggression against humankind'.[168] They demanded that 'the practice must be stopped in support of one of the highest values of Islam, namely to do no harm to another', and called for its criminalisation.[169]

While the practice continues, legal and extra-legal improvements have been made. As of the date of writing (January 2010), most western countries and many of the 28 countries in which FGC is prevalent have outlawed the practice.[170]

---

[164] ibid. Baroness Hale and Lord Bingham included in the group women who had been subject to FGC and those who had not yet been subject to the procedure. Lords Hope of Craighead, Rodger of Earlsferry and Brown of Eaton-Under-Heywood took the view that 'the particular social group is composed of uninitiated indigenous females in Sierra Leone', excluding those who have already been initiated because they could not said to be still at risk. ibid, para 56 per Lord Hope of Craighead.

[165] ibid, para 31.

[166] ibid, para 53.

[167] See 'Target's Breakthrough: Islam Outlaws Female Mutilation' (2006), www.target-human-rights.com/HP-00_aktuelles/alAzharKonferenz/index.php?lang=en&. See also UN Human Rights Council, *Intersections between culture and violence against women—Report of the Special Rapporteur on violence against women, its causes and consequences, Yakin Ertürk* (17 January 2007) UN Doc A/HRC/4/34, para 55.

[168] ibid.

[169] ibid.

[170] For a discussion of the legal status of FGC/FGM in various regions see Bowman (n 144) 140–42. For a discussion of the history of opposition to FGC see Boyle and Preves (n 80) 708–10. A similar phenomenon occurred in respect of acid burning in Bangladesh. *Report of the Sixth Session of the Committee on the Elimination of Discrimination against Women* (15 May 1987) UN Doc A/42/38, at 75, para 565 (hereinafter CEDAW Committee Sixth Session Report).

How International Law has Already Changed the Legal Response to Asylum and Domestic Violence

One way in which an international norm prohibiting systemic intimate violence may benefit victims of systemic intimate violence is through the asylum process. Many asylum seekers who have fled their home countries because of gender-based harm (or the threat thereof) are refused asylum on the basis that domestic violence is not state conduct or that abused women are not an identifiable group targeted for persecution. However, if the state component of systemic intimate violence was properly understood by immigration officials, asylum could provide a further avenue of safety for women who are unable to escape intimate violence due to a lack of state protection.[171] States may be reluctant to accept this as a basis for asylum, fearing that it will increase the flow of refugees. However, it is highly unlikely that the recognition of gender-based harm such as domestic violence will lead to an unmanageable increase in asylum applications.

In 1995 the United States listed domestic violence as a type of harm peculiar to women in the INS guidelines.[172] In 1996 in the US there was a brief moment when the possibility of asylum for domestic violence victims seemed real. Rodi Alvarado Peña, a Guatemalan woman, had been raped and beaten by her husband for 10 years in Guatemala. During their 10 years of marriage he had dislocated her jaw, attempted to cut off her hands with a machete and kicked her in the abdomen. During pregnancy, he 'attempted to forcefully abort their second child by kicking her in the spine'.[173] Despite her repeated attempts to obtain state protection, the Guatemalan police and the courts refused to intervene. When she ran away, her husband found her and beat her until she was unconscious. Ms Alvarado finally fled to the US, leaving her two children with relatives.

In the initial hearing of Ms Alvarado's asylum claim, the immigration judge granted asylum on the basis that the claimant's husband had abused her physically, emotionally and sexually, and that she could not rely on protection from the authorities by virtue of her sex.[174] Most importantly, the immigration judge determined that the claimant's husband believed that women were inferior to men and that by resisting her husband she was challenging his opinion, thereby demarcating the violence as persecution on account of her political opinion and her membership of a particular social group.[175]

The immigration service appealed to the Board of Immigration Appeals (BIA). In June 1999 the BIA reversed the decision of the immigration judge and ordered that Ms Alvarado be deported to Guatemala. The decision led to

---

[171] See Annitto (n 153) 785.

[172] Armstrong (n 149) 6.

[173] ibid.

[174] See *Re Alvarado*, No A73-753-922, slip op at 13 (Immigr Ct, San Francisco, Cal, 20 September 1996), revd, In re R-A-, Interim Dec 3403 (BIA 1999). For a discussion of this case see Annitto (n 153) 801–04.

[175] ibid.

denials of asylum protection to women fleeing a broad range of serious human rights violations, including trafficking for prostitution, gang rape, honour killings and domestic violence.[176]

In January 2001, then-Attorney General Janet Reno responded to nationwide outrage by overturning the BIA's decision. She ordered the BIA to issue a new decision in Ms Alvarado's case after the issuance of proposed Department of Justice regulations on the subject of gender asylum. In the meantime, the Department of Homeland Security accepted that a victim of domestic violence, under limited circumstances, could establish eligibility for asylum on this basis.[177]

In September 2008 Attorney General Mukasey issued a decision ordering the BIA to reconsider the case, removing the requirement that the BIA await the issuance of proposed regulations. In October 2009, 14 years after Ms Alvarado first claimed asylum in the United States, the Department of Homeland Security announced that Ms Alvarado 'is eligible for asylum and merits a grant of asylum as a matter of discretion'.[178] This brief will enable an immigration judge to grant Ms Alvarado her long-standing request for asylum.

In July 2009 the Department of Homeland Security confirmed before the US immigration courts that it regarded LR, an abused woman from Mexico, as potentially having grounds to apply for political asylum because she feared she would be murdered by her common law husband, who had repeatedly raped her at gunpoint and tried to burn her alive when he discovered that she was pregnant.[179] The applicant must prove that in Mexico violence against women is pervasive and that there is a societal perception that this is acceptable. She will then have to show that the Mexican government is unable or unwilling to protect her and that she will not be safe from her abuser anywhere in Mexico.

These cases continue, as does the enormous effort to demonstrate that the fear of domestic violence may establish a well-founded fear of persecution on account of membership of a particular social group.[180]

Similar developments have taken place in the UK. In 1999 the UK courts were required to address the case of two women from Pakistan who, because of allegations of extra-marital relations, feared persecution from their husbands if

[176] Centre for Gender and Refugee Studies, 'Documents and Information on Rodi Alvarado's Claim for Asylum in the US', cgrs.uchastings.edu/campaigns/alvarado.php.
[177] See United States Department of Homeland Security, 'Department of Homeland Security's Position on Respondent's Eligibility for Relief' (San Francisco, 19 February 2004) in the matter of *Re Alvarado* (n 176), cgrs.uchastings.edu/documents/legal/dhs_brief_ra.pdf.
[178] See United States Department of Justice Executive Office For Immigration Review, San Francisco, California, In the Matter of Rodi Alverado Pena, In Deportation Proceedings, Department of Homeland Security Response to the Respondent's Supplemental Filing of August 19, 2009, graphics8.nytimes.com/packages/pdf/national/20091030asylum_brief.pdf.
[179] See Chris McGreal, 'Obama Moves to Grant Political Asylum to Women who Suffer Domestic Abuse' *The Guardian* (London), 24 July 2009, www.guardian.co.uk/world/2009/jul/24/obama-women-abuse-political-asylum-us.
[180] See Human Rights Watch, 'US: Protecting Women Fleeing Violence: Asylum Rules for Domestic Violence Survivors have Languished for Eight Years' (December 2008), www.hrw.org/en/news/2008/12/10/us-protect-women-fleeing-violence?print.

they were sent back to Pakistan.[181] The immigration authorities recognised that the applicants feared persecution and that the state of Pakistan was unwilling to protect them. However, asylum was refused on the basis that the appellants, as women fearing violence, were not members of a particular social group because the group could not exist independently of the feared persecution and the persecution was not a response to an actual or perceived political opinion (in other words, to rely on the persecution of the group as that group's defining characteristic is circular reasoning: a group must be able to show that it exists other than by virtue of the persecution). Asylum was denied and the applicants appealed.

The Law Lords had to decide whether Pakistani women constitute a particular social group that could be defined independently of the persecution. They generally accepted that 'persecution on account of membership in a particular social group' means persecution 'that is directed toward an individual who is a member of a group of persons all of whom share a common immutable characteristic'.[182] The court accepted that the group does not have to be defined by cohesiveness, cooperation or interdependence.[183]

To what group, then, could the appellants be said to belong? The Law Lords held that in order to identify a social group, one must first identify the society of which it forms a part. As Lord Millett noted, for example,

> Westernised women may be cognisable as a distinct social group in an Islamic country in the Middle East but not in Israel; just as landowners were such a group in pre-revolutionary Russia but would not be in England today.[184]

To determine the nature of Pakistani society, the Law Lords considered reports of transnational organisations regarding the treatment and status of women in Pakistan. Citing reports by Amnesty International and the International Bar Association, the court determined that the position of women in Pakistan was such that there was legislated discrimination against women, women were vulnerable to persecution, and they would be unprotected by the state.[185]

This was particularly true of women accused of illicit sexual intercourse.[186] Pakistani law at the time provided that in rape cases the onus is on the victim to prove that she did not consent to intercourse. If she failed to prove a lack of consent, she could be convicted of illicit sexual intercourse. Moreover, in certain

---

[181] *Islam v Secretary of State for the Home Department; R v Immigration Appeal Tribunal, ex p Shah* [1999] 2 AC 629. Extracts below are taken from the judgment available at www.publications. parliament.uk/pa/ld199899/ldjudgmt/jd990325/islam01.htm (page and paragraph numbers not available).

[182] ibid, per Lord Steyn, citing the decision of the Board of Immigration Appeals in *In re Acosta* (1985) 19 I & N 211.

[183] ibid, per Lords Steyn and Hoffmann.

[184] ibid, per Lord Millett.

[185] ibid, per Lord Steyn (citing an Amnesty International report entitled *Women in Pakistan*, 6 December 1995).

cases of extramarital sexual intercourse, the evidence of women is not admissible; furthermore, it is a charge that can be made without any preliminary investigation. The result is that about half of the Pakistan's female prisoners are held on charges of extramarital sexual intercourse, being held for years notwithstanding that no evidence has ever been produced that they have committed any offence. Men frequently bring charges against their former wives, their daughters or their sisters in order to prevent them marrying or remarrying against the man's wishes.[187]

The Law Lords (with the exception of Lord Millett) accepted that Pakistani women are discriminated against because they belong to a group with immutable characteristics and are not only unprotected by the state but the state tolerates and sanctions the discrimination.[188] Lord Steyn further held that, even if he had not accepted that women in Pakistan form part of a particular social group, the appellants would then form part of a narrower group, namely women in Pakistan who are suspected of adultery and receive no protection from the state.[189] Lord Hoffmann rejected the need to refer to a narrower group because

> the legal and social conditions which according to the evidence existed in Pakistan and which left [the appellant] unprotected against violence by men were discriminatory against women. For the purposes of the Convention, this discrimination was the critical element in the persecution . . . this means that she feared persecution because she was a woman.[190]

This was echoed by Lord Hope of Craighead, holding that the reason why the appellants fear persecution is not just because they are women but because 'they are women in a society which discriminates against women'.[191]

Lord Hoffmann's explanation is enlightening:

> Discrimination against women in matters of fundamental human rights on the ground that they are women is plainly in pari materiae with discrimination on grounds of race. It offends against their rights as human beings to equal treatment and respect. It may seem strange that sex (or gender) was not specifically enumerated in the Convention when it is mentioned in article 2 of the Universal Declaration of Human Rights . . . and the concept of a social group is in my view perfectly adequate to accommodate women as a group in a society that discriminates on grounds of sex, that is to say, that perceives women as not being entitled to the same fundamental rights as men . . . I therefore think that women in Pakistan are a social group.[192]

As regards causation, that is, whether membership of that social group led to the harm in question, Lord Steyn concluded:

[186] ibid.
[187] ibid.
[188] ibid (drawing an analogy with the persecution of homosexuals).
[189] ibid.
[190] ibid, per Lord Hoffmann.
[191] ibid, per Lord Hope of Craighead.
[192] ibid, per Lord Hoffmann.

Given the central feature of state-tolerated and state-sanctioned gender discrimination, the argument that the appellants fear persecution not because of membership of a social group but because of the hostility of their husbands is unrealistic. And that is so irrespective whether a 'but for' test, or an effective cause test, is adopted.[193]

For Lord Hoffmann the question of causation, that is, the reason for the persecution feared by the appellants, comprised two elements:

First, there is the threat of violence to Mrs Islam by her husband and his political friends and to Mrs Shah by her husband. This is a personal affair, directed against them as individuals. Secondly, there is the inability or unwillingness of the State to do anything to protect them. There is nothing personal about this. The evidence was that the State would not assist them because they were women. It denied them a protection against violence which it would have given to men. These two elements have to be combined to constitute persecution within the meaning of the Convention.[194]

Lords Steyn and Hoffmann looked to the preamble to the Refugee Convention, which notes that counteracting discrimination is a fundamental purpose of the Convention.[195] The principle of equality, according to Lord Steyn, was further supported by the equality provisions in the UDHR. Lord Hoffmann noted that the grounds of persecution listed in the Refugee Convention were based on the experience of persecutions in Europe but that the 'inclusion of a "particular social group" recognised that there might be different criteria for discrimination, in pari materiae with discrimination on the other grounds, which would be equally offensive to principles of human rights'.[196]

The High Court of Australia granted refugee status to an asylum seeker who was the victim of serious and prolonged domestic violence from her husband and members of his family where the police (also in Pakistan) refused to enforce the law against such violence or otherwise offer her protection. This refusal was considered not only to be a mere inability to provide protection, but also 'alleged tolerance and condonation'.[197]

There have been other ways in which the norm against violence against women has infiltrated state practice. Many states have adopted national action plans on violence against women in an effort to coordinate activities between and within government agencies and to take a multi-sectoral approach to prevent violence.[198] In a number of countries, specialised committees on violence against women have been established, including the Turkish parliament, which recently established a commission to examine honour crimes.[199]

---

[193] ibid, per Lord Steyn.
[194] ibid, per Lord Hoffmann.
[195] ibid, per Lord Steyn.
[196] ibid, per Lord Hoffmann.
[197] Report of the Secretary-General, *Violence against Women Migrant Workers* (2007) UN Doc A/62/177, paras 49 and 55.
[198] Special Rapporteur 2006 Report (n 35) para 41.
[199] ibid.

NON-COERCIVE COMPLIANCE THEORY IN RESPECT
OF SYSTEMIC INTIMATE VIOLENCE

International law contributes to 'a whole arsenal of methods and techniques' by which human rights are protected.[200] One of the main benefits of international human rights law in particular is the way it can compel change in states' legal and social systems. Therefore, setting standards in international law in relation to systemic intimate violence can lead to changes in individual states' domestic violence policies and laws. International law has a persuasive force in galvanising change through so-called 'assimilative reform strategies'. States are encouraged to adopt a particular practice or principle of law through the slow inculcation of a supranational value without the use of coercive means.[201]

Articulating a norm in international law prohibiting systemic intimate violence does not necessarily require the existence of a central legislative and law enforcement agency; it can operate effectively through the channels described above, benefiting individuals through the establishment of legal and infrastructural support.[202] Certain forms of state conduct are more susceptible to this form of non-coercive change than others and issues of physical violence and legal equality are often the subject of the most successful international campaigns.[203] Systemic intimate violence comprises both of these components.

How has this worked out in practice? If one considers the work of the CEDAW Committee before and after DEVAW in 1993, an interesting pattern is revealed.[204] Prior to the early 1990s, the CEDAW Committee made very little reference to violence against women when considering state reports. However, after DEVAW and the increasing exposure of violence against women globally, the focus of the CEDAW Committee began to change—and with it, the focus of state parties.

---

[200] Myres S McDougal, 'The Impact of International Law upon National Law: A Policy-Oriented Perspective' (1959) 4 *South Dakota Law Review* 25, 36.

[201] For a discussion of the effect of such reform strategies in the case of female genital cutting see Boyle and Preves (n 80) 713. The idea that international law operates through several levels of actors and factors is evident in Kenneth Waltz's explanation of international relations, in terms of which the international system, the state, individuals and groups who make up the state operate interactively and not exclusively, 'like a layer cake'. Koh (n 1) 2649.

[202] According to Keck and Sikkink (n 47) 27, 'Issues involving physical harm to vulnerable or innocent individuals appear particularly compelling'.

[203] ibid.

[204] While the CEDAW Committee has issued interpretative guidance that the provisions of CEDAW include violence against women, there is no specific prohibition of violence in the text itself. See UN Committee for the Elimination of All Forms of Discrimination against Women, 'General Recommendation 19: Violence against Women' (1992) UN Doc A/47/38.

Before DEVAW

In most country reports presented to CEDAW in the mid-1980s there is very little evidence of violence against women. Where reference *is* made to violence against women, it is usually in the context of prostitution or rape (which are in the original CEDAW text).[205] For example, in the reports submitted to the CEDAW Committee in 1984, many CEDAW Committee members brought up the issue of lower wages for traditionally female jobs, the double workload of women, and facilities to encourage men to play an equal role in the family. Little emphasis was placed on violence within the family. In 1984, while discussing Hungary's report, the CEDAW Committee placed significant emphasis on the mutual support of spouses within the family.[206] However, despite being aware of the difficulties women face in private, the CEDAW Committee nonetheless did not include violence in their investigation at this point. The same is true of the CEDAW Committee's discussions in 1986 in respect of Mongolia, Ecuador and El Salvador.[207]

This is not to say that violence against women was never referenced during this period, but it was rare. Norway's report to CEDAW was one of the few that engaged domestic violence.[208] This is interesting since it was also one of the most impressive reports so far as progressive legislation and meaningful implementation of equality is concerned. For example, it revealed that Norway had implemented an incentive for affirmative action in the private sector and the Government had introduced 'the payment of a salary subsidy for six months to firms that employed women in fields heavily dominated by men'.[209] So violence against women arose as a consideration only in a state which had effective policies in place in respect of other non-discrimination contexts.

It seems that the CEDAW Committee was inclined to pursue a less common line of questioning that related to violence against women in the home.[210] Specifically, it mentioned 'the establishment of hot-line telephones and crisis centres . . . as a great step forward' and queried whether 'education on family relations was being undertaken with the young population'.[211] It is not entirely clear why violence against women would be raised by the CEDAW Committee in respect of Norway and not other countries, especially in light of the fact that most of the questions posed by the CEDAW Committee to state members were

---

[205] See eg *Report of the Fifth Session of the Committee on the Elimination of Discrimination against Women* (4 April 1986) UN Doc A/41/45 (hereinafter CEDAW Fifth Session Report), para 102, commenting on Mongolia.

[206] See eg the CEDAW Committee's discussion of Hungary in CEDAW Third Session Report (n 72) 4–10, paras 18–68, 37–38.

[207] CEDAW Fifth Session Report (n 205) 10–15, paras 69–110; Ecuador: ibid, 30–34, paras 226–264; El Salvador: ibid, 40–44, paras 314–56.

[208] See CEDAW Third Session Report (n 72) 37–45, paras 277–38.

[209] ibid, 38, para 285.

[210] ibid, 40, para 301.

[211] ibid.

quite uniform. It is possible that Norway had a sufficiently sophisticated report that enabled the Committee to consider its structures vis-a-vis violence against women. For the rest it seems that violence against women simply was not a dominant theme at the time, and only became prevalent in CEDAW Committee discussions after 1994, when the subject received attention in international law.

It is important to note that while violence was rarely raised in the CEDAW discussions in the mid-1980s, the Committee was not insensitive to many of the more opaque issues facing women within their private lives.[212] The integrity inherent in many of the CEDAW Committee reports evidences a meaningful commitment to a range of issues.

After DEVAW

Towards the end of the 1980s and in the early 1990s, the CEDAW Committee began increasingly to raise violence against women, and domestic violence specifically, in its responses to states' written reports. A wide range of countries, including Greece, Korea, Sri Lanka and Spain, were questioned on their domestic violence policies.[213]

This change in the CEDAW Committee's focus on violence against women coincided with increasing activism around violence against women, which culminated in DEVAW in 1993. DEVAW is a successful articulation of the needs of women as regards their personal safety. While it is deficient in its enforcement capabilities, there is evidence that DEVAW did improve states' responses to systemic intimate violence. The improvement was slow but, following DEVAW, there is a clear change for the better in states' domestic violence legislation and policies.

In order to determine whether this change in focus on the part of both the CEDAW Committee and Member States was related to the international pressure that was being brought to bear regarding violence against women, I examine below the reports of three states before and after DEVAW, namely those of Mexico, Nicaragua and Sweden. I consider both state submissions and shadow reports. The reports of all three states revealed a similar pattern: prior to 1993 domestic violence was a low profile concern. After 1993, however, it became a present and, at times, central focus of the reports. It is therefore likely that the international invocation of a norm prohibiting violence against women affected

---

[212] See eg the 1984 report on Egypt in the CEDAW Third Session Report (n 72) 27, para 203.

[213] State signatories of CEDAW are obliged to submit reports to CEDAW every few years. These reports are read and considered by the CEDAW Committee, which then usually poses written questions to the state in response to its report. After this exchange the state will send a representative to the CEDAW Committee hearing to respond to the Committee's questions and take note of its recommendations. See CEDAW Committee Sixth Session Report (n 170) 13–21, paras 65–129 (discussion of Greece); 21–28, paras 130–84 (discussion of Korea); 28–35, paras 185–237 (discussion of Sri Lanka); 35–44, paras 238–304 (discussion of Spain, which at the time had 17 shelters for abused women); 52–62, paras 370–451 (discussion of France).

the topics discussed in CEDAW Committee meetings and, most importantly, the changes implemented by the states themselves.

Of course the analysis is not conclusive. It is limited to a cross section of three countries and is merely a superficial reading of the laws that existed before and after DEVAW. It does, however, show a link between the change in state law and policy and the activities of NGOs and/or international bodies. This substantiates the notion that the internationalisation of systemic intimate violence may improve the manner in which states address domestic violence, especially if one considers that change happens slowly and we are only in the third decade of creating laws to mitigate violence against women.

It should be noted that the purpose of this analysis is not to suggest that the CEDAW Committee did not concern itself with violence or that it incorrectly prioritised issues such as employment, reproductive health or political inclusion. There can be no hierarchy of women's rights; the violence that women face by virtue of domestic violence is only one manifestation of the harm and discrimination that women experience. The risk women endure through prostitution, trafficking, commodification and unequal labour standards are linked to, affect, and are affected by intimate violence. Moreover, even if there is a way to rank the difficulties endured by women, it is impossible to raise all matters with equal emphasis, especially when a movement is making a tentative inroad into international law. Rather, the point of this analysis is to show how CEDAW was augmented by DEVAW, and how international law and the enunciation of norms can be effective and influence the standards applied by both national and international institutions.

Domestic Violence in Mexico Before and After DEVAW

Mexico became a member of CEDAW in 1981 and submitted its first report to the CEDAW Committee in 1984.[214] In its 1984 report, Mexico made no reference to domestic violence against women. At this stage, Mexico had no specific mechanism to address violence against women and all forms of violence, public and private, gendered or otherwise, were treated uniformly.[215] To the extent

---

[214] For a list of states that have signed and ratified CEDAW see www.un.org/womenwatch/daw/cedaw/states.htm. For a state-by-state list of reservations see www.un.org/womenwatch/daw/cedaw/reservations-country.htm. Mexico's reservation relates to the manner of implementation, which will be in accordance with Mexican legislation and available resources. Mexico signed CEDAW on 17 July 1980 and ratified it, with reservation, on 23 March 1981. It signed the CEDAW Optional Protocol on 10 December 1999 and ratified it on 15 March 2002. For a list of signatories to the Optional Protocool see www.un.org/womenwatch/daw/cedaw/protocol/sigop.htm. See also *Report of the Second Session of the Committee on the Elimination of Discrimination against Women* (27 June 1984) UN Doc A/39/45 (hereinafter CEDAW Second Session Report), 12, para 71.

[215] The CEDAW Committee expressed concern regarding the difficulties women had in accessing the courts and legal system to enforce their rights. CEDAW Second Session Report (n 214) 12, para 71. In general, Mexico expressed economic difficulties as a reason for its failure to achieve equality and to implement the provisions of CEDAW. ibid, 12, para 69.

that violence was discussed in the 1984 CEDAW report, Mexico referred to the remedy of '*amparo*', which was designed to protect both men and women against arbitrary acts committed by the state.[216] The violence women experience in private was not featured as a consideration, either by Mexico or by the CEDAW Committee.

However, in 1996, following the disapprobation of violence against women expressed in DEVAW and the concomitant international condemnation of violence against women, Mexico passed federal legislation to establish non-judicial procedures to protect victims of domestic violence and to develop strategies to prevent such violence.[217] This included the 1996 Federal District Law to prevent and assist victims of 'intrafamilial violence'.[218] The CEDAW Committee commended the progress but admonished the Mexican government for the fact that while Mexico had taken a number of legislative and administrative steps to improve the status of women,[219] many women remained unaware of their rights and lacked the facility to protect their rights due to a lack of information and education.[220]

In 1997, the Center for Reproductive Rights prepared a shadow report on the reproductive rights of women in Mexico.[221] This included a discussion of the nature and extent of violence against women. The report revealed that gender-based violence continued to be prevalent, notwithstanding the passing of federal legislation to address it.[222] It noted that, because domestic violence comprises a peculiar form of harm, Mexico's criminal law had failed to protect women from this violence.[223]

The 1997 shadow report demonstrates two important points. First, it cites a study undertaken by the federal Ministry of Health which contains statistics regarding the demographic and substantive nature of domestic violence in Mexico.[224] This investigation by the Mexican government is a fulfilment of Article 4(k) of DEVAW, which enjoins states to 'Promote research, collect data and compile statistics, especially concerning domestic violence, relating to the

---

[216] ibid, 14, para 81.

[217] Law of Assistance and Prevention of Domestic Violence, Decree of the Assembly of Representatives of the Federal District, promulgated 26 April 1996, cited by Center for Reproductive Rights (formerly Center for Reproductive Law and Policy), *Women's Reproductive Rights in Mexico: A Shadow Report* (1997), www.crlp.org/pdf/sr_mex_1297_eng.pdf, 23.

[218] *Report of the Eighteenth and Nineteenth Sessions of the Committee on the Elimination of Discrimination against Women* (14 May 1998) UN Doc A/53/38/Rev.1 (hereinafter CEDAW Eighteenth and Nineteenth Sessions Report), 34.

[219] See *Women's Reproductive Rights in Mexico* (n 217) 24 (describing the improved legislative and judicial response to rape, including the creation, in 1989, of the Attorney General's Special Agencies to deal with sex offences).

[220] ibid.

[221] ibid.

[222] ibid (noting that in 60% of cases of rape of adolescent girls 'the aggressors are close relatives of the victim, including the victim's father').

[223] ibid.

[224] ibid.

prevalence of different forms of violence against women . . . [T]hose statistics and findings of the research will be made public'.[225]

Of course this does not solve the problem of systemic intimate violence in Mexico but it does lay the foundation for improved policies and it demonstrates that, on some level, Mexico was influenced by the international condemnation of violence against women and attempted to fulfil its international obligations. The second important factor highlighted by the 1997 shadow report is the acknowledgement by the Mexican government of the obstacles impeding the implementation of legal remedies, mostly due to a lack of awareness regarding the nature of systemic intimate violence and the available remedies.[226] This echoes the CEDAW Committee's 1996 admonishment.

In the following year Mexico once again appeared before the CEDAW Committee. By this stage Mexico had signed the Convention of Belém do Pará.[227] The 1998 Mexican report described consultations 'at the local level to reform the civil and criminal codes' and the creation of special programmes to support female victims of violence.[228] Mexico had also reformed its penal system 'to facilitate proceedings with regard to violence against women in the family, including marital rape'.[229]

The CEDAW Committee praised the Mexican government for its advances, admonished it for the continued high rate of violence against women and suggested that the government 'continue to work for the adoption of nationwide legislation on all forms of violence against women, including domestic violence, adjusting state laws to national laws'.[230] Specifically, the CEDAW Committee suggested that the government

> consider the possibility of implementing an integrated, long-term plan for combating domestic violence. Such a plan could include taking legal action, training judicial, law enforcement and health personnel, informing women about their rights and about the Convention and strengthening victims' services.[231]

The positive permutations of the CEDAW Committee's remarks were evident in 2002 when Mexico once again addressed the CEDAW Committee, indicating that combating violence against women 'was one of the State's priorities'.[232]

---

[225] DEVAW, Art 4(k).
[226] *Women's Reproductive Rights in Mexico* (n 217) 24.
[227] CEDAW Eighteenth and Nineteenth Sessions Report (n 218) 34.
[228] ibid, 32.
[229] ibid.
[230] ibid, 35.
[231] In addition, the CEDAW Committee suggested that 'strong action be taken against persons who commit violence against women, and . . . it should be made easier for women to bring court actions against offenders'. ibid.
[232] Mexico created a National Programme for Equal Opportunities and Non-Discrimination against Women, PROEQUIDAD ('the linchpin of national policy on gender'), and the National Women's Institute (INMUJERES). See *Report of the Twenty-Seventh Session of the Committee on the Elimination of Discrimination against Women* (6 August 2002) UN Doc A/57/38/Rev.1, 208, para 424 (hereinafter CEDAW Twenty-Seventh Session Report).

The National Women's Institute had been established as 'an autonomous, decentralized national mechanism with ministerial rank, its own budget and a cross-sectoral impact on all government institutions, thereby mainstreaming a gender perspective within national policy'.[233]

An Institutional Panel to Coordinate Preventive Action and Attention to Domestic Violence and Violence against Women was established, which provided a national framework for coordinated action against violence against women. Within the framework, a National Program for a Life Without Violence 2002–04 was put to civil society for discussion, and legislation dealing with domestic violence was passed in 15 states within Mexico. Specific programmes aimed at dealing with domestic violence in 16 Mexican states were also created. Mexico also referred to various campaigns and national programmes against domestic violence.[234]

In 2006 Mexico presented its sixth periodic report to the CEDAW Committee.[235] The report evidences Mexico's most detailed, nuanced and progressive responses to systemic intimate violence yet. It describes steps taken by the new government to strengthen the national plan against domestic violence and the preparation of the National Programme for a Life without Violence 2002–2004.[236] Set in the context of Mexico's earlier reports, this development is staggering. In the space of 12 years, a country renowned for its hierarchical delineation between men and women had created a national network of public policies with the common aim of preventing violence against women and evaluating preventative mechanisms.[237] The report also describes Mexico's involvement in regional efforts to improve techniques to prevent violence against women.[238]

Mexico's legislative developments in respect of domestic violence are notable. Following the recommendations of the Committee's response to Mexico's fifth periodic report, 28 of Mexico's 32 states adopted laws to prohibit domestic violence and marital rape was increasingly criminalised.[239] There was a movement at the executive level to reform the Federal Civil Code on domestic violence by expanding the definition of victims and perpetrators of domestic violence[240] and to reform the Federal Criminal Code on domestic violence to ensure that women and children would not have to leave the family home in order to escape abuse.[241]

---

[233] ibid.

[234] ibid, 206, para 414.

[235] CEDAW, *Concluding Comments of the Committee on the Elimination of Violence against Women: Mexico* (CEDAW Committee Response to Mexico's Sixth Periodic Report) (25 August 2006) UN Doc CEDAW/C/MEX/CO/6, para 15 (hereinafter CEDAW Comments on Mexico Sixth Report).

[236] ibid, para 53.

[237] ibid, para 54.

[238] ibid, para 55.

[239] ibid, para 57.

[240] ibid, para 59 (a Draft Decree was intended to reform the Federal Civil Code on domestic violence).

[241] ibid, para 60. Mexico also envisaged legislative reform to create a specific crime of femicide and ensure the protection of victims of violence. ibid, paras 60–61. The National Commission on Human Rights prepared 32 proposals for domestic violence reforms. ibid, para 62.

Mexico took some practical steps too, particularly in the provision of shelters.[242] In 2002 the National Shelter Network for Women in Situations of Extreme Violence (RENARAC) operated nine shelters and by October 2004 the number had risen to 34, although only nine were run by the government.[243] Dedicated telephone lines (so-called Phone Line for a Life without Violence) were set up to provide professional care and guidance and form a national network of support services.[244] And there was a marked effort to improve inter-agency coordination by involving the Ministry of Health and focusing on vulnerable populations such as indigenous and agricultural seasonal workers.[245]

Mexico reported the establishment of the Attorney's Offices for the Defence of Children, Women and the Family and gender-specific training for prosecutors. It developed a system of detection, registration, services and follow-up in domestic violence cases and allocated the appropriate funds for its operation. Mexico provided training on masculinity and education through media campaigns, workshops and talks on gender and violence, radio spots on peaceful relationships and training in the military.[246]

In accordance with previous CEDAW Committee recommendations, Mexico included in its report information on costs, data and statistics disaggregated by gender. It reported that the Inter-American Development Bank estimates that violence against women in Mexico costs between 1.6 and 2 per cent of the Gross Domestic Product (113 billion pesos) through hospital treatment, legal processes and absenteeism.[247] Although in its 2005 budget the government invested 400 million pesos (roughly US $30 million) towards combating violence against women, representing 0.35 per cent of total federal investment.[248] The government examined mortality resulting from aggression against women living in border zones[249] and conducted a national survey on discrimination in Mexico.[250] Women reported that one of the primary manifestations of discrimination was the violation of the right to a life without violence, particularly in the home.[251] According to the survey, the main obstacles to safety were discrimination due to pregnancy or children and the lack of jobs for women.[252]

In response to this very detailed report on systemic intimate violence, the CEDAW Committee focused almost exclusively on public violence against

---

[242] ibid, paras 63–65 (it reported significant developments in the state provision and sponsorship of shelters).

[243] ibid, para 65.

[244] ibid, paras 66–69 (it also evaluates the impact of campaigns for the prevention of violence).

[245] ibid, paras 70–84, 92, 99, 417.

[246] ibid.

[247] ibid, para 106.

[248] ibid.

[249] ibid, para 110.

[250] The results show that one in every three people belonging to the interview groups claim to have suffered discrimination as a result of their condition. ibid, para 343.

[251] ibid, para 343.

[252] ibid.

women.[253] The previous emphasis on intimate violence clearly receded. The Committee did discuss violence but in the context of the connection between the pervasiveness of patriarchal attitudes and the insecurity women experience in communities, workplaces, including *maquila* factories, and territories with a military presence.[254] It mentioned specifically the widespread and systematic violence against women that takes place in San Salvador Atenco, the State of Mexico and Ciudad Juárez.[255]

The development of Mexico's policies on systemic intimate violence is extensive and dynamic, and shows how changes in international law can result in associated changes in states' domestic laws and policies. The CEDAW Committee, however, should not pull back from its insistence on policies to protect women from systemic intimate violence. It is precisely this pressure that has led to change; and, as I proposed in chapter one, continued development in international law is very much still required.

And then there is Ciudad Juárez, Chihuahua.

The rise of violence against women in Ciudad Juárez,[256] Chihuahua reveals both the capabilities and the deficiencies of international law; the phenomenon also demonstrates the manner in which the expressive function of international law operates in respect of violence against women.[257]

During the late 1990s, activists within and outside of Mexico brought a spate of gruesome murders of women in Ciudad Juárez to the world's attention. It appeared that the local authorities of Ciudad Juárez, Chihuahua had done very little to investigate the murders, apprehend the perpetrators or assist the victims.[258] The violence in Ciudad Juárez had yet 'to be understood as the urgent risk for women that it presents'.[259] The link between public and private violence, between regression and development, and between legislative equality and meaningful equivalency became increasingly clear and this triggered wide condemnation of the Mexican government.[260]

---

[253] ibid, paras 14–15.

[254] ibid, para 14.

[255] ibid, paras 14 and 16 respectively.

[256] The homicide rate for women between 1993 and 2001 rose at double the rate as that for men. ibid, para 42.

[257] ibid, para 28.

[258] For the differences between the violence against women in Ciudad Juárez and the level of violence in Mexico in general, see Inter-American Commission on Human Rights, Organization of American States, *The Situation of the Rights of Women in Ciudad Juárez, Mexico: The Right to be Free from Violence and Discrimination* (7 March 2003) EA/Ser.L/V/II.117 Doc. 44 (hereinafter OAS Report on the Situation of Women in Ciudad Juárez), para 4.

[259] ibid, para 12.

[260] ibid, para 33 ('The victims were killed brutally: many were raped or beaten before being strangled or stabbed to death. A number of the bodies bore signs of torture or mutilation'). See also Division for the Advancement of Women, 'Information Note, United Nations Work on Violence against Women', www.un.org/womenwatch/daw/news/unwvaw.html ('The conclusions of Beijing +5 testify to the fact that gender-based violence against women is now viewed as a matter of serious concern by the international community).

Following an outcry against the violence, investigations revealed that a significant number of the killings in Ciudad Juárez had taken place at the hands of victims' intimate partners. It was argued that this could only be stopped by addressing the 'root causes of violence against women—in all its principle manifestations'.[261] However, the significance of *systemic* intimate violence had yet to be acknowledged by local officials.[262] In fact much of the violence was ignored. The authorities responsible for investigating the crimes and prosecuting the perpetrators were reportedly negligent.[263] The provision of support services for the relatives of those who had been killed was negligible, and very few perpetrators were prosecuted or convicted.[264]

Advocates identified this omission as replete with 'patterns of historical gender-based discrimination' as a result of which systemic intimate violence was not approached as a serious crime.[265] Mexico responded by creating a Special Prosecutor's Office in Ciudad Juárez to deal with the killings, but the murders continued.[266]

As the murders normalised, crime in Ciudad Juárez rose. So long as officials remained incapable or unwilling to address the source of, and motive behind, the violence, the killings continued, apparently without abatement.[267] Towards the end of 2001, hundreds of NGOs contacted the Special Rapporteur about the situation,[268] concerned that 'the killing of over 200 women since 1993 had been left in impunity'.[269] Following an official visit by the Special Rapporteur, the state of Chihuahua promised to establish a number of mechanisms to improve responses to violence. These included: an emergency telephone hotline for women at risk of domestic violence and harassment in the street; the installation of more street lighting; establishing a new anonymous complaint program; and ensuring that no woman is alone on a bus or other public transport vehicle on the way to or from work.[270]

---

[261] OAS Report on the Situation of Women in Ciudad Juárez (n 258) para 11.

[262] ibid, para 12.

[263] ibid, paras 34 and 48 ('Because of the lack of basic information, family members . . . have expressed a profound lack of confidence in the willingness or the ability of the authorities to clarify what happened or pursue accountability'). See also ibid, para 54.

[264] ibid, para 70.

[265] ibid, para 36 ('The denial of an effective response both springs from and feeds back into the perception that violence against women—most illustratively domestic violence—is not a serious crime').

[266] ibid, paras 33–40.

[267] ibid, para 34 ('The organizations indicated that, because the Mexican State was allowing these crimes to remain in impunity, it was encouraging their persistence').

[268] ibid, para 33 ('the key concern set forth was that the killing of over 200 women since 1993 had been left in impunity').

[269] ibid, para 33.

[270] ibid, paras 70 and 89. See Inter-American Commission on Human Rights, 'The Law and Systems of Protection Applicable to Violence against Women in Ciudad Juárez', www.cidh.oas.org/annualrep/2002eng/chap.vi.juarez.3.htm (regarding the international law that applies to such violence. This is most useful since it formulates the right and defines the corresponding obligation of the Mexican state).

Eventually, both the Mexican government and the concerned NGOs agreed that most of the murders related to manifestations of violence with gender-specific causes and consequences.[271] While there was a public dimension to the murders, the violence was often also intimate, a fact revealed by the inter-nationalisation and subsequent discussion of the violence.[272] This in turn revealed the Mexican government's failure to devote sufficient attention to 'the discrimination that underlies crimes of sexual or domestic violence'.[273]

In 2002 Mexico once again addressed the CEDAW Committee, expressing its concern at the escalation of violence against women in Ciudad Juárez. Mexico reported the creation of a special commission to investigate the murders of women in the region. A panel was also created to coordinate Mexico's response to the violence 'with the objective of designing a plan to restore the social fabric in Ciudad Juárez, and to improve the living conditions of the children of women who had been murdered, and the city's residents as a whole'.[274]

In Mexico's 2006 CEDAW report, the government included an extensive dis-cussion of violence against women in Ciudad Juárez in response to a specific request from the CEDAW Committee.[275] Developments included the creation of the Commission for the Prevention and Eradication of Violence against Women in Ciudad Juárez. This was a decentralised administrative body, attached to the Ministry of the Interior, established to implement the federal government's policy in Ciudad Juárez via three strategies: services for victims; truth and justice; and strengthening of the social fabric. The Advisory Council on Use of the Economic Support Fund for Families of Female Murder Victims in the Municipality of Juárez, Chihuahua was established, with participation by the Offices of the Attorney General of the Republic and of the State of Chihuahua. A Special Attorney's Office was also created to monitor investi-gations into femicide in Mexico, with a budget of 150 million pesos (US $14 million), and two commissions were created to deal with murders of women.

Training and awareness-raising sessions on human rights and the gender per-spective were held for police officers and civil servants of both sexes, particu-larly those responsible for investigating and clarifying acts of violence against women. A security programme was implemented involving street patrols (in which a man and a woman would keep watch over high risk areas 24 hours a day, 365 days a year); there was an improved response by the emergency services to calls relating to gender-specific violence; and transport was made available to carry victims and survivors to participating organisations and agencies. There was also mention of draft legislation to bring the State of Chihuahua in line with the international framework on human rights, particularly the human rights of

---

[271] OAS Report on the Situation of Women in Ciudad Juárez (n 258) paras 43, 57.
[272] ibid.
[273] ibid, para 11. See also ibid, para 57 ('The killing of women in Ciudad Juárez is strongly linked to and influenced by the prevalence of domestic and intrafamilial violence').
[274] CEDAW Twenty-Seventh Session Report (n 232) 206, para 415.
[275] CEDAW Comments on Mexico Sixth Report (n 235) 146.

women, in collaboration with the World Organization against Torture. Centres providing services for violent men were also created and three shelters were established. A monitoring unit was launched to denounce sexist messages transmitted by the media and on the internet.

The Chamber of Deputies is conducting an investigation into femicide in Mexico in 11 of its states, with four investigators involved in each case. The aim is to discover what is happening in the country and to relate the murders and disappearances of girls and women to the context of each state. A diagnostic study of the incidence of gender violence in Ciudad Juárez, Chihuahua and other states was undertaken to (1) identify whether this phenomenon has spread to other cities; (2) identify the general and specific triggers of violence against women in Ciudad Juárez and the other selected cities; and (3) on the basis of the diagnostic study, prepare recommendations for preventing the continuation and spread of violence against women.[276]

None of these factors eradicated systemic intimate violence in Mexico, nor did the international outcry caused by the violence in Ciudad Juárez bring an end to the killings. However, Mexico's interaction with the CEDAW Committee maps a very clear progression of factors which today facilitates the creation, funding and support of institutions, few as they are, that assist victims of this violence.

The enunciation of facts and the articulation of norms are elements in a process of change, elements which together operate to bring relief to individuals. Expressing norms against systemic intimate violence in international law is not a panacea in and of itself. Rather, international discussions about a particular situation can expose the harm, import relief to the victims, and impose shame upon inert governments. By incremental steps the views of the international community seep into the activities of the state, potentially improving its response to those in need. The power of storytelling exposes the pain of victims, informs potentially powerful actors, and shines the proverbial spotlight on an otherwise invisible harm.

Domestic Violence in Nicaragua Before and After DEVAW

The internationalisation of concern for violence against women led to the implementation of certain reforms in Nicaragua which arguably would not have occurred but for the global discussion of domestic violence.

Nicaragua's recent history, from the poverty induced by the Cold War in the early 1960s to the overthrowing of the US-supported Somoza government by Soviet-supported Sandinistas in 1979, has had a duplicitous effect, both empowering women and leaving them increasingly vulnerable.[277] Notwithstanding an

---

[276] ibid, 147.
[277] UNIFEM-UNDP-UNFPA-UNICEF-UNAIDS-UNHCR-UNHCHR-ECLAC, 'A Life Free of Violence: It's Our Right. United Nations Inter-Agency Campaign on Women's Human Rights in

emphasis on traditional gender roles, Nicaragua's 1979 conflict was characterised by the dynamic and effective role played by women, who constituted
30 per cent of the guerrilla force.[278] However, following the rise to power of the
Sandinista there was a decrease in the power, and commensurate rights, of
women. Under the government regime following the Sandinista rule, the once
powerful Nicaraguan Institute for Women was transformed into the generic
Ministry of the Family, which was criticised for 'promoting the traditional
nuclear family and discriminating against families headed by single mothers and
common law mothers'.[279] Reports of a disquieting rate of violence against
women increased, with many concluding that violence against women in
Nicaragua was a major obstacle to development.[280] Notwithstanding the constitutional protection of equality and women's rights, women at this point constituted approximately 88 per cent of the poor in Nicaragua and were subjected
to increasing bouts of violence.[281]

The high levels of violence against women in Nicaragua began to receive international attention in the early 1980s. By 1981, Nicaragua had signed and ratified
CEDAW[282] and in 1984 Nicaragua appeared before the CEDAW Committee,
which, in an unusual line of questioning for the time, examined the unduly high
rate of gender-based violence.[283]

Latin America and the Caribbean' (1998), freeofviolence.org and specifically, Carmen Clavel and
Verónica Gutiérrez, *Nicaragua* (1998), para 117, freeofviolence.org/nicaragua.htm (hereinafter
'A Life Free of Violence)'.

[278] See 'A Life Free of Violence', ibid, 17 (the Nicaraguan women's group, the Asociación de
Mujeres Ante la Problemática Nacional (Association of Nicaraguan Women Confronting the
National Problem, or AMPRONAC), was formed in 1977 to provide civilian support to the Sandinista
platform).

[279] ibid, 118. This decline in attention being paid to women's interests was compounded by the
economic devastation following Hurricane Mitch in 1998. See also CEDAW Committee Sixth
Session Report (n 170) 37, para 196.

[280] In total, almost 30% of women who have been married at some point in their lives have experienced sexual or physical abuse. Over 50% of such women endured the abuse in front of their children and 36% while they were pregnant. CEDAW, *Fifth Periodic Report on Nicaragua* (9 September
1999) UN Doc CEDAW/C/Nic/5 (hereinafter Fifth Nicaragua CEDAW Report). See also 'A Life
Free of Violence' (n 278) 118 (describing evidence that 'sexual violence became an endemic feature
of postconflict Nicaragua, exacerbated by men returning from the war to a weak economy and high
rates of unemployment').

[281] See Luisa Pérez-Landa, *Violence against Women in Nicaragua* (Geneva, World Organisation
against Torture (OMCT), 2001) (Report prepared for the Committee on the Elimination of
Discrimination against Women Twenty-Fifth session, 2–20 July 2001) 9–10, 12. See also 'A Life Free
of Violence' (n 278) 118.

[282] On 17 July 1980 Nicaragua signed CEDAW and ratified it, without reservation, on 27 October
1981. It has not signed the Optional Protocol. For details of CEDAW and Optional Protocol signatories, ratifications and reservations, refer to the websites listed in n 216.

[283] CEDAW Committee Sixth Session Report (n 170) 37, para 195; 35, para 174. In a separate
question, the CEDAW Committee requested information regarding 'any measures that had been
taken to prevent or reduce the abuse of young girls and women, including domestic violence and sexual assault, alcoholism and drug abuse, and the care of the victims of those social ills'. ibid, 36, para
184. This line of questioning was not characteristic of the CEDAW Committee and probably arose
as a result of the international exposure of violence against Nicaraguan women.

In 1992 the post-war phenomenon of violence against women was recognised as one of the main problems facing Nicaraguan women.[284] This status quo continued well into the late 1990s, when the Nicaraguan government began to identify domestic violence as a serious health problem for women.[285] The government acknowledged that the 'grave shortcomings affecting women's access to justice'[286] were due to domestic violence, the absence of a family code, cumbersome procedures, ignorance of the law, paternal irresponsibility and delays in the payment of alimony.[287]

After 1993 the legal landscape began to change. The Nicaraguan government began to implement certain policy and legislative amendments.[288] Following DEVAW and Nicaragua's ratification of the Convention of Belém do Pará in 1995,[289] Nicaragua adopted the 1996 Law against Aggression against Women, which criminalised domestic violence, imposed a sentence of up to six years and instituted the restraining order.[290] Several modifications and additions were made to the generic Nicaraguan Penal Code (Law 230) regarding the prevention and punishment of family violence.[291] In 1997 the Penal Code was reformed to prohibit family violence, including physical and psychological violence, and the government established committees to combat violence against women.[292]

Towards the end of the 1990s, various government institutions adopted strategies to reduce violence against women, including the National Police Force,[293] the Ministry of Health[294] and the Ministry of the Family, which was responsible for formulating and coordinating government policy relating to the strengthening of the family unit.[295] Nicaragua established the Nicaraguan

---

[284] 'A Life Free of Violence' (n 278) 118 (rape laws were limited in that they did not apply to husbands, awarded paternity rights to rapists and sentences were as short as nine months).

[285] CEDAW, *Fourth Periodic Report of Nicaragua* (28 August 1998) UN Doc CEDAW/C/NIC/4 (hereinafter Fourth Nicaragua CEDAW Report), 15. See also Fifth Nicaragua CEDAW Report (n 281) 22 (describing the government's focus on violence as a health problem in an attempt to mainstream gender issues).

[286] Fifth Nicaragua CEDAW Report (n 281) 21.

[287] ibid, 21–22.

[288] 'A Life Free of Violence' (n 278) 2. The National Commission against Violence, an interinstitutional governmental agency, was created in 1990 by government decree.

[289] Nicaragua has signed and ratified the Inter-American Convention on the Prevention, Punishment and Eradication of Violence against Women (Convention of Belém do Pará) (adopted 9 June 1994, entered into force 5 March 1995) (1994) 33 ILM 1534.

[290] 'A Life Free of Violence' (n 278) 119.

[291] ibid, 2. See also *Report of the Twenty-Fourth and Twenty-Fifth Sessions of the Committee on the Elimination of Discrimination against Women* (2001) UN Doc A/56/38 (hereinafter CEDAW Twenty-Fourth and Twenty-Fifth Sessions Report on Nicaragua), 72–74, paras 277–318.

[292] 'A Life Free of Violence' (n 278) 2 (describing the 1999–2001 Strategic Plan of the Nicaraguan Institute for Women).

[293] ibid (noting that the police force established the Consultative Council on Gender and the Commissariats for Women and Children to address gender-based violence). In 1995 the national police force established the Office for Women and Children. Fifth Nicaragua CEDAW Report (n 281) 35.

[294] The Ministry of Health created the Department of Comprehensive Attention for Women. See 'A Life Free of Violence' (n 278) 2. See also Fifth Nicaragua CEDAW Report (n 281) 31.

[295] 'A Life Free of Violence' (n 278) 2.

Institute for Women as the national machinery charged with formulating and promoting public policies vis-a-vis women.[296] In 1998 the National Commission on Violence against Women was created to plan and implement solutions, which would coordinate all government departments.[297] These advances realised material, albeit limited, improvements for the victims of systemic intimate violence.[298]

In 2001, once again before the CEDAW Committee, Nicaragua acknowledged the disproportionate effect of poverty on women and the harmful social and cultural perceptions of '*machismo*', which had impeded the implementation of CEDAW.[299] While the non-equivalent roles of men and women undermined the legislative developments adopted by the government,[300] Nicaragua claimed that since its adoption of CEDAW the role of women had advanced, especially in light of developments within the country as a whole.[301]

The substance of Nicaragua's 2001 presentation to the CEDAW Committee evidenced an advanced understanding of systemic intimate violence. It noted the contradiction between the perception of the home as a place of safety and the destructive reality of a 'climate of tension and aggression within the family [which] destroys the family's meaning as a place of protection, security and support'.[302] In its fourth and fifth CEDAW reports, Nicaragua described domestic violence as a violation of the right to security of the person and the right to equality, respectively, revealing that 'intra-family violence and sexual crimes were the leading forms of crime in 1998'.[303] The Nicaraguan representative acknowledged the isolation inherent in domestic violence and the debilitating effects of psychological and physical harm,[304] factors which had led Nicaragua

---

[296] CEDAW Twenty-Fourth and Twenty-Fifth Sessions Report on Nicaragua (n 292) 73, para 280. This institute was formed following recognition of domestic violence 'as a violation of the right to life and the right to security of person'. Fourth Nicaragua CEDAW Report (n 286) 17. For a more detailed account of the advances made by the Nicaraguan Institute for Women, see Fifth Nicaragua CEDAW Report (n 281) 35–36 and the CEDAW Twenty-Fourth and Twenty-Fifth Sessions Report on Nicaragua (n 292) 74, para 292.

[297] Fifth Nicaragua CEDAW Report (n 281) 6, 37.

[298] The institutions 'provided Nicaraguan women and children with a professional body which recognizes their rights and offers expertise in all cases of rape and physical abuse'. Fourth Nicaragua CEDAW Report (n 286) 17.

[299] CEDAW Twenty-Fourth and Twenty-Fifth Sessions Report on Nicaragua (n 292) 74–75.

[300] ibid, 74.

[301] Fifth Nicaragua CEDAW Report (n 281) 4. See also CEDAW Twenty-Fourth and Twenty-Fifth Sessions Report on Nicaragua (n 292) 74, paras 287–90 (noting that while there was a lack of statistical data disaggregated by sex, Nicaragua had disseminated a handbook 'explaining the provisions of the Convention').

[302] Fifth Nicaragua CEDAW Report (n 281) 30 (noting that the violence 'affects the mental and emotional health of family members and their capacity to socialize with one another, and very often leads to the break-up of the family'). The representative of Nicaragua commented specifically on domestic violence, pointing out that it 'affected a large number of women in Nicaragua'. CEDAW Twenty-Fourth and Twenty-Fifth Sessions Report on Nicaragua (n 292) 73, para 285.

[303] Domestic violence was addressed in the Fourth Nicaragua CEDAW Report in the context of the right to security of person. Fourth Nicaragua CEDAW Report (n 286) 17. See also the Fifth Nicaragua CEDAW Report (n 281) 30.

[304] Fifth Nicaragua CEDAW Report (n 281) 30.

to develop a National Plan for the Prevention of Domestic and Sexual Violence 2001–06.[305] The representative admitted to and explained the limitations of its efforts to reduce systemic intimate violence,[306] but claimed that the criminalisation of domestic violence and the penalisation of abusers had 'led to a new openness in discussing and condemning domestic and sexual violence on the part of the Government'.[307]

The Nicaraguan representative described some of the advances the government had made in addressing domestic violence. There had been an increase in the role of female professionals and specialists with a scientific background in disseminating information regarding violence against women.[308] A national programme for women and children had been created 'to meet the needs of all those women who now have the courage to report situations of violence'.[309] Ten national offices were funded by the Nicaraguan Institute for Women and eight were funded by local initiatives.[310] The state had also published police training manuals, entitled 'Gender Violence and Citizen Security'.[311] Perhaps the most pertinent development was Nicaragua's emphasis on the role of women and civil society in developing solutions to the problem of domestic violence.[312]

In 2007 Nicaragua submitted its sixth periodic report to the CEDAW Committee.[313] The report described the formulation of a National Plan of Action for the Prevention of Domestic and Sexual Violence (2001–06).[314] In a move similar to Mexico's strategy, Nicaragua sought to incorporate a gender perspective in its public policies by strengthening cross-sectoral working groups on health, violence, education, poverty and economics, with broad government and civil society participation.[315]

The report indicated that the Ministry of Health had added violence against women to its classification of health problems and its models for dealing with them.[316] This was based on the government's acceptance that violence against women 'is internationally recognized as a determinant of health status, and its

---

[305] CEDAW Twenty-Fourth and Twenty-Fifth Sessions Report on Nicaragua (n 292) 74, para 292.
[306] The Fourth and Fifth Nicaragua CEDAW Reports acknowledged that there were contradictions and flaws in the legislation as regards protection against domestic violence. Fourth Nicaragua CEDAW Report (n 286) 8; Fifth Nicaragua CEDAW Report (n 281) 21.
[307] Fourth Nicaragua CEDAW Report (n 286) 17.
[308] ibid, 16.
[309] Fifth Nicaragua CEDAW Report (n 281) 35.
[310] ibid.
[311] ibid, 38 (this project was funded by German aid).
[312] Fourth Nicaragua CEDAW Report (n 286) 19. See Fifth Nicaragua CEDAW Report (n 281) 58 (noting 'the influence of the women university lecturers, professionals and specialists who have carried out research on women's issues such as abuse, violence, laws that discriminate against women').
[313] CEDAW Committee, *Sixth Periodic Report: Nicaragua* (5 July 2005) UN Doc CEDAW/C/NIC/6.
[314] ibid, para 43.
[315] ibid, paras 43, 51, 216, 218.
[316] ibid, paras 52, 175.

forms include domestic and sexual violence, which has an enormous impact on health; the majority of victims are women and children'.[317]

The link between the international focus on domestic violence as a health pandemic and Nicaragua's policy reform is evident. Nicaragua reformed its police structure, creating 14 women's and children's police stations, established as specialist instruments for combating and reducing domestic violence.[318] The report revealed an increase of 33 per cent in the number of complaints filed at these specialist police stations, which the government attributed to efforts to encourage reporting, awareness and education.[319] Nicaragua also seemingly incorporated the CEDAW recommendation to disaggregate data by gender, noting that women most often file complaints for the offence of battery.[320] In 2002 most complaints of violence against women occurred in the home, leading to the arrest of 7,784 perpetrators, of whom 7,028, or 90.2 per cent, were men. Women accounted for 12,818, or 52.4 per cent, of the total number of battery victims.[321]

The report recognised that, in practice, the police have become the main gateway between victims of domestic violence and the network of institutions offering medical, legal, psychological and social services to deal with the problem.[322] Targets were established for governmental and civil society organisations and technological support was enhanced.[323]

In its response, the CEDAW Committee noted the developments in law and policy but held Nicaragua to account for the continued prevalence of violence against women and the lack of condemnation of such violence.[324] The Committee urged Nicaragua to ensure that victims of violence, including poor, rural, indigenous and Afro-descendent women, have access to immediate means of redress, protection, support and legal aid.[325]

This retrospective analysis shows that following DEVAW, Nicaragua improved its legislation and policies in respect of violence against women. While the CEDAW Committee rightly highlighted that there was still work to be done on enforcement, the developments that took place between the pre-DEVAW reports and the 2007 report are significant. NGOs played a distinct role in exposing the extent of the problem and instigating legislative change, awareness raising campaigns and lobbying efforts.[326] They were also responsible for

---

[317] ibid, paras 75, 212.
[318] ibid, para 215.
[319] ibid, para 213.
[320] ibid, para 214.
[321] ibid.
[322] ibid, para 216.
[323] ibid, para 217.
[324] CEDAW, 'Concluding Comments of the Committee on the Elimination of Violence against Women: Nicaragua' (CEDAW Committee Response to Nicaragua's Sixth Periodic Report) (2 February 2007) UN Doc CEDAW/C/NIC/CO/6, para 19.
[325] ibid, para 20.
[326] 'A Life Free of Violence' (n 278) 119 ('most of the long-standing programming has been the result of action by local NGOs').

establishing shelters and services for the survivors of domestic violence.[327] The Nicaraguan government developed a strong male-focused movement to reduce violence against women, offering training workshops on *machismo* and its connection to violence against women.[328]

Of course, systemic intimate violence persists. This is due in part to Nicaragua's poverty and the fact that many state institutions prioritise needs other than gender-based violence. In addition, cultural reform vis-a-vis gender roles has been slow, partly due to a rejection of western ideologies, given the United States' contentious involvement in Nicaragua. Whatever the reason, the health and well-being of women is not a priority in many Nicaraguan communities. The state itself seems to have taken legislative steps to embrace women's rights but the extent to which this has been backed up by the necessary funding, training and material resources is uncertain.

However, one cannot ignore the progress that has been made in Nicaragua in relation to addressing domestic violence. The result of this emphasis is a slow but meaningful shift in the internalisation of the norm prohibiting systemic intimate violence. Within this state of flux, international organisations and institutions continue to research, expose and help mitigate the very high level of systemic intimate violence that is carried out against women in Nicaragua.

Domestic Violence in Sweden Before and After DEVAW

Historically, Sweden has taken an active position opposing gender discrimination. It was one of the first states to sign and ratify CEDAW (in 1980), and objected to several reservations made by other state parties.[329] In its 1984 report to CEDAW, however, Sweden made almost no reference to violence against women. While the CEDAW Committee requested information regarding rape and battering, Sweden did not supply this information.[330]

In 1993, however, in the build-up to the implementation of DEVAW, Sweden once again appeared before the CEDAW Committee.[331] This time it described significant advances in respect of domestic violence.[332] Sweden had enacted the

---

[327] ibid.

[328] ibid, 120.

[329] Sweden signed CEDAW on 7 March 1980 and ratified it on 2 July 1980. It signed the CEDAW Optional Protocol on 10 December 1999 and ratified it on 24 April 2003.

[330] CEDAW Second Session Report (n 214) 33, para 217.

[331] CEDAW, *Committee on the Elimination of Discrimination against Women, Concluding Observations: Sweden* (CEDAW Committee response to Sweden's Third Periodic Report) (1993) (hereinafter CEDAW Observations of Sweden Third Report), paras 474–522, www1.umn.edu/humanrts/cedaw/sweden1993.html.

[332] At this stage it is also clear that the CEDAW Committee takes a somewhat more holistic approach to violence, stating that 'In a time of changing social patterns, the key questions were how to change the violent pattern of male behaviour and how to reach suffering women'. CEDAW Observations of Sweden Third Report (n 332) para 501.

new Equal Opportunities Act in 1992, which established a five year plan to achieve equality, recognising that 'Violence, battering and other forms of physical abuse against women were considered to be serious expressions of the lack of equality and imbalance of power'.[333] The Act also catered for the training of professional personnel such as police officers, judges, doctors and social welfare officers and improving coordination between the authorities at the local and regional levels.[334] The most impressive component of the Act was the allocation of funds to the police to 'provide technical equipment and bodyguards for women who were subjected to threats of violence'.[335]

Since the beginning of the 1990s, Sweden has increased the number of protection orders, created government institutions and committees to examine and understand the permutations of violence against women, and passed progressive and insightful legislation in respect of systemic intimate violence. Possibly the most progressive legal provision is the revision of the Swedish Penal Code: Law on Gross Violation of Integrity and Gross Violation of a Woman's Integrity, intended to raise the penalty value of acts 'which, viewed separately, are relatively minor but when repeated may lead to substantial violation of the victim's integrity'.[336] The number of 'visiting bans' granted against men increased from 62 in 1988 to 2,295 in 1999.[337]

The Social Services Act was amended to oblige social services to facilitate alternative accommodation for women who have been subjected to violence in their home.[338] Sweden's laws make provision for the protection of personal data to ensure that the abuser is prevented from accessing information relating to the abused and, most importantly, from finding out her whereabouts.[339]

Notwithstanding these advances, however, the trend of violence in Sweden remained constant.[340] To improve this situation, at the conclusion of the 1993 session, the CEDAW Committee suggested that the Swedish government forge closer ties with grassroots organisations and facilitate the reporting of the violence.[341]

In 1993 the Government of Sweden set up a Commission on Violence against Women, to review issues pertaining to violence against women and in particular 'to present its proposals from a female perspective' (meaning the perspective

---

[333] ibid, para 480. The Act came into force in Sweden on 1 January 1992.

[334] ibid, para 480.

[335] ibid, para 480.

[336] Gun Heimer, Eva Lundgren, Jenny Westerstrand and Anne-Marie Kalliokoski (Julia Mikaelsson and Geoffrey French trans), *Captured Queen: Men's Violence against Women in 'Equal' Sweden—A Prevalence Study* (Sweden, Fritzes Offtliga Publikationer, 2002) 13, www.brottsoffermyndigheten.se/informationsmaterial/Captured%20queen.pdf/Captured%20Queen%20.pdf.

[337] ibid, 12. Sweden was the first country to criminalise marital rape. See Amnesty International (n 69) 20.

[338] Amnesty International (n 69) 21.

[339] ibid, 21–22.

[340] CEDAW Observations of Sweden Third Report (n 332) para 502.

[341] ibid.

that has emerged from feminist studies of violence against women).[342] The Commission proposed the establishment of a national centre for battered and raped women.[343] In response, the government allocated funds for the establishment of such a centre, approximately 70 kilometres north of Stockholm at the Academic Hospital of Uppsala, to provide 'medical examination, treatment and support to women subjected to violence as well as counseling around the clock'.[344] The centre, known as the RKC, constitutes an 'expert unit within the health and medical services for women who have been subjected battering and sexual assaults (*sic*)'.[345]

The RKC in Sweden is a self-contained clinic, with independent staff, commissioned to offer and develop treatment services for women who have survived battering or rape.[346] They also provide a consulting, educational, awareness-raising and research function.[347] The RKC is also able to offer a modicum of protection to victims of abuse through cooperation with the police and social services and the protection of evidence.[348]

In 2000, once again before the CEDAW Committee, Sweden affirmed its commitment to gender equality and described its role in the UN's adoption of the Declaration of the Elimination of Violence against Women and the UN's decision to appoint a Special Rapporteur on violence against women.[349] It also described improved systems of support within the state for domestic violence victims.[350] Sweden also ratified the Optional Protocol to the Convention on the Elimination of All Forms of Discrimination against Women on 23 April 2003 and, as of the date of writing, no complaints have been lodged.[351] It was therefore disconcerting when in 2005 the *New York Times* published an article describing high levels of domestic violence in Sweden, entitled 'Secret Side of Women's Lives'.[352] The article revealed that the reason for the high level of

---

[342] CEDAW, *Fifth Periodic Report of States Parties: Sweden* (18 December 2000) UN Doc CEDAW/C/SWE/5 (hereinafter Sweden Fifth CEDAW Periodic Report), 32.

[343] ibid, 33.

[344] ibid. See also Heimer et al (n 337) 22 fnn 11, 12. The report includes an informative history of the development of research and activism regarding violence against women in Sweden since the early 1980s. See National Centre for Knowledge on Men's Violence against Women (National Center for Battered and Raped Women), Uppsala University Hospital, 3 www.uas.se/templates/ page____25859.aspx (hereinafter National Center for Battered and Raped Women).

[345] ibid. It appears that there are five shelters within the County of Uppsala. ibid, 6. There are also points of refuge, referred to as 'centres for victims of crime', although the extent to which these are used by victims of domestic violence is uncertain. See also Sweden Fifth CEDAW Periodic Report (n 343) 33.

[346] See National Center for Battered and Raped Women (n 345).

[347] See ibid, 3 (the RKC plays an important role regarding the obtaining and preservation of evidence). See also ibid, 4, 6.

[348] See ibid, 4, 5.

[349] Sweden Fifth CEDAW Periodic Report (n 343) 21.

[350] ibid, 31. Victims of the crime of domestic violence are entitled to request the appointment of a so-called 'injured party counsel'. Amnesty International (n 69) 19.

[351] ibid, para 10.

[352] See Alvarez (n 50) (describing domestic violence as the 'one significant blot on the record of women's empowerment').

domestic violence is not a propensity for violence on the part of Swedish men; rather, it 'has simply been easier for them to get away with violence against wives and girlfriends . . . and harder for women to get the help they need'.[353]

In 2006, Sweden submitted its joint sixth and seventh reports to the CEDAW Committee.[354] The Government introduced a Bill in 2006 which, inter alia, highlights the problem of violence against women, particularly men's violence against women. It is also worth noting the Bill's ambition to create economic equality between women and men and to achieve equal distribution of unpaid care and household work.[355]

Gender mainstreaming through government departments, as with Mexico and Nicaragua, is a feature of the report.[356] This includes budgetary considerations, funding for shelters,[357] and crisis centres for men exhibiting aggressive and violent behaviour.[358] The report envisages better support for women of foreign origin, disabled women, and women with substance abuse problems who are subjected to violence.[359] Sweden's report focused extensively on violence in the name of honour, emphasising shelters, working with religious groups and men's networks.[360] There also appeared to be a positive focus on municipal as well as federal levels of governance.[361]

Sweden has taken specific steps to improve its police force's capacity to investigate and prevent violence against women, including developing police guidelines on assessing threat and risk in domestic violence cases.[362] The Government's ambition is that in some cases it will be possible to combine restraining orders with electronic monitoring.[363] Sweden has also reformed its prosecutorial services in terms of specialisation, training and inter-agency projects,[364] and provision has been made to involve prosecutors earlier in preliminary investigations of violence against women.[365] Gender awareness was integrated into the court system.[366] Special sections on men's violence against

---

[353] ibid. See also Sweden Fifth CEDAW Periodic Report (n 343) 32 and Heimer et al (n 337) 8, 10. For a summary of statistics of violence against women, see Amnesty International (n 69) 27.

[354] CEDAW, 'Combined Sixth and Seventh Periodic Reports of States Parties: Sweden' (14 September 2006) UN Doc CEDAW/C/SWE/7.

[355] ibid, para 7.

[356] ibid, paras 11–16, 76.

[357] ibid, paras 15, 67–68.

[358] ibid, para 67.

[359] ibid, paras 68–70.

[360] ibid, para 107–115.

[361] 70% of Sweden's municipalities have action plans in place for their work with women exposed to violence. ibid, para 99.

[362] ibid, paras 77–79. These routines and guidelines are to show, for example, how restraining orders are to be followed up, how and what information is to be given to the parties involved, and what measures are to be undertaken if the person to be protected by the restraining order reports that the order has been violated. ibid, para 79.

[363] ibid, para 80.

[364] ibid, para 81.

[365] ibid, para 83.

[366] ibid, paras 89–92.

women were included in routine professional development courses for judges[367] and work was undertaken to reduce the stress injured parties experience during the judicial process.[368] An interim report showed that the number of applications for restraining orders was rising and that the proportion of restraining orders violated had not risen since 2003.[369] Sweden's latest report reveals a progressive rehabilitative approach to men's role in violence against women.[370] The Prison and Probation Service was tasked with providing treatment for men convicted of violence against women.[371]

In its response, the CEDAW Committee went into some detail about violence against women, commending Sweden's adoption, in November 2007, of the action plan to combat men's violence against women, violence and oppression in the name of honour and violence in same-sex relationships.[372] The Committee highlighted the prevalence of domestic violence and crimes committed against women in the name of honour and the fact that Swedish crime statistics are not broken down by the sex of victims.[373] While there was an increase in shelters nationally, there were still municipalities with no shelters at all.[374] The Committee noted the appointment of a Delegation for Roma Issues but remained concerned at the forms of discrimination experienced by Saami and Roma women in various contexts and the need to integrate them into the Swedish labour market.[375]

While Sweden's battle against domestic violence is not yet won, its progressive approach to the systemic nature of this violence is evolutionary. It also demonstrates a development in the country's attempts to prevent systemic intimate violence, which is due in part to the expansive function of international law. The attention that international bodies such as the CEDAW Committee have given to violence against women has helped to crystalise the concept of domestic violence. This in turn has led to expanded responses and nuanced solutions to systemic intimate violence in Sweden.

---

[367] ibid, para 90.

[368] ibid, para 93.

[369] ibid, para 94. Around two thirds of all restraining orders issued by prosecutors are complied with.

[370] ibid, paras 101–02.

[371] ibid, para 96.

[372] CEDAW, 'Concluding Observations of the Committee on the Elimination of Discrimination against Women: Sweden' (CEDAW Committee Response to Sweden's Sixth and Seventh Periodic Reports) (8 April 2008) UN Doc CEDAW/C/SWE/CO/7, para 9.

[373] ibid, para 28.

[374] ibid.

[375] ibid, paras 28, 39.

General Examples of Improvements in Domestic Violence Laws and Policies

The functions of international law discussed above have led to significant improvements in states' responses to systemic intimate violence.[376]

Policies and National Action Plans

National action plans on violence against women are increasingly nuanced and detailed.[377] For example, Australia's national action plan on domestic violence takes into account the connection between domestic violence on homelessness and officials have proposed constructing 600 homes to accommodate the homeless, including specifically women and children escaping domestic violence.[378] Portugal's third national action plan on domestic violence includes measures to facilitate the integration of victims and survivors into the labour force.[379] Denmark has provided significant additional funds to support and treat victims of domestic violence, and measures addressing domestic violence have been integrated into Saudi Arabia's national programmes for family security.[380] For victims and survivors of domestic violence, these steps are a much needed practical solution to the violence they endure. The UK's domestic violence enforcement campaign, launched in December 2007, seeks to establish partnerships between police, charities and communities to increase reporting and to bring more perpetrators to justice. The Netherlands takes a similar approach to inter-departmental cooperation and has established a website and a privacy help desk that provides clarification on rules relating to the exchange of domestic violence data.[381] Belgium, the Former Yugoslav Republic of Macedonia and Germany are also developing guidelines relating to protection from domestic violence, including inter-disciplinary cooperation between various arms of government.[382]

---

[376] Following the General Assembly's Resolutions on the intensification of efforts to eliminate violence against women, the Secretary-General published two reports in 2007 and 2008. They discuss the improvements that have been made in national policies on domestic violence following the internationalisation of this issue, and outline various measures that states have taken to implement Resolution 61/143. UNGA, *Report of the Secretary-General: Advancement of Women, Intensification of Efforts to Eliminate All Forms of Violence against Women* (3 August 2007) UN Doc A/62/201.

[377] UNGA, *Report of the Secretary-General: Advancement of Women, Intensification of Efforts to Eliminate All Forms of Violence against Women* (4 August 2008) UN Doc A/63/214, para 14 (hereinafter Secretary-General 2008 Report). The Special Rapporteur on violence against women has noted developments in domestic violence policies in Albania, Denmark, Germany, the Netherlands, Norway, Portugal and Turkey.

[378] ibid, para 16.

[379] Secretary-General 2008 Report (n 377).

[380] This step is in addition to the budget allocated for implementation of its national action plan to combat domestic violence from 2005 to 2008. ibid, paras 17–18.

[381] ibid.

[382] Secretary-General 2008 Report (n 377) para 29.

Legislation

New legislation has been adopted in a number of countries to address domestic violence (Brazil and Greece in 2006, Albania, Switzerland, Thailand and Vietnam in 2007), forced marriages (Belgium and the UK in 2007), sexual harassment (Greece in 2006), stalking (Germany and Liechtenstein in 2007), marital rape (Greece in 2006, Thailand and Vietnam in 2007) and illegal sterilisation (Slovakia in 2005). States have added provisions that create restraining orders, provide for the expulsion of perpetrators of domestic violence from the common dwelling (the Czech Republic and Switzerland in 2007), and prohibit sexual intimidation (the Netherlands in 2006). Laws on forced marriage and female genital mutilation have been strengthened in the UK, France,[383] Jamaica and Algeria.[384] In 2007, France extended the right of residence to certain foreign women who are victims of domestic violence.[385]

Several states have revised their procedural laws and rules in order to better support victims and ensure that their cases are heard expeditiously. In some instances, victims must be notified of all procedural steps (Brazil), while in others, rules are in place that establish timelines for courts and other institutions to take action in cases of violence against women (Australia and the Former Yugoslav Republic of Macedonia).[386]

Definition of Domestic Violence

Many states have amended their laws to broaden the definition of domestic violence (such as Brazil, Japan and Turkey from 2006 to 2007). Brazil's 'Maria da Penha' law of 2006 uses a wide-ranging definition of domestic violence and San Marino is drafting a law on violence against women.[387] Laws in Chile and Thailand have been amended to broaden the definition of rape and increase the penalties for sexual violence.[388] Austria is broadening the definition of domestic violence in its 1997 Act on protection against violence by removing the requirement of a 'family-like' relationship between the perpetrator and victim of domestic violence, and is drafting a bill to create a separate offence for repeat offenders.

Criminalisation of Domestic Violence

In addition to national policies and action plans, states are taking important practical steps to reform their criminal justice systems. For example, the UK is

---

[383] ibid, para 23.
[384] ibid, para 24.
[385] ibid, para 25.
[386] ibid, para 27.
[387] ibid, para 21.
[388] ibid, para 22.

introducing new jury guidelines to disregard stereotypical myths about gender roles when adjudicating rape and sexual violence cases.[389] Its Crown Prosecution Service aims to improve inter-departmental coordination in the prosecution of sex crimes. The UK also has specialist police officers who investigate rape cases, as well as rape prosecutors, and has established 98 domestic violence courts.[390] A revision of the law in Colombia made domestic violence a crime and increased the penalties. A new criminal offence of 'recurring abuse' has been added to the domestic violence laws in Chile. Breaking a 'non-molestation' order in the UK has become a criminal offence subject to up to five years' imprisonment. Twenty-nine states in Mexico now criminalise domestic violence. In 2004 Turkey revised its law to ensure that perpetrators of honour and customs killings receive the highest punishment and Haiti reclassified sexual crimes as crimes against the individual rather than the community.[391] Chile has submitted bills to parliament to address femicide and increase penalties for crimes against intimate partners. Finland is considering making petty assault in a close relationship a public prosecution offence.

Implementing Domestic Violence Laws

Some states, including Australia, Germany and Luxembourg, have stepped up measures to monitor the implementation of laws and evaluate their legal and judicial systems' responses to cases of violence against women. As a result of the Maria da Penha law in Brazil, there is an independent monitoring body which ensures that domestic violence laws are implemented by the police, prosecutors, judges, relevant officials in the executive branch and service providers. Peru has established a working group composed of public and private sector stakeholders to evaluate existing legislation on family and sexual violence and propose improvements.[392] One hundred criminal courts on domestic violence are functioning across Brazil and the number of police precincts with expertise in dealing with victims of violence has increased significantly since 2006. All police districts in Norway are required to employ a full-time domestic violence coordinator and specialised teams are in place in the largest districts. A special prosecutor for crimes of violence against women and trafficking of persons has been established in Mexico's office of the Attorney General.[393]

Social Services

Liechtenstein's 2008 Victims Assistance Act provides counselling support services, financial assistance, and compensation from the state for both material

---

[389] See Frances Gibb, 'Beware Rape Myths, Judges to Tell Jurors' *The Times* (London), 15 June 2009, www.timesonline.co.uk/tol/news/uk/crime/article6499404.ece.
[390] Secretary-General 2008 Report (n 377) para 28.
[391] ibid.
[392] ibid, para 31.
[393] ibid, para 28.

and non-material injuries.[394] Finland's Ministry of Social Affairs and Health, together with the NGO Monika-Naiset, which assists and supports immigrant women who experience violence, has published a guidebook entitled *Immigrant Women and Violence—A Guide to Assistance Provided by the Social and Health-care Sector.* The Tukeva Perhe and KokoNainen projects in Finland provide training and have produced materials aimed at enhancing the ability of social and health services to address violence against migrant women, including honour-related violence, female genital mutilation and domestic violence.

Japan has established human rights counselling offices for foreign nationals in eight cities, where migrant women victims of violence can receive advice on legal remedies for violations of their rights, with the support of translation services. In Portugal a comprehensive online database of support resources for victims of domestic violence includes a section on services available to the migrant population. In Malaysia the *Rumah Nur*—women's services centres— serve as one-stop centres open to all women victims of violence, providing counselling, legal literacy and temporary shelter.[395]

Awareness Raising and Data

Films in ten languages and leaflets in nine languages, providing information on rights and opportunities for assistance in cases of violence against women, have been produced and disseminated in Denmark and Japan respectively.[396] Particular efforts are being made to ensure that information is accessible, and websites offering comprehensive information on domestic violence exist in the Netherlands and are being developed in Belgium and Portugal. A guide aimed at helping victims and survivors of violence through the legal process is being developed in Haiti.[397] Bahrain has published guides in eight languages that provide information to foreign workers on their rights and obligations, which are distributed during mandatory medical check-ups of foreign workers.[398]

In Finland, brochures and handbooks, available at municipal immigration offices as well as at employment offices and immigrant advisory centres, contain information in several languages about equality, orientation to working life and the use of protection orders in cases of domestic violence. Brazil and Mexico have published guides aimed at educating migrant women about their rights and at preventing all forms of violence. In Serbia, the media has provided information about legislation intended to secure safe and legal migration. Thailand has translated its Labour Protection Act into Burmese, Khmer and Lao and has disseminated relevant laws to provide migrant workers with information about their rights.[399]

---

[394] ibid, para 26.
[395] Secretary-General, 'Violence against Women Migrant Workers' (n 197) para 26.
[396] Ibid para 21.
[397] Secretary-General 2008 Report (n 377) para 32.
[398] Secretary-General, 'Violence against Women Migrant Workers' (n 197) para 21.
[399] ibid.

Data collection through surveys has improved and states, including Argentina, Belgium, the Philippines and Portugal, are responding to the challenges posed by collecting and aggregating service-based data by establishing uniform systems of reporting and registering cases of violence against women.[400] Norway's 2005 nationwide survey on domestic violence showed that one in four women over the age of 15 had been subjected to, or threatened with, intimate partner violence and 9.3 per cent of women who had ever had a partner had been subjected to severe intimate partner violence.[401] A further survey was planned in Norway in 2009. Nationwide representative surveys on domestic violence were conducted in Finland in 1997 and 2006 and in Denmark in 2004 and 2007.[402] Random sample surveys on domestic violence were conducted in Japan at regular intervals and Portugal completed its second national inquiry into gender-based violence in 2008.[403] Mexico is drafting a 'National Assessment on the Status of Gender Violence' to determine the magnitude, forms and settings of violence against women to inform government policies. It is also developing a national database on violence against women.[404] Switzerland is revising its police crime statistics to include data specific to domestic violence.[405]

Political Leadership

Political leaders are increasingly vocal in their condemnation of domestic violence. Albania's Prime Minister declared that 2008 was 'the year for the fight against domestic violence'; the Speaker of Parliament condemned domestic violence in televised public service announcements from November 2007 to January 2008, and Parliament designated 30 November 2007 the official parliamentary day against domestic violence.[406] The President and Cabinet of Finland have each expressed a commitment to strengthening gender equality and more effectively addressing violence against women. In 2008, mayors from the metropolitan region of Port-au-Prince committed to combating violence against women in the Haitian capital.[407]

On the international stage, San Marino organised a high-level event at the United Nations Headquarters in June 2008 in support of the Secretary-General's campaign to end violence against women.[408] There is also evidence of smaller but practical changes. In Portugal, only the victim's income, as opposed to the family's income, will be used to determine eligibility for legal aid, thereby increasing

---

[400] Secretary-General 2008 Report (n 377) para 61.
[401] ibid, para 58.
[402] ibid.
[403] ibid.
[404] ibid.
[405] ibid, para 61.
[406] ibid, paras 37–38.
[407] ibid.
[408] ibid, para 38.

the number of women eligible for such assistance.[409] In Ukraine, 22 centres provide psychological assistance and four centres provide medical and social services for victims/survivors of domestic violence. In Japan, authorised facilities in prefectures serve as spousal violence counselling and support centres.[410]

CONCLUSION

While international human rights law is deficient in several respects, it has been successful in a manner which is not high profile but nevertheless effective. This is augmented by the role played by non-state actors, international bodies, NGOs and transnational organisations.

In reality the legal category of women's rights is still marginalised and there is a continued reticence about applying the generic provisions and mechanisms of international law to violations of women's rights. However, the careful cultivation of the law relating to women, including the right to be free from intimate harm, is a steady theme in international law and one that ought to be pursued in the effort to reduce systemic intimate violence.

Further specification of this right by international authorities, the incorporation of systemic intimate violence into mainstream international affairs and the jurisprudential examination of the rights violated and state obligations triggered by systemic intimate violence are not only necessary in theory, they can in practice enhance the rubric of international law. This, in turn, can further advance the amendment of states' domestic laws and policies in a way that ultimately benefits the victims of systemic intimate violence in their own homes.

---

[409] ibid, para 33.
[410] ibid, para 48.

Index

violence against women (*cont.*):
    rape, and *see under* rape
    Special Rapporteur, and, 62
    women, impact on, 271–72
Violence against Women Act (1994), 83, 169,
    190
Violence (Prohibition) Bill (2003), 189

war crimes, 93–95, 270, 272
see also crimes against humanity; genocide;
    mass rape *under* rape
wars and conflicts *see under* violence against
    women
Wednesbury principles, 249
women:
    alcoholics, 129
    attitudes towards *see* cultures, traditions and
        customs; religious beliefs
    battered woman syndrome, 61, 81, 99,
        117–18, 174
    confinement of, 59, 79, 127–28, 130
    discrimination, and *see* discrimination
        against women
    domestic violence, and *see* domestic
        violence
    employment *see under* employment
    evidence giving, and, 60
    group vulnerability of, 123–34
    ICCPR, and *see under* International
        Covenant on Civil and Political Rights
    immigration, and *see* immigration
    international law, rights in *see under*
        international law
    killing abusers, 61, 80–81, 172–75
    migrant workers, as, 62, 66, 73
    murdered and missing in Ciudad Juarez,
        52–57, 81, 297–300
    subordinate status *see* discrimination against
        women

    systemic intimate violence, and *see* systemic
        intimate violence
    torture, and *see under* torture and ill-
        treatment
    traditional views of male and female roles,
        124–26
    trafficking, and, *see* trafficking
    violence against *see* violence against women
Women's Human Rights and Gender Unit, 67
Working Group on Enforced or Involuntary
    Disappearances, 277–78
World Conference on Human Rights in
    Vienna, 21
World Conferences on Women and Women's
    Rights, 18, 22, 25, 39
World Health Organization, 79, 143, 257
World Organization against Torture, 300
World Plan of Action, 18
World Summit (2005), 70
World Summit for Social Development, 74
World War II, 16, 196, 202
Wright, Shelly, 98
writings of respected authors and scholars,
    98–106
    cultural relativity, 103–105
    discrimination and violence, 105–106
    distinction between public and private,
        100–102
    states' role, 102–103
    violence against women, torture, and,
        99–100
wrongfulness *see under* elements of state
    responsibility and systemic intimate
    violence
    forced marriage, 35, 155, 156, 312

Yemen, 28
Yugoslavia, Former, 22, 93–95, 114, 132,
    269–73